| 3875 | | | NOV 5   196/ |
|---|---|---|---|
| | | | |
| | | | |
| | | | |
| | | | |
| | | | |

# A RUMOR OF REVOLT

# A RUMOR OF REVOLT

## The "Great Negro Plot" in Colonial New York

## THOMAS J. DAVIS

# FP

THE FREE PRESS
*A Division of Macmillan, Inc.*
NEW YORK

Collier Macmillan Publishers
LONDON

The Free Press
A Division of Macmillan, Inc.
866 Third Avenue, New York, N.Y. 10022

Collier Macmillan Canada, Inc.

Printed in the United States of America

printing number

1 2 3 4 5 6 7 8 9 10


**Library of Congress Cataloging in Publication Data**

Davis, Thomas J.
  A rumor of revolt.

  Includes bibliographical references and index.
1. New York (N.Y.)—Negro plot, 1741.   2. Slavery—New York (N.Y.)—Insurrections, etc.   3. Afro-Americans—New York (N.Y.)—History—18th century.   4. New York (N.Y.)—Race relations.   5. New York (N.Y.)—History—Colonial period, ca. 1600–1775.   I. Title.
F128.4.D265   1985      974.7'1      85–1873
ISBN 0–02–907740–0

To the memory of one I loved,

My Aunt Laura

(November 7, 1898–December 27, 1980)

# Contents

# CONTENTS

# Preface

Thirteen black men burned to death at the stake. Seventeen black men hanged. Two white men and two white women also hanged. All thirty-four were executed in New York City between May 11 and August 29, 1741, as part of the episode early New Yorkers called the "Great Negro Plot" or the "New York Conspiracy."

The dramatic episode laid open conflicts created by the fact that New York City ranked second, behind only Charleston, South Carolina, as an urban center of slavery in colonial, eighteenth-century British North America. In 1741 about one in every five of Manhattan's eleven thousand residents was black and, with rare exceptions, enslaved. The proportion was a bit smaller in the entire province of New York, which had roughly nine thousand blacks in its population of sixty thousand. Nowhere in the province and, in fact, few places in colonial America had so high a density of slaves as New York City, which then actually occupied less than five of Manhattan Island's total twenty-two square miles and stretched only from the harbor to just beyond Beekman Street, all south of present-day Washington Square.

The conspiracy episode underscored the troublesome slave presence and the prevailing racial attitudes in colonial New York City, but more than black-white tensions were involved as the officials in 1741 alleged that seditious whites had led the blacks in plotting. The charges developed from a series of robberies and fires and revelations that blacks frequently had congregated in an out-of-the-way place off upper Broadway and talked among themselves and with several whites about seizing freedom, money, and a measure of revenge. On hearing of the talk and seeing evidence of arson, theft, and illicit meetings, the authorities followed public opinion to draw a most threatening picture of the blacks' intentions and the motives of their white companions.

The progression of events multiplied longlived fears among the English colonists in New York. It fed their anxieties about security amid the English rivalry with the Catholic Spanish and French for domination of North America. Anti-Irish prejudices also surfaced. The reason was that Irishmen and others suspected of being Catholics and Spanish spies were among the whites accused of abetting blacks in plotting a dreaded, wholesale slave rebellion.

The episode revealed a range of animosities and patterns of everyday personal relations and interactions among blacks and whites. Indeed, a portrait of early New York emerged in the detail of the slaves' life and work—fetching water from communal wells for slaveholders to enjoy tea time, carrying foot warmers to church for their holders' comfort, or seeking their own comforts in what free time they had—and in the illustration of the nature of law and order and the functioning of institutions such as the city council and the colony's supreme court.

Scholars over the years have paid scant attention to the episode. Those who have studied it previously have fixed its significance in terms of a single question: Was there a conspiracy as the officials declared? The prevailing answer has long been no, and the consensus has dismissed not only the officials' conspiracy case as absurd but the entire episode also, as if the events contained nothing of note except the officials' being tragically wrong.

The episode's fate has thus contrasted sharply with the treatment given to similar dramatic historical events. Looking at the Salem witchcraft episode of 1692, for example, the historical question has not been were there really witches but how was it that nineteen persons were hanged and one crushed to death for suspected witchcraft. Historians have sought there to discover what the proceedings and executions revealed about the nature of Salem and colonial society, but the same type of inquiry has not been applied to New York's case.

Much of the historical neglect of the events of 1741 has stemmed from the vagaries of conspiracy. The crime is far-reaching in its implications but deceptively simple in its definition as an unlawful combination of persons. Any crime committed by two or more persons in concert involves conspiracy. For example, two or more persons who agree to commit arson also commit conspiracy. Even if they never actually set any fire, they have formed a conspiracy by agreeing to arson. Further, all the persons who agree to the arson are equally involved in the conspiracy whether all or only one of the group is to set a fire, and all are equally liable for what any one of the group says while acting in the common design. Evidence against one is evidence against all in the conspiracy.

Because agreeing to an unlawful purpose constitutes the crime, the basic evidence of conspiracy often becomes what the accused said to one another or to others. That is especially true when the unlawful purpose of the conspiracy is not carried out. For instance, if two or more persons agreed to arson and actually set a fire, there would be evidence of the fire to substantiate the existence of conspiracy; but if no fire were set, then the evidence of conspiracy might be only what the plotters said in agreeing to arson. The evidence would be the plotters' talk and agreement.

Thus, while the legal question in conspiracy is only whether the accused agreed to an unlawful purpose, other questions may arise outside the courtroom. Especially when the unlawful purpose is not fully carried out, speculation may arise about the extent of the plot and about whether the accused would have or even could have carried out the unlawful purpose. Questions may also arise about how seriously to take the plot: Was it truly insidious or idle talk?

Scholars traditionally have emphasized uncertainties about the conspiracy in dismissing the events of 1741 from serious consideration. Indeed, American historians generally have been skeptical of reported slave conspiracies, often discounting contemporary reports as signs of paranoia. The tendency has been to accept the reality of slave plots only when actually faced with white corpses or blacks up in arms; even with such evidence at hand, the threat often has been dismissed as ultimately insignificant.

The chances for blacks to overthrow the American slave system were never great, but that did not diminish the reasons for whites to worry about the dangers slaves posed. Nor did such worries necessarily mean whites were paranoid. The slave uprising in New York City in 1712, which left whites dead in the streets, like the Stono Rebellion in South Carolina during 1739 and Nat Turner's famed rebellion in Virginia during 1731, demonstrated that blacks occasionally turned to undeniably murderous action. To pose serious threats to the society enslaving them, however, blacks did not always need to be engaged in elaborate, murderous plots. The persistent patterns of slave crime demonstrated well enough to many white contemporaries that blacks harbored animosity, talked of doing harm, and would strike back against enslavement when and where the opportunity arose.

This book demonstrates beyond question that blacks in New York City during 1741 clearly talked of doing damage to the society enslaving them, expressed hopes of gaining freedom and the material benefits being denied them, and acted against the laws restraining their liberty. The talk was widespread, and some did more than talk.

Allowing the persons who were involved to speak for themselves and focusing on their individual stories, where possible, this book seeks to reconstruct the events leading to the cry of conspiracy in 1741 and the unfolding drama of the thirty-four executions and their aftermath. The quotations, including dialogue, that appear in the book come directly from historical records, principally *A Journal of the Proceedings in the Detection of the Conspiracy*, commissioned by New York's city council and published originally in 1744 as an official report on what occurred.

*A Rumor of Revolt* departs from the bulk of previous work on the events of 1741 which concentrates on pillorying the official conspiracy charges. The pages that follow demonstrate that conspiracy was, in fact, rife in 1741—in the talk, thoughts, and actions of some of the accused. Crimes of arson and theft were committed and involved conspiracy. It was not the grand conspiracy New York officials argued for in court. That never existed. But the prosecution was not wholly wrong; the officials did lay hands on perpetrators who were liable under law for the death they received.

The premise of this book is that the paramount question about the conspiracy episode is not whether the officials were simply right or wrong, but how did the events develop to put thirty-four persons in the executioners' hands. The book is a narrative history. It tells a story that aims to weave the events together with the accused, the authorities, and the public. For whatever the ultimate analysis is, the essence of the episode lies in what the New Yorkers of 1741 did and failed to do, in what they believed and feared, in how they saw one another in the light of the political, racial, religious, and social attitudes of their day.

There are connections to be drawn between the conspiracy episode and the larger context of New York and colonial history and the substantial body of literature on American Negro slavery. The classic work done on slavery in colonial America by Lorenzo J. Greene and the more recent work of Ira Berlin, Charles Joyner, Daniel Littlefield, Edmund Morgan, Phillip Morgan, Gerald Mullen, Gary Nash, Philip Schwarz, and Peter Wood, among others, offer avenues for comparison and development of trends. So do the writings on colonial New York done by Thomas Archdeacon, Patricia Bonomi, Douglas Greenberg, Michael Kammen, Bruce Wilkenfeld, and others. The citations in the Sources and Notes section draw on the larger context of the episode, indicate the correspondence to the *Journal* and, where necessary, explain its references. The rich historiography flowing from the Salem witchcraft episode illustrates the variety of approaches that may be pursued in studying an occurrence such as the conspiracy episode. But all cannot be done at once.

The historical narrative here contents itself with unfolding the dramatic events of 1741 and pursues few explicit comparisons or parallels to events elsewhere, except as the people in 1741 introduced them. I trust my fellow professional historians will find this book valuable as a straightforward, readable account that may prompt reconsideration of the significance of the conspiracy episode, but the book seeks primarily to bring the quintessential human drama of the events to a far broader, general audience.

⛓⛓⛓⛓⛓

My thanks go to many for their help during my thirteen years of researching and writing this book. To the few named here I owe a special debt: Vincent Harding's early interest in my ideas about the New York Conspiracy turned to generous help in getting me to publish on the subject. Sidney Kaplan kindly shared with me some of the fruits of his own labors on the conspiracy. Arnold C. Tovell, when editor-in-chief of Beacon Press, favored me with his personal handling of my editing and introduction to Daniel Horsmanden's journal and encouraged me to pursue the conspiracy further. Jesse Lemisch graciously invited me to present my early conception of the conspiracy to the American Historical Association, West Coast Branch, and offered me the benefit of his criticism. Henry E. Cobb fostered my work with his characteristic benevolence, which has benefited so many of his colleagues and students at Southern University. W. Augustus Low, in his capacity as editor of the *Journal of Negro History*, supplied me with suggestions for developing my early work and getting it published. Paul Sarnoff saw none of this manuscript, but his encouraging and patient tutelage contributed significantly to my writing. Mary Frances Berry, as colleague and friend, provided consistent encouragement and shared her sharp insights on the historical process. More than a decade ago, Alden T. Vaughan supervised my graduate work at Columbia University and patiently watched and waited while I took detours from my dissertation to work on the conspiracy; his genial but firm hand held me on the straight and narrow path and saved me from at least a few pitfalls. He has continued as a friend to encourage my work, and I am grateful to him, Douglas S. Greenberg, and to others of my fellow members of the Columbia University Seminar on Early American History and Culture for their comments.

To the keepers of the documents I express my appreciation, particularly to the following institutions and their staffs: the New-York Historical Society; the New York Public Library, Rare Books and Manuscripts Rooms, American History, Local History and Genealogy, and Main Reading Rooms; the Schomburg Center for Research in Black Culture; the Museum of the City of New York; the New York State Historical Association Library; the New York State Library at Albany; the Municipal Archives and Records Center, New York City; the Historical Documents Collection and Paul Klapper Library at Queens College of the City University of New York; the Library of the Association of the Bar of New York; the Columbia University Libraries and Special Collections; the Manhattanville College Library; the Earlham College Library; the Fordham University Library; the University of Maryland, College Park, libraries; the Library of Congress; and the Moorland–Spingarn Research Center, Howard University.

For financial support received over the years, I am grateful to the Ford Foundation; the Regents of the University of the State of New York; the National Endowment for the Humanities; the Academic Dean's Travel Fund, Manhattanville College; the Faculty Development Fund, Earlham College; the Faculty Research Fund, Department of History, Howard University; and the Smithsonian Institution's Office of Fellowships and Grants and the National Museum of American History.

For their special aid and encouragement, particularly on the last leg of the journey to print, I thank Joyce Seltzer and Barbara A. Chernow, who took my manuscript into the fold and shepherded it through the Free Press, along with production supervisor Celia Knight; Barbara Machtiger and Kennie Lyman, who copyedited; Norma Cole, who wielded a light but pointed pencil in reading the manuscript; Catherine McNeil Anderson, who used a fine-toothed comb to ferret out inconsistencies and solecisms; and Brenda M. Brock, who read early and often with an eye for human interest and overworked words.

Lula Johnson Davis wearied early of my toiling as what she called "a would-be writer," yet she made efforts at patience and gave aid and comfort which I appreciate.

I owe my greatest debt to the lady who spent night and day making me "get my lessons" and "encouraging me up," as she used to say. For her lifetime of love, care, and good cheer, I am and always will be grateful beyond words or deeds. This book is dedicated to her: I wish she were alive to read it.

*Note:* The eighteenth century language quoted throughout this text comes verbatim and, thus, carries the sound of the sometimes stiff and stilted colonial American tongue. To prevent tripping over it, spelling has been modernized and regularized, so that a word such as "shew" appears as "show," and British spellings have been Americanized so that a word such as "colour" appears as "color." Punctuation has been added only when the meaning of a quotation required it. The chapter titles in the text are quotations from Horsmanden's *Journal.*

# 1

## "They Died Very Stubbornly"

Caesar was the first to die. Neither hesitating nor hurrying to the gallows, he simply did what was to be done. He demanded nothing of his executioners. He requested no judge, no lawyer, no minister. He craved no mercy. He sought no reprieve. He offered no confession. Ignoring the tumult of the hateful swarm around him, he stood barefaced and unbowed, showing neither shame nor fear.

His ease enraged the whites anxious not simply to watch him die, but to see him break. He refused to bend to their will, for their shackles held his body, not his soul. By dying as stubbornly as he had lived, he meant to frustrate their desires to master him completely. His presence proved their power only to seize the life they claimed to own.

Unflinching at his final moment, he bore the only yoke he ever accepted—the hangman's noose. Then his falling weight jerked against the rope and drew the noose to break his neck and strangle him.

Caesar, chattel of John Vaarck, baker, of the City of New York, was dead. He was the first of many to die.[1]

The date was May 11, 1741.

Caesar had lived but briefly. Yet at least his later years were full—full of trouble. It was not necessarily what he wanted. It was what he got for trying to be his own man where custom and law decreed him not a person, let alone a man or in any sense his own. He was property according to the society that enslaved him, and its agents sought to yoke him to that status. But he refused to live as the society demanded: That was the trouble, and it had grown as he grew. Before he finished his teens he was notorious.

Many of New York City's two thousand blacks and nine thousand whites came to know of him. Few could say in truth that they knew him, for Caesar opened himself to few men—or women, for that matter. He went his own way, following his own rules. And although they learned better, the constables, the sheriff, and the justices marked him early as a common criminal. They jailed him and whipped him and ridiculed him, parading him through the streets, naked to his waist, his back raw, and his blood running.[2]

Breaking custom and law became Caesar's way of living. It was his choice from what was available to him and came from neither his own strength nor weakness. He had no way to pick what he most preferred. His was a contrary choice born of reaction to the strength and weakness of custom and law. He was unruly as a slave because nothing made him servile.

Seeing what manner of man Caesar was, John Vaarck asked him for little other than labor. No doubt the baker desired more and wished for the obedience to make himself master-in-fact as well as owner-in-law. But being a practical man, Vaarck seemed content so long as Caesar did his work. Indeed, he praised Caesar as his best hand and swore he had no trouble with him at home or work. What went on elsewhere certainly concerned him; but unless circumstances dictated otherwise, Vaarck turned an apparently blind eye and left the law to see to enforcing its own rules— the rules Caesar broke.

After work and away from home, Caesar moved into his own world, an underworld where almost everything he did broke New York's rules for slaves. His going anywhere except on his holder's business or with his holder's expressed permission was a crime. Meeting with his most frequent companions, Prince and Cuffee, or with other slaves in a group of three or more, except at work, was a crime. Being out unescorted after dark, except in an emergency, was a crime. Buying a drink of liquor or visiting John Hughson's tavern or any other tippling house was a crime. Seeking to gratify basic human urges for companionship and diversion by taking time to relax, to gather together and laugh and play and feel unfettered or act freely as a person for at least an hour or two was a crime because the law denied the basic humanity of slaves: It provided for slaves to be property, not people.[3]

Caesar and slaves like him repeatedly broke the law's regulations against their personal movement, for the regulations were unrealistic and, thus, unenforceable. No means existed to check the slaves' every move, not every minute of every day. Even at work and at home, few slaveholders supervised their slaves most of the time. Like Vaarck, most holders left it to the government to maintain public order. But the slaves in New York City were many and so were their opportunities to evade regulations. Policing them completely was more than the sheriff, the undersheriff, and six constables could muster, even with a citizens' auxiliary night watch.[4]

Recognizing the futility of trying to enforce every element of the regulations, the law enforcers concentrated on keeping the slaves from disturbing the peace in any major way. They usually winked at the slaves' carousing and drinking and breaking curfew. Occasionally they cracked down and raided a tippling house, fining the proprietor and forcing slaves to scamper home, often with a lick to remember. The city's official guardians believed in making lasting examples when they punished, perhaps in hopes of settling the score on what circumstances forced them to ignore.[5]

Caesar went beyond what could be ignored. He went to the underworld not simply for play, but for profit. He stretched his liberty in the dark of night and took what the law denied him by day. He broke and entered and stole.

His first fiasco taught him care. It happened in 1736 when he and Prince led other slaves one night to break into the cellar of Baker's Tavern and spirit away barrels of the Holland gin called Geneva. It raised a stink, and before it blew away, he and Prince were whipped publicly and marked by one judge as "the heads and ringleaders of a confederacy of negroes who robbed, pilfered and stole whenever they had opportunity." Caesar was caught with the goods only once more after the incident at Baker's Tavern.

He learned the ins and outs of when to steal, what to steal, and to whom to sell what he stole. The last was crucial. Like most professional thieves, Caesar seldom wanted what he stole unless it was cash. He needed buyers or he was out of business. As a slave he had no place of his own to store much loot, nor did he have means to deal directly with many people willing to buy stolen goods at usually unbeatable prices. He needed quick, quiet sales, and the fewer people he dealt with the safer for him. So he used a fence—a person who bought the bulk of loot and used or resold it profitably in ways that often looked legal.

Caesar found a fence close to home. His next door neighbor, John Romme, had ambitions larger than his legal income and respectable connections from his family that included William Romme, a city councilman and member of the New York General Assembly. John and his wife, Elezabet, enjoyed the standing of the best fences: They lived above suspicion. If found with stolen goods, they could usually bluff their way out of trouble. Thieves like Caesar seldom had that chance.[6]

Romme regularly handled Caesar's loot, particularly the big jobs, like the fifty to sixty firkins of butter—between 2,500 and 3,000 pounds—Caesar lifted from Peter Vergereau's storehouse near Long Bridge, the landing platform for ferries between Manhattan and Brooklyn. Sometimes Romme kept an item or two of clothing for his own use, but usually he stored and unloaded the lot in his capacity as a merchant.

Caesar used John Hughson as a fence also. Indeed, he preferred dealing with the taverner, who seldom bickered over shares of the profits as Romme did. But Hughson lacked Romme's capacity for big deals, so Caesar brought him trifles and light merchandise that could be moved quickly. Hughson's thus became a place of business as well as pleasure for Caesar, particularly after he met a twenty-year-old redhead who arrived from London in 1739.

Nicknamed "the Newfoundland Irish beauty," the redhead's looks attracted attention, and so did her behavior. She introduced herself as Margaret Kerry Sorubiero, although everyone called her Peggy. She said she was the wife of a soldier, but he never appeared; and when she became pregnant early in 1740, while living in the rooming house of a free Negro named Frank, tongues wagged. Her moving to Hughson's quieted the gossip a bit, for there she blended in as part of a white family and worked and waited her time without the scandal of being a white woman in a black man's house. Suspicions lingered about her and the baby born just before Christmas 1740. People whispered that Peggy was Caesar's woman and the baby was his child. Caesar gave Hughson money for Peggy and the baby, but few knew that; he never advertised his part in her life.

Caesar's relations with Peggy and his dealings with Hughson and Romme were strands for the hangman's rope that began to twist together just after midnight on the last day of February 1741, when Caesar and Prince sneaked down Jews Alley to relieve a reported bulge in the cash drawer of a small, general merchandise shop on Broad Street.

The two men expected no trouble and encountered none as they entered the shop and left with a sack of money, silver candlesticks, speckled linen, and yard cloth. They headed for Hughson's, where Prince boosted Caesar up to climb through a window into Peggy's room and haul up the loot. Then Prince went home, and Caesar and Peggy went to bed.

All seemed to have gone well. Caesar rose at dawn, gave Peggy some of the cash and cloth, did a bit of business with Hughson, and then hurried home to fire the oven before Vaarck found him absent from his bed and his Sunday chores. He might have laughed had he been able to view the scene at the shop he had visited in the day's dark beginning, but he soon discovered it was no day for laughter.

Rebecca Hogg raised hell when she entered her shop that morning. She raged at her husband, Robert, until the constables arrived. Then she raged at them, virtually demanding that they solve the crime on the spot. The lawmen recorded her complaint and assured her of a thorough investigation, but that was hardly enough for Rebecca. She turned to her grapevine and pulled in other shopowners' wives who shared a common interest in catching thieves and recovering stolen goods, because burglary at one shop invited burglary at other shops.[7]

The women put quick wits to work on extending the law's arm. Rebecca herself turned up the first lead by accosting eighteen-year-old Christopher Wilson when she saw him visiting two servants of people who lived in rooms she rented out upstairs. She remembered the boy's being in her shop and seeing her money on the previous day; and knowing he was a sailor from the hospital warship *Flamborough*, she suspected him of having at least passing acquaintance with what she considered the city's riffraff.

"I was robbed last night and lost all the goods out the shop, a great deal of silver Spanish coins, medals and other silver things," Rebecca complained and described all she remembered. "Do you know anything of these?"

"I saw the eight square piece you described," Wilson answered. John Gwin had pulled the coin from his pocket that morning at Hughson's tavern, the boy said.

Rebecca immediately got the constables to search Hughson's for John Gwin, telling them she suspected he was a soldier. But no soldier by the name Gwin nor anybody admitting to knowing a soldier by that name was at Hughson's when the lawmen went there.

When the constables returned empty-handed, Rebecca was irate and fetched Wilson to repeat his story. Insisting he had told the truth, the boy wondered aloud how the lawmen had missed the mark. What he discovered was a mistake in identity: John Gwin was not the name of a soldier but an alias of Caesar's.

Caesar was jailed that Sunday, March 1. Having suffered previous arrests on suspicion and been released when no evidence materialized, he took his cell in stride. He could hardly have foreseen the trouble ahead. He knew the constables had found nothing on him, and he was sure there were no witnesses to the burglary. He trusted Prince, as he trusted himself, to say nothing. Only death promised to open Peggy's mouth against him, and he expected Hughson also to keep quiet, because under New York law the knowing receiver of stolen goods was as liable as the thief: The ultimate penalty was the same—death.[8]

The justices examined Caesar on Monday morning and returned him to his cell after he admitted nothing. They brought in Prince for questioning, knowing he and Caesar were a team, and he also denied the burglary.

Using the fact of Caesar's being found at Hughson's—which was grounds to fine the taverner—the officials called in John Hughson and his wife, Sarah. The couple pleaded ignorance of any illegal business but failed to satisfy the justices who dispatched constables to search Hughson's house.[9]

The king's men failed to turn up anything, but Rebecca

Hogg's wily grapevine produced a piece of fruit on Tuesday afternoon, March 3, when Hughson's sixteen-year-old indentured servant Mary Burton went to buy a pound of candles at Kannady's.[10]

"Come in and warm yourself," Anne Kannady offered, recognizing the girl as one of Hughson's household and beginning to chat. "That a black child or a white child which that Irish beauty had?" Anne asked, referring to the gossip about Peggy and her two-month-old infant.

"It's as white as any," Mary quipped, seeming uninterested in entertaining the gossip.

"I heard that there was a negro who kept company with her and was the father of that child."

"There's a negro who comes there to her, but he's not the father of that child, I believe."

"I'll give you a blessing as a mother would a child, as you're a stranger in the country: Have no dealings with negroes and have no hand in thievery, for that'd be a means of bringing you to the gallows," Anne said. Then getting to the point of her chatting, she asked, "Do you know anything of the thievery of Mr. Hogg's goods?"

"No," Mary answered.

"Tell me if you do, lest you get yourself in trouble. Let me give you motherly good advice," Anne coaxed. "If you know anything of it and will tell me, I'll get you freed from your master."

"I cannot tell you now. I'll tell you tomorrow," Mary hedged, wary of the powerful bait of freedom dangled in her face. If she talked and the lure proved an empty promise, she risked being the servant of an angry master. If she said nothing and the promise was real, she risked loosing a chance to seize her heart's desire. Turning to leave, Mary goaded Anne by saying, "Your husband was not cute enough, for he trod upon the goods."

The thought of the loot being under the feet of her husband, Constable James Kannady, without his discovering it, vexed Anne. It bothered James too, when she told him that evening what Mary said. Anne refused to let him rest until he checked to see if he had been made a fool. She marched him down to Undersheriff James Mills, calling Rebecca Hogg along the way, and repeated Mary's remark. Mills and his wife, Catherine, also grumbled, because the undersheriff had led the constables in searching Hughson's. If the girl was right, Mills as well as Kannady and the other constables had been made a fool.

The lawmen had no warrant to search Hughson's again, but Anne Kannady insisted on at least talking to Mary Burton immediately and in front of witnesses. Rebecca Hogg agreed. So did Catherine Mills. And off the women went to the tavern, their husbands trudging along in tow.

The Millses entered alone to fetch Mary for questioning outside, where the Kannadys and the Hoggs waited, considering it best that they not all barge in and perhaps frighten the girl. The undersheriff and his wife failed to return promptly, however, and the other couples became impatient, standing unsheltered in the cold air that March evening.

Anne refused to wait longer. Going into Hughson's, she minced no words when she found the Millses chatting with Mary in a warm parlor. She immediately confronted the girl who loudly denied telling her anything earlier but then whispered, "I cannot tell you anything here. I'm afraid for my life. They'd kill me."

Anne and the Millses took Mary outside, where she promptly pulled from her pocket a silver coin she said Caesar gave her from the Hogg loot. With Mary and the piece of money in hand, the group rushed to Christopher Bancker, the city councilman and magistrate of their ward.[11]

Acknowledging her promise to get Mary freed in exchange for evidence, Anne prodded Alderman Bancker to put the girl in protective custody. Mary herself pleaded, "I'll be murdered or poisoned by the Hughsons and the negroes, for what I should tell you."

Bancker ordered Undersheriff Mills to put Mary up for the night at city hall, where Mills lived as jailer. Then he consulted his nearest colleague, Alderman Simon Johnson, and sent for John Hughson.[12]

The taverner started by again denying he knew anything about the goods stolen from Hogg's, but when confronted with the coin Mary had delivered and her report that Constable Kannady had "trod upon the goods" while searching the tavern, Hughson hesitantly volunteered, "I do know where some of the things are hid."

Not saying where the loot was or how he knew about it, Hughson proved himself by asking leave of Bancker and returning shortly with some of the loot. If he hoped to earn points for belated cooperation, Hughson was mistaken.

Bancker met with Mayor John Cruger and several other city councilmen and justices to discuss his finds in the morning, and the group then questioned Mary. Under oath she told the men of Caesar's climbing into Hughson's and laying with Peggy till dawn.

"My master and mistress saw the linen the same morning," the girl said, recalling her own sighting of the goods in Peggy's room and Caesar's giving a lump of silver to Hughson and a couple pieces to her, too. Mrs. Hughson hid the linen in the garret and later shifted it under the stairs—which is what the girl meant about the constable's treading on the goods while searching the house. Mrs. Hughson's mother, Elizabeth Luckstead, then carried the linen to her home in Yonkers.

"Yesterday morning, John Romme was at my master's house, and I heard him say to my master, 'If you'll be true to me, I'll be true to you.' And my master answered, 'I will and will never betray you,'" Mary reported, rankling the officials—no doubt Alderman William Romme most. They scoffed at the implication about the gentleman and sent constables to ask John Romme to come and squash the notion of his trafficking with the likes of Hughson, but they found Romme had left town.[13]

Calling in the Hughsons, the officials repeated Mary's words about Caesar's dealings at the tavern and the Hogg loot being hidden there. John and Sarah Hughson denied everything and scoffed at Mary's credibility. "She's a vile, good-for-nothing girl who was got with child by her former master," the couple declared.

Hughson's having proven himself a liar earlier by roundly denying all knowledge of the Hogg loot and then producing some of it, helped his and his wife's own credibility none. And when the officials ordered Mary to reenter and face the couple, Hughson again showed how easily his tongue turned, for he switched from cursing to blessing and tried to flatter the girl. "In the hard weather last winter, she used to dress herself in man's clothing, put on boots, and go with me in my sleigh, in the deep snows into the Commons, to help me fetch firewood for my family," he recalled.

9

Honey from Hughson held no attraction for Mary. She had bitten into the sweet promise Anne Kannady had offered, and the taste lay too thick for her to mince words. If she helped convict the Hughsons, she would be free of them and maybe freed from indentured servitude altogether. So she repeated all her stinging words to the couple's faces.

Sarah stiffened but John wilted, and the officials squeezed from him what the city recorder labeled a "confession." The taverner never spoke the name Caesar. He talked of John Gwin as the person Peggy reported getting the linen and other things from, including the silver he had surrendered to Alderman Bancker on the previous night.

Hughson said Peggy asked him to hide the linen in his cellar and later to give it to his mother-in-law. "This morning Peggy gave me a little bundle with several silver pieces in it," he added, offering to fetch the bundle from his house. Permission was granted and the delivery made.[14]

The officials asked Hughson to sign a transcript of his statement. As if recognizing too late that his tongue had wagged, he refused.

"Is it not true as I have penned it?" huffed the city's deputy clerk who read the statement aloud.

"Yes, it is. I think there's no occasion for me to sign it," Hughson muttered to explain his refusal.

Nobody pressed for the signature, and the magistrates released Hughson and his wife on bail, pending their appearance in court on the third Tuesday in April, when the next term opened. Prince also was released when his £10 bail was posted by his holder, the merchant John Auboyneau. John Vaarck did Caesar no such favor. Instead, the baker delivered a bundle of linen and plates he said he found under his kitchen floor after his slave John reported something was hidden there. The bundle contained more of the Hoggs' goods. Caesar was in jail to stay then, and Peggy also came to occupy a cell, as Hughson had abandoned her in hope of saving himself.[15]

Rebecca Hogg no doubt slept easier that night than she had since the burglary. But not Elezabet Romme. She had to fidget for her absent husband, John. Mary's mention of him was minor by itself, but John Vaarck also cast suspicion on him. "The linen and plates could easily have been put there from Romme's yard, but could not have been put there from my house without taking up a board of the floor," Vaarck swore when presenting the bundle of loot to the mayor and other magistrates. How hard it was to take up a floor board, the baker never said. What he did say was enough, however, for the magistrates to issue a warrant for John Romme's arrest.[16]

The prospects for the accused looked dim then, but not deadly. The Hoggs burglary was hardly a big deal. Even with his record, Caesar faced odds that seemed at worst to promise him a beating or banishment. What ended him on the hangman's rope was a thread of events just beginning to unwind.

The date was March 4.

# 2

## "Fires About Our Ears"

Hangovers dampened New York City on March 18, since on the previous day, Irish residents celebrated St. Patrick's Feast and the non-Irish gladly joined in by celebrating winter's coming end. Particularly among the soldiers whose ranks were thick with Sons of Eire, the popular wet and wild partying on the seventeenth was followed by a slow day of recuperation. But March 18, 1741, turned into a day that demanded everybody to come around quickly, for fire struck at New York's heart.[1]

The first alarm sounded shortly after noon on the city's southern tip, where Fort George stood. Symbolically bearing the king's name, the structure housed the royal governor and contained the colony's administrative offices; its guns guarded the harbor; its armory and barracks held materiel and men to defend against foes, foreign and domestic.[2]

Smoke wreathed the governor's house, and flames leaped from the middle of his roof. The adjoining chapel and provincial secretary's office also were ablaze at the top, as townsfolk scrambled to the scene. The first to arrive rushed to rescue the governor, his furnishings, and the province's records. Every able hand filled and fed buckets of water onto the flames, and the town's two hand-pump fire engines, dragged out from city hall, poured forth.[3]

The fire fighters did their best, but the elements mocked their efforts. Wind at gale force billowed the flames ever larger while blowing the water back to blind the people and make mud to slow their steps.

The entire fort went ablaze and quickly surrendered. The governor's house collapsed after burning for two hours. The chapel caved in next. The secretary's office crumbled, and then the barracks and the armory fell. By three o'clock all the main buildings lay burning.

Flickers scorched the shingled roofs of the houses closest to the fort. Leaping on all sides toward Stone Street, Broad, and lower Broadway—where many of the city's wealthy lived, the flames headed for the clustered forest of buildings that made up the town. Threatened householders scurried to move their clothes, furniture, paintings, rugs, utensils, and other valuables—trying to insure against losing everything if fire took their homes. Outlying neighbors and strangers lent their hands to empty the houses as all townsfolk did when faced with flames.

Even the staunchest hands began to despair. Being brave was one thing, being foolish another. And as whispers spread into rumors about flames nearing the fort's gunpowder store, a full retreat started. Fear was clear in the fire fighters' eyes as all lower Manhattan appeared destined to be lost to the surging flames.

As if again mocking the townsfolk, the mighty wind shifted at sunset and brought quenching rain that people blessed as a godsend, watching it do what they had failed to do in fighting the inferno. But just as tensions began to ease, slow combustion set off a series of grenades at the smoldering fort and panicked many again into forgetting the gunpowder store was always sealed well below ground, out of harm's reach.

Cornelius Van Horne decided to be sure the entire city lay out of any further harm's reach. A merchant by trade and a captain of militia when duty called, he summoned seventy-odd men in his company, ordered them to get their guns, and set out to patrol the streets. Many made fun of Van Horne and his men that night, tagging Cornelius with the nickname "Major Drum," but he marched undaunted with his men from dusk to dawn. Citizens later thanked him.[4]

The close encounter with what had looked like complete calamity left New Yorkers shaking their heads. The visible scars were deepest and ugliest in the ruins of Fort George. Several nearby houses had singed roofs and smoke damage, and many of the goods taken to the streets sat soaked and soiled. Replacing shingles, reroofing, and cleaning and drying promised to remove the signs of lesser damage. Rebuilding the fort would take years and much money.[5]

The trauma of having their homes, their livelihoods, and their lives threatened—evidence of the last lying in the remains of Griffith Evans, a soldier burned to death at the fort—lingered among the citizens. Many who battled the blaze from the start declared its violence unnatural, and some speculated about an evil cause like arson. Questions erupted like a rash, but the balm of answers awaited another day.

Cityfolk long remembered the dreadful Wednesday, March 18.

✷✷✷✷✷

Talk of the fire easily filled conversation during the following week, and a special week it was, too. On the old Julian calendar used then in England's empire, March 25 marked New Year's Day. Ushering out the old and bringing in the new on the eve offered another occasion for liquor to flow freely in late-night partying that usually left hangovers and a quiet day to follow on the twenty-fifth, but it unfolded as the eighteenth had.[6]

About noon an alarm sounded on the southwest end of town, not far from the burned fort. Every able man rushed to the fire as was his duty. The law required reporting promptly or paying a fine if found shirking. But the men raced not simply to avoid a fine. They hurried in fear for all they held dear in their tinderbox city which sat so that sparks all too easily darted from house to house. Those first on the scene found flames engulfing the roof of the house of Captain Peter Warren, a brother-in-law of New York Chief Justice James DeLancey.[7]

Quick hands formed a bucket brigade and wheeled out the fire engines. Soaking Warren's roof and walls and all he had, the fire fighters did what they had failed at doing a week earlier. At Fort George the flames had spread too fast and far for the people. To handle a blaze effectively, they needed to get to the flames early and keep them contained, and at Warren's they did just that. In less than fifteen minutes the fire was dampened.

Warren's house was flooded and his roof ruined, but he and his neighbors sighed thanks for the flames' not spreading further. Their moaning about the fire's start prompted a bystander to suggest a dirty chimney—a common fire hazard, for all too often sparks caught in a clogged flue and threw fire onto a roof. Warren and his neighbors firmly ruled out such a cause: His chimney had just been cleaned, Warren declared. His neighbors on all sides, facing fines for violations, claimed their chimneys were clean and dampered, too.[8]

For the second Wednesday in succession then, people went home without being sure how the blaze they battled had begun.

The next Wednesday was April 1, All Fools' Day. Before it was over many New Yorkers felt sure someone was playing the fool with them, because fire struck again, roaring through Winant Van Zant's warehouse near the docks on the city's East River.

The blaze belched out toward the neighboring wharves and houses, which lay like kindling. After the first spark, no hope flickered for saving Van Zant's building: Its weather-worn, dry-rotted wood frame fit the definition of a firebox, and its hay, fir, and pine contents made good tinder.

A fire fighter early on the scene said it looked "impossible to hinder spreading further." But the frantic bucket brigade wet everything in reach, and helped by having the river close at hand, the people succeeded in confining the flames and marvelled at the feat.

In the questioning of how the fire started, passers-by reported seeing a pipe smoker near Van Zant's hay moments before the alarm. Investigators found, however, that the fire began in the roof on the opposite side of the building from the hay. The smoker breathed easier, but few shared his relief. Not having him to blame left the townspeople without a clue to the fire's cause.

Nobody had to await another Wednesday to see if the near holocaust of the previous three weeks would strike again. Three days after Van Zant's, fire darted through Quick and Vergereau's cow stable at the foot of Maiden Lane. Filled with cut and dried fodder, the building sat sure to feed fire to the east end's recently enlarged produce market and residential section called the Fly.

Flames already leaped from the middle of the stable's floor to the roof when a passer-by answered the cows' cries and sounded the alarm.

Racing up rather than out, the fire failed to spread widely before the first hands arrived, and their fast work confined the damage to a stack of hay and part of the stable's roof.

The area's merchants and residents immediately suspected arson because hay was piled halfway to the roof. But they had no time to prove the point.

Another alarm sounded only steps away, at Ben Thomas's house. The crowd on hand had no trouble squelching the fire or determining its source. "The fire had been put between a straw [mattress] and another bed laid together" in the kitchen loft where a slave slept, an investigator found.

An angry neighbor accused Thomas's slave of setting the fire. Thomas countered by suggesting that burning his bed and shelter seemed unreasonable even for a slave. He speculated that somebody else's slave had set the fire for spite, which enlarged suspicion to the slaves of Thomas's closest neighbors, Agnes Hilton and Jacob Sarly.

The approach of midnight halted debate, and the citizens headed home, agreeing slaves behaved strangely at times and leaving till the morrow the task of deciding which slave to blame.

Morning brought only fresh worries. A whiff of smoke at the coach house and stables of the prominent attorney Joseph Murray, Esq., on lower Broadway caught the eye of a passer-by who investigated and discovered coals burning at the base of a haystack. Kicking the embers away, he ran to get Murray and his neighbors.

The remnants of danger were clear as a crowd gathered to inspect the dying coals and smother from the singed hay. The passer-by became a momentary hero, as had his counterpart at Quick and Vergereau's on the previous night. His acting quickly was credited with forestalling major damage, for had the stack ignited, the blaze would surely have spread to Murray's home and the expensive neighborhood.

Like the Fly Market's merchants and residents, Murray and his neighbors wanted to know how the embers got to the haystack, and having daylight and time—unlike the previous night—they found an answer.

Coals and ashes were "traced along from the fence to a neighboring house next adjoining the stables, which caused a suspicion of the negro that lived there," an investigator reported.

The suspicion of slaves having a hand in the recent fires was strengthened later on that Sunday, April 5. While looking out her window, Abigail Earle saw three black men talking and gesturing as they strolled up Broadway toward her house. Drawing back to avoid their seeing her, she eyed them and listened.

"Fire, Fire, Scorch, Scorch, A LITTLE, damn it, BY-AND-BY," one black said, boldly thrusting up his hands to emphasize the words. His companions laughed.

Uneasy at the sight and sound, Abigail stayed hidden until the blacks were out of sight. Then she dashed to her closest neighbor, Lydia George. Repeating the scene, Abigail mimicked the black speaker's swaggering. "He threw up his hands and laughed," she huffed. The rendition chilled Lydia.[9]

Not knowing who the blacks were or where to find them, Abigail hesitated to go further for help. She feared being made to seem a public fool who cried wolf without being able to produce one or at least a witness to back up her claim of having seen one. How could she ask people to search for three black men in a city where hundreds were likely to fit the description she was then able to give? Lydia sympathized.

Neither woman wanted to let the incident simply pass, but what could they do? To walk the streets looking for black men was unthinkable and as impractical as mounting a public search with the little they knew.

On the chance of the blacks' returning down Broadway, the women went to Abigail's window to wait and watch. And about an hour later, their vigil was rewarded.

Abigail immediately recognized the three and pointed out the one she said spoke so brazenly. Lydia knew him: Quaco was his name. Former assemblyman John Walter was his holder.

Throwing on their coats and hats, Abigail and Lydia rushed to the nearest magistrate, and on Monday morning he delivered their report to a full meeting of his fellow councilmen who, like most citizens, were convinced the blazes were arson.

⛓⛓⛓⛓⛓

"It was natural for people of any reflection to conclude that the fires were set on purpose by a combination of villains . . . [seeking] to have the opportunity of making a prey of their neighbor's goods, under pretence of assisting in removing them for security from the danger of the flames," declared one stiff council member. Householders around the fort, Warren's, Van Zant's, the Fly, and Thomas's had, he noted, all "complained of great losses of their goods and furniture."[10]

Before the council could act on the report, a fresh alarm sounded as smoke billowed from Sergeant Burns's house, opposite the fort garden. People burst in with buckets in hand, expecting to find fire where there was smoke. They discovered only a smother.

The sergeant fumed. The insides of his house lay ruined, because what the smoke had not damaged his neighbors had trampled in their eagerness to help him.

Nobody found a clue to the cause. The standby of a dirty chimney was suggested, but Burns dismissed it by declaring his chimney was swept three days earlier. "There were grounds to suspect a villainous design," muttered one neighbor sympathizing with Burns.

A new alarm sounded before the crowd dispersed. Next door to Ben Thomas's, where people had rushed on Saturday night, the roof of Agnes Hilton's house was aflame. Quick work saved the house from having more than a badly burned patch of shingles, but the fire fighters refused to leave the scene without satisfying themselves about the source of the flames.

"The fire must have been purposely laid on the wall-plate adjoining to the shingle roof, for a hole had been burnt deep in it, near that part of the roof where the fire had taken hold to the shingles. And it was suspected that the fire had been wrapped up in a bundle of tow, for some was found near the place. The fact was plain," concluded one investigator.

Arson appeared the only answer for the broken fibers of hemp or flax being stuffed where they were. The question was who did it?

Standing in just about the same spot where they had debated the origin of the fire at Thomas's two days earlier, the citizens again concentrated their suspicions on the neighborhood slaves, and the consensus focused on Jacob Sarly's Juan.

Neighbors recalled Juan's grumbling about being sold as a slave after his capture in the crew of a Spanish sloop seized as a prize of war in 1740. He and his mates spoke little English, but they insisted clearly enough that they were "free men in their own country."

"Behaving himself insolently upon some people's asking him questions," as one townsman put it, Juan was dragged to jail. And he did not go alone. Angry citizens raised a hue and cry: "The Spanish negroes. The Spanish negroes. Take up the Spanish negroes."[11]

The neighborhood magistrate headed off the mob by ordering the constables to pick up Juan's shipmates "in order for their safe custody and examination," and he and his fellow city councilmen tried to take charge of the situation, meeting after lunch to interrogate the Spanish Negroes who were hustled in. All else was tabled. Indeed, the officials concentrated so intently on the scare about the foreign blacks that, for the moment, they completely forgot about Abigail Earle and Lydia George's lead to Walter's Quaco.

Just as the magistrates were about to start questioning the Spanish blacks, another alarm sounded. From their chambers the councilmen themselves saw what one described as "fire running up the shingles, like wild fire, from near the bottom to the top of the roof" of the Philipse warehouse on the waterfront. The sight scared the officials. Philipse's "was the middlemost of three large storehouses next each other in a row, old timber buildings, and the shingles burnt like tinder," a councilman noted.

The proximity to city hall, located at Broad and Wall Streets, allowed the fire engines to be on the scene and pumping in minutes. The river offered all the water needed, and hands turned out fast. "The fire, to one's great surprise, [was] . . . soon extinguished," a townsman exclaimed.

Philipse's storehouse was a ruin. It was destined to be one from the first sight of the flames which were well placed for a conflagration. Indeed, many people thought the flames too well placed.

"These storehouses were not inhabited, nor had they a chimney in them, but were at a great distance from any," one official explained. "The houses nearest them [sat] opposite to the wind, [and] there was a large space of garden ground between them; so, no spark from these chimneys could have occasioned this mischief. The fire must have begun inside."

The investigator's commonly shared conclusion was simple— arson. "The difficulty was to discover by whom the fire was put," he said.

While the crowd considered the implications of arson at Philipse's, the fourth alarm of the day sounded. Most of the fire fighters rushed to the new scene, but Jacobus Stoutenburgh was unable to, for he was perched on a roof adjacent to Philipse's.

Inching his way down to follow the others, Stoutenburgh noticed a Negro sneak out the window of a near-by storehouse and begin to run. He tried to quicken his descent to catch the fleeing black man but hit a snag. "I was hindered by a nail catching hold of my breeches," he later explained. Rather than tear his pants or let the Negro escape, he yelled, "a negro, a negro."

"The negroes are rising," screamed whites who heard Stoutenburgh from afar. Glimpsing the fleeing black man, they immediately gave chase with their cry. A few closer to Stoutenburgh hurriedly explained the pursued was a lone black whom they saw well enough to identify as Adolph Philipse's slave Cuffee, and the cry was changed to "Cuff Philipse, Cuff Philipse."

A crowd surged to Philipse's home where Cuff was found and, according to one witness, "dragged out of the house and carried to jail, borne on the people's shoulders."

Seizing Cuff failed to quiet the crowd. The cry that "the negroes are rising" had voiced many whites' deep anxiety, and although they had abandoned the words, the echo persisted.

⊛⊛⊛⊛⊛

The four fires that Monday proved too much for the citizens, especially after the Wednesday series which started with the ruin of Fort George. That the fourth fire of the day—the alarm that sent people scrambling from Philipse's storehouse—was but a flicker snuffed out easily by a few hands comforted almost no one.

Word of there almost being a fifth alarm, when the chips in the cellar of a baker near Coenties Market—the city's fish center—briefly caught afire, was no comfort either.

So citizens did not stop with Cuff. Mobs swept black men off the streets and jailed them, too. And it was not a matter of a night's cooling off. As one official noted without sympathy, the blacks "were continued some time in confinement before the magistrates could spare time to examine into their several cases."

City hall cells seemed safer for some blacks than being outside among the mob, but jail held its own dangers. For more than a few, the time turned long and hard.

Among the blacks awaiting their fate was Walter's Quaco. When the magistrates got around to questioning him, he immediately confessed to saying, "Fire, Fire, Scorch, Scorch, A LITTLE, damn it, BY-AND-BY," as Abigail Earle reported. But he declared his meaning was far different from what he knew the whites suspected.

Quaco claimed his words and gestures intended simply to show his companions how great he thought the recent news of English Admiral Edward Vernon's defeating the Spanish at Jamaica's Porto Bello in Caribbean fighting. The victory was "but a small feat to what this brave officer would do by-and-by," he cooed to his interrogators.[12]

None of the magistrates wished to impugn the praise of Vernon and the victory or challenge Quaco for touting the patriotism being urged on citizens and slaves. Yet few believed him.[13]

"Considering that it was but eighteen days after the fort was laid in ashes that these words were uttered, and that several other fires had intervened, [others] were apt to put a different construction upon Quaco's words and behavior," scoffed one official. He interpreted the words as meaning that "the fires which we had seen already were nothing to what we should have by-and-by, for that then we should have all the city in flames, and he would rejoice at it."

Quaco's deft construction secured his release, and others like him also talked their way from jail. None of the blacks walked without a cloud of suspicion, however, for whites worried that a dark conspiracy was afoot.

The date was April 6.

# 3

## "There Were Great Complaints"

T HE TUMULT AROUSED BY the many fires and mobs displayed the anxiety and short temper for which New York was noted. The city's characteristic hustle, with everybody seeking an edge and somebody seeing every move as a personal gain or loss, often rubbed residents raw. Outbursts of anger in the streets, lingering resentments, and deep suspicions seemed endemic.[1]

Manhattan's multiplicity of peoples sat uneasily with each other. The Dutch who founded the original city, New Amsterdam, were viewed by others as clannish and haughty—an image reinforced by their disproportionate wealth and the strength of their family alliances, often achieved through intermarriage. The Dutch themselves saw the English as interlopers trying to push ahead while holding the Dutch back with imperial rule, particularly in commercial matters. Surrendering the city along with their province of New Netherland in 1664 never signified their subjection, Dutch residents suggested; they saw themselves as having yielded only allegiance, and indeed, they had retained title to their property. They clung tenaciously to their interests.[2]

The English, for their part, continually suspected the Dutch. The recapture of the city in 1673 during the Third Anglo-Dutch War (1672-1674) and the rebellion Jacob Leisler led with his

Dutch connections in New York during 1689 left a legacy to stoke the suspicions. The noted individualism of the Dutch prickled against English legalism and pushed Dutch residents into court on charges of contempt for authority with a frequency exceeding their relative number. The success of English merchants bolstered by their connections in London and what the Dutch viewed as self-serving maneuvers of English officials in the city and province sparked recurrent feuding.[3]

As rulers, the Dutch had been tolerant. Free trade was their main concern, and their open commerce had brought to the city Spanish and Portuguese Jews, Frenchmen, Englishmen, and Africans as slaves. The variety of religions that persisted under English rule was evidence of the polyglot basis the Dutch laid. Name the sect and it probably had followers in the city, although after the English takeover, Roman Catholics were wholly unwelcomed.[4]

Under English rule the size and proportions of the population shifted. Scotch, Irish, Hugenots—French protestants fleeing their Catholic homeland, and some Germans flocked to New York. The Dutch declined from being more than 80 percent of the city's white population in the 1670s to being around 40 percent by the 1730s, although they continued to dominate the city's wealthiest ranks. The English and Hugenots filled out the upper ranks and together accounted for about 40 percent of the city's whites in 1730s. Among the remainder of the whites, there was a growing number of Irish often stuck in the lower ranks as soldiers, sailors, and laborers.[5]

Most of the Irish and the few dozen Jews were easy to spot by name, but the shared surnames among the Dutch, English, and French and the increasing use of English spellings that changed Marius into Morris, or Pels into Pell, and Roos into Rose, along with marriage among the three major groups, made precise accounting of ethnicity impossible. But the blending of names did not melt ethnic animosities.[6]

A handful of Indians lived in the city; usually arriving as captives from the continual raiding that marked colonial life, they served as slaves. Blacks formed the bulk of slaves; indeed, as elsewhere in England's American colonies, Negro and slave were synonymous. A few managed liberty on Manhattan through manumission, but their number was small and formed a dwindling proportion of the population as blacks brought to the city in the slave trade, particularly between 1700 and 1740, and those born into slavery grew. The rising number of blacks worried many whites, for by the late 1730s they were approaching one-fifth of the city's total population.[7]

Seizing black men, as the mobs did on April 6, was an act most of the city's whites could easily agree on, regardless of their ethnic background. Arson and theft were two of the most common crimes committed by blacks; and even those among the roughly 900 holders in the city who seemed sure their own slaves were safe, worried about the unruliness of others' slaves. Recent troubles with slaves in other colonies heightened the worries. The slave uprising in Stono, South Carolina, during 1739 particularly lingered in New Yorker's memories.[8]

Reports that Carolina blacks were plotting to rise forcibly and join up with the Spanish enemies of England who were raiding along the coast and frontier from their bases in Florida were rampant in early 1739. Four blacks and an Irish Catholic servant had, in fact, stolen horses and headed for Florida in February 1739. One of the blacks was killed, but the others made it to St. Augustine, where the Spanish received them gladly. Encouraging more defections, the Spanish published a proclamation declaring "Freedom to all Negroes, and other slaves, that shall Desert from the English Colonies."[9]

Then on the morning of the second Sunday in September 1739 a couple of dozen blacks gathered at a point on the Stono River, about twenty miles outside of Charleston. Breaking into Hutchinson's store in Stone Bridge, the rebels armed themselves with muskets, powder, and shot. They left the heads of two white men on the store's steps as evidence of their intentions and headed south, burning and taking what they could along the way. Joined by other blacks, their number swelled to around a hundred shouting "Liberty!"

By mid-afternoon that Sunday, armed whites responded to the black threat. In a shoot out about ten miles from where the rebels started, the band was broken. About half escaped. Some of those captured pleaded that they had been forced to join the group; those few were allowed to live. The others not killed in the fighting were shot and, according to one account, the whites "cut off their heads and set them up at every mile post they came to."[10]

A manhunt followed. By Wednesday, about twenty more

blacks were killed in fighting, and forty were captured. The last group was caught on Saturday, thirty miles south of Stone Bridge. A few were spared as innocents. The rest taken alive were shot, hanged, or strung up to die slowly.

Nobody kept the body count, and unsure how may rebels there were in all, whites stayed on guard. The blacks had killed about a dozen white men and a couple of white women. But not every white the rebels met was put to death. They spared a tavernkeeper named Wallace, reportedly because "he was a good man and kind to his slaves." Thomas Rose, another white man, also was spared when a few slaves hid him from those wanting him dead. The South Carolina settlers rewarded the slaves who saved Rose. They also put a bounty on the heads of any remaining rebels whose scalps might be brought in.[11]

The fear raised by the rebels remained high. At Christmas 1739 whites in Charleston worried over what one called, "a conspiracy that has been detected to have been carrying on by some of our Negroes in town but has been discovered before it came to any maturity. We shall live very uneasy with our Negroes," he wrote.[12]

In June 1740 white Carolinians were again up in arms over a purported black conspiracy near the rice-growing district between the Ashley and Cooper rivers. The great Charleston fire in November 1740 and suspicions about slaves engaging in arson continued to feed the fears—and not only in South Carolina. New Yorkers followed the news with dread, considering their own troublesome blacks.[13]

⛓⛓⛓⛓⛓

The man sitting in the New York governor's seat was himself alarmed by the tumult in his capital, and following the mobs on April 6, the Monday of the many fires, he called out the garrison and ordered the troops to stand night watch until further notice.[14]

He hesitated to do more. In New York's factious politics almost any action held the potential of political fallout, and he wanted to generate no more than he already had. He wanted nobody to accuse him of usurping the powers of the city's officials who were increasingly jealous over home rule since the municipal charter of 1731 had allowed the mayor to join the aldermen and assistants of the seven wards as an annually elected, instead of gubernatorially appointed, member of the Common Council that conducted the city's affairs.[15]

He looked to keep his distance and allow the magistrates a chance to soothe the anxieties developed during the twenty days since the fall of Fort George, but he saw the issue as much more than angry citizens suspecting arson and turning ugly against blacks.

From his view the fires were only the latest in a rash of calamities that had set New Yorkers to scratching and clawing. Recent bad weather had besieged them. Ruin threatened their economy. An unpopular war had further aggravated them. Discontent and insecurity seeped throughout the city and lay like oil on water, awaiting a spark to ignite. The outburst over the blazes showed how anxious people were to blame others for their misfortunes. The situation left the government's head worried about his own seat.

He already sat uncomfortable. Burned out of house and office at the fort, he had lost many cherished possessions. Yet nothing matched his loss in May 1740, when Anne Hyde Clarke, the wife of his youth and a source of his strength, had died. The people had loved her, much more than they ever loved him. Her absence from his side after more than thirty years of being there left him groping. Without wife and without home, his personal discomforts were many at that moment in his sixty-fifty year, and his job offered little solace.[16]

He cringed at his own official title, for although he occupied the governor's chair and acted as governor, he was called governor only for convenience. Technically, he was lieutenant governor: That was all the king appointed him to be and all the assembly paid him for being.

He, George Clarke, Esq., felt he had the experience to be full titular governor of New York. He had served as the right-hand man of governors from the widely loved Robert Hunter (1710–1719) to the roundly hated William Cosby (1732–1736). He had served as president of the governor's council, secretary of the province, and more. But he had lacked the political backing to win an outright, full appointment.[17]

Clarke encountered trouble from the moment he assumed the duties of acting governor, amid controversy when Cosby died in March 1736. Virtual civil war had faced his accession. Rip Van

Dam, one of New York's powerful Dutch politicians, had claimed the role of acting governor since he was senior on the council before Cosby suspended him—unwarrantedly, he alleged—in November 1735. Prominent citizens, both Dutch and English, who had opposed Cosby—men such as James Alexander, Phillip and Gilbert Livingston, Lewis Morris, and William Smith—backed Van Dam. John Peter Zenger's newspaper the *Weekly Journal*, which had so adamantly opposed Cosby—leading to the libel case in 1735 that became a landmark in the freedom of the press—also backed Van Dam. Stephen DeLancey and his sons, including the chief justice, and other powerful men such as Adolph Philipse and Cornelius Van Horne—the "Major Drum" of the fort fire—who had supported Cosby backed Clarke; so did others who owed their positions to Cosby, men such as Attorney General Richard Bradley and Supreme Court Justice Daniel Horsmanden.[18]

Setting himself up in Fort George and putting the garrison on alert with additional gunpowder, Clarke was a besieged man by early October 1736. The struggle for power seemed headed for the street. Only the arrival of royal orders on October 13, confirming Clarke as council president and then, on October 30, appointing him lieutenant governor forestalled violence.[19]

Clarke was on trial and he knew it. He wanted to win full appointment as governor. In his own view, he had dedicated his entire career to promoting the province's well-being, and he had long hoped to one day be in charge. His opponents claimed he had dedicated himself only to lining his pockets and, in fact, he had amassed a fortune since first arriving in modest circumstances during 1703. He now had the chance to prove himself.

Pitiless fate elevated Clarke to let him see himself as, perhaps, the right man at the wrong time because he came to office in lean years that promised any governor trouble, for New York was unhappily on its bottom.

⛓⛓⛓⛓⛓

Clarke could do nothing about the weather, but it certainly was a problem. Coming early and leaving late, the winter of 1740–1741 gripped New Yorkers in a season more frigid than even the oldest had ever heard of or seen. For Christmas the city received what people came to call "the great snow." Three feet fell on that single, silent night, and the blizzard refused to cease on the following days until it had dumped ten feet of snow on the city. Violent winds piled drifts even higher and almost buried some of the smaller houses and shacks.[20]

The weather, in effect, closed down the city. Bitter cold and ice accompanied the snow and invited only the most hardy, the foolish, or the desperate to venture out; and even they braved the elements only briefly, for every step outside became an adventure fraught with danger. Simply to push past their front doors demanded a struggle for most people, and if they succeeded, frostbite soon nipped at them.

All normal traffic halted. Snow blocked the byways and the once busy thoroughfares and made the town a virtual prisoner. Solid ice shut the harbor. The Hudson, which townsfolk called the "North River," lay frozen for sixty miles—from Manhattan past Poughkeepsie. Neither by land nor by water was the city open, and its people suffered.

From the overseas merchants and large landowners standing at the top of New York's economic ladder down the rungs to shopkeepers, craftsmen, laborers, servants and slaves, the pain of the frozen grip was clear. As no ships entered or exited the port, ocean trading and all dependent on it were in misery. No sailing meant seamen out of work. It meant empty pilothouses and idle pilots. It meant stevedores had nothing to load or unload. It meant idle caulkers, ship painters, and scrubbers.

All business was afflicted. Merchants without fresh merchandise made few new sales. Shopkeepers found their stores going bare. More hands went idle and conditions worsened as pockets went empty. Without the flowing lifeblood of trade, New York's economic arteries froze, and its heart withered.

The stroke of weather pushed people toward hibernation, and had they been able to spend the winter in a dormant state, many might have been spared much suffering. Even to sit or sleep out the winter, however, people needed first to eat, and for many the larder was bare. Almost empty stalls met them at the Broad Street Market and at the Old Slip Market on Burger's Path. No fish flowed into Coenties Market on the docks nor into the Fly Market on Maiden Lane, which had little of its usual meat, and the Meal Market at the foot of Wall Street offered only sparse measures.[21]

The food for sale came mostly from a few outlying farmers enterprising and well-equipped enough to hazard a potentially lucrative ride by horse and sleigh on the fickle roads. Hawkers, who managed to procure provisions by means only they knew, also provided a bit. But supply nowhere neared demand. Scarcity ruled; and a cruel ruler it was, creating a seller's market where common people cursed the prices as criminal.[22]

People with money enough to buy bought, evidently considering being robbed better than being hungry. The bulk barely scraped by on what a few pennies scattered on their plates. The city's usual mass of penniless suffered most, for when hard times hit, they were hit hardest. A few packed tightly into the two story, brick poorhouse built in 1736 off the city's Common. Others begged. Some stole, obeying the law of survival. Society's law at least promised the poor thief a chance of ending up fed and warm in a city hall cell, if caught. Few forgot that grim winter.[23]

Not everyone suffered equally. The produce of their gardens saved some, putting preserved fruits and vegetables on their tables when others had none. Those who kept cattle and chickens—not uncommon, even on Broadway—fared better. Their cows gave them milk, cheese, and butter; their chickens offered eggs; and their pigs provided meat. These people had to worry about finding feed for their animals and about keeping them safe from hungry thieves and those seeking to steal for slaughter and sale. The prayerful among them no doubt thanked God for such worries.

Some New Yorkers had few worries at all because wealth stocked them well. Even with the cursed weather freezing their businesses, they had money enough to buy whatever was available. Food was no problem for them, nor was firewood. Where others lacked even scraps to ease their hunger or a flicker to fight against the cold invading their houses, almost everyone in the homes of the rich sat down to satisfying meals and luxuriated in warmth, including the slaves.

With eyes widened by cold and hunger, some cityfolk saw more sharply than ever before the merciless contrast between rich and poor, and they beheld the well-off with resentment. They marked the haves who showed no apparent concern for the have-nots and, also, the mean who profited from others' pain by charging exorbitantly for food and fuel, paying attention only to cash and ignoring the cry of human misery. Some saw, too, that slaves—their black rivals for all manner of labor and livelihood— were often sitting better fed and sheltered than they were.

That winter's scene occasioned more than a little muttering. Some townsmen simply got angry. Others waited to get even, keeping score of the haughty, the hoarders, the profiteers, and all the people whom they felt had hurt them or just not helped.

❦❦❦❦❦

The weather's effects on the social fabric worried Clarke. Nobody blamed the winter on him, but the frigid economic climate was another matter. The signs of gloom accompanied him to office in 1736. From the farm lands to the city streets, New York had settled into a depression, as once-bustling commercial avenues carrying its chief cash crop turned bare. Where once golden harvests of wheat garnered wealth for the city and countryside to share in good measure, they had come to trade woes and little more. In good times each had chided the other about its rich share, but by 1741 they had virtually nothing to share, and each charged the other as the culprit.[24]

Complaints hit Clarke from all sides, and after four years in office, he still saw no relief in sight. The depression was not his doing, but the people charged him with finding someway to undo it, and soon. They demanded a return to prosperity, and they wanted it almost instantly. But he offered no quick fix. Lecturing the people on the chronic ills that had laid them low, Clarke prescribed a slow process of rehabilitation. Few people cared, however, to stomach the slow-acting prescription.

Over long years New Yorkers had largely filled their fields and their ships with a single commodity, wheat. Making flour and meal their big-volume exports, they diversified little and refused to turn away from the grain that brought the colony its early bread. Everybody had wanted more—from the farmers hiring hands and clearing land to plant growing acres of the white seed all the way to the merchants cramming ships on the waves of high prices, for wheat had spread profits throughout New York.

Millers had hired carpenters and masons and millwrights to build new mills and enlarge old ones to grind the grain. They hired more hands to tend their grindstones. They bought more barrels from coopers to pack their product and ordered more wagons from wainwrights to haul it and hired more draymen to drive it. New York City had hummed, happily matching the tune from the farm lands and mills. Workers crowded the wharves as stevedores loaded the ships hurrying in and out of port. From shore to sea, New Yorkers had sailed continuously busy in the wheat boom.

Success bred competition. Rivals from New Jersey and Pennsylvania, particularly, grew as challengers in the prime markets of the West Indies and the South. A price war resulted, and to survive New Yorkers had to cut prices; but that cut their profits and pushed them to try selling larger volumes to offset the cuts. When the price fell a tenth, they rushed to sell a tenth more, desperate to reach the income level they had counted on to pay for their new lands and mills and ships and everything else they had built on the projections of prosperity.[25]

Clarke groaned early and often about New York's going awash in wheat. He pleaded with the people to listen to the knells. "The markets for your flour, the present staple of the Province, are already so much overdone by the great importations that are made of them from this and the other northern colonies that, unless some manufactures be set on foot that are wanted in Great Britain or do not interfere with theirs, there will be no way to employ the people to any advantage," Clarke warned in 1737. Few heeded him; the majority sailed full speed with their wheat as the siren of profit lured them with hope of weathering the sinking prices.[26]

Time proved Clarke woefully right. New Yorkers began to drown in their once-precious grain as prices lurched, and refusing to let go of their heavy hold, they sank slowly and stubbornly. Waves of depression swelled throughout the province and particularly in New York City, which was being dragged under by both the weight of lost profits from the Hudson valley's wheat and lost profits from the port's slipping position in the flour-and-meal-carrying trade.[27]

Rivals in Philadelphia and Baltimore surged ahead on the strength of cheaper wheat floated down the Delaware and Susquehanna rivers. The falling profits, lower wages, and rising unemployment left New Yorkers seeking someone to blame, and prominent as culprits in many whites' eyes stood slaves who competed in almost every area of work from common labor to crafts.[28]

Considering it prudent public policy and sensible politics, Governor Clarke himself attacked blacks in repeated calls to make New York a white man's land—a prospect he saw dimming in light of the population trends, particularly in New York City. During the 1730s the flow of white immigrants to the colony slackened because of the depression, but importations of slaves were

relatively brisk: 1,065 slaves entered the Port of New York between 1730 and 1737. Not all of the imported slaves remained in
New York, but the number of blacks in the city was creeping up.
In 1737 the city contained 8,945 whites and 1,719 blacks. The importations slowed between 1738 and 1741, as 329 slaves entered
the port, but even then the rate of increase in the black population
promised to double the number of blacks in the city twenty times
by the time whites doubled once.[29]

By 1741, one of every seven persons throughout the province
was black. In New York City the proportion stood higher, near
one in every five. About one in four of all the city's males aged sixteen to sixty years was black. That really worried Clarke. Black
men, particularly those between sixteen and thirty years of age—
like Caesar, Cuff, and Prince—often proved troublesome. They
were the ones who usually packed tippling houses like Hughson's,
who had hands in burglaries, and who were generally what whites
called "insolent." They created other social problems, too. Black
men outnumbered black women in the city by a ratio of 110 to
100, while white women outnumbered white men by 100 to 91;
that increased worries about relationships like Caesar and Peggy's. The troublesome black men were also the most prized slaves
of holders, because they were used mostly in business, as opposed
to domestic service where women predominated. Clarke himself
held a black woman slave as cook and maid and a black boy for
use around the house, but like many white men, he scorned the
growing tendency to have black men working at trades in the
city.[30]

New York needed to be "replenished with white people,"
Clarke declared. In commenting on petitions from white skilled
craftsmen in 1737, he emphasized that "the artificers complain
with too much reason of the pernicious custom of breeding slaves
to trades. The honest and industrious tradesmen are reduced to
poverty for want of employ[ment]. And many of them are forced
into other countries."[31]

A sure way to get and keep more whites, in Clarke's view, was
to reduce the competition and growing number of black men
that frightened off potential immigrants and also scared settlers.
Especially at times of general unrest, many whites feared blacks as
potential enemies ready to join foreign foes in an attack. New
Yorkers were, in fact, worried about just such an attack in 1741,
for they were at war.

Spanish sailors chopped off the ear of English merchant sea-man Robert Jenkins in the Atlantic during 1739, and the outraged British Parliament demanded satisfaction. When none came through diplomatic channels, King George II declared war—The War of Jenkin's Ear. The conflict carried over into Europe's War of the Austrian Succession (1740–1748). English colonists in the Americas came to call the hostilities King George's War, a title that captured the popular sentiment that it was the king's fight, not theirs.[32]

New Yorkers protested not only that the war was none of their business, but that it threatened to destroy their businesses by interdicting an already suffering trade with many of their best grain markets in the West Indies. Trading with their old Spanish and French customers had become treason. Merchants intent on conducting business as usual faced the risk of privateers and men-of-war from England, France, and Spain concentrating in the Atlantic shipping lanes leading south. Running the gauntlet successfully still left the risk of falling into unfriendly hands on the trading docks that shifted with the tides of battle. The war then complicated the province's already confused commerce and promised to cost the city dearly in lost trade.[33]

The imperial ministers expected New Yorkers to show loyalty as the king's subjects by absorbing any business losses and by helping to pay the costs of the fighting: They expected too much. Their demand of a war levy produced a political battle in the colony, and Clarke became the unhappy man in the middle. Duty called for him to follow his instructions from the king and ask the assembly for the money, but sad experience warned him of an angry reply from both the province's legislature and the people.[34]

The issue became part of a growing debate about London's authority to tax American colonists. Only the people's elected representatives had the power to lay and collect a legitimate levy, the assembly resolved. If New York paid anything to the king, it would be as a gift not as a tax, the people's representatives contended. A few actually suggested sending nothing, but for most assemblymen the question became how much. Showing its character as an independent deliberative body, the assembly took its time to decide.[35]

Clarke was caught in the middle. London raged over New

York's delay, as the ministers queried if he were governing or not? When he pushed for payment, the assembly questioned if he were serving the people or their oppressors? After two years of haggling, Clarke succeeded in striking a compromise: While not paying all that was demanded nor what it viewed as a levy, the assembly voted £2,500 to enlist and equip as many companies of New York men as volunteered for war.[36]

A paradox emerged. Unpopular as the war was among New Yorkers, about 3 percent of the white males sixteen to sixty years old rushed to enlist. The explanation was simple: The pay for soldiering, meager as it was at thirty pence a week, attracted the depression-stricken from city and countryside to troop off to battle, but the effect deepened domestic worries.

With close to six hundred of the colony's men departing to the West Indies front, fears mounted about being unprotected at home. Particularly in the city, New Yorkers recalled how Charleston, South Carolina, had been attacked by the Spanish and French during Queen Anne's War (1702–1713). They remembered, too, that New York City itself had fallen captive to foreign fleets. The English themselves had taken the city and province virtually by sailing into the harbor in 1664. The Dutch did the same in 1673, recapturing the city and yielding it only after a peace treaty. The possibility of being invaded again preyed on many minds.[37]

⛓⛓⛓⛓⛓

Fort George's fall and the fires that followed led some New Yorkers to suspect an enemy was already afoot and attacking the city from within. The seizing of black men off the streets resulted then from more than a whim about arson. Citizens were angry, afraid, and depressed in the face of many troubling questions, and they had arrived at the point of demanding some answers.

Clarke urged the people to search themselves and seek guidance from God to answer their complaints and make amends. Looking to the future, he proclaimed Wednesday, May 13, as a day of "public fasting and humiliation" for what he termed "the calamities with which we have of late been visited."[38]

The appointed day lay more than a month away, and before it arrived some answers indeed were arrived at and some searching done.

The date was April 10.

# 4

## "A Scheme Was Proposed"

NEW YORK'S CITY COUNCIL sat in an extraordinary session on Saturday, April 11. All seventeen members had witnessed the wrath poured out in the streets the previous Monday. The fires had shaken the councilmen, too; and like their fellow residents, the councilmen were anxious to settle the source of the blazes. In responding so far, however, they were a step behind the people.[1]

The crowds at the homes of Ben Thomas, Joseph Murray, and Agnes Hilton and the mobs after the fire at Philipse's storehouse had marched on the popular suspicions of arson. Fingering Spanish blacks and then black men in general, the people had pulled the city's leaders into action. Alderman John Pintard headed off the mob moving against the Spanish blacks clustered in the East Ward, ordering constables to arrest them for protection and interrogation. Neither Pintard nor his fellow magistrates were quick enough after Philipse's.

The mobs had roughed up the blacks and delivered them to jail for the officials to deal with. But questioning the near hundred brought in yielded no immediate answers, and the council's eagerness to solve the riddle of fires had grown with each passing day. The men sought to placate the people before the muttering turned louder and jeopardized their own positions as leaders.

The popular suspicions about black men and the fact that the fires concentrated in the downtown and east side areas where slaves were thickest sharpened the council's focus. The Montgomerie Ward, stretching north from Golden Hill between William Street on the west and the East River, held the largest number of slaves—about one-sixth of the city's total. The wharves were located there, and it was where Winant Van Zant's burned warehouse sat. South of Montgomerie was the East Ward, bordered on the west by William Street, which became Smith south of Maiden Lane. It was where the Fly Market section stood and where the fires had struck most frequently—at Quick & Vergereau, Thomas, Hilton, and Philipse's. It also held about one-seventh of the city's slaves. Another one-seventh of the slaves were in the West Ward which ran north from Fort George up Broadway and out to the Hudson. Joseph Murray's house struck by fire sat near Trinity Church in that ward. So did Hughson's, although it was in the lower reaches by the riverside. Slightly more than half the city's blacks lived then in the Montgomerie, East, and West wards, and their aldermen—John Marshall, John Pintard, and Christopher Bancker—were particularly pressed for answers.[2]

None of the city's seven wards were without slaves, however. Because slaves lived in their holder's household, they were just about everywhere in the city. They clustered in the best sections with the wealthy who had money enough to buy and maintain most of them. Dock Street and its extension, Queen Street, running through the East and Montgomerie wards along the East River were a rich residential strip with many slaves. So was lower Broadway in the West Ward. The Dock Ward had its clusters, too, particularly along Broad Street and along Pearl Street. The Out Ward on the city's northern edge was the only section without a heavy concentration.[3]

Aldermen Simon Johnson, John Moore, William Romme, and Gerardus Stuyvesant were as anxious as Bancker, Marshall, and Pintard then to reassure their constituents. Most of the city's nearly fifteen hundred white families held no slaves and saw no reason to be bothered by them. The bulk of the nine hundred or so individual slaveholders who had only female slaves or male slaves younger than sixteen years for use basically in housework saw no reason either to be bothered by the black men suspected as the likely culprits. The holders of men slaves were themselves eager to have the group purged, so as to keep their own property safe. Also, as holders were liable for their slaves' jail costs, the holders of black men taken up by the mob wanted whoever was responsible for the suspected arson punished as soon as possible, limiting the damage to their own pockets.[4]

Aldermen Marshall, Moore, and Pintard and Mayor John Cruger—himself once a slave trader—personally understood the holders' eagerness, for they had men slaves. Many prominent citizens did, using them as butlers and coachmen and in business. Such slaves were badges of social status as well as significant investments that paid handsomely in added comforts and control of labor costs. In line with their status as the city's wealthiest group, merchants often held black men. So did tradesmen such as bakers, butchers, house painters, and smiths who frequently preferred holding blacks rather than using white indentured servants or wage workers who might move on with the benefits of their training and even start competition. The pressure to sort through the jailed blacks then was not simply to find culprits but, also, to get the rest back to work.[5]

The council's success or failure promised to reflect on all the men—including the seven assistants, one from each ward, who served with the aldermen. John Chambers, the prominent lawyer appointed city clerk by the governor, also wanted an effective resolution to protect his property, which included slaves; having no vote in the council's decisions and not facing voters, however, he seemed less pressed than his elected colleagues.[6]

Mayor Cruger had already responded to the thefts accompanying the rash of fires by revoking John and Sarah Hughson's bail and jailing them. It evidently made no sense in Cruger's mind to leave implicated accomplices of thieves at large when stealing was rife. He wanted every suspect in hand and, like his fellow councilmen, planned to use the law fully to discover the cause of the fires and satisfy the people.[7]

⛓⛓⛓⛓⛓

No councilman sat more stubborn on law and order than forty-seven-year-old Daniel Horsmanden, Esq. "Taking notice of the several fires which had lately happened in this city, the manner of them, the frequency of them, and the causes being yet undiscov-

37

ered," he declared, "[we] must necessarily conclude that they were occasioned and set on foot by some villainous confederacy of latent enemies amongst us." He demanded punishment.[8]

The politics of strict social control ruled in Horsmanden's world. The eldest son of a pastor in Purleigh, England, he was a blue-blooded king's man who claimed heritage through his mother's line from the French emperor Charlemagne. He came to New York in 1731, bearing letters of recommendation from influential men in London and had been, in his contemporaries' phrase, "bred to the law" at the famous Inns of Court in England.

Royal government was Horsmanden's career, and as a dedicated loyalist, he rose rapidly in the ranks of provincial officials. Within two years of his arrival, he won appointment to the governor's council. Within five years he was the city's recorder and, thus, an *ex officio* member of the city council; a judge on the Court of Admiralty which had jurisdiction over New York, New Jersey, and Connecticut; and third justice on New York's Supreme Court of Judicature, the province's highest tribunal.

Horsmanden scrambled from post to post. None satisfied him because none paid much by his standards. The £50 a year he earned on the Supreme Court was the most he got from any of his jobs, and their total amounted to a scant income to support the style he demanded for himself. So he continually scraped for pennies and cursed his fate. He was still a bachelor because, in his estimation, he lacked the money to marry. He was an ambitious man who craved the independence of wealth and the influence of power.

His pursuit of fortune was eased later in his life when he wed a rich, older woman whom he survived. As for his quest of fame, people who recalled his name at all in later generations came to identify Daniel Horsmanden, Esq., as the most prominent personality in the investigation of the fires and thefts in 1741.[9]

Horsmanden seized the council's Saturday discussion. Using his closeness with Governor Clarke for backing, he addressed his fellow city councilmen with a characteristically superior and sometimes patronizing tone. "A proclamation should be issued by the government, promising proper rewards to such person and persons as should make such discovery of the incendiaries, their confederates and accomplices, as that they should be convicted thereof," he instructed.

The message carried in his stiff lawyer's language was simple: Offer money to loosen tongues. All agreed to the idea, but bickering arose over who was going to pay and how much. The elected councilmen hesitated to pay out of the townspeople's pockets, sensitive to the perennially sore issue of city spending and taxes.

Being appointed by the governor, Horsmanden faced no prospect of having to answer at the polls. He supported Clarke's position on the fires' being the city's business even though the burned fort was crown property. In any case, the governor controlled no money to offer the city; the assembly held the colony's purse strings, and with a stingy hand.

The city's men understood the familiar facts of life. Their country cousins usually cried poor and called for cooperation when trouble struck themselves but went deaf and dumb when trouble struck the city. The rural folk expected the urban throng to put a lion's share into the pot and then eat like a church mouse. The council majority deplored the traditional state of affairs, but the men had no recourse and voted to offer rewards from the municipal treasury.[10]

Deciding the amounts and conditions became the problem. Had all persons been considered equal, a simple answer might have sufficed. But equality was anathema and akin to anarchy in the councilmen's eyes. Their society's law and order recognized persons by different degrees, and their "proper rewards" did likewise, discriminating by color and status. A white person was offered £100. Not half as much was offered a nonwhite, and the sum depended further on condition: A free black, a mulatto, or an Indian was offered £45; a slave was offered £20, but manumission accompanied the money as the slave's holder was to receive compensation of £25—more money than the slave.[11]

Despite the inequity, the scale was relatively generous and indicated how desperately the council wanted information. A reward of £100 represented about one-fourth of the city's total £439 revenue from franchises and properties during the five year period from 1736 to 1740. The sum was at least five years wages for the average white person lucky enough to have steady work during those hard times. A reward of £45 was four to five years' pay for an average, free nonwhite; £20 was a small fortune to a slave; and being set free was, no doubt, the best of the bargain and beyond measure in money. Thus, the councilmen fashioned an attractive offer, and they added a promise of immunity from prosecution and a pardon for any crime connected with the fires.[12]

Using the majority's reluctance to pay up, Horsmanden ventured on bolder action by urging ''a general search of all houses throughout the town, whereby . . . probable discoveries might be made, not only of stolen goods, but likewise of lodgers that were strangers and other suspicious persons.'' Seeing a chance to keep their money by finding any culprits themselves, the councilmen agreed to the scheme and delayed proclaiming the rewards.

The men made themselves virtual wardens in planning to assault the privacy of every home, searching without warrants and demanding that townsfolk answer for their persons and possessions. In seeking out ''strangers and other suspicious persons,'' the officials' broad hands also carried the smack of xenophobia; for despite the immigrant character of the city, suspicion of newcomers and fear of outsiders prevailed.

The council hoped the citizens would accept the draconian measures. Anticipating anger and wanting to prevent any warning, however, the men agreed to hold the scheme secret among themselves and Governor Clarke, who offered to order out the militia on the day chosen.

It was too late that Saturday to start the search. Violating Sunday was unthinkable. So Monday, April 13, became the day.


Armed men cordoned the city at dawn and halted all traffic. Their orders were ''to stop all suspected persons that should be observed carrying bags or bundles, or removing goods from house to house,'' Horsmanden noted.

No person or place was supposed to escape as the aldermen and assistants probed each house in their own among the seven wards—a task they did more or less thoroughly, depending on how well they personally knew the owner, his reputation, or his social standing. The magistrates prayed that their familiarity as the citizens' elected representatives would blunt the shock of invasion.

Townsfolk muttered, but with troops in the streets, nobody resisted, and the initial inspections went smoothly. The officials soon discovered trouble, though, for in laying their plans they overlooked a crucial point—time. To cover the twelve hundred homes and boarding houses in the city between dawn and dusk left the men ten minutes per house; meeting that pace led to cursory looks that thwarted the purpose in most places.[13]

The results frustrated the councilmen. "There were not any goods discovered which were said to have been lost, nor was there any strange lodger or suspicious person detected," Horsmanden lamented. City clerk John Chambers was more embarrassed than anyone, however, for "some things were found in the custody of Robin, Mr. Chambers' negro, and Cuba, his wife, which the alderman thought improper for and unbecoming the condition of slaves, which made him suspect they were not come by honestly," Horsmanden explained.

Chambers's slave couple joined the horde in jail as he sat chagrined with the council. To deflect criticism and put the day's effort in a favorable light, Horsmanden suggested the lack of discoveries confirmed what lawmen often claimed: The vast majority of people were law-abiding and had nothing to hide. But he had also to look at the search in the light of the constables' repeatedly unfruitful searches of Hughson's, which showed that unless a house were turned inside out, with every nook and cranny emptied and every board and brick tested, stolen goods were likely to remain undetected.

⛓⛓⛓⛓⛓

Having gambled and lost, the councilmen became more anxious for a score. They turned to more intense interrogation of the dozens of slaves remaining in the city hall jail, seeking to settle accounts in that way if they could.

Led by Horsmanden, the men pressed especially hard against Cuff Philipse. Most of them were familiar with him and his reputation as a spoiled slave who abused the privileges he had as houseboy of the New York Assembly's wealthy and powerful seventy-six-year-old speaker, Adolph Philipse.[14]

The questioning focused on Cuff's hiding inside an empty building near the fire at the Philipse storehouse and then racing away when spotted—the action precipitating the cries of "the negroes are rising." The men suspected Cuff bolted because he was guilty of starting the blaze.

Cuff had dealt with the likes of his questioners often enough to know they wanted him to confess to arson or say something to prove himself guilty; and when they pushed him to talk, he offered only a bare account of what he had done on the day of the Philipse fire.

"I was at home all that afternoon, from the time I returned from Hilton's fire, where I'd been to assist and carry buckets. I was at home when the bell rung for the fire at [the] storehouse," Cuff claimed.

Neighbors attested to Cuff's peeping out the door at home moments before the alarm sounded. When he failed to join in the rush to the flames, people knocked at the door to be sure he knew of the fire.

"It's supposed to be at your master's storehouse," the neighbors had told Cuff. Seeing him make no move to leave, they had demanded, "You going with the buckets?"

"I'd enough of being out in the morning," Cuff quipped.

The neighbors well remembered. They had marked Cuff's response as impertinent. No matter how long he had been out at Agnes Hilton's fire that morning, they thought a good and faithful slave ought to have run his fastest to help save his holder's property.

Cuff's reported reluctance prompted people to wonder if he had eventually helped or only hid at the Philipse fire. There was no doubt about his being somewhere on the scene, but exactly where and when?

An old white man named John Peterson swore he had stood next to Cuff during the blaze, but not everyone believed the account at first because Peterson was notoriously nearsighted. Seeing the doubts, however, he described the blue coat with red lining that Cuff had worn and insisted he knew what he was talking about.

Peterson recalled having to prod Cuff into helping at the blaze by asking, "Why don't you hand the buckets?" The question suggested Cuff again had acted badly, but nothing so far tied him to arson.

Horsmanden questioned Cuff's opportunity to set the blaze during the time between the fire at Hilton's and the storehouse alarm. Adolph Philipse answered in part by saying he ordered Cuff to saw wood until lunch and then sent him to sew a vane on the Philipse sloop on the day in question.

A white boy who worked with Cuff recalled the welding job on Philipse's small, one-masted boat, and assured the councilmen that he and Cuff were together at the dock most of the afternoon of the fire. "I stood by him to see him sew [the vane]," the boy swore. "I left him but a little before the bell rung for the fire."

Cuff seemed to have an alibi then, but Horsmanden continued to puzzle over how much time intervened between Cuff's leaving the boy and appearing home. "Upon the whole it was thought proper Cuff should remain in confinement to await further discovery," he noted.

Horsmanden and his colleagues were at a stalemate, for as he soon complained, "a great deal of time [was] spent by the magistrates in the examination of the negroes in custody, upon account of the fires, but nothing could be got out of them."

⛓⛓⛓⛓⛓

No hope remained for a quick solution. Nearly two weeks were gone since the Monday of the mobs and mass jailing of black men, but the councilmen still had nothing to satisfy citizens. Their general search had succeeded only in aggravating anxieties and provoking leery neighbors into further distrusting each other and those they did not know. The muttering from the search was not soon quieted, and tittering about Chambers's embarrassment lingered. Some said it served him right to have his slaves jailed and wished, perhaps, that other councilmen had been tripped in their own scheme. People wondered too about how many holders, like Chambers, did not know what was in their slaves' possession or how it got there. The release of slaves who passed the magistrates' questioning did not help the suspicions.

With most of the black men back out on the streets and nobody punished or firmly fingered for the fires as yet, an uncertain calm hovered about the city. Cuff's remaining in jail prompted no popular sense of the officials' having anyone in hand. Considering his owner's power, some townsfolk suspected that Cuff, no doubt, would walk free as former assemblyman Walter's Quaco had with what they thought was a clearly contrived excuse for his overheard remark, "Fire, Fire, Scorch, Scorch, A LITTLE, damn it, BY-AND-BY."

How far holders were willing to go to protect their slaves provoked consternation in the city on occasion. Irritated by having to compete with slaves for work and seeing slaves in the better homes, apparently living in a manner many free men could not afford, common folk resented what they considered privileged treatment of slaves. They were not alone. Governor Clarke and other officials sympathized with them.

Horsmanden, who held no slaves, himself argued repeatedly that New York's slaves had too much liberty and were too little grateful for what he considered their undeserved good fortune of being given a standard of living which most whites never reached. In his view, blacks had been done a favor by being taken from backward Africa and brought to a civilized and developing society. More than once he spoke of slaves' "ingratitude" and said blacks were a naturally degenerated people. Pointing to their repeated crimes, he once called slaves "enemies of their own household." He believed their presence endangered society, and like his ally Governor Clarke, he wanted to rid New York of blacks or, at least, put them under stricter control.

The roundup of black men had offered an opportunity for a crackdown on slaves, and the suspicions and lingering resentment provided popular support for a further move against slaves. During the fires, even slaveholders seemed willing to press for exemplary punishment. If slaves were publicly caught redhanded it was in the holders' interest to see them chastened, so as to maintain discipline and to reassure safety. No holder wanted himself pictured as harboring proven public enemies. Certainly no influential man like Adolph Philipse would court popular ill will by trying to protect his slave in the face of clear wrongdoing. The officials and people simply needed a clear case against slave suspects such as Cuff and Quaco.

The evidence so far was circumstantial. Investigators at several of the fires had found enough signs to prove arson. The straw mattresses stacked in Thomas's loft, the tow stuck in Hilton's outside wall, the hay piled to the roof of Quick & Vergereau's, and the coals in Murray's stable all pointed to deliberate attempts to burn the buildings. The initial Wednesday pattern starting at Fort George, then striking Warren's exactly a week later and Van Zant's the following week had spread the notion that there was a design. The four fires on Monday, April 6, left no doubt in the popular mind about the fact of crime; the only disputed issues were who set the fires and why.

Accident played no part in the people's thinking after eight fires struck in the six days from April 1 to April 6. Many were willing enough initially to attribute the catastrophe at the fort to chance, but in the face of the ensuing fires a consensus developed that they were a product of some level of coordinated activity, not isolated events. The thread of intent was still thin, and the individuals involved were not pinpointed, but the existence of an unseen connection seemed certain to the cityfolk and the officials.

Random human behavior was not something most New Yorkers in 1741 accepted. In their world view everything had a cause and purpose and happened for a reason. Any unusual events separated by little time and small distances were seen as a signal worthy of note. Either God was sending a message of good or ill, or evil was besieging them. Governor Clarke's proclamation of a day of fasting and humiliation reflected the common assumption that the city was being tested in some way that citizens considered not yet fully understandable.

Perplexed and frustrated, people visualized a common strand in their troubles. In addressing New Yorkers on what he called "the calamities with which we have late been visited," Clarke himself lumped together the hostilities with Spain, the severe winter, the economic losses, and the "fires about our ears, without any discovery of the cause or occasion of them." With no remedies at hand for slumping business, the weather, or the war, citizens had only the blazes as a focus for their immediate anger and action.

The desire to lay hands on somebody was natural, and the fact that slaves were the citizens' first targets simply reflected the blacks' vulnerable position: They lay open to whatever physical abuse the society allowed. It reflected also the stereotype of slaves as stealthy, for whites often considered blacks furtive in their behavior and accused them of mischief done outside public view or in secret.

But citizens did not confine themselves to blaming dark deeds on blacks. They believed all their enemies, led by the devil himself, schemed at secret machinations. Repeated news stories carried rumors of their Spanish foes sending out spies and plotting the destruction of English colonists. Fear of a constantly suspected Catholic conspiracy hatched by the pope to gain worldwide dominion also preyed on Protestant minds.

The apprehensions that erupted on the fateful Monday when whites mobbed blacks were extended by the city council's general search for what Horsmanden called "strangers and other suspicious persons." The failure to come up with any leads intensified, rather than diminished, suspicions. The officials and the people generally worried that if the source of the fires and accompanying robberies were so well hidden as to escape immediate detection, something truly dark and deep was afoot.

Few whites rested easily, and the councilmen were especially unnerved. Only Cuff was in custody for any connection with the fires. The arrest of Chambers's Robin and Cuba had no clear tie-in with any recent robberies. The only ones in jail on a count of theft were Caesar, Peggy, Hughson, and his wife. But the Hogg burglary for which they were arrested occurred more than two weeks before the first fire. Caesar and Peggy were in cells during all the blazes, in fact, although the Hughsons were not jailed until after the outburst of April 6. Prince was still out on bail. Nothing so far suggested any of the five had a hand in the city's troubles since March 18. The officials had simply drawn a blank.

⛓⛓⛓⛓⛓

Quitting empty-handed was unthinkable for the council. Citizens were virtually up in arms. Cornelius Van Horne's decision to order his militia to the streets on the evening of the fort fire was not forgotten, and the Monday mobs had reinforced the spreading sense of urgency. People were expecting answers from their officials, but the council found itself in no position to deliver.

Being part-time and mostly unpaid for their public duties, the majority of the councilmen were less than eager to commit more energy to a search that had proven futile and had already cost them nearly two weeks from their private businesses. They looked to shift the burden of inquiry from their own shoulders without appearing to shirk their duty, and there they turned to Daniel Horsmanden, Esq.

As recorder, Horsmanden was essentially the city's lawyer and his fellow councilmen knew he remained eager to investigate the fires. Also, as a judge, he was paid to sift through the evidence of crime. With the help of a grand jury, petit juries, and prosecutors, he had access to means the council lacked. Pushing the search for suspects into the colonial supreme court where Horsmanden sat then, the council could announce its participation in an enlarged probe while relieving itself of the actual investigation.

Horsmanden himself welcomed the shift. He had pushed for a crackdown, and handling the probe in his court afforded his zeal full sway. His scorn for slaves and all whom he viewed as the crown's enemies cast him as ideal to hunt the suspected culprits. The possibility of political gain if the probe proved the position he, Clarke, and others had taken on slave men being inherently dangerous made him eager to pursue the task.

The judge knew his colleagues were likely to seek credit if the judicial investigation succeeded and abandon him to ridicule if it failed. But he was confident that there were, in fact, culprits to be found and that once they were in hand, citizens would rally to support the probe and whatever punishment the court meted out. He showed no worry about factionalism, perhaps for good reason: Citizens seemed united against a suspected common foe, and the issue appeared black and white. If further probing produced nothing, all the officeholders were likely to have to answer to the people. There seemed little prospect then of Horsmanden's suffering any backlash alone.

If a conspiracy was afoot, Horsmanden and his fellow officials needed a witness to reveal the plot. Someone tying the fires or accompanying thefts to a secret plan promised the most useful results, for the question was not if damage was intended. Damage already was done. The pressing question was whether one or more persons had combined to inflict damage: That was the essence of conspiracy, a combination to do an illegal or simply harmful act.

Agreeing to harm anyone or to commit an illegal act was itself a crime, whether or not the intended act was accomplished or attempted. If anyone had talked of setting fires that was conspiracy, and whoever had talked in that way and consented to the idea was criminally involved and equally liable for any arson one of them committed. If one such person or someone overhearing him turned evidence, then conspiracy could be proven in court. With broad leeway under the law, the prosecutors would need to prove only that the talk had occurred. Getting the first person to talk was the key.[15]

The money and immunity the city council had agreed on April 11 to offer aimed at enticing a witness to come forward and tell the purpose, design, and identity of any plotters. Having failed in any other way to get the break they needed, the officials fell back on their offer in conjunction with Horsmanden's projected probe, and Governor Clarke released the proclamation of rewards.

The date was April 17.

# 5

**⛓⛓⛓⛓⛓⛓⛓⛓⛓⛓⛓⛓⛓⛓⛓⛓⛓⛓⛓⛓⛓⛓**

# "To Discover the Contrivers"

JUSTICE HORSMANDEN SAT anxious to proceed as the Supreme Court opened its regular spring session at city hall on Tuesday, April 21. The calendar called only for impaneling a grand jury and instructing its members to investigate accusations of crime and to indict any person against whom it heard sufficient evidence. The task held special significance in Horsmanden's view, because to proceed as he saw fit required the jurors to cooperate fully. He wanted to be sure the seventeen men understood their roles, but he had to hold his tongue.[1]

Being junior in rank although senior in age among the court's three judges, Horsmanden was relegated to being seen but not heard in court that day. The opening belonged to Second Justice Frederick Philipse since a royal commission had called Chief Justice James DeLancey away to Rhode Island.[2] But Horsmanden's desire to have a suitable note sounded was certainly satisfied; for although he and Philipse did not always see eye to eye, that day the two judges shared the same perspective.[3]

"The many frights and terrors which the good people of this city have of late been put into by repeated and unusual fires and burning of houses gives us too much room to suspect that some of them, at least, did not proceed from mere chance or common accidents but, on the contrary, from the premeditated malice and wicked pursuits of evil and designing persons; and therefore, it greatly behooves us to use our utmost diligence, by all lawful ways and means, to discover the contrivers and perpetrators," Philipse declared, leaving no doubt that he, too, believed in a plot.

"We have the happiness of living under a government which exceeds all others in the excellency of its constitution and laws," Philipse explained with a tone of chauvinism. "Yet if those to whom the execution of them is committed do not exert themselves in a conscientious discharge of their respective duties, such laws which were intended for a terror to the evildoer and a protection to the good will become a dead letter and our excellent constitution turned into anarchy and confusion, everyone practicing what he likes and doing what shall seem good in his own eyes," he warned.

To forestall the social chaos he envisioned required a simple remedy—"exemplary punishment of the guilty (if any such should be so found) that may deter others," Philipse said. Elaborating particularly on the consequences of unchecked arson, he emphasized that "the crime is of so shocking a nature that if we have any in this city who, having been guilty thereof, should escape, who can say he is safe or tell where it will end?"

Pushing what he suspected as a source of the trouble, Philipse directed the jury "to find out and present all such persons who sell rum and other strong liquor to negroes." He said, "It must be obvious to everyone that there are too many of them in this city who, under pretense of selling what they call a penny dram to a negro, will sell to him as many quarts or gallons of rum as he can steal money or goods to pay for."

The complaint carried the tone of a latter-day tirade against a rampant drug traffic with alcohol as the illicit substance and blacks as the addicts. Philipse's concern fixed on neither the drug itself nor its effects on blacks themselves. Holding no brief against liquor or against blacks addicting themselves to death, Philipse worried only about his society's being threatened at every turn by what addicted blacks did to support their habit. "The many fatal consequences flowing from this prevailing and wicked practice are so notorious and so nearly concern us all that one would be almost surprised to think there should be a necessity for a court to recommend a suppressing of such pernicious houses" as dealt illicitly with blacks, he declared.

The call for a crack down against places such as Hughson's underscored the reason the traffic thrived: Money. The promise of large and quick profits lured people to ignore the law and human misery. But the promise existed only because a lapse of vigilance allowed the rewards of crime to outweigh the punishments, Philipse suggested. And he demanded the imbalance be corrected, not with added laws or added penalties, but with stricter enforcement. He saw that more law did not make crime less if existing penalties were seldom imposed. Only sure and swift punishment, in his view, tipped the scales against crime's paying.

Law was "intended for a terror to the evildoer," Judge Philipse insisted; and he instructed the grand jurors to assist the terror's reign by presenting for punishment "all conspiracies, combinations, and other offenses, from treasons down to trespasses." He wanted every offender, whatever the crime, to pay the price. "I pray to God to direct and assist you in the discharge of your duty," he concluded.

The grand jury certainly understood. All seventeen men had fought the flames and lived with the fears—some more than others. Winant Van Zant had lost a storehouse in the fires. John Cruger, Jr., had witnessed the political heat the blazes caused his father, the mayor. David Provoost and Adoniah Schuyler held slaves jailed on account of suspicion connected with the fires. They already knew the recent trouble, perhaps too personally. Their hearings began the next morning.[4]

❆❆❆❆❆

Calling indentured servant Mary Burton, the grand jurors anticipated starting with her repeating the earful she had given the magistrates before the fires to make the Hogg burglary an open and shut case against Caesar, Prince, Peggy, and John and Sarah Hughson.

Mary snubbed the first summons to city hall. "I'll not be sworn, nor give evidence," she told the jury's messenger.

A constable armed with a warrant delivered the girl later that morning, but when ushered into the hearing room, she sulked and repeated, "I'll not be sworn."

"She seemed to be under some great uneasiness or terrible apprehension," Horsmanden noted. The jurors tried to assure Mary that she had nothing to fear; and worried that their large number intimidated her, the seventeen divided.

"Do you know something concerning the fires that have lately happened?" one group asked the girl. When she refused to respond, the men suspected they had their answer. "Speak the truth and tell all you know," jury foreman Robert Watts exhorted. The clerk read the rewards proclamation, emphasizing the money, immunity from prosecution, and protection if she talked.

Mary still said nothing.

Exasperated by the girl's stubborn silence, the grand jury ordered her jailed for contempt, and a constable took her away. But with Peggy, the Hughsons, and the blacks there, jail was not a place Mary wanted to stay. Before the constable could lock her up, she was ready to talk, if not tell all.

"I'll acquaint you with what I know relating to the goods stolen from Mr. Hogg's, but I'll say nothing about the fires," Mary declared on returning to the hearing room.

The jurors marked her opening as significant. It suggested she in fact knew something about the blazes: Why else would she declare she would say nothing? They pleaded and threatened for an answer from Mary, but "she remained inflexible," Horsmanden complained.

"[Consider] the heinousness of the crime which you would be guilty of, if you were privy to and could discover so wicked a design as the firing of houses about our ears, whereby not only people's estates would be destroyed, but many persons might lose their lives. This you would have to answer for at the day of judgment, as much as any person immediately concerned, because you might have prevented this destruction and would not. . . . A most damnable sin would lie at your door," the jurors admonished Mary. If she feared not God's hand, but evil human hands quicker to hurt, the men again assured her of protection.

Something the jurors said worked, because Mary began to talk. Recounting the burglary story she was originally called to tell, the girl added new details about Caesar's heisting beeswax and indigo on the same night as the Hogg job. The men listened politely to boost her confidence, but their real interest now focused on getting her to tell about the blazes. Their patience was rewarded.

"Caesar, Prince and Mr. Philipse's negro man, Cuffee, used to meet frequently at my master's house, and I've heard them talk frequently of burning the fort and [say] that they'd go down to the Fly and burn the whole town. My master and mistress said they'd aid and assist them as much as they could. In their common conversations they used to say that when all this was done, Caesar'd be governor and Hughson, my master, should be king. Cuffee used to say that 'A great many people have too much and others too little. My old master has a great deal of money, but in a short time, he should have less and I should have more,'" Mary quoted.

"At the meetings of the three negroes—Caesar, Prince and Cuffee—at my master's house, they used to say that when they set fire to the town, they'd do it in the night and as the white people came to extinguish it, they'd kill and destroy them. . . . I've known, at times, seven or eight guns in my master's house, and some swords, and I've seen twenty or thirty negroes at one time in my master's house. At such large meetings, Cuffee, Prince and Caesar were generally present and most active. They used to say, 'The other negroes dare not refuse what we command them.' And they were sure they had a number sufficient to stand by them," Mary said, emphasizing the black trio as ringleaders.

"Hughson and my mistress used to threaten that if I ever made mention of the goods stolen from Mr. Hogg, they'd poison me. And the negroes swore, if ever I [revealed] the design of burning the town, they'd burn me whenever they met me," Mary confided, explaining her reluctance to talk earlier.

The jurymen repeated their assurance of her safety and closed the session by asking Mary if she knew any other whites involved in the scheming she had reported.

"I never saw any white person in company when they talked of burning the town, but my master, my mistress, and Peggy," the girl answered. She still seemed unsettled, but if she had not yet told the jurors all she knew, Mary certainly had told them enough to send them scurrying.

⊕⊕⊕⊕⊕

"This evidence of a conspiracy, not only to burn the city, but also destroy and murder the people, was most astonishing to the grand jury. And that any white people should become so abandoned as to confederate with slaves in such an execrable and detestable purpose could not but be very amazing to everyone that heard it; what could scarce be credited," Horsmanden declared.

Neither the judge nor the jury questioned Mary's credibility. Everything she told the magistrates in March about the Hogg burglary had proven true. That inclined the men to believe her now. Also, her initial reluctance to talk to the jurors made what she finally said appear as a hard-won prize the men were loath to reject. More than anything else, though, they accepted her story because it corroborated their suspicions. Horsmanden himself had long believed that, as he said, "the several fires had been occasioned by some combination of villains."

Using Mary's story as proof of his being right from the start and of the investigation's needing to muster an all-out attack against a conspiracy, Horsmanden immediately enlisted Judge Philipse's support. Together they summoned "all the gentlemen of the law" living in New York City to a special session in the Supreme Court chambers.

All the lawyers appeared except for the province's aged and ailing attorney general, Richard Bradley. Horsmanden briefed them on Burton's testimony and appealed for them to serve as deputy prosecutors in the investigation. Not one demurred. "The gentlemen of the law generously and unanimously offered to give their assistance on every trial in their turns," the judge recorded.[5]

The official cast was thus set. Mayor Cruger and the city council had already taken their positions. Governor Clarke had agreed to act when called upon, and the province's assembly consented to watch in silence after convening at city hall on April 14. The grand jury was hard at work, and now the prosecution was in place. Attorney General Bradley would be lead prosecutor when his health allowed. James Alexander, John Chambers, Abraham Lodge, Joseph Murray, Richard Nicolls, and William Smith became Bradley's backups. The only remaining lawyer in the city was William Jamison, the sheriff. Horsmanden and Philipse were ready to sit in judgment.

Making way for swift and sure punishment of all possible plotters, the king's men agreed on the suspicion that "this was a scheme of villainy in which white people were confederated with negroes and most probably were the first movers and seducers of the slaves," Horsmanden explained. "From the nature of such a conjunction," he said, "there was reason to apprehend there was a conspiracy of deeper design and more dangerous contrivance than the slaves themselves were capable of. It was thought a matter that required great secrecy, as well as the utmost diligence . . . that a matter of this nature and consequence should be fathomed as soon as possible." None of the men wanted any slip-ups, for they well recalled the backlash that struck a generation earlier during an episode which itself bolstered belief in a present slave conspiracy.

⛓⛓⛓⛓⛓

In 1712, on March 25—New Year's Day on the old-style Julian calendar—a group of enslaved Cormantines and Pawpaws, not long from Africa, drank and talked in a tavern like Hughson's. What they said became clear just after midnight on April 6 when at least twenty-five slaves gathered outside Peter Vantilborough's house in the city's east ward. Two slaves set fire to a near-by building and then waited with their fellows for whites to swarm to the alarm.[6]

Wide-eyed citizens from prominent families died that night. Adrian Beekman caught a pistol shot in his heart. Henry Brasier, Jr., had his neck broken by an ax blow. Augustus Grasset's throat was cut. Stabs to the chest killed William Echt, Adrian Hoglandt, and Joris Marschalk. John Corbett and Johannes Low were bludgeoned, hacked, and stabbed to death. Lawrence Reade and David Coesart also suffered multiple critical wounds from knives, staves, and swords and seemed dead on the spot; and ten other white men came to carry the scars of the slaves' attack.[7]

The sounds of terror awakened the entire town. Governor Robert Hunter ordered the fort's biggest cannon fired to signal the danger and dispatched troops to the scene. Their surprise ended, the rebels scampered without a wound to themselves, but their northward retreat to the woods of Harlem was neither orderly nor safe.

Only the cover of darkness protected the blacks' flight, and when dawn came vengeful whites pounced. A half-dozen blacks allowed only their bodies to be brought back. One black couple died together, the man serving the fatal blow to his woman and then to himself. Four more followed in suicide. Others continued to scatter. The troops and militia from the city and its northern neighbor, Westchester County which at the time included the Bronx, seized nineteen fugitives.

The uprising "put us into no small consternation, the whole town being under arms," admitted one townsman. The excitement increased at the news of a rampage by seven Cormantine slaves on the West Indian island of Jamaica. Within six days the

54

city had "about 70 Negro's in custody," one witness noted. Another added. " 'Tis fear'd that most of the Negro's here (who are very numerous) knew of the Late Conspiracy to murder the Christians. Had it not been for the Garrison . . . [the] City would have been reduced to ashes, and a great part of the inhabitants murdered."[8]

Prosecution was swift. Spilled white blood required a full measure of black blood in the eyes of May Bickley, then New York's attorney general. Fourteen slaves hanged. Two burned at the stake. Eight to ten hours over a slow fire roasted another to death. Another died broken on the wheel. Whipped and set to starve in public, the last lingered for three days before dying. Nineteen slaves were thus executed.[9]

Not all whites relished such revenge, nor were such pitiless punishments reserved only for blacks. Jacob Leisler's rebellion in New York during 1689 resulted in brutal sentences for Leisler and six of his followers who were condemned to be hanged by the neck, cut down before they died, and gutted. Their bowels were to be burned before their faces. Then their heads were to be cut off and the remaining corpses cut into four parts. Governor Henry Sloughter mercifully reprieved five of the men and commuted Leisler and the sixth man's sentences to hanging and beheading. Governor Robert Hunter himself criticized Attorney General Bickley's apparent thirst for blood in 1712, calling him "a busy waspish man," and secured his removal from office as citizens and the king's London counselors ridiculed the prosecution for acting summarily.[10]

❦❦❦❦❦

Memory of 1712 remained vivid in New York. Bickley's fate particularly impressed Horsmanden and his cohort in 1741, and to protect themselves in handling what they feared was a plot to imitate the uprising, they resolved to provide what Bickley had not offered—full jury trials.

Neither generosity nor justice alone prompted the decision. The king's men had no choice if whites were accused: The law required jury trials for them. But a single judge's word sufficed to decide a black's guilt and to punish him on the spot; the mayor or any magistrate in the presence of five freeholders also had the same power of summary justice. Extending trials to blacks and whites alike was not legally necessary then. It was simply prudent.[11]

Jury trials provided complete due process and what the law called twelve "good men" to determine the facts in every case. To punish anyone would require both the grand jury to indict and a trial jury to convict the accused. The outcome would not rest then solely on Horsmanden and his fellows' shoulders. Citizens would share the burden of judgment and be involved from case to case. That promised the judges and prosecutors a measure of insulation against charges of proceeding arbitrarily.

Full, public trials would also allow Horsmanden and his cohort to proceed piecemeal. If their investigation did not crack the conspiracy all at once, they could put whatever accused they had in hand on trial and await further developments to present a public view of the whole plot. In that way, the prosecution could keep the people's attention and build popular momentum from case to case.

The decision of the king's men to have jury trials then was self-serving. It promised to strengthen their hand, protect them from public criticism, and also put the supreme court center stage with a spotlight on the officials' working in defense of society.

With all the attorneys in town already on the prosecution's side, whoever was accused had little prospect of defense during the trials. No blacks like Caesar, Cuffee, and Prince or whites like the Hughsons and Peggy had money to hire an out-of-town lawyer; nor did any volunteer their services, deterred perhaps by knowing an appearance to defend supposed public enemies was unlikely to be well received and, also, by having the trouble of traveling to the city without knowing how long the proceedings would last.

Horsmanden had no qualms about the fairness of the projected trials. His immediate worry was about how long it would take to apprehend the as yet unnamed plotters that he was sure were lurking in the city. He expected the action certainly to run beyond the regular one week spring term of his court, and he received a month's extension from Governor Clarke. He received notice also to extend his secrecy and suspicion, for an apparent leak had sprung in the investigation.[12]

Since disappearing on March 4, when Mary Burton and John Vaarck connected his name with the Hogg burglary, John

Romme had eluded arrest. Alerted by the warrant for him however, New Jersey authorities discovered a clue to his whereabouts by intercepting a letter which they immediately forwarded to New York's magistrates. Written in Dutch by a female hand and dated "Nieu York den 21 April," the translated message said:

> Beloved Husband John Romme,
> This is to tell you I received your letter from the bearer hereof, and I understand from it that you intend to return home. My beloved, I want you to do your best to get farther away. Don't come to New York, and don't make yourself known where you are, for John Hughson and his wife are this day going on trial. The servant maid is king's evidence against both. She has brought your name likewise into question, and I'm afraid John Hughson and his wife will be hanged, from what I can hear. The sheriff and bumbailiffs seek you everywhere. Vaarck's negro holds his word steadfast for you. Brother Lucas is chosen one of the jurymen, and he learns how it is in the hearings. No more for now, but I remain your loving wife, Elezabet Romme, even to death.

When questioned, Elezabet Romme denied everything—writing the letter, her husband's being involved in illegal activities, her knowing his current whereabout, and knowing anybody named "Brother Lucas." The letter belied her, but bespeaking the Rommes' social position, Elezabet was released without charges.

Horsmanden fretted over the implication of an informer among the grand jurors, who were the only jurymen so far impaneled. None of the members was named Lucas, and neither John nor Elezabet Romme had a brother-by-birth among the men. "Brother Lucas" was either a code or a nickname, but for whom?

Several of the seventeen jurymen escaped suspicion. Nobody imagined the culprit being the mayor's son, John Cruger, Jr., or Winant Van Zant, who had lost a warehouse in the fires, or Robert Watts, the prominent merchant and jury foreman. But as city and court officials and the other jurymen themselves wondered about the informant, suspicion fell heavily on the remaining fourteen: Henry Beekman, Isaac DePeyster, Thomas Duncan, Rene Hett, Abraham Keteltass, Jeremiah Latouche, John McEvers, John Merritt, David Provoost, Joseph Read, Anthony Rutgers, Adoniah Schuyler, George Spencer, and David Van Horne. Particularly the men of Dutch heritage were watched because of the letter's language, the Rommes' Dutch background, and distrust between English and Dutch New Yorkers.[13]

57

Each juror was left to prove his own loyalty. If any protested too much against the direction of the king's men, he opened himself to charges of treachery. But the test of following the prosecution's lead failed to satisfy Horsmanden's scruples, and lingering suspicion produced its natural effect: It created an inside group among the insiders.

The date was April 28.

# 6

## "The King Against . . . Slaves and Others"

THE TRIALS BEGAN on Friday, May 1, and townsfolk flocked to city hall eager to hear what the king's men had discovered about the now widely rumored conspiracy by slaves and others to burn and rob the city. People from Boston to Savannah who followed the news of Fort George's burning and the rash of fires and thefts were also eager for a solution to the mystery and waited to hear exactly who and what were involved in the New Yorkers' troubles.[1]

Horsmanden and his fellow officials were not ready, however, to make a case for conspiracy. They had only Mary Burton's word as testimony about a plan to set fires, and nothing she said so far identified any arsonist—Cuffee's flight from Philipse's fire was the authorities' closest link so far. Their case for theft was a different matter. The chain of recovered loot from the Hogg burglary, with John Hughson's bumbling and Mary's leads, made the case against Caesar, Prince, Peggy, Hughson, and his wife seem simple. And Mary's testimony that the five had talked of setting fires along with Cuffee and dozens of unnamed blacks suggested a link between the burglary and the plot. The king's men decided to start then with the burglary.

The prosecution opened against Caesar and Prince. Two felony counts faced them. The first was for the Hogg burglary. The second was for theft of beeswax and indigo from Abraham Meyers Cohen. Both blacks pleaded not guilty.

Attorney General Richard Bradley and Joseph Murray called fourteen witnesses for the king. The Hoggs and Cohen in turn identified their goods and had their ownership attested to by subsequent witnesses. The two constables who took the Hoggs' burglary report and Undersheriff Mills testified to their searching Hughson's and arresting Caesar on the tip from the young sailor Christopher Wilson, who repeated in court that he saw Caesar at Hughson's with coins from the Hogg loot. The city council's deputy clerk read Hughson's statement that Caesar gave Peggy goods stolen from Hogg's. A reluctant Peggy also testified but admitted little more than knowing Caesar. Mary concluded the testimony for the prosecution with her account of Prince's boosting Caesar to Peggy's window and handing up goods in the early hours of March 1, the day the Hogg burglary was reported.

Neither Caesar nor Prince took the stand formally in their defense. The law forbade blacks' taking any oath and, thus, they had no power to testify. No witnesses appeared for Caesar, but Prince's holder, John Auboyneau, and two friends of Auboyneau's—aldermen Christopher Bancker and Simon Johnson—served as character witnesses for Prince.

In summation, Attorney General Bradley argued the case was open and shut. Caesar and Prince repeated their denial of the charges. The trial jury returned a quick verdict: Guilty.

Court adjourned without a hint of conspiracy charges, but the fears of a black plot were inflamed over the weekend by what Horsmanden called, "a melancholy and affrighting scene" in neighboring New Jersey.

An hour before dawn on Saturday, May 2, an alarm sounded in Hackensack, and whites rushed from their beds to find seven barns ablaze with flames threatening to spread throughout the sleepy, little town. "In a short time [the barns] burnt down to the ground," one man reported. The fire fighters blocked the flames' advance but discovered they had more than fire to contend with.

Two blacks with guns appeared. One got off a shot. The other was seized before getting his gun loaded. Interrogated immediately, one black confessed to setting fire to three barns; the other black confessed nothing. Neither slave implicated anyone else, yet the whites imagined more than the two were involved.

A clear, quick message went out from Hackensack's citizens to their slaves: The two blacks burned at the stake. The episode was thus ended by the time the news from Hackensack crossed the Hudson. Some New Yorkers openly admired the dispatch as they puzzled over the failure so far to bring anyone to justice for New York City's rash of fires.[2]

* * * * *

The king's men remained mute about the plot on Wednesday, May 6, when they convened to try Peggy, Hughson, and his wife on a felony count of having knowingly received stolen goods from the Hogg burglary. But there were shouts enough about conspiracy.

Just as the trial started, an alarm sounded. A stable behind the burned Philipse storehouse was ablaze. Court recessed as men rushed from city hall. The flames failed to get far before being doused, but the scare sent townsfolk wailing about a plot when a quick investigation revealed arson: Burning sticks had been stuck into the stable boards.

''This was a bold attempt after all that had happened, and was conjectured to be a scheme contrived in favor of the Hughsons,'' Horsmanden noted. If the fire was part of a plan for escape or for postponing the prosecution, it failed.

Court resumed promptly. Attorney General Bradley made the king's case simple. The evidence in the Hogg burglary linked Caesar and Prince to the Hughsons and Peggy; so, as the two slaves were already proven guilty on the basis of that evidence, the three whites also had to be judged guilty, Bradley argued. Having the jury believe a guilty verdict in the prior case demanded a guilty verdict in the present case was a convenient prosecution tactic. It required only one verdict to start a chain stretching however far the king's men wanted. To be sure of forging that crucial link, the prosecution called fourteen witnesses.

The testimony was largely a rerun from the trial of Caesar and Prince. The faces changed but the story remained the same. The key parts were Mary's revelations and Hughson's performance for the magistrates, which Mayor Cruger, Aldermen Simon Johnson, John Moore, and William Romme recounted. As a servant indentured to Hughson, Mary did not testify, but foreman Robert Watts repeated her statements in the grand jury's hearing. The defendants offered no direct testimony and made little case in their defense. The Hughsons called four character witnesses. Nobody testified for Peggy. The outcome never seemed in doubt. The jury's verdict was guilty.

The verdict did nothing to reduce popular anxieties. Indeed, the two trials so far only increased tensions because the officials said not a word about a plot. If they had aimed to heighten the suspense, the king's men could have hit on nothing so effective. The indications that they had the plot clearly in their sights without having yet felled it was pushing people into a frenzy. But drawing out the suspense was not without danger for the king's men, for townsfolk were angered that fires like the one that morning were still breaking out. The people's patience was running short.

The king's men needed to produce plotters soon or suffer the consequences of popular indignation. But they had nothing in fact to offer except Mary's unsubstantiated tale of blacks' meeting at Hughson's and talking of arson. Horsmanden craved a witness to corroborate Mary's story by repeating incendiary talk from Hughson's. If Cuff or someone Mary identified as being at Hughson's confessed to an act of arson, that would be ideal. Even if blacks such as Jacob Sarly's Juan and Joshua Sleydall's Jack—whom popular suspicions picked as the likely incendiaries, the first for the fires at Ben Thomas's and at Agnes Hilton's and the second for laying the coals in attorney Joseph Murray's haystack—were connected to Hughson's, Horsmanden saw a plausible chain to strengthen the conspiracy idea. But making the initial link severely strained the king's men until they got a break: One of the city hall prisoners turned informer.

Arthur Price, an indentured servant of merchant Captain Vincent Pearse, was looking for a way out of the charges against him for filching some of Governor Clarke's goods saved from the flames at Fort George and left at Pearse's. Price thought he found the way out when he and Peggy began to talk in jail.

Virtual solitary confinement made Price and Peggy's chatting almost natural. As whites they occupied part of the upper floor, segregated from blacks crammed below ground in dungeons. Walls and a solid door enforced isolation and privacy for the sexes, as only a shuttered opening in the door provided a view from the hall or the facing cell. By shouting for all to hear the prisoners might talk to others in cells along the hall, but only those in cells facing each other, like Price and Peggy, could talk in conversational tones. Thus, the two occasionally opened up to one another, as Peggy did when the strain of the trials unnerved her.[3]

"I'm very much afraid of those fellows telling or discovering something of me. But if they do, I'll hang them every one, but I'll not forswear myself unless they bring me in," Peggy whispered, referring to some of the blacks being questioned by the authorities.

"How forswear yourself?" Price probed.

"There's fourteen sworn," Peggy blurted.

"What? Is it about Mr. Hogg's good?"

"No, by God, about the fire."

"Were John and his wife in it?"

"Yes, by God, they were both sworn as well as the rest."

"Aren't you afraid that the negroes will discover you?"

"No, Prince, Cuff and Caesar, and Vaarck's negro [Bastian] are all truehearted fellows," Peggy answered. But after her testifying and seeing Caesar and Prince convicted, she complained to Price about Mary Burton. "I've no stomach to eat my victuals. That bitch has fetched me in and made me black as the rest about the indigo and Mr. Hogg's goods. . . . If they do hang the two poor fellows below, they'll be revenged on them yet. But if they send them away, it's another case."

"I don't doubt but they'll endeavor to poison this girl that has sworn," Price prodded.

"No, I don't believe that. But they'll be revenged on them some other ways," Peggy declared. "For your life and soul, you son of a bitch, don't speak a word of what I've told you."

Price ignored Peggy's threat and repeated her every word, first to Undersheriff James Mills, the jailer, and then to Judges Philipse and Horsmanden.

Peggy suspected she had said too much and changed her attitude toward Price. She was moved, and the Hughsons' nineteen-year-old daughter, named Sarah like her mother, came to occupy the redhead's former place.

"I've been with a fortune teller who told me that in less than five weeks time I'd come to trouble if I didn't take good care of myself, but after that I'll come to good fortune," young Sarah confided to Price when arrested on general suspicion immediately after her parents' conviction. She had no idea of what had passed between Peggy and Price.

"What of your father's fortune?" Price pumped.

"My father was to be tried and condemned, but not hanged. His punishment's to go over the water." Sarah sounded confident of her father's being banished unharmed, which implied her also escaping harm.

"Some of the negroes who were concerned in the plot about the fires have discovered," Price said, playing on what he learned from Peggy and trying to deflate the girl's hope.

"I don't know of any plot," Sarah retorted.

"They that were sworn in the plot have discovered and brought them, everyone, in," Price persisted.

"Do you know who it was? When did you hear it?" the girl fidgeted and flushed, beginning to believe the man.

"I heard it by-the-by. It was kept private," Price improvised.

"It must be either Holt's negro or Todd's. We were always afraid of them and mistrusted them, though they were as bad as the rest and were to have set their own master's houses on fire. I wish that Todd had sent his black dog away or sold him when he was going to do it," the girl moaned.

"You'd better tell everything that you know, for that may be of some use to your father."

"No, they're doing all that they can to take his life away. I'd sooner suffer death and be hanged with my daddy, if he's to be hanged, than I'd give them that satisfaction of telling or discovering anything to them. I was to have gone up into the country," Sarah said in a rueful reference to her grandfather Hughson and uncles' place in Yonkers. "Like a fool that I am, I didn't go, but now I'd go up in the country, and I'd be hanged if ever they should get me in [New] York again. If they've no better care of themselves, they'll have a great deal more damage and danger in York than they're aware of. And if they do hang my daddy, they'd better do something else," Sarah fumed.

"They've been picking out of me what they could concerning the fire at the fort and think that I know something of it," Price complained himself. "But I took God to be my judge that I didn't know anything of it."

"As to the fire at the fort," the girl offered, "they didn't set the saddle on the right horse."

Price ran to the authorities with what Sarah said and also repeated a threat Peggy hurled at him when she had chanced to see him.

"Don't you discover anything for your life, for if you do, by God, I'll cut your throat," the redhead flared. Price scoffed as if Peggy's hand lacked the strength to slash his jugular, not considering that a flick of her tongue in the right place might do him harm enough.

<hr />

Price's reports raised Horsmanden's hopes but failed to move him as the informer hoped. The judge wondered if the man were not himself involved in the plot. "Upon the supposition that Arthur knew nothing of the secrets of the conspiracy before he came to jail, he acted with more than ordinary acuteness, for one of his station, in pumping so much out of Peggy and Sarah, and their confidence in him, if he were a stranger to them, was somewhat extraordinary," Horsmanden noted.

The names Peggy and Sarah dropped to Price offered the prosecution leads. Caesar's housemate Bastian was arrested, and constables went for Robert Todd's Dundee and Henry Holt's Joe. A testy Todd confirmed that he had threatened to ship Dundee off in the fall, and like young Sarah, he wished he had, as the lawmen arrested the slave. But dancing master Holt, perhaps sensing ill winds, had set sail with his slave Joe for a more suitable climate.

When the constables put Bastian and Dundee in cells, Peggy no longer needed to guess if Price had talked; and sitting convicted of a felony, she knew only bad fortune awaited her unless she somehow forestalled it. So she decided to do her own talking about a plot and gave Undersheriff Mills and a jail secretary what Horsmanden labelled a "voluntary confession."

Saying she saw ten or twelve blacks meeting at John Romme's, particularly during December 1740, Peggy named seven attendees: Philipse's Cuff, Peter Jay's Brash, John Pintard's Caesar, Alderman Moore's Cato, Henry Breasted's Jack, William English's Patrick, and Cornelius Tiebout's Curacoa Dick. "The rest of the names that were in the combination, I cannot remember, or their master's names. . . . They proposed to burn the fort first and, afterward, the city, and then steal, rob and carry away all the money and goods they could . . . to Romme's. . . . All the rest of the negroes in city and country were to meet in one night. They were to murder everyone that had money," Peggy explained. "The reason why I didn't make this discovery before [was that] Romme swore them all never to discover, and swore me, too. I thought I'd wrong my soul if I discovered it."

Peggy's story differed from Mary's in numbers, names, and places. The redhead counted a dozen blacks at the meetings, not the servant-girl's twenty to thirty. Mary named only three blacks—Caesar, Cuff, and Prince; Peggy named seven, putting Cuff on her list but refusing to implicate her Caesar or Prince. Also, where Mary named John Hughson and his wife as principals and their tavern as the plotting place, Peggy never mentioned the Hughsons and set the scene at Romme's.

Horsmanden seized what Peggy said to corroborate the existence of a plot, but he wanted more from the woman. "She seemed now to think it high time to do something to recommend herself to mercy, and this confession coming voluntarily from her, it gave hopes that she was in earnest and would make some material discoveries," the judge noted. He wanted more detail and, especially, more talk of Hughson's instead of Romme's. In hope of getting it, Horsmanden himself interrogated Peggy, with Judge Philipse present.

"Dare not to say anything but the truth or to accuse innocent persons. We have dived so far into this mystery of iniquity already that we can easily discern whether you prevaricate or not; and if you do, you must not flatter yourself with hopes of being recommended to mercy," Horsmanden huffed. "Disingenuous behavior will but deceive yourself and make your case desperate."

Peggy appeared to heed the warning, for Horsmanden noted that "she put on the air of sincerity, as if to make a discovery, but seemed to be under terrible apprehension." She talked under oath for two days.

Beginning with the autumn of 1740, when she lived at the free Negro Frank's on the Battery, Peggy reported visiting John Romme's—about three or four doors away—to have a pair of boots made. During the frequent fittings, she became acquainted with Romme and his wife, Elezebet.

"Many different negroes [were] there at several different times [and] used to resort there to drink drams, punch and other strong liquors. Romme [was] keeping a public house. Often numbers of them have continued at the Romme's house till two or three o'clock in the morning, to my knowledge, drinking, singing and playing at dice," Peggy opened.

"Returning home by the way of Whitehall" close to midnight on Sunday, November 2, the redhead recalled, "I saw two negroes coming towards me, each of them with a firkin upon their shoulders, and [I] saw them turn into Romme's gate sixteen firkins. I stayed under [Obidiah] Hunt's shed . . . because I suspected them to be stolen goods." The goods were in fact stolen, and although she refused to admit knowing or being able to identify the two black thieves, they were Caesar and Prince.

"One evening, some time about last Christmas, I was at the house of John Romme where I saw, in company with Romme and his wife, ten or eleven negroes, all in one room. And Romme was observing to the negroes how well the rich people at this place lived and said if they (meaning the negroes, as I understood) would be advised by him, they (including himself and the negroes, as I understood) should have the money. To which Cuff, Mr. Philipse's negro, replied 'How will you manage that?' 'Well enough,' said Romme, 'set them all a light fire, burn the house of them that have the most money, and kill them all as the negroes would've done their masters and mistresses formerly,'" Peggy recalled. Horsmanden noted the reference to the 1712 uprising.

"Romme'd be captain over them till they'd get all their money, and then he'd be governor," Peggy explained. "Cuff said they couldn't do it. 'Yes,' says Romme, 'we'll do well enough. We'll send into the country for the rest of the negroes to help, because I can write, and I know several negroes in the country that can read.' And he encouraged them and said, 'I'll stand by you. The sun'll shine very bright by-and-by. Never fear, my lads.' 'The Devil take the failer,'" Cuff chorused, according to Peggy.

Romme had it all planned, even a getaway. "If it should happen that anything should come out, I'll make my escape and go to North Carolina, Cape Fear or somewhere thereabout or into the Mohawks country, where I've lived before. Besides, the Devil can't hurt me, for I've a great many friends in town and the best in the place will stand by me," Romme boasted, according to Peggy.

He offered the blacks an out, too. "If the fire didn't succeed, and they couldn't compass their ends that way, then he proposed to the negroes present that they should steal all that they could from their masters. Then he'd carry them to a strange country and give them their liberty and set them free," Peggy reported. Romme asked the blacks, " 'Will it do?' Cuff answered, 'There's great talking and no cider'." At that point the meeting broke up, with few of the blacks responding to Romme's exhorting, Peggy said.

"John Romme insisted upon my being sworn to secrecy that I wouldn't discover anything that I knew had passed in his house, either relating to the butter, or the fire, or discourse at the meeting, which I accordingly was [sworn] and kissed a book. What book it was, I know not," Peggy claimed. "Romme's wife was by, all or most of the time, during the meeting and discourse, and when Romme insisted that I should be sworn, [he insisted] as well on his wife." So both women were sworn to secrecy, although the redhead said that, like herself, "Romme's wife didn't at all join in any of the discourse."

The detail of Peggy's statement impressed Horsmanden, but he suspected her of thinking the fugitive Romme was a safe target and of switching the scene from Hughson's to Romme's. Only with apparent reluctance did the judge concede that, in his words, the plot "might have been brooding at both places. One may be persuaded from the course of the evidence that Romme was apprized at least of the conspiracy."

Elezabet Romme was again brought in for questioning, and again she denied almost everything. She said she knew nothing about any conspiracy to fire the fort and the town and murder people nor anything about an oath of secrecy imposed by her husband on herself or Peggy.

Elezabet admitted that her husband received some firkins of butter but claimed to know nothing about them. As for blacks coming to the Rommes' house, she said Cuff Philipse's father kept game fowls at the house and "used to come there to bring them victuals, but [he] never used to stay long." Other blacks also came to the house for a drink, but Elezabet claimed they never stayed long and at no time were there more than three—the legal limit.

"Vaarck's Caesar used to come morning and evening often; Auboyneau's Prince sometimes; Mr. Moore's Cato once or twice, and no oftener, as I remember; [I] never saw Breasted, the hatter's negro, there at all, nor Mr. Jay's Brash, nor English's Patrick, but [I] have seen Vaarck's Bastian there, and Mr. Pintard's Caesar," said Elezabet, when pushed to name the blacks who visited her house.

Elezabet was jailed, and so were the blacks Peggy named. Cuff was already in a cell, of course, but not the other six. The redhead identified them as they were brought in, and she caught a mistake when English's Cork was arrested instead of his housemate Patrick.[4]

The mix up prompted Horsmanden to pen a note that revealed his disposition on judging blacks.

> Cork was unfortunately of a countenance somewhat ill-favored, naturally of a suspicious look and reckoned withal to be unlucky too. His being sent for before the magistrates in such a perilous season might be thought sufficient to alarm the most innocent of the negroes and occasion appearance of their being under some terrible apprehensions. But it was much otherwise with Cork, and notwithstanding the disadvantage of his natural aspect, upon being interrogated concerning the conspiracy, he showed such a cheerful, open, honest smile upon his countenance (none of your fictitious hypocritical grins) that everyone that was by and observed it (and there were several in the room) jumped in the same observation and opinion, that they never saw the fellow look so handsome: Such an efficacy have truth and innocence that they even reflect beauty upon deformity!
>
> On the contrary, Patrick's visage betrayed his guilt. Those who are used to negroes may have experienced that some of them, when charged with any piece of villainy they have been detected in, have an odd knack or (it is hard what to call or how to describe it) way of turning their eyes inwards, as it were, as if shocked at the consciousness of their own perfidy; their looks, at the same time, discovering all the symptoms of the most inveterate malice and resentment. This was Patrick's appearance, and such [was] his behavior upon examination, as served to induce one's credit to what Peggy had declared so far at least that

he was present at a meeting when the conspiracy was talked of and was one of the persons consenting to act a part in that infernal scheme.

The mix up with Cork and Patrick boosted Horsmanden's hope of Peggy's truly cooperating, as she clearly knew the blacks she named. But the judge remained troubled by the discrepancies between her story and the servant girl's, for after eyeing the six blacks Peggy had fingered, Mary said she recognized none as ever being at Hughson's. The judge saw his choice as either believing Mary or Peggy or believing them both. For the moment he leaned toward both which, in his words, meant that "this villainous scheme was carrying on at Romme's as well as Hughson's."

Horsmanden seemed momentarily pleased with Peggy, especially when she finally mentioned Caesar and Prince. They "used much to frequent Romme's house in the evenings and to stay often late in the night, drinking and playing at dice," the redhead said. But she insisted, "I never heard any discourse among them concerning burning the fort or setting fire to the town."

Caesar and Prince stood beyond protection when Peggy mentioned them, for on Friday, May 8, they received their sentences from Horsmanden and Philipse, the second justice delivering the decree with bluster.

"You have been convicted by twelve honest men upon their oaths, so the judgment of God has at length overtaken you. I have reason to believe that the crimes you now stand convicted of are not the least of those you have been concerned in, for by your general characters you have been very wicked fellows, hardened sinners, and ripe, as well as ready, for the most enormous and daring enterprises, especially you, Caesar," Judge Philipse declared.

"The time you have yet to live is very short. I earnestly advise and exhort both of you to employ it in the most diligent and best manner you can, by confessing . . . and praying God of his infinite goodness to have mercy on your souls; and as God knows the secrets of your hearts and cannot be cheated or imposed upon, so you must shortly give an account to him and answer for all your actions. And depend upon it, if you do not truly repent before you die, there is a hell to punish the wicked eternally," the judge said, coming to the bottom line.

"You Caesar and you Prince . . . are to be hanged by the neck until you be dead. . . . And [it is] further ordered that after the execution of the said sentence, the body of Caesar be hung in chains."

On Monday the two went to the gallows, and afterward Caesar's corpse was fixed on a platform near the city's powder house. "They died very stubbornly, without confessing anything about the conspiracy and denied they knew anything of it to the last," Horsmanden noted. "These two negroes bore the character of very wicked idle fellows . . . and were persons of most obstinate and untractable tempers, so that there was no expectation of drawing anything from them which would make for the discovery of the conspiracy, though there seemed good reason to conclude— as well as from their characters as [from] what had been charged upon them by information from others—that they were two principal ringleaders in it among the blacks. It was thought proper to execute them for the robbery and not wait for the bringing them to a trial for the conspiracy, though the proof against them was strong and clear concerning their guilt as to that also. And it was imagined that as stealing and plundering was a principal part of the hellish scheme in agitation among the inferior sort of these infernal confederates, this earnest of example and punishment might break the knot and induce some of them to unfold this mystery of iniquity in hopes, thereby, to recommend themselves to mercy," Horsmanden explained.

The date was May 11.

# 7

## "Some of Them to Unfold This Mystery"

Arthur Price's talking encouraged Horsmanden. His informing provided apparent leverage to make suspects turn king's evidence or to move them to implicate themselves and others. Price boosted the officials' prospects for sustaining conspiracy charges, particularly after they moved Philipse's Cuff into the same cell with him.

The jailer supplied Cuff and Price with "a tankard of punch now and then, in order to cheer up their spirits and make them more sociable, [which] produced the desired effects," Horsmanden explained.[1]

"What could be the reason that Peggy's called down so often?" Cuff worried in his cups.

"I think Peggy's discovering the plot about the fire," Price milked.

"She can't do that unless she forswears herself, I know," Cuff muttered. "I'm one of the Geneva Club that was sworn. . . . Hughson swore Quack three times."

"I believe I know this Quack. He lives with a butcher."

"No, he don't live with a butcher but lives with a painter, who lives within a few doors of a butcher. . . . Quack's married to a negro wench who's cook to the fort, to the governor," Cuff rambled on without apparent suspicion at his being in a cell with a white man or at the sudden hospitality of the jailer.[2]

"How could Quack do it?" Arthur reached, trying to tie the black to the fort fire.

"I can't tell how he did it, but Quack was to do it and did do it."

"Don't you think the firing will be found out?"

"No, by God, I don't think it ever will."

"Weren't you afraid that the two negroes who were to be executed on Monday would discover?"

"I wasn't afraid of that, for I was sure they'd be burnt to ashes before they'd discover it. I'd lay my life on it," Cuff crowed but still worried. "I wonder why they only took up the Long Bridge boys and didn't take up those of the Smith's Fly. For I believe if the truth be known, [the Smith's Fly boys] are as much concerned as [the Long Bridge boys]."

Butcher John Roosevelt's Quack, one of the Smith Fly boys, was arrested on Tuesday, May 12.

⛓⛓⛓⛓⛓

May 13 was the day Governor Clarke had proclaimed for "public fasting and humiliation," and Judge Horsmanden reported that "the same was reverently and decently observed, particularly in this city, by persons of all persuasions. The shops were all shut up, and persons of all ranks resorted to their respective places of divine worship." Himself a vestryman, Horsmanden attended services at Trinity Church, but he did not linger: His own shop was open to receive a fresh delivery from Mary Burton.[3]

The girl reported that a day or two after her testifying to the grand jury on April 22, Vaarck's Bastian accosted her as she walked by Vaarck's house on Broad Street and asked if she told the authorities anything about the fires. She said she lied and told him no. "Damn you, it's not best for you [to talk], for fear you should be burnt in the next [fire]," Bastian threatened. The girl claimed this housemate of Caesar's was among the blacks at Hughson's who promised to burn the fort and the whole city.

None of the king's men asked Mary why she took three weeks to speak up about the incident. They apparently took for granted that only now that Bastian was in jail did she feel safe enough to finger him. Grateful as they were to have her talking, Horsman-

73

den and his cohort continued to accept Mary's tendency to speak only against persons who were already implicated and in hand.

The men pictured Mary's motives as simple: She wanted her freedom, which the reward proclamation offered, but fear made her cautious, in their view. They marked her hesitancy as a sign of her youthful sixteen years of age and an understandable fear from having spent almost a year in what was being painted as Hughson's den of iniquity. Her resemblance to the girls who lied so murderously in the Salem witchcraft episode in Massachusetts during 1692 seemed to have eluded the officials. They showed no sign of thinking she was lying, although they clearly suspected she was not telling them the whole truth.

To see if the girl was holding back on other blacks, Horsmanden had her look at several prisoners. She identified Roosevelt's Quack as a pal of Caesar, Cuff, and Prince's and said she saw him often outside Hughson's but never inside. She identified candle maker Joshua Sleydall's Jack also, and insinuated that he was intimately acquainted with young Sarah Hughson. "From the kindness shown him by Hughson, his wife, and daughter, I've great reason to think [Jack] was in their secrets," Mary said. When asked directly if Jack was among the plotters, however, she admitted never actually seeing or hearing him talk of a plot.

In trying to make herself useful to the judge, Mary sometimes sounded as if any black in or around Hughson's was party to a plot. She talked, for instance, of seeing as many as thirty blacks together at Hughson's particularly on Sundays, when slaves had most of their free time. But she reported that they usually played dice, not plotted. The gambling was illegal but hardly interested Horsmanden, although he saw the slaves' identities as leads. The girl promised him continuing help by saying, "I'd remember their faces if I saw them."

Mary did recall a few names. Vaarck's Jonneau and the widowed butchery owner Elizabeth Carpenter's Albany drank at Hughson's, but the girl said she heard neither talk about setting fires or killing whites. However, the Long Islander Thomas Ellison's Jamaica was among "some country negroes [who] were concerned in the conspiracy about the fires," she reported: That pricked Horsmanden's ears, for hearing that slaves outside the city were involved enlarged his notion of the plot.

The girl also elaborated on the Hughson-Romme connection. She mentioned John Romme's name at the beginning of March, in the initial investigation of the Hogg burglary, but had since fallen silent about him. Now she reported his frequenting Hughson's and being fast friends with the family. Romme and John and Sarah Hughson often went up to Peggy's room and talked in Dutch, which Mary did not understand.

"Romme used to tell Hughson he was afraid of me," but Hughson told him, " 'She's bound to me and dare not tell, for if she did, I'd murder her,' " the girl reported. Romme refused to drop his guard, evidently, for Mary said that when she was around he never did or said anything directly about the plot. The girl could not swear then that Romme was part of the plot or that he had actually done anything illegal.

Hughson, his wife, daughter Sarah, Peggy, and many blacks were not so cautious as Romme. They took an oath in front of the girl to keep "the secrets about firing the fort, the houses at the Fly and the whole town and about murdering the white people," Mary reported:

"Now you must take care, for you're all sworn," Hughson told the blacks.

"Don't tell," Caesar cautioned Mary. He, like Romme, apparently had his doubts about her.

"She dare not," Hughson scowled.

"Damn my blood if I'll tell any if I am burnt," Cuff interjected.

"Caesar, can you get any others to help?" Hughson asked.

"I can get enough who dare not but go if I speak," Caesar boasted. And, according to Mary, the talk was hardly idle. He paid Hughson £12 to buy weapons, and the taverner procured "seven or eight [long] guns, three pistols and four swords, which were hid away under the boards in the garret floor in Hughson's house," the servant girl informed Horsmanden.

❊❊❊❊❊

While Mary talked in hopes of winning freedom, Peggy sat in fear of losing her life or her baby if she failed to please both the king's men and the Hughsons, whose kin held the infant.

Horsmanden himself remained hard on Peggy, pressing her to fulfill his images of the scenes at Hughson's. She shifted to accommodate him but continued to move gingerly. Resisting his full desire, she still focused on the absent Romme, yielding only by

75

mentioning the Hughsons and fingering the now dead Caesar and Prince.

Peggy recalled that Romme dropped in at Hughson's one day early in February 1741. Hughson was off cutting firewood. Disappointed not to find him home, Romme ordered punch, warmed himself, and started chatting with Mrs. Hughson about the harsh winter.

"I've money enough myself, yet I can't buy wood for it. But I've a parcel of good children who bring me wood almost every night. So I've done well enough hitherto," Romme crowed.

"It's poor enough with us. You're a gentlemen and can live without work," Mrs. Hughson retorted. Her manner moved Romme to explain his visit: He wanted Hughson to hide some butter.

"The weather's so hard and the ground so frozen that I don't know how to hide them away. And as no vessels can go out, I can't ship them off. I believe gammon would do better. My brother's going to Carolina and he can stow them in his cabin when there could not be room to stow there fifty or sixty firkins of butter."

"I don't know, but I believe my husband won't have a hand in it."

"Oh, I want to talk to him myself, for I know how circumstances are with you. Towards the evening I'll come again and talk to him, for I want a load of wood," Romme replied.

The butter and gammon, hams and sides of bacon, were stolen from Peter Vergereau's storehouse and delivered to Romme's by Caesar and Prince, Peggy explained. Romme often got goods from them and from Cuff, his brother, and the young white boy Christopher Wilson, nicknamed Yorkshire. They were the "parcel of good children" Romme was probably referring to, the redhead said.

Peggy's continuing implication of the fugitive drew particular attention on Monday, May 18, when John Romme was returned to the city after being captured in Brunswick, New Jersey.

Interrogated immediately, Romme positively denied knowing anything about a plot. He admitted blacks had brought firkins of butter to his house, but he claimed his wife took them in and he knew nothing more about them.

Quick on her husband's heels, Elezabet Romme was brought from her cell. She again denied knowing of any plot. She was hardly pleased at her husband's return or his contradicting her by saying that she, not he, had taken in the butter. On returning to her cell, Elezabet showed her sore displeasure. "Going by her husband's apartment, and he putting his head out of the wicket, she civilly saluted him with a smart slap on the chops," Horsmanden reported.

John Romme was questioned repeatedly, but "not a word would he own about the conspiracy," the judge grumbled. Peggy's word alone stood against Romme, for although Mary Burton and John Vaarck suggested probable illicit activity by Romme, only Peggy actually depicted the gentleman as little more than a well-heeled fence.

The redhead refused to relent at the fugitive's return. Pouring out more detail, she left no doubt about Romme's handling the stolen butter. Portraying him as a lazy dog that nosed around after work was done, Peggy confirmed that his wife took the night delivery because Romme lay in bed. But he made the deal, haggling to pay fifteen shillings each for the firkins while Caesar insisted on and got twenty shillings each, Peggy said. She listed other loot Romme bought from Caesar: twenty pieces of eight, a shirt, stockings, and the coat he was then wearing as she confronted him.[4]

The details convinced Horsmanden's colleagues of Peggy's sincerity, but the judge grumbled about her trying "to provide for her own safety, if she could do it so cheap as by amusing us with a narrative of the plot." He complained particularly that she still had said virtually nothing about the Hughsons and that, in his words, she "shifted the scene and laid it in the wrong place." He spoke as if the woman's evidence mattered only against Hughson and not against gentleman John Romme.

Hughson was certainly a more convenient target, for if Romme were put firmly in the plot, the king's men faced the prospect of prosecuting a gentleman from a respectable, old Dutch family, rather than simply a lower class taverner with no significant political or social ties. The black-white confrontation seemed more straightforward with Hughson who could be dismissed as what Horsmanden called "scum." Romme could not be dismissed so easily. If he were part of the plot, his class standing would cast him as the natural leader and his connections promised to aggravate Dutch–English tensions and political bickering. Horsmanden clearly preferred to steer clear of Romme and drive against Hughson.

Peggy's insistence on fingering Romme frustrated Horsmanden, as did her refusal to come bare on Hughson. Bent on having his way with her, the judge sent her to stand with Hughson and his wife to face the first indictments for "conspiring, confederating and combining with divers negroes and others to burn the City of New-York and also to kill and destroy the inhabitants thereof." He suggested convicting Peggy of conspiracy to get her "to make an ingenuous confession in order to save herself."

The king's other men made the judge compromise his desire, and he agreed to recommend Peggy for a pardon. The papers were prepared for Governor Clarke to sign and seal for delivery, but there was a catch. Horsmanden got the other officials to agree to wait and see if the woman "should be thought amply to have merited [pardon]," and he was to decide what constituted the final merit.

Peggy was left ignorant of the document drawn for her on Wednesday, May 20. She continued to sit in isolation with thoughts of how to ransom herself and her baby from death and with the haunting spectacle of Caesar's nine-day-old corpse, no doubt plaguing her lonely days and lonely nights.

❈❈❈❈❈

A growing harvest of suspected conspirators caused many besides Peggy to fear the grim reaper, and like her, they talked in hopes of saving themselves. Carpenter's Albany wasted no time in trying to shift suspicion from himself when the constables arrested him. He admitted no direct knowledge of any plot but did confess to having heard something about the fires.

"Niblet's Sarah told me that [her housemate] Sandy had been concerned in setting the fort on fire; that he'd likewise set Machado's house, next door to [Niblet's], on fire; and had also thrown fire over Alderman Bancker's fence," Albany claimed.

The officials checked the slave's source, Thomas Niblet's Sarah. She denied having said anything like what Albany claimed and found herself in jail. The king's men retrieved Niblet's Sandy and jailed him also for further questioning after he denied knowing anything about any fires or a conspiracy. Thus did fear form a progression: One suspect spoke and three now sat in jail.

"If you will speak the truth, the governor will pardon you though you have been concerned [in the plot]. This is the time for

78

you to save your life by making a free and ingenuous confession,'' the grand jurors told Sandy, when questioning him.

"The time before, after that the negroes told all they knew, then the white people hanged them,'' the sixteen-year-old retorted, remembering the black history of 1712.

"That's false. The negroes which confessed the truth and made a discovery were certainly pardoned and shipped off,'' the jurors huffed.

Evidently accepting the men's promises of good faith, the boy recited a litany of dozens of slaves' uttering sentiments similar to Cuff's cursing once, "Damn me, hang me or burn me, I'll set fire to the town.'' And they did more than talk. Cuff and Roosevelt's Quack burned the Philipse storehouse. Quack also burned the fort after trying to recruit Sandy to help. The boy said he told Quack, "No, I'll not run the risk of being hanged, but you can go to hell and be damned.''

Sandy fingered several others by name, too. "William, Captain Lush's Spanish negro, told me if they didn't send him over to his own country, he'd ruin the city,'' the boy reported. "Curacoa Dick said he'd set fire to Mr. Van Zant's storehouse, and he was to be a captain. Captain Sarly's Juan said he'd set fire or help to set fire to Hilton's house and was to be a captain of the Fly company. Captain Bosch's Francis threw fire into Mr. Bancker's yard and told me so. Mr. Peter DeLancey's Antonio said he'd burn his master's house. McMullen's Augustine said he'd burn his master's house and was to have been an officer. [Gerardus Comfort's] Jack and an old man [Comfort's Cook] said they'd set fire to their master's house and assist in their designs. Gomez's Cuffee said he'd burn his master's house and was to have been an officer in the Fly company.

"Just by Coenties Market, I heard Mr. English's Patrick and Colonel Moore's Cato say they'd set fire to their masters' houses. Wilkins' Fortune was to set fire to his master's house. Vaarck's Caesar, that was hanged, was concerned and was to have been captain of the Long Bridge company. About a fortnight before the fire at the fort, at Comfort's house, I overheard Jack and the old man Cook, in company with four other negroes I didn't know, talk about the rising of the negroes,'' Sandy said. His words settled the old suspicions about the Spanish blacks and fixed suspicions on the slaves of several prominent citizens such as Chief Justice Delancey's younger brother Peter and Alderman John Moore.

"What was it the negroes proposed by rising and doing all this mischief?" the jurors wondered.

"Their design was to kill all the gentlemen and take their wives. Quack and Cuffee were particular persons that talked so," Sandy answered.

"Was Mr. Walter's Quaco knowing or concerned in the affair?"

"No, though he was always cursing white people," Sandy replied about the slave who had said, "Fire, Fire, Scorch, Scorch, A LITTLE, damn it, BY-AND-BY."

"You had much acquaintance with Danby, the governor's negro?"

"Very little."

"Does he know anything?"

"I believe not." Sandy thus cleared Clarke's slave boy, but his words cast thunderclouds over many other black heads.

✷✷✷✷✷

The king's men conjured up a scene more threatening than even Horsmanden had so far projected. Particularly Sandy's mentioning officers and subordinates alarmed the officials, as they imagined massive organization among disgruntled slaves. Construing the boy's words literally, the judge himself noted that "several of the officers were appointed captains" and pictured blacks mustered into paramilitary units with at least three companies of men to match the number of captains Sandy listed. Marking a hundred per company meant nearly half the city's black males age sixteen or older were in the plot by the judge's reckoning.

Sandy's story also strengthened the notion that both Mary and Peggy were telling the truth—the girl about Hughson's and the redhead about Romme's. The boy's referring, as Cuff had, to blacks being grouped into the Smith's Fly Boys in the city's northeast end and the Long Bridge Boys in the southwest, around Bridge Street, inclined the king's men to believing that, as the judge put it, "the conspirators held their cabals at Romme's as well as at Hughson's." Romme's on lower Broad Street was convenient for the Long Bridge Boys and Hughson's off upper Broadway for the Smith's Fly Boys. The two places provided access to both the largest pockets of slaves and of wealth in the city.

Pulling together the scenes described by Sandy, Peggy, and Mary, the king's men projected a plot that ran beyond arson or theft. They envisioned a general slave revolt. The frightening image turned more terrible as the officials' considered the blacks being assisted by what Horsmanden called, "the most flagitious, degenerated, abandoned, scum and dregs of the white people."

The blacks were threats enough in the officials' mind, but believing them limited in their thinking, they feared only haphazard or desultory violence from them. White leadership, however, darkened the portents. And the more Horsmanden and his cohort heard of the plot, the more they imagined long-term, large-scale planning. The officials' initial talk of a simple rash of fires had given way to talk of all New York City being burned and, in Sandy's words, the killing of "all the gentlemen and tak[ing] their wives." The plot turned then from simple disorder and thievery into the darkest danger of social destruction.

The possibility of Sandy's lying completely was settled in the officials' mind when the grand jury questioned John Wilkins's Fortune, whom the boy had implicated as one of the slaves set to burn his holder's house. Fortune said Roosevelt's Quack talked of burning Fort George and after the fire admitted setting the blaze and named as accomplices Sandy and Lewis Gomez's Cuffee. Fortune said Sandy himself confessed to him of having a hand in the fort fire.

Recalling his returning home after running an errand on Broadway during the evening before the fire at the Philipse storehouse on New Street, Fortune also added to the officials' notes against Philipse's Cuff and the Spanish blacks. "I came by the house of Captain [Jacob] Phoenix at the corner of New Street. I saw Cuffee and two more negroes at some distance from him. But being dark, who they were I didn't know. I believe one of the two negroes was a Spaniard, because when I left Cuffee, I heard one of them call to him '*Ven aquí, señor*,'" Fortune mimicked the Spanish for "Come here, mister."

Fortune said he asked Cuff, "What you doing here so late?"

"I'm waiting here for my master. He wanted something out of the storehouse and was to come and bring the key with him," Cuff replied although old man Philipse's actually fetching a key seemed unlikely. The inference Horsmanden drew was that Cuff and a couple of Spanish blacks had laid the preparations for the next day's fire.

"Are you acquainted with Hughson and his family?" the jury asked Fortune.

"I was frequently asked by Caesar, Prince, and Philipse's Cuffee to go there [to Hughson's], but never did go. I was told that they'd a dance there every other night."

"Did you ever go to Romme's house or know what negroes frequently resorted thither?"

"I never went there myself, nor am I acquainted with those that did," Fortune answered. The jury gave him that Friday night in jail to recollect his thoughts, and in the morning the men questioned him again.

"Don't you remember some others concerned in the late fires, besides Quack, Sandy, and Cuffee? If you do, it's expected you should name them, without any regard to persons, be they white men or negroes."

Fortune repeated that he knew nobody else involved but gave the men a bit more on Sandy, perhaps hoping to make the boy regret having mentioned him.

"My master's going to send me to Albany," Sandy pouted.

"For what?"

"I set fire to the house three times, but my master discovered and extinguished it and, therefore, is resolved to send me away," the boy confessed a day or two before his arrest, Fortune reported.

The jurymen recalled Sandy to answer questions raised by Fortune, but the boy tried to deflect accusations from himself by implicating other blacks and elaborating on talk of violence.

"Going by Comfort's one Sunday evening, about a month before the fort was set on fire, Jack called me in. About twenty negroes were there. I only knew Jack and the old man [Cook], Vanderspiegle's Fortune, Peck's Caesar, Cowley's Cato, and [Mary] Burk's Sarah, the only negro woman there. Upon my coming into the room, they gave me drink and then asked me to burn houses, and I not giving a ready answer, Sarah swore at me and the [other] negroes did also, and with knives in their hands. They frightened me. I feared they'd kill me. I promised I'd assist and burn the Slip Market," Sandy claimed. "They swore to be true to one another on the oath that 'God Almighty strike the [failers] dead with the first thunder.' . . . Sarah and Vanderspiegle's Fortune were to have set fire to the meal market."

"Did you use Hughson's and Romme's house with the other negroes?" the jurors asked.

82

"I never was at either of their houses."

"Who told you of what you related?" the men asked, because the boy hinted at events in places he now denied visiting.

"Jack did and one of the Spanish negroes who were concerned."

"Did you assist in setting the fort on fire?"

"No, only before it Quack did ask me to help him, and I gave the answer mentioned before. Then Quack said he'd do it," Sandy insisted. He denied having tried to set his holder's house on fire, too, and in an apparent effort to change the subject, Sandy told the grand jurors a grisly story about a slave who lived next door to Niblet's.

"Diana, in a passion because her mistress was angry with her, *took her own young child from her breast and laid it in the cold [so] that it froze to death*," Sandy declared. Horsmanden himself underscored the horror. The men asked no more of the boy that day.

Calling in Burk's Sarah, the jurymen confronted her with Sandy's allegations of her threatening him and being in the reported plot. The woman held her tongue except to spit out that the boy once told her, "God damn all the white people. If I had it in my power, I'd set them all on fire."

⛓⛓⛓⛓⛓

Thus, blacks started pinching one another and leaving Horsmanden and his men to pick among the squealing. Sandy's admission that he was party to the plot, even if he entered under duress as he claimed, made him a prize for the prosecution. As an insider, his word alone could serve to convict other blacks whom he identified as being involved. The willingness of Carpenter's Albany and Wilkins's Fortune to talk suggested, however, that Sandy's word would not have to stand alone. Fortune's difference with Sandy about the boy's own part and about which Cuffee— Gomez's or Philipse's—was involved at the fort seemed insignificant to Horsmanden. The important point was that both corroborated the story that blacks had set Fort George on fire and talked of setting other blazes. An official roundup of blacks began then, and unlike when the mobs had pounced in April, there seemed evidence enough to make a case in court.

Even under the loose rules of conspiracy law, however, the king's men wanted more than they had at present to proceed against white suspects. Peggy's confession that she took an oath of secrecy, Arthur Price's reports that Sarah Hughson acknowledged the plot, and Mary Burton's testimony about meetings at the tavern provided enough for a conspiracy indictment against the Hughsons and Peggy. But to settle the case in court, Horsmanden wanted to reconcile the differences between Mary and Peggy's stories.

If the redhead agreed with the girl or another white corroborated the girl's story, the king's men would have what they wanted: Two witnesses against Hughson as the chief conspirator. That was the strongest case in the officials' eyes, because of the evidence confirmed by the Hogg burglary. Peggy's own story about Romme seemed headed nowhere because his social standing and Mary's saying nothing that definitely tied him to a plot left him in the background, if not in the clear. That was what drove Horsmanden to get Peggy to talk about the Hughsons. If she refused to shift her story, she was likely to be damned by her own confession which implicated her in a plot, but if she did shift, she was almost sure to get a pardon although Horsmanden refused to let her know that.

Young Sarah Hughson was a possible second witness, but she refused to tell the king's men anything that might jeopardize her parents. Horsmanden tried to push the nineteen-year-old to confirm what Price reported her saying in jail and confronted her with the informer. The girl admitted talking about her fortune teller's readings and acknowledged that Price advised her to tell what she knew about a plot, but she insisted she knew nothing. Horsmanden was sure she was lying and noted that "when Price vouched the thing to her face, she did but faintly contradict what he said."

The king's men were not ready then to try the Hughsons and Peggy for conspiracy, but they were ready to move against the blacks. Cuff's slip in jail with Price had put Roosevelt's Quack in the officials' lap as the arsonist at Fort George. Sandy and Wilkins's Fortune finished any remaining question about Quack and further named other blacks as arsonists: Sarly's Juan at Hilton's and Cornelius Tiebout's Curacoa Dick at Van Zant's. Their notes on Cuff added to the suspicion of his having a hand in the Philipse fire and, perhaps, also in the fort fire. Horsmanden had not only his solution to at least three of the eleven fires of March and April, but also identities and two willing witnesses.

Cuff's regret was clear. "After Quack was committed, Cuffee never mentioned anything . . . but read sometimes and cried much," Price informed Horsmanden. The privileged slave of the speaker of New York's assembly seemed doomed, and not him alone.

The date was May 28.

# 8

❦❦❦❦❦❦❦❦❦❦❦❦❦❦❦❦❦❦❦❦❦❦❦❦❦❦❦❦

# "To the Place of Execution"

On Friday, May 29, the king's men finally opened their conspiracy case to the public. Horsmanden presided on the Supreme Court bench with Frederick Philipse. Attorney General Richard Bradley led the prosecution, backed by Joseph Murray and William Smith, two of the most successful lawyers in New York City. Huddled as defendants stood Adolph Philipse's Cuff and John Roosevelt's Quack, each facing two felony counts—one for arson and one for conspiracy.[1]

"This is a cause of very great expectation, it being, as I conceive, a matter of the utmost importance that ever yet came to be tried in this province," the attorney general told the packed chamber at city hall. More than the two slaves were clearly on trial as Bradley outlined the prosecution's case. He spoke not of simple arson or the slaves' agreeing to set isolated fires; he suggested a holocaust.

"You will hear from the mouths of our witnesses that these two negroes, with divers others, frequently met at the house of one John Hughson, in this city. It was there they were harbored; there was the place of their general rendezvous; and there it was this hellish conspiracy was brooded, formed, consented, and agreed

86

to. It was there that these two negroes and the rest of the conspirators came to a resolution of burning the king's house at the fort, and this whole town, and of murdering the inhabitants as they should come to extinguish the flames,'' the attorney general asserted.

"The eyes of the inhabitants of this city and province are upon you, relying on and confiding in you, that by the justice of your verdict in this cause this day the peace and safety of this city and province may for the future be secured to them—which at present, until some examples are made, seem very precarious,'' Bradley told the jurors. "Gentlemen, it is in you the people in general place their hopes and expectations of their future security and repose, that they may sit securely in their own houses and rest quietly in their beds, no one daring to make them afraid.'' He left no doubt about what was demanded of the twelve.

Eleven witnesses testified for the king's case.

Mary Burton repeated her story of blacks' meeting at Hughson's, emphasizing Cuff's closeness with Caesar and Prince and quoting his saying, "A great many people have too much and others too little. My old master has a great deal of money, but in a short time, he'll have less and I'll have more.''

The indentured servant girl tied the talk to a fresh encounter by suggesting Cuff once tried to molest her. "About three weeks after I came to Hughson's, which was about midsummer last [year], the negroes were there talking of the plot, and some of them said perhaps I'd tell; and Cuffee said, 'No, she won't. I intend to have her for a wife.' And then he ran up to me. I had a dishcloth in my hands, which I dabbed in his face, and he ran away,'' the sixteen-year-old whined to her sympathetic audience in a way that denied Cuff's advance being simply playful. The white men scored the incident on their growing list of reported sexual threats by black men against white women.

Arthur Price followed Mary and recited the jailhouse conversations in which he said Cuff talked about himself, Quack, and their vow to start fires.

Sarah Higgins testified to seeing Cuff and three other blacks lurking at Abraham Kipp's brewhouse, near her home behind the Philipse storehouse, on the night before it burned. "I imagined they were upon some ill design and, therefore, got Captain [Jacob] Phoenix's sons to go along with me with small arms, and they went with me and searched Kipp's brewhouse for the negroes but didn't find them,'' the woman swore.

Old man John Peterson repeated his story of Cuff's trying to shirk at the Philipse fire, and Isaac Gardner corroborated Peterson in part, testifying that "when the buckets came to Cuffee, instead of handing them along to the next man, he put them upon the ground and overset them. . . . When the flames of the house blazed up very high, Cuff huzza'd, danced, whistled and sung. I said to him, 'You black dog, is this a time for you to dance and make game upon such a sad accident.' He only laughed and whispered to Albany, Mrs. Carpenter's negro, who stood next [to] him on the other side,'' Gardner swore. Jacobus Stoutenburgh followed to relate the hue and cry at Cuff's fleeing the storehouse ruins.[2]

Attention then shifted to Quack and the fire at Fort George. Daniel Gautier, a carpenter who was among the first to reach the flames at the governor's house, refuted early suspicions that a plumber carelessly sparked the blaze while soldering a leaky, leaden gutter at Clarke's on the morning of the fire. Noting that "there was no fire within, I believe, twenty foot of the end next the chapel,'' where the plumber had worked, Gautier testified that the fire "couldn't have been occasioned by the plumber's working there.''

The plumber David Hilliard took the stand to defend his reputation. "I was very careful of the fire I carried up, and I had a soldier to attend me. My fire-pot was set on a board which laid over the gutter, from the chapel to the house. . . . I don't think that any sparks of fire flew out of the fire-pot, for it was an enclosed pot, like a dark lantern, with an opening only to put my soldering iron in. And I was careful to put the back of it towards the wind. The fire was on the other side of the roof, not near where I was at work.''

Assistant prosecutor Murray called Wilkins's Fortune and Niblet's Sandy to offer what the attorney called "negro evidence,'' noting that although the law prohibited blacks from giving formal testimony, it did allow them to speak in court to give "evidence good against each other.''[3]

Fortune recounted seeing Cuff near Captain Phoenix's on the night before Philipse's fire, corroborated by Sarah Higgins's sighting, and he repeated his conversations with Quack and Sandy about the fire at the fort.

Sandy repeated his story of Quack's asking him to help burn the fort and of Cuff and Quack's talking of burning Philipse's storehouse. "They two particularly talked of killing the gentlemen and taking their wives to themselves," the boy added.

In their defense Cuff and Quack called ten witnesses. Adolph Philipse repeated his opinion that Cuff's working on the sloop vane denied him the opportunity to set the storehouse fire. But refusing to cover his slave completely, Philipse said, "As to his character I can say nothing." The politician was playing it safe; he was going to argue neither for nor against his slave.

John Roosevelt and his son Nicholas testified that Quack also lacked the opportunity to set the fire as accused. "He was hardly ever out of our sight all that morning, but a small time while we were at breakfast, and we cannot think he could that morning have been from our home so far as the fort," the senior Roosevelt declared.

The prominent merchant Gerardus Beekman and ship captain James Rowe added a favorable note on Quack's character by recalling that he did a good job and minded his business when they had recently used him for work on the new battery. Four others also served as character references for either Quack or Cuff. Thomas Niblet, Sandy's owner, also appeared for the defense and suggested that his sixteen-year-old slave was not always to be believed.

To rebut the Roosevelts' testimony, the prosecutors produced Private James McDonald who said Quack visited the fort frequently to see his wife, Governor Clarke's cook, and had indeed come about eleven o'clock on the morning of the fire and talked his way in.

"I knew that the governor had some time before forbid Quack coming to the fort and, therefore, I scrupled to let him in," McDonald explained. "Not long before that, I was posted one night at the same gate, and Quack came up in order to go to the governor's house. . . . I opposed his entrance within the gate. But Quack was resolute and pushed forward."

" 'Whether you will or not, I'm coming in,' " McDonald re-called Quack's saying. "I then bid him to take what followed and clubbed [him with] my firelock and knocked him down. Then Quack got up and collared me and cried out, 'Murder.' I was go-ing to strike him again, but the officer of the guard, hearing the bustle, called to me and forbid me striking him any more, and then Quack ran indoors, into the governor's kitchen. We went and fetched him and turned him out of the fort."

The Roosevelts could only shake their head, as the sentry seemingly proved Quack's opportunity to set the fort afire and, perhaps, his motive—to settle a grudge against the governor who tried to keep the slave from visiting his wife.

Quack's being at the fort and Cuff at the storehouse provided circumstantial evidence, at best, but the prosecutors rested their case and offered nothing firmer to tie either slave to arson. On the conspiracy charge, where the rule of legal fact was loose, the king's men offered a tighter case. The reports by Mary, Price, Fortune, and Sandy that Cuff and Quack had, at least, discussed illegal acts was sufficient for a conspiracy conviction—if the four were believed.

Determining the facts was the jury's job. In this case, both the rule of law and the pressure of popular opinion pointed to a fore-gone conclusion. The sentiment among the jurors' peers swelled on the side of the king's men, as the spectre of conspiracy haunted the entire city with images of holocaust, bloody corpses of white men, and ravished bodies of white women. The burden of proof that fell on the defense also had the effect of inclining the jurors to the prosecution's side. No presumption of innocence nor dictum of reasonable doubt favored the accused. The remnants of trial by ordeal lingered to the degree that those charged with crime were required to overcome all obstacles to demonstrate their own inno-cence. The fact was that both in the prevailing legal thought and in the popular mind, until proven otherwise, the defendants were guilty.[4]

Attorney General Bradley made the case personal to the jurors from the outset, suggesting that as white men they were destined for death in the blacks' plot. He aimed not only to muster the ju-rors' support, however. He wanted also to disarm any potential alliance of slaveholders intent on defending their property, and he tried to do that by casting holders also as victims. To defend slaves then, holders risked the appearance of undermining their own and their neighbors' security. John Roosevelt did protest in Quack's behalf, but not too much. Politically astute Adolph Philipse protested not at all—seemingly thinking it better to yield Cuff to the popular will than suffer any possible backlash in his position as speaker of the New York Assembly. The prosecution's ploy made the issue simply blacks against whites.

Cuff and Quack thus sat isolated without defense. They had no help from their holders, and they could count on no sympathy from the jurors. They had no legal counsel to rebut the prosecutors and no hope of support from the bench—not with Judge Horsmanden sitting with Judge Frederick Philipse. Cuff's being held as property by Judge Philipse's uncle seemed not to matter, nor did the fact that the judge himself was the owner of record for the storehouse Cuff was accused of burning. Nobody charged conflict of interest or openly questioned if the justice was disinterested and dispassionate. The bench was, after all, the king's bench, and the judges and prosecutors alike served the same master, shared the same interests, and pursued the same end. That meant defendants tried in the king's name needed to battle both the bench and the opposing bar. Only bleak prospects faced the prisoners then.[5]

Exploiting their advantage, the prosecutors used the two blacks as props to set the stage for the full, official rendition of the plot. Their theme portrayed the ugliest tragedy imaginable to the king's men, as William Smith indicated in his summation to the jury by fashioning a *bête noire*—the image of a revolting black beast ravenous for money, power, and sex.

Projecting full scale revolution, Smith enlarged on sixteen-year-old Sandy's comments about the blacks' organization and objectives and connected them to Caesar and John Hughson. "No scheme more monstrous could have been invented nor can anything be thought of more foolish," the prosecutor declared. "What more ridiculous than that Hughson, in consequence of this scheme, should become a *King*! Caesar, now in gibbets, a *Governor*! That the white men should be all killed and the women become a prey to the rapacious lust of these villains! That these slaves should thereby establish themselves in peace and freedom in the plundered wealth of their slaughtered masters!" Smith scoffed.

"It is hard to say whether the wickedness or the folly of this design is the greater, and had it not been in part executed before it was discovered, we should with great difficulty have been persuaded to believe it possible that such a wicked and foolish plot could be contrived by any creatures in human shape. Yet, gentlemen, incredible as such a plot would have seemed to have been, the event has in part proved it to be real. Whence else could so many fires have been lighted up all around you in so short a time, with evident marks of willful design? A design that could not be executed but by several hands,'' Smith contended, trying to assure his audience that while the plot sounded unreal, the knell of experience echoed its existence.

Conceding the prosecution's lack of direct and positive evidence, Smith emphasized the legal rules of inference. ''From the facts proved and circumstances attending them, there appears violent presumption of guilt which the law esteems full proof,'' he noted. And in the prevailing legal system based on believing the accused guilty unless and until innocence was proven, Smith was right: What was deemed the legitimate and natural tendency imbedded in the law directed the judges and the jury to conclude that a crime was as the prosecution contended.

''By divers parts of the evidence it appears that this horrid scene of iniquity has been chiefly contrived and promoted at meetings of negroes in great numbers on Sundays,'' Smith noted. ''This instructive circumstance may teach us many lessons, both of reproof and caution, which I only hint at and shall leave the deduction of the particulars to everyone's reflection,'' he declared, as he proceeded to lambast what he perceived as inordinate leniency toward slaves and the inherent dangers they posed.

''The monstrous ingratitude of this black tribe is what exceedingly aggravates their guilt. Their slavery among us is generally softened with great indulgence: They live without care and are commonly better fed and clothed and put to less labor than the poor of most Christian countries. They are indeed slaves, but under the protection of the law, none can hurt them with impunity. They are really more happy in this place than in the midst of the continual plunder, cruelty, and rapine of their native countries,'' Smith continued, apparently blind to the contradiction between the very case he was arguing and his reasoning that blacks were happy and ought to have been grateful to be in bondage in America.[6]

''Notwithstanding all the kindness and tenderness with which they have been treated among us, yet this is the second attempt of the same kind that this brutish and bloody species of mankind have made within one age," Smith said, alluding to the city's slave revolt of 1712. "That justice that was provoked by former fires and the innocent blood that was spilt in your streets should have been a perpetual terror to the negroes that survived the vengeance of that day and should have been a warning to all that had come after them. But I fear, gentlemen, that we shall never be quite safe till that wicked race are under more restraint or their number greatly reduced within this city," Smith warned, recommending harsher slavery or fewer slaves as his general solution for the security of the city. His specific request in closing his summation to the jury was simpler: "I make no doubt but you will bring in a verdict accordingly and do what in you lies to rid this country of some of the vilest creatures in it."

After receiving their instructions, the jurors filed out and after a few minutes returned with the expected verdict: Guilty. Judge Horsmanden immediately pronounced sentence.

"You both now stand convicted of one of the most horrid and detestable pieces of villainy that ever Satan instilled into the heart of human creatures to put in practice. You and the rest of your color, though you are called slaves in this country, yet are you all far from the condition of other slaves in other countries; nay, your lot is superior to that of thousands of white people. You are furnished with all the necessities of life—meat, drink, and clothing—without care, in a much better manner than you could provide for yourselves were you at liberty—as the miserable condition of many free people here of your complexion might abundantly convince you. What then could prompt you to undertake so vile, so wicked, so monstrous, so execrable and hellish a scheme as to murder and destroy your own masters and benefactors, nay to destroy root and branch all the white people of this place and to lay the whole town in ashes?" Horsmanden asked rhetorically.[7]

"I know not which is the more astonishing, the extreme folly or wickedness of so base and shocking a conspiracy, for as to any view of liberty or government you could propose to yourselves upon the success of burning the city, robbing, butchering and destroying the inhabitants, what could it be expected to end in in the account of any rational and considerate person among you but your own destruction?" the judge queried, eyeing the obvious fact that whites from near and far in England's North American colonies promised to descend without question if black rebels succeeded against all odds in taking the city.

93

Horsmanden recognized that the might of the entire political system maintained slavery. To be free, in fact, slaves needed to slay the oppressive Hydra itself. Killing individual slaveholders or seizing a community promised no lasting relief, for the monster's heads were many and never distant. Cutting off one head only spawned more vicious growths.

Nothing made slaves' thinking and scheming to reach freedom wholly unreasonable, however, even if the end exceeded their grasp. Nor was the gap that yawned so great as to leave citizens without fear. Even whites like Horsmanden, who seemed sure the Almighty insured their rule, worried about the death and destruction rebelling slaves might inflict. The threat was not the slaves' succeeding at revolution, but the violence of their trying.[8]

Horsmanden focused on the bloody potential and played, as Prosecutor William Smith had, on the popular sense of outrage at blacks being ungrateful for the benefits of slavery. "You that were for destroying us without mercy, you abject wretches, the outcasts of the nations of the earth, are treated here with tenderness and humanity, and, I wish I could not say, with too great indulgence also. You have grown wanton with excess liberty, and your idleness has proved your ruin, having given you the opportunities of forming this villainous and detestable conspiracy—a scheme compounded of the blackest and foulest vices, treachery, blood-thirstiness, and ingratitude. . . . We ought to be very thankful and esteem it a most merciful and wondrous act of Providence that your treacheries and villainies have been discovered," the judge declared, stressing for the benefit of his fellow citizens the idea of New York's being saved from slaughter.

Having invoked a deity in his own image and likeness, Horsmanden urged Cuff and Quack to confess fully in hope of saving themselves from hell's fire. His own final judgment was fixed: "Each of you shall be chained to the stake and burnt to death."

The execution was set for the morrow—an example, indeed, of swift and sure justice.

Swarms descended on the city's Common that May Saturday, camping for a clear view of the spectacle scheduled between one and seven o'clock in the afternoon. Executions were commonly popular events that drew people from near and far to behold the law's exemplary punishment. In a society where mass entertainment was rare, almost everyone able attended.

Sympathy sometimes marked executions as onlookers identified with the condemned or their cause. Curiosity was common, as people sought to witness death firsthand and see if in dying the condemned showed signs of guilt or innocence. Hatred also flared when the crimes were heinous or the convicts despicable, which was how the officials labelled Cuff and Quack and the charges against them. The prisoners were pictured as enemies of the people; and feeling ran high against them, particularly as the day dragged on and anticipation made the crowd edgy.[9]

No shadow of doubt loomed that day about the trial's being fair, the verdict just, or the sentence humane. The trial was, in fact, correct to the letter of the law, and few citizens seemed to worry if the path of law and the path of justice had diverged, or if Cuff and Quack had only boasted a bit too much with bad talk against the whites. The two were held strictly accountable for what they had reportedly said, as if being tied to the Biblical stricture in Matthew, 2:36–37, that "Every idle word that men shall speak, they shall give account of in the day of judgment, for by thy words thou shall be justified, and by thy words thou shalt be condemned."

If all men were truly made to answer for their bragging and bantering and, particularly, their loose talk in taverns, few could escape conviction for conspiracy. As for arson, presumption rather than proof prevailed against the blacks. Yet, as the prosecutors suggested and the judges and jury agreed, the law of the day allowed the presumption to suffice. The townsfolk rallied without question to Horsmanden's call of fire for fire.

Eyes eager to see vengeance locked on Cuff and Quack as the two trudged to the stakes about three o'clock, and the sight of the kindling and the crushing crowd scared both condemned men.

Cuff once puffed about burning before he would tell any secrets, but faced with the reality, he proved his earlier words only bluster. Chained, with faggots heaped knee-high, both slaves confessed back to back: Quack to his holder, John Roosevelt, and Cuff to provincial deputy secretary George Joseph Moore, because Adolph Philipse had washed his hands of the slave.

"I did fire the fort," Quack confessed. The Roosevelts were wrong and McDonald right. The slave said he sneaked from home on the morning of the blaze and also on the previous evening. "I thought the fort would've been on fire the night before, for I took a firebrand out of the servants' hall and carried it up into the garret on the seventeenth at night, St. Patrick's [Day], and when I came up the next morning into the garret, I found the brand alight, and then went away again," Quack explained.

Agreeing that Hughson contrived the plot and held meetings at his tavern, often on Sunday afternoons, Quack said that "Hughson desired the negroes to bring to his house what we could get from the fire, and he was to bring down country people in his boat to further the business, and would bring in other negroes. Forty or fifty, to my knowledge, were concerned, but their names I can't recollect." Roosevelt pressed, however, and got a list of seventeen names. "Mary Burton spoke the truth and can name many more, and Fortune and Sandy, too. Sandy can name the Spaniards and say much more," Quack sighed.

"What view had Hughson in acting in this manner?" Roosevelt wondered about his fellow white man.

"To make himself rich" Quack retorted. Then he tried to provide for his own and a few others by declaring, "Ellison's Jamaica wasn't concerned that I know of, although he was frequently at Hughson's with his fiddle. Danby [Governor Clarke's black boy] knew nothing about the matter. . . . My wife was no ways concerned, for I'd never trust her with it."

Like Quack, Cuff named Hughson as the chief plotter and listed eight black names, although he agreed that about fifty were involved. He vouched for Sandy and Fortune's having information to give. The two were hardly innocent, Cuff said. "Fortune knew and was as deeply concerned as me, and Sandy was concerned and knew the Spaniards. Sandy set fire to Mr. Machado's house: Niblet's negro wench [Sarah] can tell it, and Becker's Bess knows it.

"I set fire to the storehouse. When my master went to the coffee-house, I ran out of the other door and went the back way into the storehouse, having lighted charcoal in my pocket between two oyster shells. I put the fire between the ropes and the boards and left and went home," Cuff confessed. "There was a design to kill the people, but [it was] not told to all. Hughson's people were to raise a mob to favor the design."

Horsmanden delighted in the confessions. He had what he had sought—confirmation of Mary's words about Hughson's and the design of the plot. Feeling certain that Cuff and Quack could tell more than they had in their last hour, the judge considered them worthy of a reprieve and, perhaps, a pardon under the terms of the reward proclamation.

Deputy secretary Moore agreed and, with the confessions in his hands, rushed to the governor. Clarke authorized a conditional stay of the blacks' execution, but time ran short as Moore raced back to the Common, for impatient with all the talking and the delay, the crowd was howling.

Sheriff Jamison cut Moore off to say the mob was near being out of hand. "Carrying the negroes back would be impractical, and if that's his honor's orders, it cannot be attempted without a strong guard which cannot be got in time enough," the sheriff insisted. Thus, as Horsmanden noted with minor regret apparent, "the executions proceeded."

Cuff and Quack bought barely two hours of life by confessing, but their words circulated like currency for months to come. They had damned others and failed to save themselves, for the kindling flared at their feet shortly after five o'clock. Singeing their hair, then searing their flesh, the flames swallowed the two from head to toe. Their screams drowned in the mob's howling, but the stench of the burning men seeped into the pores of the people and the city on what deserved to be a memorial day.

The date was May 30.

# 9

$$\text{⛓⛓⛓⛓⛓⛓⛓⛓⛓⛓⛓⛓⛓⛓⛓⛓⛓⛓⛓⛓⛓⛓⛓}$$

# "The Devil's Agent"

HORSMANDEN HASTENED to make capital of Cuff and Quack's dying declarations and ordered the arrest of the blacks they named. By midnight May 30, the constables had grabbed all on Quack's list of seventeen, except for the slave he called "Old Butchell"—nobody recalled anybody by that name. The lawmen also had Cuff's eight, except for Frederick Becker's Bess who disappeared. The judge himself worked on the names on Monday, June 1, calling in Niblet's Sandy and Wilkins's Fortune to divulge more, as Cuff and Quack suggested.[1]

Sandy obliged Horsmanden without hesitation. He listed eighteen blacks by name and ten others whom he said he knew only by sight. Six of the unnamed were Spanish Negroes. Three others were a brother, a cousin, and a nephew of Comfort's Jack whom Sandy called "country negroes." The remaining one unnamed was Comfort's old Cormantine woman: She was called Jemmy, the judge later discovered. The boy mentioned only six of the eighteen names during his previous sessions with questioners, and Horsmanden marked the additions as progress.

The sixteen-year-old slave alone had now implicated thirty-nine blacks, counting the four dead. He offered Horsmanden

98

more help by detailing a mass meeting of blacks he claimed Comfort's Jack dragged him into on Sunday, February 8.

"Damn you, do you cry? I'll cut your head off in a hurry," Jack threatened him, Sandy recalled.

"He deserves it if he won't say yes," Burk's Sarah barked, as Jack and other blacks pressed Sandy to join in plotting.

"The knives are dull and wouldn't cut," the men complained, as Jack distributed a dozen rusty knives after taunting the boy.

"My knife's so sharp that if it comes across a white man's head, it'll cut it off," Jack boasted, after leading the men to sharpen the blades on a whetstone.

"If you want to fight, go to fight the Spaniards. Don't fight with your masters," Sandy said he objected.

"We haven't men enough this year, but next year we'll do it," Jack retorted. Others chimed in to say their fight was indeed against those who held them slaves, not against the enemies of the English.

"Everyone present is to set his master's house on fire first, and then do the rest at once, and set all the houses on fire in town. When we've done that, we'll kill all the white men and have their wives for ourselves," Jack declared.

"Let the first thunder that comes strike us dead if we don't stand to our words," blacks around the room swore.

"If the captain won't send us back to our own country, we'll ruin all the city, and the first house we'll burn will be his. We don't care what they do," Spanish blacks said, referring to the townsfolk enslaving them and cursing their captor, Captain John Lush. "Damn that son of a bitch. We'll make a devil of him."

To check Sandy's recollections, Horsmanden called in Fortune who, like the boy, had to harbor hopes of saving himself by winning favor from the king's men. Fortune failed to match Sandy however and added nobody new to his own bare list of eight—Sandy, Gomez's Cuffee, the four dead blacks, and two glimpsed in the dark with Philipse's Cuff at the storehouse. Fortune mustered only the dead Quack's telling Gomez's Cuffee, "Meet me to burn the house, and if the white people come, shoot them with pistols." He offered nothing on which house, where the pistols were to come from, or on the blacks' having hidden guns.

Disappointed, Horsmanden tried Burk's Sarah, who carried

the reputation of being a bitch. "This was one of the oddest animals among the black confederates and gave the most trouble in her examinations. She was a creature of outrageous spirit. When she was first interrogated upon this examination about the conspiracy, she absolutely denied she knew anything of the matter, threw herself into most violent agitations, foamed at the mouth, and uttered the bitterest imprecations. . . . She, no doubt, must have had extraordinary qualifications to recommend her to the confidence of the confederates, for she was the only wench against whom there was strong and flagrant evidence of having consented to and approved this execrable project," the judge noted.

"I never was at Comfort's in my life nor know where's his house," Sarah retorted to questions raised by Sandy.

"You can entertain no hopes of escaping with life or recommending yourself to mercy but by making an ingenuous confession," Horsmanden told her.

Sarah stood silent for awhile, perhaps taking measure of the judge. "I was at Comfort's house, in the kitchen, about five weeks before the fort was fired. A great many negroes [were] sitting around the table, between twenty and thirty. . . . I stayed there about an hour, and rum was there," Sarah admitted. Then she offered her own version of the Sunday meeting Sandy had spoken of earlier. She described what sounded like a house party that turned wilder as the liquor flowed.

"We'll go and set fire along the docks," some of the men said, as they sharpened their knives.

"The fort first," Jack insisted.

"No, they'd find us out if we do," countered old Cook, but others disputed his advice. Sarah explained that "Quack was pitched upon to fire the fort, [and] others having refused, Quack undertook it. . . . Everyone was to set their masters' house on fire. Clopper's Betty carried me there. We swore and said we wished thunder strike us to the hearts if we told. . . . All that made the right bargain swore. The rest were to come the next day. Comfort's Jack drew out his knife and threatened Sandy, on which he consented. . . . I bid them cut his head off if he didn't drink."

"We'll kill the white men and have the white women for our wives," some of the black men said, Sarah reported. Her version closely matched Sandy's on the dialogue and also on the characters at Comfort's.

Sarah named thirty-three blacks: twenty-eight men and five women other than herself. Seventeen matched names on the boy's list, and Horsmanden savored the concurrence until Sarah retracted eleven names by explaining that the persons "went away before the bargain was made." All of her five black women were among the people she tried to excuse, and they were helped by Sandy's remembering Sarah as the only woman he had seen. Of all those the woman tried to clear, only two were on both lists.

Sarah's reducing the names tightened the match. Horsmanden scored the reversal, however, as a mark against her credibility. He complained that "her conduct was such upon the whole that what she said, if not confirmed by others or concurring circumstances, could not deserve entire credit." Thus, the black woman returned to jail, no doubt worrying about what she needed to do to save herself.

⛓⛓⛓⛓⛓

John Hughson also worried on that first day of June. His scheduled conspiracy trial with his wife, daughter, and Peggy was only two days away, and he was clearly uneasy at the prospect.

"I want to speak to the judges and to open my heart to them," Hughson told Undersheriff Mills about noon.

"What is it you wanted?" Horsmanden asked Hughson, after summoning him later in the day.

"Is there a Bible that I might be sworn?"

"No oath will be administered to you. If you have anything to say, you have free liberty to speak," Horsmanden declared. But he hardly seemed ready to listen and conveyed little hope that confession would help Hughson.

"[Look at] your wicked life and practices, debauching and corrupting negroes, and encouraging them to steal and pilfer from their masters and others, and for showing your children so wicked an example, training them up in the highway to hell," the judge reproached the convict. "You, your wife and Peggy stand convicted of a felony for receiving stolen goods of negroes, and nothing remains then but to pass sentence of death upon you and to appoint a day for your execution." And as for the conspiracy, the judge continued, "the evidence will appear so strong and clear against you in this particular that there is little doubt of your being all convicted on that head also."

"May I be sworn?" Hughson persisted.

"No."

"I know nothing at all of any conspiracy. I call God as my witness. I'm as innocent with respect to that charge as the child unborn, and also my wife, daughter, and Peggy, for aught I know," Hughson protested, matching Horsmanden's scowl with a smile.

The judge dispatched the man back to his cell.

On entering the encounter for the record, Horsmanden seemed to wonder why Hughson had wasted his time. He conjectured that either the man never seriously intended to confess or others in jail dissuaded him after hearing his request to see the judges. Horsmanden offered no excuse for his delay of three hours to hear Hughson, and he noted no connection between his hectoring and Hughson's not talking.

The chance to hear whatever the man, whom the king's men had made the leader of the plot, might have wanted to tell before his conspiracy trial was lost. But the chance to reflect on his life and the lives of his wife, his oldest daughter, and Peggy remained in the forty hours before they faced the judge, the jury, and the verdict Horsmanden had already announced as a foregone conclusion.

⛓⛓⛓⛓⛓

Hughson grumbled repeatedly about his tortuous life in the city and his wishes to return to the predictable life of hard but honest labor in the rural world where he grew up farming with his father and five brothers in Westchester County. To have land of his own to husband and raise a family on was a natural desire for a farm boy, as natural as the desire he developed for the Yonkers' girl Sarah Luckstead.

Sarah's idea of living contained no notion of struggling from harvest to harvest, however. The bustle of the biggest town, in her view, offered the best prospects for her and the man she married, and with her sure and unshy self, Sarah led her John to New York City.

Reluctantly entering the hand-to-mouth world, Hughson muttered when he moved with Sarah into a place off the docks on the city's lower east side. To provide for her, the four daughters she bore him, and himself, he tried his hand where a dollar was to be made. His familiarity with hard work and the skill he developed as a cordwainer, making and mending shoes and other leather goods, eased his struggle somewhat.

Sarah saw to their making and saving a bit of money; and to get ahead, she labored with John at turning their home into a public house by taking in lodgers and serving food and drink. Hughson's, as the place became known, developed a reputation as a warm spot for a clientele not welcomed everywhere: Sailors and soldiers frequented the tavern, and so did slaves although it was illegal for them to be there drinking or together in more than three's or after dark.

Sarah's rules counted neither condition nor color, so long as customers put the right coins on the counter and kept their hands off her and her helping daughters. The crowd known throughout town as ruffians seldom gave Sarah problems when John was present, for his more than six foot frame, toughened in the fields, and his apparently friendly manner drew enough deference to control the rowdies. When he was out doing odd jobs for more cash, Sarah proved strong enough to hold her own with the best of the crowd.

The Hughsons' life hardly developed as Sarah had dreamed or as John had desired, but it kept their family together and their bills paid. Like others on the lower side of white society, no doubt, John and Sarah believed in a Protestant ethic that propagated the desire to line their own pockets, not make others rich. They wanted to be proprietors, not renters or wage earners all their lives, and they preferred their oldest daughters, Sarah and the three-years-younger Mary, to work at home rather than be servants of others till they married. The stigma of catering to those whom self-righteous Christian citizens in their class-conscious society called "unsavory characters" failed to detract from the blessings the couple counted and tried to enlarge on while eyeing the growing suffering of many in New York's depression.

The Hughsons managed to prosper enough by 1739 to get a bigger place for themselves on the upper west side, off Broadway. In the summer of 1740, they bought the sixteen-year-old indentured servant girl Mary Burton to help with the work of their growing business. To keep their larder filled and cash flowing, John and Sarah handled filched scraps from Caesar and others, and that proved to be part of their undoing, for lawmen began to visit the house on hardly social calls.

"There was a cabal of negroes at Hughson's," Constable Joseph North recalled, describing a raid on the place in 1740. "Ten, twelve, or fourteen of us . . . went down there in order to disperse them, and when we came there, we went into the room where the negroes were round a table, eating and drinking. There was meat on the table and knives and forks, and the negroes were calling for what they wanted."

"Peggy was waiting on them and had a tumbler in her hand for them to drink [from]," Constable Peter Lynch noted, with apparent distaste for the white woman's serving the black men.

"We saw [Caesar,] the negro who's now hanged in gibbets, at the time, waiting at the door in order to get in, as we took it," North added.

"At our appearance, the negroes made off as fast as they could. North laid his cane to them, and [we] soon cleared the room of them," Lynch recalled.

"We'd heard frequent complaints of Hughson's entertaining negroes there," North explained, suggesting John and Sarah's neighbors frowned on the couple's boisterous crowd. "Hughson was at the door as we came away and we reproached him."

"I can't help it. It's my wife's fault," John whined, according to the constables.

For breaking the liquor laws and letting slaves congregate, the Hughsons faced arrest and a fine—seldom more than £5, which was nothing to be sneezed at but a small price to pay for the profits from black business. Because the offense was officially their first, the couple got a break and received only a warning.[2]

John and Sarah needed to be careful from then on, but they proceeded with business as usual and reportedly joined their customers who muttered in their mugs and called for more than the droppings from the province's upper crust. They had no more trouble until the constables came searching for Caesar and the goods stolen from Rebecca and Robert Hogg's shop on Sunday, March 1, 1741. They remained in the clear until their fresh servant girl started wagging her tongue at the scent of freedom.

John's apparent incapacity to talk his way through tight spots alone was what got the Hughsons and Peggy into real trouble. With Sarah at his side, he turned away Undersheriff Mills and the constables' searching and questioning about the Hogg loot; but when called on the night of March 3 to answer Alderman Christopher Bancker's questions, Hughson found no help, and he failed himself and others.

"Do you know anything of the matter?"

"No," croaked Hughson.

"If it is within your power, tell me who committed this piece of villainy," Bancker fished, showing the skill of a man practiced at baiting and playing out his line with a sense of when to let up and when to pull in fast and hard. Hughson was out of his depth and his circling closed as the alderman fed his line and repeated, "Do you know anything of the matter?"

"I do know where some of the things are hid," Hughson plunged, only later feeling the full force of being hooked. Groping for a way to free himself, he dragged in not only a small bundle from his underworld but also his mate and family and companions. "Peggy delivered to me sundry silver things in a little bag," Hughson wriggled, in apparent hope of sticking the barb to the redhead, who, with her baby, were virtually members of his family.

Reporting his catch to Mayor Cruger, Bancker agreed with his fellow city councilmen to let John continue to open his mouth, and Hughson responded by sinking himself further with the weight of a proven liar. At that time, during the first week of March, the officials saw little use for Hughson, who seemed to have spilled his guts. They allowed him to roam free on bail until the wave of fires and thefts pushed the mayor himself to order John and Sarah hauled into a cell on April 8.

The angry flood that swept the city in the wake of the blazes and looting washed John, Sarah, Peggy, Prince, and Caesar into a deadly vortex. The two blacks hanged ten days after being convicted on May 1 for the Hogg job, and the tide of talk kept the two Hughsons and Peggy swirling even after their conviction on May 6 for having hands in the Hogg mess. The currents also caught nineteen-year-old Sarah Hughson in the indictment for conspiracy, launched against her parents on May 12, against Peggy on May 15, and against the girl herself on June 2.

The charges swelled and gained intensity until the four's trial. John, wife Sarah, and Peggy started out being indicted for "conspiring, confederating, and combining with divers negroes and others to burn the City of New-York and also to kill and destroy the inhabitants thereof." Then the three were arraigned with daughter Sarah on a count of "conspiracy for abetting and encouraging the negro Quack to burn the king's house in the fort."

Added against the quartet was a count of "conspiracy for counselling, abetting, etc. the negro Cuffee to burn Mr. Philipse's storehouse."

Daughter Sarah stared at two felony counts then, and her previously convicted parents and Peggy faced three counts. Each charge carried a possible death penalty. The only lesser punishment likely for all four was exile in disgrace. Hughson stood a chance of being whipped and ridiculed as well. But not the women. Custom forbade the lash on female flesh, at least when it was white. No prison term threatened either. New York's lawmen saw no sense in feeding, clothing, sheltering, and supervising criminals for any extended period at public expense; such an idea smacked their minds as a scheme to tax the good to sustain the bad. The likes of Horsmanden believed firmly in punishing, not coddling, convicts.[3]

The judge's virtual refusal to let John confess for pardon, wife Sarah's determination to remain mum, daughter Sarah's concern about jeopardizing her parents, and Peggy's continuing dilemma about what more to say, left the four with only one apparent hope for emerging from their coming trial alive: They had to have a sympathetic jury.

❈❈❈❈❈

The Hughsons and Peggy's conspiracy trial opened shortly after ten o'clock on Thursday morning, June 4. Justices Philipse and Horsmanden presided. Flanked by assistants James Alexander, John Chambers, Joseph Murray, and William Smith, Attorney General Bradley prosecuted. The four accused had no counsel.

"Cryer, make proclamation," the court clerk began.

"Oyes! Our sovereign lord the king doth strictly charge and command all manner of persons to keep silence upon pain of imprisonment," the cryer announced, and when the stirring of spectators stopped, he continued. "If anyone can inform the king's justice or attorney general for this province on the inquest now to be taken on behalf of our sovereign lord the king, of any treason, murder, felony, or any other misdemeanor committed or done by the prisoners at the bar, let them come forth, and they shall be heard, for the prisoners stand upon their deliverance.

"Oyes! You good men that are impanelled to inquire between our sovereign lord the king and John Hughson, Sarah his wife, Sarah Hughson the daughter, and Margaret Sorubiero, alias Kerry, the prisoners at the bar, answer to your names," the cryer declared.

The prospective jurors assembled.

"Hold up you hands," the clerk ordered the Hughsons and Peggy to identify themselves officially. Then he told the four, "These good men that are now called and here appear are those which are to pass between you and our sovereign lord the king, upon your lives or deaths. If you, or any, or either of you challenge any of them, you must speak as they come to the book to be sworn, and before they are sworn."

"You the prisoners at the bar, we must inform you that the law allows you the liberty of challenging peremptorily twenty of the jurors if you have any dislike to them, and you need not give your reasons for so doing; and you may likewise challenge as many more as you can give sufficient reasons for; and you may either all join in your challenges or make them separately," Judge Philipse said, doing the bench's duty toward the four. As whites they had recognized rights and privileges, and the law insisted on their being at least informed of the basics they were allowed, although it offered not a hint of legal aid for their defense.[4]

The Hughsons and Peggy groped as the most distinguished, experienced, and high-priced attorneys in all New York watched and waited to battle them. Circling themselves, the defendants settled on John to handle their challenges and speak for them. They had no alternative: He was the only man among them, and they needed a man in that time and place, because women were seldom listened to seriously in public on crucial questions—sex, like race, was a handicap for all not male and white.[5]

Hughson peremptorily challenged sixteen prospective jurors. His daughter expressed confidence in his sallies, but his wife and Peggy held reservations. His exclusion of a young gentleman from the panel prompted Peggy to protest, "You've challenged one of the best of them all."

The spectators snickered, but Hughson's picks were no light matter. The final jurors included four who held slaves then sitting in jail on suspicion of conspiracy and a fifth, Peter Vergereau, who owned half the cowstable partially burned on the night of

April 4 and the storehouse from which Caesar stole firkins of butter. Almost half the jury had direct personal interests in the issues
of the case before they heard a single witness.

❈❈❈❈❈

Attorney General Bradley outlined the king's case. "A great
number of negroes and the rest of the conspiracy" met at
Hughson's with the taverner, his wife, daughter Sarah, and Peggy
and "entered into a most wicked and hellish plot to set on fire and
lay in ashes the king's house [Fort George] and this whole town
and to kill and destroy the inhabitants," Bradley told the jurors.

"Gentlemen, such a monster will this Hughson appear before
you that, for the sake of the plunder he expected by setting in
flames the king's house and this whole city and by the effusion of
the blood of his neighbors, he—murderous and remorseless he!—
counselled and encouraged the committing of all these most astonishing deeds of darkness, cruelty, and inhumanity. Infamous
Hughson! Gentlemen, this is that Hughson! whose name and
most detestable conspiracies will no doubt be had in everlasting remembrance to his eternal reproach and stand recorded to latest
posterity. This is the man! This that grand incendiary! That arch
rebel against God, his king, and his country!" the attorney general exclaimed. "Gentlemen, behold the author and abettor of all
the late conflagrations, terrors, and devastation that have befallen
this city."

A parade of eleven prosecution witnesses commenced.

John Roosevelt testified to Quack's confession, and George Jo-
seph Moore, who served as court clerk as well as deputy secretary
of the province, testified to Cuff's confession and to Quack and
Cuff's conviction for arson and conspiracy. Constables John
Dunscomb, Peter Lynch, and Joseph North reported the raid on
Hughson's during May 1740.

Mary Burton then took the stand and repeated her general
story about the Hughsons and Peggy. But for all her talk of the
plot, the servant girl conceded that she never saw the defendants
swear to any plot. "One of Hughson's daughters [did] carry a Bible upstairs, and the Hughsons carried the negroes into a private
room. When they came down again to the rest of the negroes,
Hughson said they were all sworn," the girl started weakly.

"Now you are found in a great lie, for we never had a Bible in the world," Hughson's wife interrupted, while Hughson sat confused because he had earlier insisted he and his wife did have a Bible.

The spectators laughed at the muddled defense, and Mary resumed her testimony.

"I saw Vaarck's Caesar pay John Hughson £12 in silver Spanish pieces of eight to buy guns, swords, and pistols; and Hughson went up into the country, and when he returned, brought with him seven or eight guns and swords and hid them in the house. I've seen a bag of shot and a barrel of gunpowder there. . . . The negroes were to cut their masters and mistresses' throats, and when all this was done, Hughson was to be king and Vaarck's Caesar governor. The negroes used to say to Hughson when I was in the room and heard them talking of burning the town and killing the people that 'Perhaps, she'll tell.' Hughson said, 'No, she dare not.' The negroes swore if I did they'd burn and destroy me. The Hughsons often tempted me to swear and offered me silks and gold rings in order to prevail with me, but I wouldn't," the girl asserted, giving herself an air of steadfast innocence and the plot a more ominous appearance with her suggestion of hidden guns.

"You very wicked creature. You lie," the Hughsons and Peggy protested together, throwing up their hands and rolling their eyes, as if astonished by Mary's words. But they failed to shake her story.

Arthur Price then took the stand and recited his jail conversations with Peggy, daughter Sarah, and Cuff. Constable John Schultz followed and said that when Cuff and Quack returned to jail immediately after being convicted for conspiracy, Cuff reproached Hughson by saying, "We may thank you for this, for this is what you've brought us to." Undersheriff Mills and Constable Cornelius Brower corroborated the statement; and Mills, Dunscomb, Lynch, and Schultz each recalled Hughson's seeming eager to unburden his soul on the previous Monday. "Hughson said he wanted to speak to the judges and open his heart to them that they should know more, and [he] was very urgent that somebody should go to the judges to acquaint them therewith," Mills testified. Nobody even hinted at how Horsmanden confronted Hughson and dismissed his request to talk under oath.

The prosecution rested.

"If you have any questions to ask these witnesses, now is your time to propose them; or if you have any witnesses to produce to your characters, let them be called," Judge Philipse informed Hughson.

John neglected the chance for cross-examination. He was no match for the king's men in court. He was literate enough to sign his name, but he never read law nor proved himself able to handle rough questioning. In fact, his previous showings in front of Alderman Bancker and the mayor and magistrates provided little enough reason for faith in his abilities. The defense proceeded then on hope alone and simply called five character witnesses.

"Me and my husband lodged two months in Hughson's house last winter," Eleanor Ryan testified about herself and Private Andrew Ryan. "I saw no negroes there but Cuff and the negro that was hung in gibbets, three or four times. I never saw any entertainments there for negroes, but I lay sick in bed in the kitchen almost day and night all that time."

"I saw Hughson give a dram to a negro, but I thought him a civil man," neighbor Andrew Blanck testified, knowing that giving a slave a shot of liquor was a crime.

"I know nothing of the character of Hughson's house, but I never saw no harm of him," offered Peter Kirby, another neighbor.

The king's men let not even this lukewarm trickle pass unchallenged and, seizing a moment when Hughson hesitated in the defense's flow, put the cooper Francis Silvester on the stand.

"When John Hughson lived next door to me upon the dock, he kept a very disorderly house and sold liquor to and entertained negroes there. I've often seen many of them there at a time, at nights as well as in the day time. Once, in particular, I remember seeing in the evening a great many of them in a room, dancing to a fiddle, and Hughson's wife and daughter along with them. I often reproached Hughson with keeping such a disorderly house which very much offended his neighbors. Hughson replied to me that his wife persuaded him to leave the country where he subsisted his family tolerably well by his trade [as a cordwainer] and his farm, but his wife said they'd live much better in town, though he wished they'd return to the country again, for he found their gains so small and his family so large that they soon run away with what they'd get. Hughson said his wife was the chief cause of having negroes at his house and he was afraid some misfortune would happen to him and he'd come to some untimely end," the former neighbor declared.

"Have you any more witnesses?" Philipse prompted Hughson.

"Yes sir, we desire that Adam King and Gerardus Comfort may be called.

"Of late I took Hughson's house to be disorderly, for I saw whole companies of negroes playing at dice there; and [Benjamin] Wyncoop's negro [London] once carried a silver spoon there that was hammered down," King testified, hardly helping the defense. He did add what he perhaps thought was a kind word for Hughson by saying, "I saw no harm of the man himself."

"Have you any more such witnesses as this?" the attorney general mocked Hughson.

Comfort then stepped forward. The defendants no doubt hoped the man's word would bring what his name signified. The king's men certainly recognized the name, particularly from the reports of a mass meeting in Comfort's kitchen on a Sunday in February. Comfort's slaves Jack and Cook sat in jail at that very moment because of the talk, and the man himself, at least in Horsmanden's view, needed to clear his own name.

"I saw nothing amiss of him," Comfort testified, but he covered himself by adding, "My business is a cooper, and I'm often abroad and very seldom go to his house."

"Mr. Comfort, you are a next door neighbor to Hughson. You live opposite to him, and surely you must have seen negroes go in and out [of] there often, as the witnesses have testified that there were frequent caballings with the negroes there," Horsmanden interrupted. His questioning sounded more like that of a prosecutor than a judge.

"I have seen nothing amiss of him. I have seen no harm there," Comfort repeated. He was then dismissed from the stand but not from Horsmanden's memory.

"Have you any more witnesses?"

"We have no more, sir," Hughson responded. In summation of the defense, he added simply that "All the witnesses said against us was false. We call upon God as our witness."

William Smith then summed up for the prosecution, as he had at Cuff and Quack's trial. Emphasizing the city's being saved from destruction "by the blessing of heaven and the uncommon diligence of the magistrates," he played on the citizens' feelings of outrage at the reported plot and made the case against the Hughsons and Peggy sound open and shut.

"Gentlemen, nothing remains to be considered of by you but the credit of the witnesses—against which I can see no reasonable objection; if they are to be believed, then the prisoners are guilty and you now behold at this bar the authors, abettors, and contrivers of those destructive fires which your eyes have seen. . . . The witnesses declare the principal contriver of those mischiefs to be that wicked man John Hughson, whose crimes have made him blacker than a negro, the scandal of his complexion, and the disgrace of human nature!" Smith exclaimed.

Judge Horsmanden charged the jury. "It is needless for the court to observe further to you, after what has been said by the counsel for the king, concerning the nature and destructive tendency of so execrable a piece of villainy as this conspiracy now charged upon the prisoners at the bar. It has been sufficiently and properly enlarged upon. Nor is it any more necessary for the court to recapitulate the evidence given in the case, for that has been clearly stated by the gentlemen at the bar. Now, gentlemen, if you cannot credit the several witnesses for the king, if that can be the case, you will then acquit the prisoners of this charge against them and find them not guilty. But, on the other hand, as the evidence against them seems to be so ample, so full, so clear and satisfactory, . . . I make no doubt but you will discharge a good conscience and find them guilty," Horsmanden said, without apparent hesitation about sounding injudicious.

The constable sworn to attend the jury led the men out for their deliberation, and minutes later they returned with their verdict: Guilty.

The date was June 4.

# 10

⛓⛓⛓⛓⛓⛓⛓⛓⛓⛓⛓⛓⛓⛓⛓⛓⛓⛓⛓⛓⛓⛓⛓⛓⛓⛓

# "Mercy on Your Souls"

THE CONVICTIONS ENCOURAGED the king's men. Their piecemeal approach was producing results. After their frustrating initial interrogations about the fires and general search for loot, strangers and suspicious persons, Horsmanden and his fellows had now proven in court an outline of conspiracy involving blacks and whites. They had delivered public enemies that suited and enlarged the image the mobs had conjured up in early April. Promising citizens more, the judge and prosecutors acted confident of getting to the bottom of the plot by following the Hughson's connection.[1]

The indisputable facts that Caesar and Prince stole and that Hughson, his wife, and Peggy received stolen goods established a black-white criminal connection that was essential to the officials' conspiracy case. That Hughson's tavern served as a hideaway for loot and a hideout for slaves like Caesar also established an important meeting place connection.

In Cuff and Quack's trial, the king's men opened two more crucial connections—the arson link and the formal conspiracy link. The first coupled Quack's arson at Fort George and Cuff's at the Philipse storehouse to the notion that the March and April fires were in fact a series set by black hands. The second used Cuff and Quack's reported talk of their intentions to set fires as evidence to satisfy the legal minimum for criminal conspiracy: Two persons had spoken of and agreed to commit a crime. The links were sealed in the confessions at the stake, for the two slaves admitted to arson in such detail as to erase any doubt that they had indeed set the blazes at the fort and storehouse. Their statement that Hughson and blacks who frequented his tavern were in on the fires thickened the black-white connection, the meeting place connection, the arson connection, and the conspiracy connection.

Attorney General Bradley, his assistant William Smith, and Horsmanden enlarged on each connection and made a chain to capture all elements of the plot they envisioned. They talked of the city's being burned and plundered, not simply of blacks setting fires and looting. They projected New York in ruins with the white men slaughtered and the white women enslaved to black men's passions. And they anchored the links to a general slave uprising led by John Hughson.

Tying a white man to the plot was essential to the chain. With the social prejudice that denied blacks' intellectual capacity to plan seriously, the king's men needed someone to blame as the brains of a scheme that had taken them from mid-March to late May to unravel. To justify the delay, they had to produce more than a simple version of "the negroes are rising," which citizens had shouted when mobbing blacks on April 6.

The prosecutors built on popular sentiment then. Pillorying Hughson as an "arch rebel against God, his king, and country," the attorney general had cast him as "the author and abettor of all the conflagrations, terrors, and devastation that have befallen this city." Bradley drew New York's troubles then into a catchall of evil, treason, and rebellion. He centered the devilish combination at Hughson's, as Horsmanden had from the start, and stressed that it extended far beyond the people's early suspicions.

Smith continued the theme. In summing up the king's conspiracy case against the Hughsons and Peggy, he had spoken of a "barbarous, unjust, and cruel design." Feeding the old fears of the March–April blazes, he stirred in a measure of self-credit and deserved gratitude. "The circumstances attending these fires convinced everybody that the most of them did not proceed from accidental causes, but from a malicious and wilful design," he said. The people were right to have seen a conspiracy, but getting to the bottom of it required "the blessing of heaven and the uncommon diligence of the magistrates," Smith asserted.

Horsmanden reiterated the official themes at every turn, and his colleague Judge Philipse joined him. In sentencing the Hughsons and Peggy on Monday, June 8, the second justice extended the ominous sounds of the black-white and meeting place connections. Philipse stressed Hughson's tavern as an example of what officials called "disorderly houses" and pointed up the dangers such places posed to social order. Whites who catered to blacks as customers were, in the judge's view, "guilty not only of making negro slaves their equals but even their superiors by waiting upon, keeping with, and entertaining them."

Philipse underscored what he saw as the ultimate evil: Whites making common cause with blacks against society. Lashing the Hughsons and Peggy for encouraging "these black seed of Cain to burn this city and to kill and destroy us all," the judge exclaimed, "Good God! When I reflect on the disorders, confusion, desolation, and havoc which the effect of your most wicked, most detestable and diabolical councils might have produced, had not the hand of our great and good God interposed, it shocks me!"

Condemning the four for crimes "one would scarce believe any man capable of committing, especially anyone who had heard of a God and a future state . . . [and] who have been brought up and always lived in a Christian country and called themselves Christians," Philipse ordered Hughson, his wife, daughter Sarah, and Peggy to be hanged on Friday, June 12, and Hughson's body afterward to be hung in chains, next to Caesar. "I pray God of his great goodness to have mercy on your souls," the judge finished.

⛓⛓⛓⛓⛓

The officials' reconstruction had come full circle, but their chain of conspiracy was not yet complete. Horsmanden and his cohort had enlarged the connections too broadly to close with only two blacks and four whites convicted of conspiracy. They needed more than a half-dozen to flesh out the plot. Indeed, almost as soon as Philipse sentenced the Hughsons and Peggy, a parade of accused began in court.

Immediately doubling the number set for conviction, the king's men put Peck's Caesar, Gomez's Cuffee, Comfort's Cook and Jack, Ellison's Jamaica, and Chambers's Robin on trial for "conspiring, combining and confederating with divers negroes to burn the whole town and City of New-York and to kill and destroy the inhabitants thereof."

Attorney General Bradley, John Chambers, and Joseph Murray prosecuted. George Joseph Moore and John Roosevelt testified for the king's case, repeating Cuff and Quack's confessions which said Peck's Caesar and Gomez Cuffee set the fire at Van Zant's storehouse. Both dead blacks had also fingered Jack and Cook for agreeing to set fire to their holder's house. Cuff implicated Robin, too; and his arrest for having suspected loot found during the general search lent further credence to the charge that he was in with the gang at Hughson's.

Mary Burton testified against Jamaica. "He used to be very forward at the meetings at Hughson's in talk about the conspiracy; particularly once when they were talking of burning the town and killing the people, Jamaica said he'd dance or play over the whites while they were roasting in flames," the girl said and, for emphasis, quoted Jamaica as saying, "I've been a slave long enough."

As "negro evidence," Sandy and Burk's Sarah recalled the Sunday meeting at Comfort's. The boy particularly reported Peck's Caesar for saying, "I'll kill the white men and drink their blood to their good health." Fortune added his piece about Gomez's Cuffee helping Quack to burn the fort.

No witnesses appeared on the slaves' behalf. Not one of their holders offered a word. In fact, John Chambers was assisting in the prosecution of his slave Robin. Jamaica alone had a bit of indirect defense, for only Burton testified against him, and in confessing at the stake, Quack had declared, "Jamaica's not concerned that I know of but was frequently at Hughson's with his fiddle."

William Smith offered no summation in this case. Instead, he sat on the jury, and he and the rest of the twelve hardly left the courtroom to decide the verdict: Guilty.

Horsmanden sentenced the six immediately: "The said Jack, Cook, Robin, Caesar and Cuffee shall be chained to a stake and burnt until they shall be severally dead, and the said Jamaica shall be there hanged." He ordered the five burned the next afternoon, between one and seven o'clock; the hanging he set for Friday. Five more blacks were arraigned on the conspiracy charge before court adjourned.

Comfort's Jack fretted on the evening of his conviction, which was also the eve of his execution, and begged to tell the king's men all they wanted to hear to save his life. Horsmanden agreed to listen.

Listing him as "Captain Jack," the judge noted the slave as being "a crafty, subtle fellow"—the sort of black he pictured as troublesome. Jack was "too much at liberty . . . and might be captivated with the fine promises and hopes given him of being not only a free but a great man, a commander in this band of fools," Horsmanden wrote with clear sarcasm.

Jack lived across from Hughson on lower Stone Street, which ran up from the Hudson River to Broadway, just above Trinity Church. So he had easy access to the tavern and ample opportunity to visit with little likelihood of being stopped. His holder was often away on business, repairing barrels and casks as a cooper "for days and weeks together," Horsmanden complained. And with the river forming a dead end, few people wandered by his part of the street. Most of the regular traffic were slaves sent to fetch water from Comfort's well or an occasional customer to use Comfort's dock. Thus, Jack often came and went much as he pleased, and he described his visits and visitors for the judge.

Willing as Jack was to talk, Horsmanden grumbled about almost needing an interpreter because, he said, the slave's "dialect was so perfectly negro and unintelligible." But considering the stake, the slave managed at length to make the judge understand him.

Jack recalled vividly what he said was his initial meeting with blacks' talking of rising up. Setting the scene at Hughson's, he described the taverner and slaves acting much as the prosecution had already portrayed in court, but his detail added to the arson connection and opened new links—a slaveholder murder connection and an invasion connection. According to Jack, slaves throughout the city had pledged to set fires, arm themselves, and murder their own holders; and they had tied their action in part to a hope of a Spanish-led attack on New York.

Jack said Alderman John Marshall's Ben introduced him to the talk, while fetching water one afternoon at tea time.

"Countryman, I've heard some good news."

"What news?"

"There're Spanish negroes at Hughson's who told me they've designs of taking this country."

"What they'd do with this country?"

"Oh, you fool! Those Spaniards know better than York negroes. . . . They're more used to war, but we must begin first to
set the houses on fire," Ben snorted. "Brother, go to Hughson's.
All our company's come down."

Jack said he followed the summons and found Hughson's
packed with blacks. The taverner, his wife, daughter Sarah, and
Peggy were all there.

"Who'll be headman for the rise?" Hughson asked.

"Me, I'll stand for that. I can find a gun, shot, and powder at
my master's house. My master doesn't watch me. I can go into
every room," Ben answered, pushing himself in front of the other
blacks.

"What'll you stand for?" Ben asked Hermanus Rutgers's
Quash.

"Whatever, I don't care what I do, but I can kill three, four,
five white men before night. I can get two half-dozen knives, three
or four swords. I'll set my master's house on fire, and when I've
done that, I'll come out to fight."

"I'll kill my mistress before I come to fight, for she scolds me,"
Abraham Marschalk's York yelled, as other slaves joined in with
pledges.

"Before I come to fight, I'll set his house on fire," added
Marschalk's London.

"I'll set my mistress's house on fire before I go out to fight,"
volunteered Mrs. David Van Borsom's Scipio.

"I'll set my mistress's house on fire and, as the houses stand
all together, the fire'll go more far," John Shurmur's Cato offered.

"I'll come out to fight, too, but first I'll kill my mistress, for
she's always cross and works me hard and won't give me even
good clothes," complained Mrs. Carpenter's Tickle.

"I'll get my master's sword and then set the house on fire and
go out to fight," said John Provoost's Cato.

"I'll set my master's bakehouse on fire," declared Cornelius
Kortrecht's Caesar.

"Will you stand to help?" Quash asked Vaarck's Bastian.

"Yes, you know I will. That's why I'm here."

"What'll you stand for?" York prompted Jonneau, another of
Vaarck's blacks.

"I'm not able to fight, but I'll burn my master's house and the
neighbors.' "

"And what'll you do Jack? Will you set your master's house to flames?"

"No, I'll set his shingles on fire and then go to fight," Comfort's Jack reported himself shilly-shallying.

"I'll burn the storehouse," Jack's housemate Cook declared.

"Will you burn your master's house?" Ben was asked.

"No," the hopeful headman retorted. "If we conquer this place, I'll keep that to live in myself."

"I'll get my master's gun and fire his stable," Cornelius Tiebout's Curacoa Dick joined in but cautioned, "Everyone must stand to his word."

"Damn us if we fail!"

"God damn us all!"

"By God, if you be true to me, we'll take this country," Hughson exhorted. "I'll stand by you and be your king."

"By God, I'll do my part," Jack admitted swearing.

"We'll wait a month and a half for the Spaniards and French to come, and if they don't come then we'll begin at Wenman's, next to [New York Chief Justice James] DeLancey's, and go on down Broadway. We'll do it on one and the same Sunday, when church's gone in for the morning [service]. And if all's not done in that one day, we'll go on the Saturday following," the blacks agreed. They apparently hoped for an invasion by England's enemies, but their talk sounded like a weekend rebellion with time for their jobs in between.

"If the Spaniards and French didn't come, we were to do all ourselves. . . . We waited until the month and a half was up, and then the fort was burnt. . . . I met Provoost's Cato the night that Hilton's house was burnt and asked him 'What's news? I heard there's been a fire at your end of town.' 'I done it,' Provoost's Cato said," Jack told Horsmanden.

As those who stood trial with him prepared to march to their execution, Jack sat still talking. He corroborated the other reports that Gomez's Cuffee set fire to Van Zant's storehouse and Sleydall's Jack to Murray's haystack. He fingered a couple of Spanish blacks also for the grand jury—Becker's Pablo for providing the knives distributed at Comfort's and Peter DeLancey's Antonio for distributing something to throw on houses to make them burn.

By the time he finished talking, Jack had named thirty blacks and corroborated Sandy and Sarah's reports about the meeting at

Comfort's. He, the boy, and woman all agreed on twelve names at the Sunday meeting at Comfort's; he agreed on two more each with either Sandy or Sarah.

Jack's report confirmed Sandy and Sarah's identification of Antonio and Pablo but still left the king's men with a problem of confirming the other Spanish blacks, because Sandy and Sarah failed to agree on which of them were involved. Shown a line-up of six, the woman pointed out only Abraham Filkins's Will, a slave who preferred his name José. She said she recognized none of the others. Sandy fingered all except José and McMullen's Augustine.

A case against the Spanish blacks fit neatly with the hue and cry, "Take up the Spanish negroes," that people launched when seizing Sarly's Juan on suspicion of arson in the Fly neighborhood. It fit also with the notion of strangers fomenting trouble and offered a possible tie in with a Spanish invasion. But the linkage was still as uncertain as the unconfirmed identifications of the Spanish blacks who might have had a hand in a plot: The king's men had more work to do there.

⛓⛓⛓⛓⛓

Horsmanden accepted the concurrence of Jack, Sandy, and Sarah's stories as further evidence to prove a far-reaching chain of conspiracy. And determined to pursue the connections down to the smallest link, the judge wanted to find every person who could be associated with the fires or talk about them at Hughson's. He seemed ready to pump the slaves personally until he got the last detail he wanted.

Hearing Abraham Leffert's Pompey, after listening to Jack, made the judge even more anxious to interrogate all the slaves who were implicated; for in confessing that Quack and Hermanus Rutgers's Quash recruited him to set Leffert's house on fire, Pompey reported his last instructions coming from Quack only two or three days before Quack's arrest on May 12.

Horsmanden wondered if the blacks were still plotting, even then. He surely hoped for the scene on the Common that Tuesday, June 9, to deter them. The sight was certainly grisly: Peck's Caesar, Gomez's Cuffee, Comfort's Cook, and Chambers's Robin were burned to death at the stake.

The spate of executions and continuing fears opened all the old sores whites nursed against blacks. The weeks of mystery about the fires' sources had built up venemous pools of resentment, too. Rather than slaking a popular thirst for blood then, the two hangings and six burnings so far prompted only a lust for more. Feeling sure now that blacks were indeed the cause of their problems, citizens virtually cheered on the prosecution's flow.

The judge postponed Jack's execution to June 12, hoping for the continuing threat of death to keep the slave talking. He reprieved Jamaica also, until he had more than Mary Burton's word on which to hang him. Like his fellow officials, Horsmanden wanted no controversy about the proceedings and had been careful so far to have at least three persons offer evidence to support judgments for death. He was not ready to abandon that formula now. If slaves like Jack continued to confess in hopes of saving their lives, the judge expected no problems in getting the evidence he wanted.

The slaves already had confessed enough to keep the grand jury busy handing up indictments and the constables busy making new arrests almost daily. After the executions on June 9, for instance, the grand jury indicted four more slaves and nine others were jailed.

The trial of the four—Carpenter's Albany, Vaarck's Bastian, Tiebout's Curacoa Dick, and Bosch's Francis—occurred the next day, Wednesday, June 10. The four got at least the semblance of a break by being allowed to challenge Ben Thomas from sitting on the jury: His house being partially burned in the fires attributed to the plot made his impartiality reasonably suspect. Removing Thomas, however, hardly resulted in an impartial panel. Seven of the twelve men seated had already rendered their verdicts on the conspiracy charge at hand, for they had served two days earlier on the jury that convicted Jack, Jamaica, and the four blacks burned on the previous day.

Attorney General Bradley, Joseph Murray, and William Smith prosecuted, presenting Mary Burton and three other witnesses along with Sandy and Burk's Sarah as "negro evidence." Mrs. Carpenter and her neighbor Robert Hogg testified for Albany, and Cornelius Tiebout testified for Curacoa Dick. Edward Sherlock interpreted for Francis, who was Spanish. The trial was brief and the verdict swift: Guilty. The four were sentenced to burn at the stake on Friday, June 12.

Vaarck's Bastian, like Jack before him, refused to go quietly into the night before his death and offered to confess. Starting his story with the party at Hughson's on Sunday, January 18, Bastian corroborated what Jack had said. He, too, mentioned the invasion connection which the king's men were now anxious to hear more about, and he helped answer a growing question: How did so many slaves apparently become involved in the plot?

Focusing on his own recruitment, Bastian blamed his dead housemate Caesar for getting him involved. He suggested how intimidation and inducements were used to draw blacks into agreeing to help in the reported scheme.

"Will you join along with us to be our own masters?" Caesar asked Bastian, while tapping a pistol on his chest during the meeting at Hughson's.

"Join with you in what?"

"In the plot," shot Caesar. "We've designed to take the country, and we've a parcel of good hands for it. . . . The Spanish negroes'll join us. War'll be proclaimed in a little time against the French, and the French and Spanish'll come here. We'll join with them to take the place."

"No," Bastian blurted. "I'll not join."

"Damn you, if you won't, you'll not leave here alive. Take a drink." Swallowing hard, Bastian accepted the offered whiskey and the deal he no longer dared refuse. "He's but a weak-hearted dog, but set his name down and I'll encourage him up," Caesar sneered to Hughson.

Bastian slouched down with the others and settled his stomach on the bellyful of duck, goose, mutton quarter, and veal spread out on a long table. After the meal, Hughson produced a Bible.

"The first thunder strike them dead that discover or don't do as they promise," Hughson declared. Then he swore himself, his wife, daughter Sarah, and the blacks. All kissed the holy book and said they would "burn the town and murder the people, but we were to stay till the Spaniards and French came—about a month and a half; and if they didn't come in that time we were to begin ourselves. We were to begin with the fort first. . . . Hughson was to have the goods that were stolen from the fires," Bastian explained to Horsmanden.

In rendering his version of the activity at Hughson's and at Comfort's, Bastian implicated twenty-eight blacks. Thirteen he named for being at both Sunday meetings; eight he put at

Hughson's only, and seven at Comfort's only. Of the total of twenty he placed at Comfort's, twelve were persons listed by at least two previous witnesses. He agreed with Jack on six that Sandy and Burk's Sarah had not named and matched one additional name with Sandy and one with Sarah.

From the four listings a total of twenty-seven blacks emerged as positively identified by at least two witnesses as being at Comfort's meeting. Eleven of the blacks Bastian placed at the Hughson's meeting matched Jack's report; and all nine of the blacks Mary Burton had fingered as being at Hughson's were on either Jack or Bastian's list.

Horsmanden delighted in the corroborating evidence. His star witness, Mary Burton, was proving true at every turn so far. Bastian even confessed to cursing and threatening her as she reported. The matching words among Bastian, Jack, Sandy, and Burk's Sarah also boosted their stock somewhat with the judge. He seemed particularly pleased with Bastian and noted that he "seemed by his looks and behavior to be touched with a remorse for his guilt and was very ingenuous in his confession." Bastian's reward was a week's reprieve.

Mrs. Carpenter's Tickle and Sleydall's Jack followed Bastian's example in confessing. Both their stories corroborated what others had said but added some fresh detail.

Tickle opened his story to Horsmanden at a date six months earlier than anyone else, saying he was recruited for the plot in June 1740, a couple of weeks after the constables' May raid on Hughson's.

"Will you do as we do?" Pemberton's Quamino and Rowe's Tom accosted Tickle.

"What's that?"

"Set fire to both rows of houses in Stone Street," Quamino explained. "I'll find powder and pistol and ball."

"I don't know," Tickle stalled. "I'll think about it." And he did, quickly.

"Agree or I'll cut your throat," Quamino threatened, pulling out a razor. Thus Tickle joined the plot, and he recalled attending two meetings at Hughson's—the big Sunday gathering on January 18 and one in the middle of that week in 1741.

"Now's a proper time to make the plot. There's so many of us here together. Burn the town. Burn the fort. Burn Stone Street.

. . . And kill the white people as they come to put out the flames,''
Hughson opened.

"Almost everyone agreed," Tickle told the judge and admitted to agreeing to burn Mrs. Carpenter's house. He recalled further that "Hughson brought out a great book and swore himself
and Peggy first and then all the negroes. Damn them that fail or
tell," they all swore. "Rowe's Tom was to be a drummer, to give
notice on firing the houses, to kill the people and plunder. . . .
The Spaniards had black stuff to set houses on fire. . . . The tall
man, DeLancey's Antonio, and Sarly's Juan had it. . . . Juan
owned to me in company at Comfort's that he set fire to the house
of Ben Thomas." The neighbors had suspected that at the time of
the fire. Tickle corroborated the talk about Gomez's Cuffee, too.
"I've done what I promised. I set Van Zant's storehouse on fire,"
Cuffee told Tickle.

"We were to bring all the goods we'd get at the fires to
Hughson's house, and after all [was] over, Hughson was to carry
us off." The taverner offered free liquor to attract blacks to meetings and kept a roster of who was to do and get what, Tickle noted
in closing.

Sleydall's Jack also recalled Hughson's Sunday meeting, but
his statement differed markedly from the other slaves', at least in
form, for it came to the judge already written out—an apparent
arrangement between Jack and Joshua Sleydall, designed to serve
both their interests if it succeeded in saving the slave his life and
the slaveholder his investment. Sleydall invited others to witness
while he wrote and Jack talked.

"Captain Marshall's Ben sat at the head of the table. . . . Mr.
Philipse's Cuff played on the fiddle, and after we'd done dancing,
we made a bowl of punch and drank for some time. We said,
'Let's set fire to the town and kill the white people and, then, we'll
make our escape.' We all agreed to it and swore on a book and
kissed the book. I told them, 'If you do it, I try to help,'" Jack recalled. He listed the names of eleven blacks at the meeting and,
also, confessed to the arson Comfort's Jack accused him of. "On a
Saturday night, I took some ashes and coals from the house, in a
little kettle, and put it under Mr. Murray's haystack. Mr. DePeyster's Pedro told me to do it and said that after the stack was on
fire, the others would set other parts of the town on fire,"
Sleydall's Jack admitted.

Horsmanden and his fellows grabbed the slaves' confessions as full proof of a plot. The lists of names given separately by Comfort's Jack, Niblet's Sandy, and Burk's Sarah closely matched, and so did the talk they reported from Comfort's Sunday meeting. The reports from Vaarck's Bastian, Comfort's Jack, Sleydall's Jack, and Carpenter's Tickle on Hughson's Sunday meeting matched twenty names with at least two witnesses, and the talk the four recalled was much the same. The admission by Sleydall's Jack that he tried to burn Murray's stable, like Quack's admission about burning the fort and Cuff's about Philipse's storehouse, convinced the king's men that their prosecution was on the mark.

The fact that the details from the slaves matched so well, not only with names but in the talk they reported, was indeed convincing that those who had talked so far were telling the truth. Jailed at different times as they were, interrogated separately, and not all held together in the same cells, the slaves had little opportunity to concoct similar stories. Their agreement was clearly based on a shared experience, not an elaborate lie. Cuff, Quack, and Sleydall's Jack were too specific about how they set fires to be lying. And talking in the face of death as they had, confessing a lie that might be found out offered no real escape. What the slaves were saying was true, as far was it went.

The confessions confirmed Hughson's guilt in the eyes of the prosecution and the townspeople. Clearly the taverner had at least talked seditiously with the blacks and agreed with them on evil purposes, Horsmanden insisted as he reviewed the evidence. Legally, the meetings held at Hughson's and the meeting at Comfort's, too, constituted conspiracy. No doubt existed that the meetings occurred. Mary Burton said at the start that forty to fifty blacks convened at Hughson's, and the blacks that turned king's evidence verified her claim by naming forty-five. The judge sat satisfied then, as the Hughsons and Peggy awaited the hangman.

Cuff and Quack's dying words damned Hughson, for in connecting him to the crimes they confessed, they made him as guilty as themselves under the law of conspiracy. Yet the prosecution circumvented the law by introducing the slaves' confessions as evidence in the conspiracy trial of Hughson, his wife, daughter Sarah, and Peggy, because the word of a black was technically inadmissible against any white in court. Using George Joseph

Moore and John Roosevelt to repeat what the slaves confessed failed to change the essential fact: The evidence remained tainted, but the judge ignored the point. In pursuing what he thought of as justice, Horsmanden's apparent belief was that moderation was no virtue and excess no vice.

Only cold comfort faced the Hughsons and Peggy then. Unlike the blacks convicted one day and burned the next, the four whites had a week between their verdict and the gallows. But without legal counsel and a change of venue to escape the climate in the city, they never had any reasonable prospect of acquittal; and convicted in the highest court of the land, they had no appeal. John, his wife, and Peggy sat dead to rights after being convicted of receiving stolen goods. Yet if that charge alone had faced them, they and daughter Sarah might have escaped the stare of death.[2]

Not a tear of pity fell for John, and all hope for him evaporated with the tirades of the king's men and the blacks' identifying him as the plot's ringleader. A glimmer of clemency for the three women remained, because in concentrating so completely on John, the prosecutors proved little against them. The slaves' confessions referred only briefly to the women, and the sentiment in the city tended to run against executing females. Wife Sarah's stubborn refusal to talk or cooperate in any way killed sympathy for her, however compassion lingered for Peggy and especially for daughter Sarah.

Peggy earlier had reached the edge of release, and a pardon remained ready for her if she switched her tale from Romme's to Hughson's, but the redhead never knew how close she was. She tried during her conspiracy trial to play on sympathy by having her infant in court, sucking at the breast, until Horsmanden ordered the baby removed. The sight failed to move the jury in her favor. So Peggy's dilemma grew as the shadow of the gallows neared.

The redhead killed her own last hope by telling Undersheriff Mills that she gave false witness against John Romme. He was a fence but nothing else. "All that I said about Romme and his wife was false, excepting as to their receiving the stolen goods of the negroes," Peggy told Judge Philipse. Horsmanden took her retraction as proving his initial judgment that she had shifted the talk of plotting from Hughson's to Romme's, and he declared there was no reason now for "taking any further pains with her, since there could be no dependence upon what she should say."

Daughter Sarah's youth made even Horsmanden reluctant to hang her. His colleagues, like Judge Philipse, viewed the girl as simply the unfortunate offspring of bad parents and wanted to pardon her. Horsmanden saw the girl as an ideal witness to complement Mary Burton's testimony, and he wanted to use her to flesh out all the elements inside Hughson's. He hoped that once her parents and Peggy were dead, Sarah would confess to save her own life. He agreed then to give her a reprieve until June 19.

Thus, as the Friday sun reached its noon, daughter Sarah sat alone in her cell as her father, her mother, and Peggy rode the hangman's cart.

Hughson stood up during the ride, looking round and lifting up his hand as high as his shackles allowed, as if expecting to be rescued. He declared that some remarkable sign would show his innocence, but aside from a rash of red spotting his pale face, no sign appeared. If he expected help, none came.

John seemed resigned when he reached the gallows. He admitted deserving to hang for receiving stolen goods but protested innocence of conspiracy. His wife stood like a lifeless trunk throughout, saying not a word and scarcely moving. Peggy was less resigned than the other two, and for a moment she seemed ready to say something, but Mrs. Hughson gave her a shove and silenced her.

The crowd gathered for the hanging also watched three more blacks burn to death. Nine others were arrested for conspiracy that day.

The date was June 12.

# 11

━━━━━━━━━━━━━━━━━━━━━━━━━━━━━━━━━━━━━━

# "We Have Still Daily New Discoveries"

In the six weeks since May 1, the king's men had tried six cases—one for robbery, one for receiving stolen goods, and four for conspiracy. The juries convicted all eighteen defendants in the six cases. Comfort's Jack and Vaarck's Bastian turned king's evidence and, along with the younger Sarah Hughson and Ellison's Jamaica, received reprieves. The others convicted met death: Caesar, Prince, John Hughson, his wife, and Peggy hanged; the remaining nine—all blacks condemned for conspiracy—burned at the stake. Yet the prosecution had only just begun.[1]

Horsmanden saw much more to be done, and so did his fellow officials. They had hammered out their formal conspiracy and meeting place connections by making Hughson's the center of the plot and by nailing down the talk of illicit designs there, but the other basic links in their chain of conspiracy remained unforged.

The arson connection had netted specific culprits for five fires—Quack at the fort; Gomez's Cuffee and Peck's Caesar at Van Zant's; Sarly's Juan at Thomas's; Sleydall's Jack at Murray's; and Cuff at Philipse's; but the other seven fires in the rash of twelve were not yet resolved to the townspeople's satisfaction.

The slaveholder murder connection was also yet to be plumbed, and the notion of specific whites being targeted for death made both the officials and the citizens anxious to identify any slave who had talked of killing his holder. The possibility of being marked for death individually struck more real terror among people than being a casualty in the random mass slaying the king's men initially projected.

The invasion connection particularly interested Horsmanden. He saw it as giving the plot even greater dimensions, coupling as it did the terror of domestic insurrectionists with the fear of England's foreign foes. If the king's men demonstrated a link between the slaves and the hated Spanish or French, the judge expected everyone surely to see that New York had been in extreme danger. Such a link promised also to underscore his arguments against slavery; for like William Smith, Horsmanden pictured blacks as perennial domestic enemies and wanted them entirely removed or greatly diminished in number for the security of New York.

Continuing the parade of implicated slaves was, in the judge's view, the best way for the king's men to examine all who were involved and to find any real links to the invasion connection and, also, to fill out the arson and murder connections. His colleagues agreed and picked up their pace in prosecuting the slaves and pumping them for evidence.

Five more were tried for conspiracy on Saturday, June 13. Attorney General Bradley made it immediately clear that he, like Horsmanden, stood ready to root out every element in the plot. He also joined the judge in suspecting that there was more behind the blacks than had so far been revealed. "It cannot be imagined that these silly unthinking creatures could of themselves have contrived and carried on so deep, so direful and destructive a scheme as that we have seen with our eyes and heard fully proved, . . . without the advice and assistance of such abandoned wretches as Hughson was—that never to be forgotten Hughson, who is now gone to his place as did Judas of old," Bradley told the jurors.

Not letting yesterday's dead rest, the attorney general flailed Hughson and hinted at there being others like him and the blacks already executed. "The number of conspirators is very great; for besides these five negroes, fourteen others, and four white people . . . [who] have already been convicted and received sentence of death, we have still daily new discoveries of many more. But [we] have now, God be thanked, encouragement to hope that we shall soon reach to the bottom of this mystery of iniquity," Bradley declared.

John Chambers and Joseph Murray carried the prosecution against the five. Mary Burton, Comfort's Jack, Niblet's Sandy, Vaarck's Bastian, Carpenter's Tickle, Leffert's Pompey, and Sleydall's Jack appeared for the king's case. The defendants produced no witnesses or evidence, and the case was shut almost as soon as it opened. The jury reached the predictable verdict: Guilty.

Horsmanden sentenced the five: Marshall's Ben, who reportedly styled himself as a headman at Hughson's, and Rutgers's Quash, who had boasted of his ability to get a dozen knives and a few swords, were condemned to burn at the stake. Cowley's Cato, Provoost's Cato, and Vanderspiegle's Fortune—all named by several witnesses for swearing to burn their holders' houses—were to hang.

The constables arrested four more blacks that Saturday afternoon. One of the four was Gabriel Crooke's Prince, and he immediately fed Horsmanden's worries that the plot was lingering afoot, for he reported blacks' talking of rising up even as Cuff and Quack were being burned on May 30.

"Look at the great number of white people present," Crooke's Prince confessed he had marvelled to Marschalk's York while perched at a distance to watch the execution.

"Now's a fit time for us to rise," declared York.

"I don't think so. There's a great number of them. Perhaps we'd kill only one or two, and then we'd be taken and hanged for it. It's not a right time to begin now; there's too much trouble in town," Prince said he cautioned York, who was clearly angered by the sight of his fellow blacks being burned to death and of whites' reveling in the light of the flames.

Could the slaves still be set on doing violence? Horsmanden wondered, and so did the grand jury pressing to get every name and detail it could for indictments. The jurors marked York for questioning, but many stood ahead of him in the interrogation line.

The jury's particular concern at the moment was Carpenter's Tickle who, in naming blacks at meetings he attended, said, "They had a list of them on paper."

"Who had the list?"

"Ben had it, and there was a list of them at Hughson's, as well as Comfort's," Tickle answered. Others before him suggested such lists existed, and the king's men were eager to lay their hands on them as physical evidence and as a timesaving in their efforts at identification.

Ben denied having or knowing about such a list. He refused, in fact, to say much of anything as he faced death on that day— Tuesday, June 16.

The grand jury indicted six more blacks for conspiracy, before adjourning for the spectacle of Ben's burning with Quash and the three hangings.

In the eighteen days since May 30, the king's men had now killed seventeen persons for conspiracy.

⛓⛓⛓⛓⛓

On Wednesday, June 17, the five most frequently mentioned Spanish blacks came to trial in *The King against DeLancey's Antonio, Mesnard's Antonio, McMullen's Augustine, Sarly's Juan, and Becker's Pablo*. The defendants preferred their full names: Antonio de San Bendito, Antonio de la Cruz, Augustine Gutierrez, Juan de la Sylva, and Pablo Ventura Angél. Merchant Mordecai Gomez translated the proceedings for them.

Captured aboard prizes, like the sloop *La Soledad*, by Captain John Lush and others and sold into slavery between May 1740 and January 1741, the five and fourteen of their shipmates protested their treatment. They claimed they were free men, not bondsmen, and considered themselves properly prisoners of war. Their fair-skinned, clearly European-featured mates were, in fact, handled as prisoners of war awaiting exchange. But the Court of Admiralty condemned the dark-skinned nineteen, counting their African features as *prima facie* proof of slave status.[2]

The question of legal status loomed, in fact, as a major issue in the trial. Under the peculiarities of New York law, the issue affected the evidence and the conspiracy charge itself. If judged as free men, the defendants were entitled to be considered as whites, not as blacks. The legal inference stemmed from the very argument used to condemn the defendants as slaves: If being black meant they were necessarily liable for sale as slaves, then not being liable for sale as slaves meant they were not black. The logic in both directions was flawed, but the argument followed the ruling legal presumptions. The issue affected the evidence because the law prohibited blacks from testifying against whites. Thus, in this case, the defendants technically would face only Mary Burton's testimony; none of what any of the blacks had told the officials or might say in court would be legal evidence.

Also, if the five were judged as captured free men they were entitled to be treated as prisoners of war, like their fellow crewmen. Although the conventions applying to such prisoners were not codified and agreed to on all sides at the time, a general understanding prevailed that such prisoners were entitled to try to escape and that any hostile act on their part was not to be considered criminal conspiracy, but an act of war. And public opinion was sensitive on that issue as New Yorkers with sons, brothers, and husbands off fighting the Spanish in the West Indies wanted to avoid any cause for retaliation against their kin liable to capture.[3]

Horsmanden showed less concern for the status question than others did. For him the case was a step toward establishing a connection between the plot and England's perennial enemies. He was not yet ready to argue publicly that the connection existed, but he noted hints that Spain, through Catholic allies or foreign agents, had planned to stir up New York blacks. That the Spanish blacks had plotted was beyond doubt in the judge's mind; he saw no legal problems with the prosecution and expected the king's case to be clear enough to satisfy concerned citizens.

The prosecutors seemed more cautious than the judge. Attorney General Bradley pleaded the infirmities of age and left the case to James Alexander, John Chambers, and Joseph Murray. They opened by calling Mary Burton, and she made exactly the points Horsmanden wanted made, testifying to the Spanish blacks' presence at Hughson's and their participation in the plot talk.

"I've seen DeLancey's Anthony often [at Hughson's] at nights. He was there when they talked about fires. I think I saw Anthony there about new year, but I'm sure I saw him there often in March. He often spoke to me in English, and I heard him say, 'The York negroes kill one, the Spanish kill twenty,' " Mary said. She mentioned no other defendant by name but swore, "I've seen all the prisoners at Hughson's when they were talking about the plot, and they were consenting."

Sandy reinforced what the girl said. Repeating his story about Spanish blacks' cursing Captain Lush and joining in the talk of setting fires, the boy quoted DeLancey's Antonio as saying, "Damn that son of a bitch, if he no carry us to our own country, we ruin the city and play the devil with him." Sarly's Juan agreed to help burn Lush's house and do Sarly's himself. McMullen's Augustine also agreed to burn his holder's house at the same time. Becker's Pablo was with the others during the talk, and Mesnard's Antonio and McMullen's Augustine were at the meeting at Comfort's. "One of them rolled something black in his hands and broke it and gave [some] to the rest to throw on the houses, to set fires to the shingles," the boy said.

George Joseph Moore bolstered Sandy's credibility by testifying that Cuff and Quack confessed most of the Spanish blacks were in the plot. "They did not name any names but referred to Sandy who, they said, could name them all," Moore noted.

Comfort's Jack also corroborated part of Sandy's story and drew Spanish blacks into the plotting. "DeLancey's Antonio said he had stuff to throw on the houses to make them get fire," Jack told the court. Confessing it was true that he had distributed knives during the February meeting at his holder's house as Sandy had reported, Jack said, "I let nine have knives that had none. I bought the knives off Pablo for half a crown." But he did not remember everything being as the boy said, for he reported, "There were only two Spaniards there [at Comfort's], Mr. DeLancey's Antonio and Becker's Pablo."

Like Sandy, though, Carpenter's Tickle recalled more Spanish blacks' being at Comfort's. "I saw Juan and Augustine there. . . . There were two rooms full of negroes. Some were in the kitchen and some in the shop," Tickle said. He also recalled that "DeLancey's Antonio had something black which he said was to throw on houses to set them on fire, and he cut it in pieces and gave to several of the negroes."

Vaarck's Bastian also said, "DeLancey's Antonio had something black in his hand, which he cut and gave to other negroes to throw on houses to set them on fire." Like Jack, Bastian named only DeLancey's Antonio and Becker's Pablo, but along with Tickle, he noted the blacks were not all in the same place at Comfort's. "Some were in the kitchen, some in the shop," he said.

Bastian and Tickle's remarks about blacks' being in two separate rooms at Comfort's partially explained why they and others differed on who was there. Being in one room or the other limited who anyone saw, for there was no way to see everyone in the kitchen and the shop at the same time; and even in moving between the rooms, which were not side by side, a person might have missed seeing others—particularly if those who attended were coming and going, as Burk's Sarah had suggested. Different times of arrivals and departures also helped to explain why the reports did not all name the same people.

In Horsmanden's view the key point about the five Spanish blacks on trial was made, for at least two persons placed each of the five at Comfort's. The consensus was complete on DeLancey's Antonio and Becker's Pablo being there. And the two were portrayed not only as being present but as advancing the talk of burning and killing: Antonio by distributing a reported incendiary and Pablo by supplying the knives Jack distributed. McMullen's Augustine and Sarly's Juan were both tagged as agreeing to set fires.

Juan was fingered for the fire at Ben Thomas's house. Popular suspicions also had fixed on him for the fires at Agnes Hilton's and at the Quick & Vergereau cow stable—all within steps of Sarly's house in the Fly neighborhood. Juan was not on trial for arson, however, and the king's case contained no evidence of his actually setting any fire. The prosecutors simply stressed his talk of setting fire.

On Mesnard's Antonio the king's case contained nothing, however, about his having uttered even a single untoward word. The witnesses confirmed only that he was at Comfort's during the meeting there. That was more than enough evidence for conviction in the judge's mind.

To assure the case's withstanding protests about the defendants' being free men, the prosecutors focused on the issue of status. The proof was *pro forma*, because the essential fact was that the five were slaves if the king's men said they were slaves. And the king's men had, in fact, said the five were slaves. The prosecutors called Deputy Register of the Admiralty Richard Nicolls and Mayor John Cruger, in his role as port venue-master, to attest that the five were lawfully condemned and sold.

To cinch their case the prosecutors called three final witnesses. Captain John Lush testified that DeLancey's Antonio and Sarly's Juan spoke enough English to be understood—an important point, considering that Burton and the blacks who reported against the five understood no Spanish and could repeat only what was said in English. William Douglass testified to serving on a ship that sailed to Havana, where a Cuban gentleman purchased a captured brother of DeLancey's Antonio and said he knew Antonio and his family as slaves from Cartagena, the city on the Caribbean coast in Spain's South American colony of Nueva Granada. City councilman Robert Benson, partner in a merchandise shop with Frederick Becker, Pablo's holder, recalled having "a parcel of clasp knives" fitting the description of those Comfort's Jack said he bought from Pablo. Benson said he had only one knife left but was not sure what happened to the others.

That was the king's case. Without the blacks who turned king's evidence, the prosecutors had only the barest evidence against the five for conspiracy, and that evidence turned on the issue of status.

The five defended themselves by insisting that they were free men and innocent. They called eleven witnesses, but their first line of argument fell flat, for chief among their witnesses stood their holders whose interests opposed all denials of slave status. Yet the holders' interests in protecting their property did contribute to the second line of defense.

Peter DeLancey, the absent chief justice's thirty-six-year-old brother, testified that there was no way his man could have been in a plot to burn Fort George. He told the court, "My Antonio went to my farm in the country last fall and did not return till two days after the fire at the fort. I was not there all the while myself, but was frequently there and saw him lame, his feet being frozen. I do not think he could have come to town in that time."

Abraham Peltreau, one of DeLancey's workmen, confirmed part of the alibi for Antonio. "The negro went up with Mr. De-Lancey to the farm before Christmas and came down with him after the fort was burnt. His feet were frozen after the first great snow, and I don't think he was in town all winter," Peltreau said. Challenging the workman rather than DeLancey himself, the prosecutors got Peltreau to concede that Antonio's feet were well some time before he came down from Westchester on March 20.

Mrs. Sarah Mesnard produced much the same alibi for her Antonio, as DeLancey had for his. "He was not downstairs from November till the seventeenth of March. I believe it not possible for him to be abroad at that time," the woman testified.

Doctor Francis DePuy, Sr., confirmed the affliction. "Antonio's feet were frozen, and I dressed them during December and January," the doctor said. His son, Doctor Francis DePuy, Jr., elaborated: "From the latter end of November and December last, this negro was ill. I saw his toes in December and they were then so bad that he could not walk."

The prosecutors did not contest the doctors' diagnosis, but they did press on the dates, and the younger doctor conceded their point. "I do not know whether he was able to walk in February or not. He came to my father's house the beginning or middle of March; I cannot say the time exactly, but it was before the fire at the fort."

The king's men also pressed Gilbert Budd about Mesnard's Antonio. "I dressed this negro from the middle of November to the fifth or sixth of March," Budd said. "I think Mrs. Mesnard told me that he came downstairs about the latter end of February, when his feet grew bad again, for they had been better before."

As with DeLancey's Antonio, the witnesses for Mesnard's Antonio left unanswered the crucial question of his being able to get to the two big meetings where the king's evidence had placed the defendants on the dates of January 18 and February 8.

The time factor and health were also questions in the case against Pablo, for Frederick Becker offered the alibi of illness for him, too. "My negro was brought into this country by Captain [William] Boyd in January last and was sick in my house till some time in March," Becker said.

James McMullen and two of his lodgers, William Quinland and Thomas Palmer, repeated the alibi for McMullen's Augustine who they said was sick all winter with violent fever and fits of shivering from ague, which reportedly confined him to bed during February.

Whether Augustine was bedridden in January was left unanswered, and as with his codefendants, his opportunity for mischief after the fort fire was left open. The prosecutors pushed the implications and the presence of a motive by getting McMullen to concede that Augustine was captured and brought to the city by Captain Peter Warren, whose house flared a week after the fort fire.

Opportunity was less an issue in the case against Juan. The question was more about his character. His holder, Captain Jacob Sarly, offered him no alibi of illness but spoke of his being well behaved and closely supervised. "I never had a more faithful servant, and when I'm home, the negro cannot be out after nine at night," Sarly told the court. His wife also spoke well of Juan and credited him with being the first to discover the fire at Ben Thomas's house, next door to Sarly's.

The king's men construed the fact that Juan was the first to yell fire as an indication he had set it. They pressed Sarly on exactly how close his supervision was, too. "I'm not always at home," the sea captain admitted. Nobody asked Mrs. Sarly about her reason for praising Juan or what he did on the many nights her husband was not home.

The defense rested.

In summation the prosecutors cited the statutes covering prizes and prisoners of war. Chambers recapped the king's case against the two Antonios and Pablo, and Murray handled Augustine and Juan.

For their part, the defendants again insisted they were free men and declared themselves innocent of conspiracy. Repeating their alibis, they also denied that they spoke English and claimed they never kept company with slaves.

The case was now for the jury to decide, and in his charge Horsmanden told the twelve men that the issues were simple. Noting that none of the five defendants entered a formal protest when condemned and sold as slaves by the Court of Admiralty, the judge contended that their raising the question of status now was only a ruse and made no practical difference in this case. "Be they free men or be they slaves, the main question before you is whether they or any or which of them are guilty of . . . conspiring with other slaves and persons to burn the house in the fort, to burn the town and murder and destroy the people," he declared.

Conceding that the prosecution had only Mary Burton as a formal witness, the judge told the jurors that "one witness is sufficient, and if you give credit to her testimony, you will no doubt discharge a good conscience and find them guilty. If you should have sufficient reason in your own minds to discredit her testimony, if you can think so, you must acquit them."

Horsmanden crushed even that sop to judiciousness, however, by instructing the jury that "The prisoners seem all to be equally involved by [Mary Burton's] testimony in this unparalleled and hellish conspiracy, and there is no room to make any difference between them; therefore, you will either acquit them all or find them all guilty."

The jury took half an hour to return the verdict: Guilty.

⛓⛓⛓⛓⛓

Horsmanden fitted the convicted Spanish blacks into an image of rotten, foreign apples. With bad seeds, such as Caesar, they had spread the corruption fostered by John Hughson and soured the city's home-grown blacks, the judge suggested. That image was easy enough for people to understand and accept, but it left unexplained how the infection had apparently corrupted so many blacks.

Explaining how the plot, as they had pictured it in court, extended from a small, rotten core was indeed one of the essential tasks remaining for the judge and his fellow officials. Thus, they were very much interested in learning more about how and why blacks joined in the scheme. Horsmanden expected no deep reasoning on the blacks' part. He believed they were, as Attorney General Bradley had called them, "silly, unthinking creatures." The other officials and the people-at-large also accepted that characterization.

Under questioning, arrested blacks had offered the beginnings of two patterns in their recruitment that Horsmanden found useful. One explanation was that blacks joined after being plied with liquor; another was that they joined because they were threatened.

Benjamin Moore's Tom offered the officials a story on Thursday, June 18, that illustrated the two elements of explanation. Starting his recollections near Christmas 1740, Tom said Philipse's Cuff treated him to punch at Hughson's. A week later, Cuff again took Tom to the tavern, and Vaarck's Caesar and Auboyneau's Prince joined them for a drink.

"Will you join us in what we're about to do?" Prince asked Tom, while Caesar and Cuff stepped outside for a moment.

"What's it you're about to do?"

"You'll find out when Caesar and Cuff return," Prince said.

"What's it you're about to do?" Tom repeated when the two came back.

"We're going to burn houses. I'll burn my master's house. There's money enough there, and you'll have a share of it," Cuff explained.

"No, I dare not. The white people will play the devil with you," Tom balked.

"You needn't fear that. We've people enough to stand by us," Cuff declared.

"I'll consider on it," Tom said. Then he drank up and left. Five days later Caesar chanced on him in the street and offered to buy him a drink again at Hughson's.

"Join us," Caesar urged after a round.

"No, I don't like it," Tom persisted and drained his mug. Caesar ordered another and let Tom finish that one, too.

"Why won't you concern yourself with us? Last time you said you'd consider it," Caesar prodded.

"I'll join with you," Tom relented. Caesar called Hughson, who brought the book and swore in the recruit. The liquor made him yield, Tom suggested.

"When you coming down again to Hughson's?" Cuff asked a few days later.

"I'll go there no more. I'm sorry I went there at all. What you're going to do is a great sin," Tom huffed.

"Fool, if you think it a wrong thing or a sin, I know a man who can forgive you," Cuff taunted, as Caesar approached.

"Damn you," Caesar cursed when he heard Tom's talk of backing out. "If you do or speak a word of what passed among us, I've a pocket pistol that'll be the death of you. If you're in any pain about what we're going to do being a sin, there's an old man in town we know can forgive them." Tom said he never learned the name of the man with the reported power to forgive sins, but he remembered Caesar's teaching him a lesson at Bayard's wharf a few days later.

"I'll throw you into the river if you fall off from us or inform anybody what we're going to do," the husky slave hissed and snatched Tom to the water's edge.

"I'll be true to you," the shrinking slave whimpered, and when Caesar let him go, he scurried home. From then on, Tom said, he avoided the trio who propositioned him.

"One Sunday I'd a mind to disclose this design . . . to Mr. Ogilvie [Rev. John Ogilvie, an Anglican missionary] and went to him. I told him I had something to tell him which was a very great sin and would surprise him, but he answered that he was going to church and bid me come when church was out and he'd hear me. I didn't go to Mr. Ogilvie after church was out nor did I ever say anything to him about it," Tom confessed to the grand jury.[4]

Tom's tone of contrition and his talk of being plied with liquor and threatened sat well with the officials, and they readily accepted his explanation. How many were there like him? That general question seemed much on people's mind. A more specific question also developed from what Tom said: Who was this man who slaves said could forgive sins? The claim sounded like witchcraft to righteous Protestants like Horsmanden.

#####

At ten o'clock on Friday, June 19, court resumed with Shurmur's Cato, Kipp's Harry, and Marschalk's London and York standing trial on the conspiracy indictment. John Chambers and Joseph Murray prosecuted. Comfort's Jack, Vaarck's Bastian, Carpenter's Tickle, and Niblet's Sandy offered their evidence. George Joseph Moore read Cuff and Quack's confessions which named Kipp's Harry as a plotter. Jane Lovell also testified, reporting a conversation she had with a couple of slaves.

"You! All this trouble was occasioned by you," Lovell recalled her own accosting of Shurmur's Cato and Groesbeck's Mink outside her house on April 6, the Monday of the many fires and mobs.

"I wish all concerned were tied to a stake and burnt," Mink assured the woman.

"You a fool! If you knew as much as me, you'd hold your tongue," Cato rebuked Mink, Lovell reported.

Neither slave offered any reply to the woman in court. In fact, all four defendants said little, and none of them had anyone to testify in his behalf. They defended themselves simply by denying the talk against them. Chambers and Murray summed up the king's case, and a reporter noted, "the court having charged the jury, they withdrew and after a short stay returned and found the prisoners *guilty*."

Five more slaves were indicted for conspiracy that Friday, and the occasion proved noteworthy because two—Edward Kelly's London and Peter Lowe's Indian slave Wan—pleaded guilty, a first in all the arraignments. Wan immediately confessed to being at Hughson's once in June 1740. He said an Indian named John, then a slave but since freed by his holder Cornelius Cosine, took him to the tavern.[5]

"We drank a mug of beer and paid for it. Then John went away, but Hughson stopped me and told me a law was made to sell no liquor to slaves and bid me not tell, and I said I wouldn't and I put my hand on the book and swore after what Hughson said: To burn my master's house and to kill my master and mistress and to assist to take the town. Tickle and Bastian were there when I swore."

"Anyone else?" the grand jury asked.

"None," Wan answered. "John, the Indian, met me afterwards and, seeing me melancholy, asked me 'What's the matter?' I told him what I'd done. He said, 'That's good for you.' Gomez's Cuffee and Bosch's Francis told me they were to set their masters' houses on fire and one day asked me if I was ready. I told them 'Yes.' "

"What were you going to do when you took the town?" asked the jurors.

"We were to kill the white people, the men, and take their wives to ourselves," Wan answered. His repeating the accepted idea of the plot, his talk of drinking, and his note of remorse satisfied the officials who thought they were now getting a handle on how the plotting had spread among the slaves.

James Debrosse's Primus bolstered the officials' thinking when he too confessed to the grand jury that afternoon. Starting his story at the week before Christmas 1740, Primus said much the same as Moore's Tom and Wan. A couple of slaves had invited him to Hughson's, they drank awhile, and then Hughson asked him "to rise and to kill the white people."

"I said I'd help them but cared not to kill my master and mistress as they're kind to me," Primus confessed. Only that one time was he at the tavern and, he said, the only details he knew were that Hughson kept a list of those who agreed to help in the uprising and that Peck's Caesar told him that he and Gomez's Cuffee set Van Zant's storehouse on fire.

⬤⬤⬤⬤⬤

Primus's story, like that of Tom and Wan, fit the meeting house connection the king's men had established and helped to explain the large number of blacks reported to be in the plot. It also offered the officials a convenient division among the slaves—those who were hard core and had recruited others or engaged in actual arson or theft and those who had been drawn in by liquor or threats and had done nothing except agree to the plot.

Hoping to encourage more like Primus to talk and speed a final round up to end the proceedings that were now entering their third month, the king's men agreed on Governor Clarke's issuing a proclamation promising mercy and pardon

> to any and every person and persons, whether white people, free negroes, slaves, or others . . . concerned in the said con-

spiracy, who shall on or before the first day of July next, voluntarily, freely and fully discover and confession make of his, her or their confederates, accomplices, or others concerned in the said conspiracy, and his, her and their part or share, actings and doings therein, so [long] as the person or persons making such discovery and confession are not thereof before convicted, arraigned, or indicted for the same.[6]

But the actual results were hardly what Horsmanden and his colleagues anticipated.

The date was June 19.

# 12

## "Now Many Negroes Began to Speak"

Slaves scrambled to confess as if the pardon offer were their last lifeboat in the continuing swell of prosecution that had now killed nineteen. Seven confessed to the judge on Monday, June 22, and the number multiplied in the following days.

So heavy was the rush of blacks' talking to save themselves that Horsmanden and his fellows became virtual scriveners. Even so, their efforts to hurry the blacks' words to paper failed to meet the demand and forced a two day extension of the pardon offer.[1]

By the original deadline of July 1, the judge and his benchmate Frederick Philipse personally managed to take a total of twenty-two confessions. Prosecutors Richard Nicolls and Abraham Lodge collected fifteen on June 27 alone and added nine more during the next four days. In all, between June 20 and July 3, the king's men gathered seventy-one confessions.

Constables swept the city almost daily for fresh blacks during the two weeks of confessions, netting thirty-four the first week and seventeen the second. The fifty-one added to the scores already crammed into city hall cells. "The jail began to be so thronged it was difficult to find room," Horsmanden noted during the dragnet.

"It seemed very probable that most of the negroes in town were corrupted," the judge declared. And, in fact, more than half the city's black males sixteen years of age or older—nearly two hundred in all—found themselves in jail by July 4, as the cries of April to jail all the black men echoed anew. The more blacks revealed of what they said and did among themselves and at places such as Hughson's, the more the officials and townsfolk widened their picture of a horrible plot. Instead of moving the proceedings to a swift conclusion then, as the officials had hoped, the pardon offer gave rise to a fresh wave of anxiety among both the king's men and the people.

Not simply the increasing number of blacks implicated in the talk of plotting, but also the identity and position of some of the implicated blacks, intensified concern about who the chief blacks were, about how recruitment had proceeded, about who had incited the plotting among blacks, and about what the blacks had agreed to do. Who confessed and what they said was of great interest then, as the king's men tried to fit together a full and final explanation of the conspiracy.

The confessing blacks seemed willing enough to tell the king's men what they wanted to hear, and for several reasons Horsmanden and his fellow officials accepted almost everything confessed as true. First, the rush of words left officials little time to check every detail. Second, the details checked in the fourteen confessions taken before June 19 were largely corroborated. Third, the confessions fell into patterns where the repetition of detail itself provided corroboration. Fourth, the patterns themselves confirmed the links the king's men had postulated in the arson, meeting place, and murder connections.

Three patterns of revelations emerged. One marked several of the king's men themselves as targets in the conspiracy by suggesting that their own slaves were involved in the plotting. A second repeated the theme of earlier confessions in which blacks said they had heard about or even agreed to join in the plotting but had not really wanted to be involved. Both allowed a glimpse into the world of resentment among slaves and alarmed holders who seemed unable to imagine their own slaves—members of their own households—harboring enough anger to plot murder. The third provoked the most alarm, for it suggested that whites other than the Hughsons and Peggy were involved in the plotting.

Peter DeLancey's Pompey opened the confessions on June 22 and stirred the officials by indicating that the plotting had reached further into houses of power and wealth than the king's men suspected. Slaves of prominent New Yorkers, including Peter DeLancey's Spanish black Antonio, had been implicated earlier, but they had been few. Governor George Clarke's Danby, although suspected during the early days, managed to sustain his innocence and avoid arrest; he owed much of his saving grace to Quack's dying words. Others were not so fortunate. Yet only three suffered punishment so far: New York Assembly Speaker Adolph Philipse's Cuff died in the first burning at the stake, after being convicted in the first conspiracy trial. Assistant Prosecutor John Chambers's Robin was burned on June 9. Alderman John Marshall's Ben also was burned at the stake, on June 16.

Pompey immediately enlarged the count and brought the king's men to worry that they themselves had been direct targets in the plot. Admitting he attended the big meeting at Hughson's and the one at Comfort's, Pompey said Hughson asked him to steal long guns, pistols, and swords. DeLancey's strong locks closed the possibility of getting the arms at home, but nothing kept Pompey from slipping into the plot and swearing, "Devil take me if I don't stand [to help]."

Pompey recruited others, too, notably Mayor John Cruger's Deptford, and Hanover, a slave of the mayor's son Henry. He said his own recruiter was Sam, a slave of Frederick Van Cortlandt—a scion of the landed Westchester family that ruled Cortlandt Manor, just south of Yonkers. Frederick's brother Philip sat on the Council of the Colony of New York, which advised the governor and acted as an upper legislative house. Pompey also fingered Chief Justice James DeLancey's Othello.[2]

Alderman John Pintard's Caesar followed Pompey and implicated twenty blacks, including those of two more city councilmen—John Moore's Cato and Robert Benson's Mars. Describing his initiation at Hughson's "soon after the Cuba men were gone," Pintard's Caesar spurred townsfolk who nayed earlier, when hundreds of New York's men sailed for war on the West Indian front, and now nagged that the men's departing, the trouble with the Spanish blacks, and the reports of plotters awaiting an invasion of the city were all connected to the conspiracy.

Pintard's Caesar did reassure the officials a bit. Noting that the nightwatch intercepted him on occasion, he indicated that the city's security forces unknowingly disrupted meetings at Hughson's. Also, he suggested that not every slave was ready to commit arson, even if willing to kill for freedom. "I told Hughson I'd not set any man's house on fire, that I'd only fight and kill the white people," the slave confessed. He personally recruited sixteen others, among them Comfort's Jack.

Unlike Pintard's Caesar and DeLancey's Pompey, Alderman Moore's Cato cast himself as a reluctant rebel, describing his initial recruitment by Alderman Marshall's Ben and Hermanus Rutgers's Quash—both already burned at the stake.

"Join us!" Ben and Quash urged Cato, after telling him that "the negroes are to rise against the white people."

"I've no occasion for it. I live well enough," Cato replied.

"I live as good or better than you," sneered Quash.

"So do I! But it's a hard case upon the poor negroes who can't so much as take a walk after church-out but the constables take them up," Ben declared. "In order to be free, we must set the houses on fire and kill the white people."

"I'm not willing to do that," Cato insisted. But in time he relented, attended the big meetings at Hughson's and Comfort's, and swore to be true. Whatever his earlier commitment, Cato now implicated thirty-three blacks by name.

John Furman's Harry echoed Cato's halfheartedness as he recalled being recruited while getting a shave from Comfort's Jack.

"You could set your master's bakehouse on fire," Jack said, in a break from his usual barber's chattering. "Your master'd never know you did it."

"No, my master do me good," Harry retorted.

"I'll cut your throat if you don't agree," Jack threatened.

"If you set your master's house on fire first, I set mine's," Harry compromised. Sitting in bib and lather and with a honed edge over him, he was in a poor position to argue. Duress alone accounted for his agreeing to the plot, Harry insisted. Aside from Comfort's Jack, he implicated only former alderman Stephen Bayard's Ben, who disappeared, as did Henry Cruger's Hanover.

Robert Todd's Dundee added a note against Comfort's Jack and against Alderman Moore's Cato, while offering another glimpse of how slaves entered the plot. Sent to Comfort's to fetch water but lingering for hours on what proved an unlucky summer

Sunday for him, Dundee lost about twenty-five pence to Comfort's Jack, Jenny, and Cook in a card game called papa at a penny per pot. Jack won most of the money and played generous winner by treating Dundee to a pint of rum at Hughson's. "I got almost drunk and Jack helped me [home] with the water," the young black admitted. He recalled little of that day's talk of the plot, but he remembered what happened the next day, when he and Jack returned to Hughson's.

"Whose boy is that?" Mrs. Hughson questioned Jack about Dundee.

"Mr. Todd's. Never fear him. He's a good boy."

"What's your name?" John Hughson inquired of the youngster.

"Dundee."

"Stay a little while till I fetch a book," said Hughson, who then disappeared for a couple of minutes and returned asking, "What you say your name was?"

"Dundee," the boy repeated.

"Lay your hand on the book."

"For what?"

"You must swear to help us set fire to houses and to tell nobody of it."

"The devil fetch me and damn me if I tell. What I'm to do?" Dundee asked Hughson and Jack.

"Set your master's house on fire. The fort's to be burned first. Quack's to do it. You must help burn the rest of the houses and destroy the people. . . . There are too many guns in the fort; so we burn that first. We're to burn the fort on St. Patrick's Day. You fire your master's house the same evening after the fort's destroyed. . . . When the whole city's on fire, we're all to meet together and destroy the people as fast as they come out. We'll have penknives to cut their throats. I'm to provide them," Jack explained, offering Dundee a knife.

"I'll buy one," said Dundee, apparently not liking the looks of the blade Jack offered. "I'll cut my mistress's throat, in the night. She scolds me when I stay [out]," he whined, and Jack offered to kill Mr. Todd for following Dundee to Comfort's on occasion and complaining about the slave's lingering when fetching water.

"Bring wine in the cask as often as you come for water," Jack suggested, with an eye on emptying Todd's well-stocked cellar.

147

"I've no opportunity, else I would," Dundee hedged. When the fires came, he forgot his promises and made no move on Mrs. Todd or the house. "I was afraid I'd be catched and hanged," Dundee confessed to the listening whites.

"The day the fort was burnt, [English's] Patrick, me, and Alderman Moore's Cato was on the mount. I said, 'I'm sorry the governor's house is burnt.' Patrick said, 'Not me, I wish the governor burnt in the middle of it.' Cato wasn't present then but came just after and said, 'By and by this'll be put in the news, that the fort's burnt, and then the Spaniards'll come and take us all,' " Dundee reported.

The blacks' repeated references to a Spanish attack and also the ambivalence among them—some seeming eager but others reluctant to strike whites—intrigued the interrogators. The men, like Horsmanden, acted as if they genuinely failed to understand why slaves would wish English enemies well or think of assaulting their holders themselves. That not all the slaves expressed the same feelings for their holders further confused the issue. More than fretting about the blacks' motives, the king's men grew increasingly worried if a Spanish plan was afoot against New York.

Sterling, a slave of city councilman Samuel Lawrence, suggested again that resentment was a prime motive among blacks as he confessed to joining the plot and offered two notable details on the fire at Fort George. "When the governor forbid Quack coming to the fort," denying him visits to his wife, the slave determined to burn the place and planned the fire for March, "when the wind blew hard," Sterling reported. That confirmed Quack's confession and townsfolk's early belief that late winter winds billowed the blaze not by chance alone.

Like most of the blacks who confessed, Sterling centered his story on others. Johannes Tiebout's Jack tried the same tack and repeated the resentment theme in his story of Anthony Ward's Will inviting him for a drink in March and asking him to build a boxed candleholder that let Will hide the light when he wanted.

"Mr. Van Horne won't allow a candle," Will told Jack, referring to elderly Abraham Van Horne, a member of the governor's council and holder of the slave Will called wife. "Van Horne won't allow me to come to my wife, but before long I'll show him a trick. The negroes here are cowards. They've no hearts as those in Antigua," Will complained. His mates on the Leeward Island—from which he came in 1736, after a major rebellion—continually pricked their slaveholders in ways New York's blacks never managed, the West Indian black suggested. He particularly ridiculed Alderman John Pintard's Caesar, who had fumbled and left a gun to be picked up and turned in by a soldier soon after the fort burned. "Pintard's negro's a fool for undertaking a thing which he couldn't go through with. I give him the gun to take care of," Will scoffed. Also, according to Tiebout's Jack, Will refused to help extinguish the flames at the Philipse fire and declared, "I'd sooner see all the houses burnt down to the ground before I'd lend a hand."

Neither the angry nor the ambivalent talk by blacks stopped at the city line, as the reports about Frederick Van Cortlandt's Sam suggested. Not only that Westchester slave was involved, according to Steven Evans who implicated several blacks: Ulster Assemblyman Johannes Hardenburgh's Will, Borough of Westchester justice of the peace and former assemblyman Gilbert Willet's Robin, and John Dorland's Jack. Evans overheard the slaves talking in the summer of 1740, he recalled.

"What you think of . . . the plot?" Hardenburgh's Will asked Robin.

"Damn it! I'll have nothing to say to it. If they burn their backsides, they must sit down on the blisters. But let them go on and prosper," Robin answered.

Letting them know he overheard them, Evans accosted the blacks on the spot and tried to find out exactly what they meant.

"It's a plot. If it go on, you'll hear more of it. Can't do less than hear of it," Robin told the white man, but refused to say any more. Even those few words had returned after a year to haunt Robin, as whites such as Evans dredged their memories for unseemly bits of black conversation.

Wanting to be neither martyrs who died by choice nor heroes who died by chance, some slaves surrendered themselves by trying to speak before anyone spoke against them. Among those appearing to make their own separate peace with the king's men was merchant Robert Bound's Scipio, who negotiated with such apparent sincerity that Justice Horsmanden later commended him as "a fellow that did not want sense."

"Who's your master and what's your name?" the officials opened their routine questions.

"Master, don't you know me?" Scipio addressed Richard Nicolls personally, concentrating the man's focus on their previous relationship. "I'm Scipio, belonging to Mr. Robert Bound and formerly belonging to Dr. Nicolls," the slave said formally to the kinsman of his former holder who sat now among the interrogators.

"How did you come to be concerned in the conspiracy?" Nicolls asked, recognizing the slave.

"It's true, sir. I ought to have known better. My first master, Dr. Nicolls, brought me up from a child, sent me to school and had me taught to read. He intended to give me to his son, who was bred a merchant, for which reason he put me to a cooper to learn that trade; but his son going to live in the country, he had no use for me in that business. My old master therefore sold me to my present master, Mr. Bound, who has likewise been very kind to me," Scipio said. His recounting showed him to be a slave who, as Horsmanden noted, "had a better education than most of his color."[3]

"It was with me as it is with all my color who are never easy till they get a dram, and when they have one want more. This was my case on meeting with Comfort's Jack who carried me to Hughson's where from drinking one dram I drank more till I was bewitched with it," Scipio continued, his tone sounding contrite as he blamed liquor for what his questioners considered his acting ungrateful for the favors bestowed by his holders.

The slave's tact impressed Richard Nicolls and the others around the table. "Those gentlemen declared this fellow seemed to be the most sensible of any they examined and appeared very penitent and sorry for what he had done. He had, when examined, his bible in his bosom, which he said he read in jail as often as he could," Horsmanden noted.

Joseph Murray's Jack brought no Bible to his confession, but like Scipio, he adopted a penitent tone as he described his recruitment by Vaarck's Caesar and Hughson, while running an errand to Comfort's well on January 18, the Sunday of the big meeting, and indicated that his holder, the outspoken prosecutor, was slated for death in the plot.

"Hughson proposed that we meet at Mr. Murray's house that night. I was to be in the kitchen and open the back gate where [the others] were to come in; and Adam [another of Murray's slaves] and me were to come downstairs to them, and we were to proceed to set fire to the house, murder my master and mistress, and the white people in the house. But I was interrupted by [Murray's housekeeper] Mrs. Dimmock accidentally coming down into the kitchen and sending me up to bed. . . . I came down again, went into the yard, and opened the back gate, and stayed in the yard half-an-hour, expecting the others. They not coming after my waiting so long time, I went up to Mr. [Mayor] Cruger's corner and there saw [Walter's] Quaco and the other negroes who had engaged to come to my master's house, but they said they couldn't come then, for they must go down to Hughson. I returned home and went in at the kitchen window and slept there till the first cock-crowing and then opened the kitchen door and fetched in wood to make the fire to make the family believe I got up early and came downstairs." Jack made it sound as if Murray and his family narrowly missed getting their throats cut in their sleep.

Prosecutor Murray, who was present during the confession, pressed for more details from his slave, perhaps having trouble believing his ears.

"Destroy Mr. Murray, Mrs. Murray and all the family with knives. All of you have knives?" Hughson asked the group, Jack recalled. "We all said we had and pulled them out of our pockets. Adam pulled out a long knife, and all the rest had long knives but me. I had a short one, a penknife. . . . Hughson called me aside and told me, 'After you and Adam have murdered the whole family, steal the plate out of the beaufets [fashionable post-1720 cupboards set in a recess for china and crystal], the kitchen furniture, wearing apparel, linen, guns, swords, and everything of value and bring them to my house.' Adam was to kill the master and mistress, Mrs. Dimmock and her daughter, and I was to kill Caesar, Congo and Dido," Jack reported, suggesting for the first time in all the talk that blacks planned to kill other blacks, in this case housemates, for the trio he mentioned were slaves also held by Murray.

The attorney rushed home to confront Adam, well remembering the slave's recent odd behavior and the long, sharp knife found in his possession during the general search. Even before Murray arrived, however, one of his law clerks had noticed Adam's seeming particularly distracted and decided to test his fledgling lawyer's instincts by questioning Adam himself.

"Do you know anything concerning the plot?"

"No, but I'm afraid some dog or another owe me a spite and bring me in. People talk a great deal of me," Adam pleaded to the clerk. He was clearly worried. And he had reason to be.

The slave continued to insist he was innocent when Murray arrived to question him, but he was immediately sent to jail, where Horsmanden and others interrogated him.

"I'm innocent," Adam told two of Murray's clerks when they visited the jail to help the prosecutors. "Nothing but damned lies brought me here. I know who authored them and I'll be revenged if I die for it."

"If you're innocent, insist upon it and don't be afraid. You may be sure of having justice done you," the clerks replied but added a caution. "If you're guilty, denying it will signify nothing, for we know as much about the plot as they that are concerned in it. The only way to recommend yourself to favor is by making a full confession."

"Who accuse me?"

"We believe it's Jack."

"I'm a dead man. I was afraid the dog serve me so," Adam wailed and banged his head repeatedly against a post. Getting hold of himself, he stripped the silver buckles from the knees of his breeches and his shoes and said, "Give these to my brother Caesar [another of Murray's slaves]." The clerks turned to leave, but Adam cried, "Stay."

"We've no occasion to stay to hear you repeat the same things over again," one clerk responded.

"What you have me say?"

"Speak sincerely. Are you guilty or not?"

"I'm guilty," Adam answered, but he was not ready then to confess. "The information that he gave came from him slowly and by piecemeal, which was very tiresome and gave so much trouble that he was several times remanded to jail and told that what he said would do him little service," Horsmanden complained in his notes.

⊗⊗⊗⊗⊗

Adam's story started with his first meeting Hughson at a cockfight at Adolph Philipse's house in January 1738 and his visiting the taverner's old place on the docks and the place off the Hudson where Hughson later moved. The plot talk began back then, the slave suggested, as he recalled Hughson's propositioning him that night.

"I'll find arms and powder, but I want you to get some too," Hughson told Adam.

"I've no money to buy them," the slave protested.

"Steal some," the taverner urged.

Adam noted other slaves having money and access to weapons. "I've a key to my master's things and can come at what I please and can get some of my master's swords and guns," Cuff Philipse once boasted. Adam explained, "I've often seen Cuffee and Prince have plenty of money about them, silver and gold. Cuffee had once two doubloons . . . and Prince had once eight or nine Spanish dollars." That was a tidy sum for Auboyneau's slave or any slave, and Cuff's reported cash amounted to even more, as the Spanish gold coin called a doubloon ranged in value from five to sixteen dollars.[4]

Describing parties at Hughson's and a couple at a free Negro's house on Bowery Lane, Adam implicated two dozen blacks. Among those he fingered was Chief Justice DeLancey's Othello. "I spoke to Othello about the plot a few days after Hughson had proposed it to me at the cockfight at Mr. Philipse's house. I asked him to be concerned. He said he would, and laughed as if he knew of it before," Adam reported.

Walter's Quaco—the black who had whooped, "Fire, Fire, Scorch, Scorch, A LITTLE, damn it, BY-AND-BY"—also made the list. "We used to play marbles together," Adam noted. But being a friend since childhood won Quaco nothing, for his one-time playmate cast him in the inner circle: "Quaco undertook to burn his master's house and cut his throat. Quaco was as great a rogue as any of them," Adam declared.

The slave seemed coldhearted indeed, as he confirmed his housemate Jack's confession about the two of them planning to kill everyone in the Murray household, including the lawyer's other three blacks. "I was to murder Congo, and Jack was to murder Caesar and Dido," Adam admitted without hesitating on the fact that Murray's Caesar was his brother.

Adam insisted on Caesar, Congo and Dido's being completely innocent. "I don't believe they know anything of it," he said. His and Jack's talk of murdering the three proved recommendation enough for the authorities to clear those slaves without question; so, perhaps, Adam did his brother a good turn after all.

Horsmanden made a special note of Adam's mention of De-Lancey's Othello, particularly after Adam said, "Me and the rest of them who were to murder Mr. Murray's family were to assist in murdering the chief justice." Horsmanden wanted to be sure the facts were clear against his colleague's slave, who had been out of town with his holder since early March.

The image of the chief justice's being murdered, of Prosecutor Murray slated for death, and of Mayor Cruger and many of the city councilmen having implicated slaves brought the reported plot home to the officials. Indeed, Adam and the other blacks confessing made clear that the officials themselves were targets of the plot. To Horsmanden the confessions proved that, as he put it, "slaves were enemies of their own households."

There were no good slaves in the judge's view, for either they were willing to engage in mischief or all too easily induced to mischief. He wanted to rid New York of them all; failing that he wanted surely to get rid of those he called "the head negroes" who pushed or led others in acting or talking against the ruling society. But even more abominable to Horsmanden were whites such as Hughson who made common cause with blacks.

Murray's Adam fed the judge's distaste by offering fresh, white suspects as he confessed that "One time at Hughson's was one of Hughson's brothers, a boatman. He had a boat there, and I saw John Hughson give him a small box to put into it to carry up the river," Adam said. Four of Hughson's five brothers—Nathaniel, Richard, Walter, and William—were sitting in jail in Yonkers, along with their father, Thomas, pending full investigation of their possible connection with the crimes for which John died.

"I saw Holt, the dancing master, at Hughson's about the new year holidays, at a meeting with the negroes, and another white man belonging to him whom they called 'Doctor,' " Adam said. The so-called doctor was Henry Holt's indentured servant whose surname was Hamilton; his nickname, "Doctor," was so frequently used that nobody seemed to know for sure what his first name really was.[5]

"Holt's Joe told me not once but a hundred and a hundred times that I needn't be afraid, for his master was concerned in the plot," Adam continued and recalled a conversation he had with Hughson, Holt, and Holt's Joe.

"I've guns of my own but not enough powder," Holt complained.

"You needn't make yourself uneasy about that; I've seven or eight barrels," said Hughson.

"Your master have any arms?" Holt asked Adam, after promising pistols to his own slave Joe.

"He's some pistols," Adam answered.

"Get some."

"I will, but I can't get powder."

"We'll supply you," Holt and Hughson both promised.

Two other white men figured in Adam's story. One was John Romme, who still sat in jail. "Cuffee Philipse told me that he used often to talk to John Romme about the plot. . . . I know that Cuffee used frequently to go there [to Romme's]," Adam reported. But his mentioning Romme was shrugged off for three reasons: It was based on hearsay; it was only a black's word against a white's; and Peggy's retracting her claim that Romme was in the plot had not only cleared him of her charges but made the officials even more wary of proceeding against him without the firmest evidence.

Adam's word on a second white man was not shrugged off. Being shown a prisoner named John Ury, the slave said, "I saw a little short man four or five times at Hughson's. He used to teach school at Campbell's. Hughson told me the man was one of two priests who could forgive sins. I saw him twice in the room at Hughson's whispering and talking with him when many negroes were there, and I suspected then the little man knew of the plot and was concerned in it; but I don't remember Hughson or the negroes talking out concerning the plot when the man was present."

Was Ury the sorcerer promising blacks supernatural forgiveness of their sins and, thus, encouraging dark deeds? That was the prime question in Horsmanden's mind, and the possibility of the answer being yes filled him with anticipation about revealing the enormity of the plot.

Eager as the judge and prosecutors were to focus on the whites lingering in the background, they concentrated on finishing with the throng of implicated blacks. Indeed, their efforts to clear away the slaves began as the flood of confessions crested. Forty-four slaves were indicted between June 20 and July 1; and showing the shift since the pardon proclamation, thirty-three of the forty-four pleaded guilty and threw themselves on the mercy of the court. The remaining eleven awaited trial.

Sentences began to flow again on Wednesday, July 1, when Horsmanden sentenced ten slaves convicted before the pardon offer. He ordered all five Spanish blacks hanged and five other slaves also, although they had confessed since their convictions. Marschalk's York was one of the second five. He admitted acting as a captain in the plotting, and his corpse was ordered hung in chains on the gibbet, joining John Hughson's three week old remains and those of Vaarck's Caesar, still hanging since May 11.

Chief Justice James DeLancey returned from his special commission in Rhode Island just in time for the last acts. He understood the outlines of the proceedings from his mail and the newspapers, but he knew little of the detail except that sent to him about his slave Othello, whom he had shipped to New York City a week before arriving himself. He heard of his brother Peter's slaves Antonio and Pompey being implicated along with one of his father's slaves. His own firsthand experience began on July 2, when for the first time during the proceedings the Supreme Court had its full complement: thirty-eight year old DeLancey, forty-three-year-old Philipse, and forty-seven-year-old Horsmanden.

All three judges worried, along with the king's other men, that conditions in jail threatened the city with an epidemic of yellow fever or one of the kindred infections that constantly plagued the city and preyed on residents' minds particularly after the smallpox scare in June 1738.[6]

"The season began to grow warm, as usual, and it was to be expected that the heat would be increasing upon us daily. So the judges found there was a necessity of bethinking themselves of taking such speedy measures as should upon deliberation be thought advisable for ridding the jail of such of them as should by their confessions be thought most deserving of recommendation of mercy. It was feared such numbers closely confined together might breed an infection," Horsmanden noted in explaining the situation.

People with money enough regularly fled the city in the late spring and returned in early autumn to miss the summer's heat and the diseases it spawned. In an ordinary year, the court itself did only a week's work in late July, leaving DeLancey and Philipse to retire to their estates in Westchester. Horsmanden's means offered him no retreat, however, and the threat seemed to bother

him especially, as he commented on the conditions of those confined to the city. Noting that the situation was "very offensive to
the poor debtors imprisoned in the city-hall, which from the necessity of the case could not have been prevented or remedied," the
third justice almost apologized.[7]

To reduce the problem, the judges decided "to examine the list
of negroes committed as confederates in the conspiracy—many
whereof had made confessions of their guilt in hopes of pardon in
consequence of the proclamation—and others who were pardoned
and turned evidence, and to mark out such as should be thought
proper to recommend to his honor the lieutenant governor to be
pardoned upon condition of transportation," Horsmanden explained. On the first Saturday in July, the judges sent Governor
Clarke an initial list of forty-three blacks to be pardoned and
shipped abroad.[8]

Among the slaves on the list were Mayor Cruger's Deptford
and the slaves of several city councilmen: Pintard's Caesar, Benson's Cato, Lawrence's Sterling, and Moore's Tom. Assemblyman Clarkson's Fortune also made the list. Robert Bound's
Scipio—no doubt still clutching his Bible and showing the jailers
his contrite spirit—also was named. So was Thomas Ellison's Jamaica, for although he was convicted and sentenced to hang in
early June, Jamaica never confessed and Horsmanden found nobody but Burton to accuse him. Burk's Sarah, the only black
woman implicated, made the list too, for although her confession
in early June came grudgingly at first, she helped corroborate crucial testimony.

Grumbling surfaced about the lenient handling of the politicians' slaves, but the citizens' cries for blood were fading now that
half the city's black men were in jail and the rush of penitent admissions had apparently revealed the dark side of the plot. Still,
the burnings and hangings were deserved, exemplary punishment
in most whites' eyes; and whites remained ready to see any lingering black leaders receive the same.

The growing sense among townsmen was that the blacks were
now under control. Once frightened neighbors had their culprits
for arson at all the fires except the smothers at Sergeant Burns's
house and the Coenties Market bakery, the alarm after the Philipse storehouse blaze—all on April 6, and the barn burning behind Philipse's on May 6, the day of the Hughsons and Peggy's
first trial.

The only questions nagging most citizens were whether all the troublesome blacks were in hand and how the plot was developed and masterminded to the degree it was for so long. Horsmanden and the prosecutors had more explaining to do to satisfy the people on the source and scope of the plot that had been presented in court.

⛓⛓⛓⛓⛓

Confessing thus saved some slaves. But not all. Admitting his guilt sent Anthony Ward's Will to burn at the stake. Horsmanden explained Will's fate by noting that the slave was implicated in two conspiracies in the West Indies, one on St. John and the other on Antigua in 1736, where Will turned king's evidence and received a pardon on condition of being transported from that colony. He landed in New York City in late 1736 but was soon sent to Providence, Rhode Island. Not working out there, he ended up back in Manhattan. "It was thought high time to put it out of his power to do any further mischief," the judge remarked, after noting the slave's history.[9]

Will showed no intention of dying quietly and talked at the stake, trying to save himself. Naming a dozen blacks, he confirmed that he knew of the plot and had discussed it with others; but shunning his own part, he focused on Alderman Moore's Cato and Alderman Pintard's Caesar, and for a moment he clouded the credibility of confessions made by blacks during the prior two weeks.

"Cato advised me and [DePeyster's] Pedro to bring in many negroes, telling Pedro he'd be certainly burnt or hanged if he didn't confess but if he brought in a good many, it save his life. 'I found it so myself. You must say you was to set your master's house on fire. That'll make the judges believe you,' [Cato said.] Pintard's Caesar said much the same," Will claimed, perhaps bitter that the aldermen's slaves were slated to live while he stood in death's clutches. He spoke sourly, too, of Jacob Goelet's Quack and John Tiebout's Will for bringing him into the plot. Yet he did not speak ill of all: "DePeyster's Pedro is innocent for what I knows," he said and added, "[Comfort's] Jack's a true evidence."

Horsmanden immediately dismissed the notion of any of the confessions not being valid. Suspecting Will of trying to cover his own guilt, the judge noted that DePeyster's Pedro confessed three days earlier that Will himself had offered the advice he attributed to Moore's Cato and Pintard's Caesar. "So rare it is to get the truth from these wretches!" scoffed Horsmanden. Yet the judge snatched what Will said about several more whites.

"William Kane, a soldier belonging to the fort, knew of the plot. I heard him say, 'I don't care if the fort's burnt down.' Since the plot was discovered, I told Kane I'd make a discovery, and Kane gave me three pounds in bills and told me not to," Will declared. In apparent confirmation, the money was found in the slave's room at Ward's. Will confessed to doing more than that bit of business with Kane and also implicated Kane's wife and a soldier named Edward Kelly.

"My mistress lost a silver spoon which I stole and carried to Kane's wife. She gave it to her husband in my presence, and he sold it to Peter Van Dyke, a silversmith, and gave me eight shillings of the money. Kane and Kelly asked [Roosevelt's] Quack to burn the fort and said, 'If that's done, we'd have our liberty.' Kelly said, 'You must do it with wet cotton. That'll make no smoke.' " The reasoning seemed curious, but the soldiers were serious, Will insisted.

"I talked of the plot with Kane and Kelly often and been to Kane's house and heard that other soldiers were concerned, but I don't know them. I've seen . . . some money . . . collected at a meeting at Kelly's, which money was to be paid to Hughson," the slave sputtered as he tried to escape the flames.

"The pile being kindled, this wretch set his back to the stake, and raising up one of his legs, laid it upon the fire, and lifting up his hands and eyes, cried aloud and several times repeated the names Quack Goelet and Will Tiebout, who he had said first brought him into this plot," Horsmanden noted. Thus, like Philipse's Cuff and Roosevelt's Quack at the stake a month before him, Ward's Will bought himself a little time by confessing, but not life.

The date was July 4.

# 13

## "Popish Priests Lurking About the Town"

THE RUSH OF CONFESSIONS left the king's men feeling they finally had the bulk of blacks in hand. They wanted to sort out any remainder of what Horsmanden called "head negroes" and to make a few more examples, as they had in burning Ward's Will at the stake. But their most pressing interest was in pursuing the freshly implicated whites.[1]

Since the first reports about a plot, both the officials and the townsfolk had been convinced that the blacks were led by whites. Attorney General Bradley announced the common sentiment in saying that "It cannot be imagined that these silly unthinking creatures could of themselves have contrived and carried on so deep, so direful and destructive a scheme."

Bradley, Horsmanden, and the king's other men had already pilloried John Hughson as the blacks' leader, but questions of his being the only white man involved had persisted. John Romme's name continued to be bandied about, but since Peggy had retracted her accusations about him before her execution, he had become only a background figure sulking away in jail. However, the mentions of Hughson's brothers, dancing master Henry Holt, Holt's indentured servant "Doctor" Hamilton, the soldiers William Kane and Edward Kelly, and schoolteacher John Ury gave a new edge to the suspicions about white leadership.

Judy Pelham from the landed Westchester family was among the people greatly worried about whites being involved with the blacks, and she offered a sworn statement about a soldier named Thomas Plumstead whom she had heard in early March declare, "There'll be bloody times in York before harvest, and I must be in the middle of it. There'll be no time granted to take leave of wives or children."

When Horsmanden sought to question Plumstead, he found the soldier had disappeared. Holt and his servant were also gone. Kane, Kelly, and Ury were on hand, however, and among them the judge put Ury at the top of the list.

John Ury's troubles began before Murray's Adam identified him as "a little short man . . . [who was] four or five times at Hughson's, " for his arrest occurred three days prior to the slave's comment.

Noting the initial reason for detaining the man, the judge wrote: "Intimation having been given for some time past that there had of late been Popish priests lurking about the town, diligent inquiry had been made for discovering them, but without effect. At length information was given that Ury, who had lately come into this city . . . was suspected to be one. . . . He was taken into custody this day [June 24] and not giving a satisfactory account of himself was committed to the city jail."[2]

Horsmanden himself pictured Ury as the person several slaves alluded to as having the power to forgive sins, and he worked at fitting the man into that image, treating his case almost like a jigsaw puzzle. The judge began with only a few pieces that outlined Ury's arrival in town during October 1740 and his work as a tutor until April 1741, when a local schoolmaster named John Campbell took him in as a junior partner to teach Greek and Latin. But the man's background and the detail of his life remained unsorted.

Few townsfolk seemed able to place Ury. Only a handful initially recalled ever seeing him, and most of them pictured the man vaguely as short, swarthy, dully dressed, and given to blending into the surroundings. A couple of the families he worked for recommended him as able but noted that he acted a bit eccentric—a fact they earlier attributed to his being a teacher. He shied away from conversation and, appearing to prefer privacy, often withdrew to his boardinghouse room where he seemed to stay to himself. Even after eight months, the man seemed to have few friends and still appeared a stranger in the city.

The shadowy image cast Ury as someone who slipped into Manhattan and moved about without taking root. The small-town mores beneath the comparatively cosmopolitan capital and market center's veneer of sophistication marked the man for suspicion then. People expected a person of his apparent education to seek out his peers and make himself known among the better classes. Yet the man failed even to advertise himself as a teacher or to attract students publicly. People wondered also why he had not presented himself socially, for he appeared to be an eligible bachelor. Ury's failure to follow the community's expectations for newcomers fed sinister speculations.

The man stood as an outsider in a town where many residents sat frightened by the current stories of private and deadly scheming. He faced chronic xenophobia which projected strangers in the popular mind as people who caused trouble; and worse, Ury came in for questioning at the moment when people like Horsmanden were searching, in the judge's words, for "strangers and other suspicious persons." The strikes against Ury increased as people recalled that a schoolteacher named Elias Neau was implicated in the city's slave revolt of 1712 and wondered if the new schoolteacher was involved in the present plot.[3]

Ury lacked even a clergyman to vouch for him, and in many minds that itself was a sin on a man's part, because it meant he had joined none of the city's congregations. The manner of his worship of God became a major question in fact, for religion ranked as an important test of loyalty. Ury's apparent failure even to attend church put him in a precarious position where his fate might depend on his beliefs.

The judge himself was quick to emphasize Ury's mastery of Latin, the language of the Roman Catholic Church. Hated by Horsmanden and the king's men everywhere, the Church of Rome haunted many New Yorkers' minds like an evil specter: It lurked as the religion of England's centuries-old foes Spain and France and as the dominion of the Pope, whom Protestants often imagined as an Antichrist striving to reduce the world to his single faith.

Throughout Great Britain's realm a belief persisted that a constant Catholic conspiracy was afoot to subvert the crown and the Church of England; and with war raging in the West Indies and Spanish attacks on the Georgia–Florida borderlands and sorties as close as Charleston, South Carolina, at least some New Yorkers worried about Ury's being a Catholic spy for Spain. Horsmanden suspected the man of being a priest in disguise. Again recalling the slaves' talk about a man who forgave sins, the judge suggested a rhetorical question: Who but a priest pretended such power?[4]

If Ury were proven a priest, Horsmanden and others thought that would explain the reported conspiracy. Neither the judge nor anybody else was prepared immediately to prove that Ury was a priest involved in the plot. Their notion was simply that a priest was an agent of the Church of Rome and, therefore, an ally of the Spanish crown; both connections cast such a person in the role of an enemy likely to have a hand in the death and destruction so many slaves admitted intending for the city.

Horsmanden broached the Catholic connection even before Ury's arrest by remarking that John Hughson's wife "was bred a Papist, and Peggy was much suspected of the same persuasion." To couple religion to the elements of race and rebellion already linked in the plot, the king's men looked to cast Ury as a Catholic and as a conspirator.

The judge called Mary Burton to testify if she had seen Ury at Hughson's. In April she had told the grand jury, "I never saw any white person in company when they talked of burning the town, but my master, my mistress, and Peggy." When shown Ury after his arrest, however, Mary changed her story.

"He is the same person I've often seen at the house of John Hughson. . . . I saw him there first some time about last Christmas when for a fortnight together he came there almost every night and sometimes used to lie there but was always gone in the morning before I got up. . . . After the fortnight I believe he didn't come to Hughson's for about a week. Then he came again frequently, almost every night, until the time of the stealing of Hogg's goods. He used to strip himself and go to bed as if he was to lie there all night," the sixteen-year-old servant girl declared about Ury.

"When he came to Hughson's he always went upstairs in the company of Hughson, his wife and daughter, and Peggy with whom the negroes used to be at the same time consulting about the plot. I've often heard Hughson, the rest of the white people, and the negroes talk in the presence of Ury about setting fire to the houses and killing the white people of this city. And often when such conversation was going on, I saw Ury whispering to Hughson. . . . I understood [him] to be joining in the conspiracy with them. I thought it looked very much like it, though I can't say I ever heard him speak out. But I esteemed his actions and behavior to signify his approving and consenting to what was carrying on by the company touching the conspiracy, and this not one time in particular but a great many," the girl swore.

Ury often seemed uneasy when she was around, and he joined the Hughsons and Peggy in trying to lure her into the plot, Mary said, further recalling parts of conversations with him.

"Take an oath," Ury and the others once instructed Mary.

"What for?"

"Swear first. Then we'll tell you."

"No."

"You're a great fool if you don't," Peggy scoffed.

"Hadn't you better swear and go fine, than go as you do?" Ury chided Mary. The girl explained to the judge that "They offered me silks and a deal of fine things. . . . At my refusal they were angry and turned me out of the room."

Mary offered two more incidents when she said Ury spoke to her with what she thought were strange words.

"God forgive me!" the girl recalled exclaiming one day, when several molesting slaves provoked her to swear at them.

"That's a small matter. I can forgive you a great deal more sins than that. That was nothing," Ury told her.

"I wish you black toads to the devil!" Burton exclaimed on another occasion.

"Let them be black or what they will. The devil has nothing to do with them. I can forgive them their sins and you yours too," Ury declared, according to the girl.

Mary claimed now to remember not only Ury's being present during talk of the plot, but several other whites also. One was the taverner's sixteen-year-old daughter, Mary Hughson. Horsmanden showed no interest in John's second child, but he was interested when the girl said schoolmaster John Campbell came to Hughson's in February with a man named Garrit Van Emborough.

"Campbell used to go into the room below, with the Hughsons, Peggy, Caesar, Prince, and Cuffee. When they met, the Hughsons used to turn me upstairs. But I can't say I ever heard them talking of the plot before Campbell; but I strongly suspected that he knew of it from his keeping company with the Hughsons," the girl declared.

Mary sounded as if she now believed a person's simple presence at Hughson's constituted a connection with the reported conspiracy. Not even Horsmanden was ready to go that far. The girl conceded that she had not seen the whites she named take any oath nor heard them talk about the plot. Doubt about the value of her word crept in then, particularly as her list of names began suddenly to grow.

Horsmanden moved cautiously on the whites against whom he so far had only Mary's word. For example, he pressed no conspiracy charge against Campbell. The schoolmaster had standing in the city, after all. But he also had debts. The judge arranged simply to jail him for nonpayment and continued to investigate.

What Mary said about Van Emborough was of no immediate help to the judge, because the man had disappeared, but her words about Ury were a help because they corroborated what Murray's Adam said about Ury's at least being at Hughson's. Neither the slave nor the girl reported hearing or seeing Ury actually talk of the plot or swear to it, but their common sighting of the man was enough for Horsmanden.

The soldier William Kane was not on Mary's list, but in confessing at the stake, Ward's Will implicated him. Horsmanden questioned Kane after church on Sunday, July 5, and Chief Justice DeLancey sat in to get his first direct look at the examination of anyone accused in the plot. The session started with routine questions about Kane's background, and the soldier tried to parlay the opening into an autobiography that began with his birth at Athlone on the Shannon River in central Ireland and his coming to America at age six. The judges took little interest in all of the soldier's forty-odd years and cut the life story short.

"What about the silver spoon?" Horsmanden asked, recalling Will's confessing to stealing a silver spoon and taking it to Kane's wife who gave it to her husband, who fenced it and gave the slave eight shillings.

"My wife brought home a silver spoon out of the fields, which she had of one of the Cuba men. This was about the time of their embarking. My wife can tell the name of the man. I carried the spoon to [Peter] Van Dyke, the silversmith, to sell. The spoon was battered up, and I told Van Dyke I believed it was a stolen spoon, but he answered he'd buy it . . . and gave me a milled Spanish piece of eight, and seven or eight shillings in pennies, as best as I remember," Kane said.

The soldier's glib answer left little room for accusation. His wife needed only to agree that she got the spoon from one of the men who sailed with the expeditionary force. If pressed for a name, she had her pick of those reported killed in the fighting. And to shield himself, the silversmith needed only to assure the authorities that he thought his deal with Kane innocent. That promised to shield the soldier also, for with Ward's Will dead, no one remained to contradict Kane directly on the spoon.

"What about John Romme?" Horsmanden asked, moving quickly to other issues.

"I've no acquaintance with John Romme. I never was at his house at the Battery in my life."

"John Ury, the Papist?"

"I never was in company with Ury now in jail. Nor have I any acquaintance with him. I never was in any congregation or meeting where Ury either preached or prayed. I myself am a Protestant of the Church of England, and I never was at any Roman Catholic congregation in my life," declared the soldier, trying to cut short any connection between himself and Catholicism or Horsmanden's candidate for the priesthood.

"And Connolly, Peter Connolly, the soldier in jail?"

"I've no acquaintance with Connolly than common for one brother soldier with another. I never was at his house in my life," Kane answered, referring to his fellow Irishman who, along with Private Edward Kelly, was taken from the garrison, on religious suspicions around the day of Ury's arrest.

"What of Kelly? Were you ever at his house and saw blacks there?" the judge probed, using the connection Ward's Will made at the stake to link Kane, Kelly and other soldiers to blacks in the plot.

"I never was at Kelly's in my life," Kane said. Aside from the two being soldiers together in the fort garrison, the only connection between them was that a family named Spotten boarded with him after living at Kelly's, Kane maintaned.

"I've heard Thankful Spotten, wife of James Spotten, say that she once saw a large company of negroes at Kelly's house, dancing to a fiddle," Kane explained and reported a scene from that night.

"What business you have here? I'll kick you into the fire if you don't go away," a black man threatened Thankful at the party. Thankful fled upstairs, where she continued to watch the blacks dance. The same black man menaced her there, too. But a mulatto slave "huffed the negro fellow," and told Thankful to relax, she said—according to Kane, who told Horsmanden that the woman herself had told him the story.

Kane's Irish tongue seemed to serve him well as he again glibly slipped by the questions, using denials padded with plausible explanations. His answers reflected only distant light on himself and cast shadows thick enough to allow those he mentioned to hide themselves from trouble. Just as he gave his wife and the silversmith Van Dyke an out on the spoon, Kane offered the same to the Spottens and the Kellys: He placed Thankful as an innocent victim and left her husband and Edward Kelly unmentioned. Mrs. Kelly alone appeared on the spot from Kane's words, but only indirectly since he supplied simple hearsay about her allowing a black entertainment at her house. If questioned about the reported party, she could deny remembering or confess to an innocent diversion; as a woman, she stood liable for little punishment, and her husband had the out of pleading total ignorance.[5]

Kane overlooked one person—Mary Burton. Horsmanden called her in and asked if she ever saw Kane at Hughson's. The servant girl immediately enlarged her story again by adding the soldier to her growing list of whites she suddenly remembered being at the tavern.

The third justice never questioned the girl's apparent leaps of memory, but the chief justice seemed less accepting. Cautioning Mary, DeLancey asked if she understood "the nature of an oath and the consequences of taking a false one, more especially as it affects a man's life?"

"I'm acquainted very well with the nature of an oath, and I'd not take a false one on any account," Mary assured DeLancey.

He then ordered Kane delivered to hear the accusations which the girl repeated to the soldier's face.

Kane nearly fainted as he listened to Mary's talk of his frequenting Hughson's and plotting along with others. The color drained from his ruddy Irish cheeks and his voice croaked as he tried to protest. To revive his tongue and no doubt his wits, the soldier asked for a glass of water and sipped it dry. Then he tried to counterattack by hitting at the girl's credibility, but Mary refused to waver. Both judges counted his reaction as proof he was lying.

Horsmanden argued for breaking Kane by giving him no time to regain his composure, and DeLancey was satisfied enough to permit continuous interrogation.

⛓⛓⛓⛓⛓

"Don't flatter yourself with the least hopes of mercy, but by making a candid and ingenuous confession of all that you know of the matter," Horsmanden warned.

"I'll tell the truth," Kane responded after a pause. Then he described how he first heard talk of burning the fort when he started going to Hughson's around Christmas 1740.

"I was sentry at the governor's door. Being dry, I asked Jerry Corker, who tended in the governor's stable, for some beer. He said he'd get some. He had rum in his pocket and said he'd make flip, which he did in a copper pot with loaf sugar. I drank a draught, and when I was relieved at nine at night, Corker came into the guard room and asked me if I'd go to [John] Croker's, at The Fighting Cocks, where there was to be a christening by a Romish priest.

"When we went there the people didn't come that night. We stayed till past ten. The next night we went again, and they weren't there. The third night we went to New Street, to the house of [John] Coffin, a peddler. They had a child and christened it. Three acted as priests and handed the book about. . . . One of those who acted as priest was a little man that lodged at Croker's," Kane said. Ury was a little man and he lodged at Croker's.

"About four days later, Corker and I were on guard and Corker said, 'By God, I've a mind to burn the fort.' I'd heard Corker, John Coffin, and Daniel Fagan [another Irishman in the garrison] talking about burning the town," Kane continued. "They drew me behind the church [Trinity on Broadway] to a meeting and would've had me to rob houses with them and go off."

Admitting that he lied earlier, the soldier confessed to keeping company with his garrison mates Peter Connolly and Edward Kelly and to frequenting Hughson's. "Connolly, on Governor's Island, owned himself to've been bred a priest and was often in company with Ury. Kelly is a Roman. Connolly and he were intimate," Kane said. Then he recalled a conversation between himself and Kelly at the beginning of January.

"Would you go to Hughson's?" Kelly asked Kane.

"What for?"

"Something's to be done there?"

"What?"

"Something you've heard of before."

"What's that?"

"Don't you know what Jerry Corker said to you before Christmas about burning the fort?"

"What, is that in agitation still?"

"Yes, and it ever shall be till the fort's burnt down," Kelly declared. All this was according to Kane, who reported accompanying Kelly to the tavern.

"I was at two meetings at Hughson's about the plot. The first was the second day of Christmas, and the second the last Sunday in February. . . . Corker, Fagan and Coffin were at the first meeting. At the second I was sworn to secrecy by Hughson. The first to discover was to be hanged at low-water mark; his privy parts were to be cut out and thrown in his face, his belly ripped open, and his body eaten by the birds of the air," Kane revealed, in part to explain his hesitance to confess earlier.

The soldier listed the names of a dozen blacks he said he remembered from the meetings. Among them were Walter's Quaco, whom Horsmanden had long wanted condemned, and Niblet's Sandy who denied ever being at Hughson's and whom nobody but Kane so far said was there. He recalled three Spanish blacks, but only Sarly's Juan by name.

"Some black stuff was cut among the negroes, which I . . . heard was to set fire to the roofs of houses in dry weather. I've seen Harry, a negro doctor that lives on Long Island, bring that stuff. I've seen him several times at Hughson's, and at the two meetings. He was to bring the negroes poison to use before they were executed, if they were taken. . . . I've seen Harry give a large quantity to Hughson," Kane said. Walter's Quaco offered to sneak the poison to those in need, using as cover his holder's having the food concession at the jail: "I'd not be suspected and might go to the prison and carry victuals, and so give the poison to those that were condemned, to prevent their execution," Quaco said, according to Kane.

"I saw all the negroes sworn," the soldier continued and described the ceremony. "There was a black ring made on the floor, about two feet and a half diameter, and Hughson bid every one pull off the left shoe and put their toes within the ring. And Mrs. Hughson held a bowl of punch over their heads as the negroes stood round the circle, and Hughson pronounced the oath: 'Thunder and lightning, God's curse and hell fire fall on them that first discover the plot.' Every negro repeated the words after Hughson, and then Hughson's wife fed the negroes with a draught out of the bowl."

Elements of witchcraft shrouded the oath ceremony Kane reported. The fact that Hughson's mother-in-law, Elizabeth Luckstead, was a fortune teller whom people sometimes thought was crazy and other times claimed was a witch added to the sense of there being an evil invocation of the supernatural at the meetings. But in this case Horsmanden and the other officials had no inclination to suspect any sorcery other than that which they attributed to Catholicism. Kane already had done his part there by limning the baptism, and he continued with his detail of the plot.

Mentioning three of Hughson's brothers and his father, Kane said, "Me and those men and Sarah Hughson the daughter were sworn together. We were to burn what we could of the city and get what money and goods we could and carry them to Mr. [James] Alexander's house, which was to be reserved for Mr. Hughson [John's father]. We were to kill the principal people. If any people came from the country or West Indies to conquer us, we were to kill the people belonging to the vessels here and go to Spain. Our design was to wait for the French and Spaniards, whom we expected; and if they didn't come in six weeks, then we were to try what we could do for ourselves."

Echoing the slaves' confessions, the soldier confirmed the talk of arson, murder and robbery. He added a specific tone that suggested a plot not against all whites, but against "the principal people," men such as attorney James Alexander, a long-time member of the governor's council. Neither was the whole city slated for burning, only part. Kane's rendition carried the sound of plotting by have-nots against the haves. It was not blacks against whites, but struggling whites against the wealthy and slaves against masters. "Most of the negroes, I believe, would've joined us if we were like to succeed," Kane explained.

Class more than race was the issue in the soldier's view, and that clashed with the perspective drawn by Horsmanden and his cohort, who publicly shunned any prospect of economic grievance or envy spawning rebellion among whites, as if such an idea were unthinkable. To explain the Hughsons and Peggy's reported plotting with blacks, the king's men said simply that such whites were deluded, and since Ury's arrest, they increasingly attributed the delusion to the effect of what in their view was an insidious religion.

Kane continued to contribute to the religious theme. "The priest, the little man that lodged at Croker's, was several times at Hughson's, and many negroes were christened there by him. He endeavored to seduce me to the Romish religion at Coffin's house," Kane claimed, recalling the encounter.

"Can you read Latin?" Ury asked.

"No," Kane answered.

"Can you read English?"

"No," the soldier admitted being completely illiterate and unable to serve the man's need as a reader.

"It's a fine thing to be a Roman [Catholic]. They [the priests] can forgive sins . . . [so we] shouldn't go to hell," Coffin commented, after stepping in to do the reading.

"I'd not believe that on any man's word," Kane said. His response provoked an argument and prompted his leaving the house. "I don't know but they would've seduced me, the priest and Coffin pressed me so," the solider told Horsmanden.

The judge pressed Kane to confess that Ury, frequently referred to now as "the priest," also plotted.

"I've not heard the priest say anything of the conspiracy, but from Corker's account, I believe he knew it. . . . Corker told me that Hughson and him had designed to burn the English church [Trinity] last Christmas Day but that Ury the priest said they'd better let it alone until better weather, [when] the roof might be dry and there'd be a larger congregation. Their full design was to burn the English church. They had a greater spite against that than any other, especially Ury," Kane said.

Evidently unable to comply completely with Horsmanden's demands, the soldier had offered only hearsay and conjecture on Ury's having a part in the reported plot, but Kane had more on others. Explaining how the winter's heavy snow blocked the designs of destroying the church where Horsmanden served as a vestryman and where most of the king's men worshipped, the solider suggested that spring's coming allowed the burning of Fort George to proceed. He noted Jerry Corker's being the soldier who assisted the plumber at work on the governor's roof on the morning of the fort fire.[6]

Kane added also to the hearsay about the absent dancing master Henry Holt. "That cursed dog my master is the greatest rogue in the world. He'd burn all the town to get money. If you knew what was between him and Hughson it'd make you stare," the soldier quoted Holt's Joe telling him once about Holt's part in the plot.

The soldier further reported that after being arrested and seeing Kane in jail, the schoolmaster John Campbell said, "Though I can pay the debt I'm in for, yet I believe they won't let me out, on account of the priest Ury that lodged at my house."[7]

Campbell's words sounded innocent enough, except for the reference to Ury which provoked a question: Had Campbell himself actually called Ury "the priest" or had Kane added the words?

Horsmanden had those words and the whole confession read back to assure no mistake was made, and Kane swore every word "was true and signed his mark for his name," the judge noted.

⛓⛓⛓⛓⛓

The constables went out in search of the men Kane named who were not yet in jail. Jerry Corker eluded the lawmen: He had quit the garrison for work in White Plains shortly after the fort blaze and now was nowhere to be found. Private Daniel Fagan slipped away, absent without leave. The peddler John Coffin was the only catch that Sunday night.

DeLancey and Horsmanden questioned Coffin on Monday, July 6. "The fellow seemed to be under terrible apprehensions, trembled and cried, but denied everything alleged against him by Kane. Particularly he protested that he did not know nor was anywise acquainted with John Hughson or ever saw him until he was hanged," Horsmanden noted.

"I never had any acquaintance with Kane nor was ever in his company but once, when I drank a mug of beer with him at Eleanor Wallis'," Coffin insisted, claiming he did not know what the soldier was talking about. The woman he mentioned ran a little tavern with not the best of reputations. Despite the peddler's protest, he was in jail to stay—unless Kane's story proved a lie, and nobody else implicated him.

After a hard ride to Nassau, Long Island, where the black "Doctor" Harry lived, the constables delivered him for questioning on Tuesday, July 7. Horsmanden noted that "The doctor was a smooth, soft-spoken fellow, and like other knaves affected the air of sincerity and innocence, but was of a suspicious character. Well known to the magistrates of this city, he had a few years before been forbid [in] the town for malpractice in physic, upon the penalty of being severely whipped if he was seen here again."

Kane confronted Harry, as did Murray's Adam who told the judge, "The doctor was sworn of the plot. . . . I seen him once in town about three weeks before the fort [was] fired and once going down to Hughson's since the fort burnt. I heard he came over in a little canoe."

"I never was at Hughson's, nor have I been in town since I was ordered out by the magistrates," Harry insisted. But the current suspicions simply fed the residue lingering from the malpractice case that resulted in his being banished earlier, when a married daughter of the prominent merchant John Watts died. Harry argued that the young woman, Mrs. John Riggs, died from no medicine he gave her. He claimed, in fact, not to have given her anything directly. The culprit was one of Watts's female slaves, according to Harry, for he explained that he "gave Mr. Watts' wench stuff to hinder any person being got with child, but whether she gave it to her young mistress I know not; . . . Mrs. Riggs did not die of what I gave the wench, but she died of something the wench gave her."[8]

The interrogators persisted, but as Horsmanden complained, "the doctor was stout and denied all." Despite his protests, Harry joined the crowd in jail.

The judges redoubled their efforts to pick out blacks for pardon on condition of transportation, and the grand jury joined in the effort to clear the jails. During that first full week of July, the jurors began releasing a few blacks on the grounds of insufficient evidence.

But the conditions remained cramped and forced a breach in the usual segregation when, to accommodate the throng of men, young Sarah Hughson was celled with Burk's Sarah. The arrangement caused trouble for Hughson's daughter because the slave woman, not knowing she had already made the pardon list and apparently desperate to secure herself a spot, reported that in her cell chatter the girl admitted to being sworn into the conspiracy.

Since her scheduled hanging with her parents on June 12, young Sarah Hughson had received repeated respites from the judges who hoped to get her to confess. Horsmanden particularly expected her to be able to unveil the entire plot and the whole cast of characters at her parents' home. But she continued to frustrate all the authorities' hopes.

Seeing no reason for more patience, Horsmanden ordered her to hang on July 8. Having not yet questioned the girl himself however, Chief Justice DeLancey called her on the morning set for her finally to go to the gallows, and Justice Philipse and others sat in on the session—but not Horsmanden.

The hangman awaited then, as the girl confronted the ready snarls of Burk's Sarah, and clearly fearing to follow the fate of her parents, she confessed to knowing of the plot.

"I saw William Kane sworn one Sunday evening, some time before Christmas. I can't tell exactly. He threatened to kill me if I discovered, and the negroes threatened me the same. My father charged me to say nothing about it. They were first to begin with burning the fort with a good wind. After that they were to begin at the upper end of the town with an east wind, so as to burn the whole town, to destroy the whites and, after, to keep the town and send notice to the Spaniards that they might come and hold it, so that it couldn't be taken from them again. I think my mother knew of it," the girl said, still showing reluctance to focus guilt fully on her parents.

"I can't remember them all, but I'd know them if I saw them," young Sarah said as she offered a handful of blacks' names. On whites she said, "I've seen a middle-sized white man that called himself a doctor, with black hair always cut, of a short chin, talking with the negroes and drinking with them." The description fit Holt's man "Doctor" Hamilton, but no positive identification emerged. "I think I've heard the name Coffin: He's a fresh colored, long-haired man who was often at our house among the negroes.

"The first time I saw Ury was with Campbell, about a fortnight before May Day, when they came to see the house," the girl continued. The two schoolteachers indeed inspected Hughson's before Sarah's arrest on May 6. Sent as prospective tenants by the landlord, the men said they wanted to rent the place for classes. With her parents in jail, Sarah was the oldest left at home and received the men who appeared ready to snatch the house from under her, her three sisters, and Peggy's baby. The encounter spawned no love in Sarah for either Campbell or Ury.

Horsmanden scoffed when he reviewed the girl's statement and underscored her offering nothing the king's men did not already have. All the blacks Sarah named were dead, except Walter's Quaco, and his days seemed already numbered in the third justice's view. All the whites she named were in jail, and she added nothing on Kane that he had not confessed himself nor given more than he had on Coffin, Campbell, and Ury. In fact, her mention of both schoolteachers contradicted the testimony of the soldier and Mary Burton, who claimed Ury visited Hughson's long before Sarah's reported first sighting him in mid-April.

"This confession was so scanty, and came from her after much difficulty, [and] with [such] great reluctance that it gave little or no satisfaction; and . . . it was said [that] after she returned to jail, she retracted the little said and denied she had any knowledge of a conspiracy," Horsmanden complained in arguing for "a necessity of ordering her execution." He yielded, however, to allow a "last experiment to bring her to a deposition to unfold this infernal secret, at least so much of it as might be thought deserving a recommendation of her as an object of mercy." Sarah thus escaped the hangman that day, but he continued to stalk.

⬤⬤⬤⬤⬤

Horsmanden, DeLancey, and the grand jury in turn called Kane and Mary Burton for further questioning. The soldier and the servant girl both fingered another Irishman from the garrison, after his arrest on the previous day, Wednesday, July 8.

"I know Edward Murphy, now in jail. I've seen him several times at Hughson's and know he was concerned in the late conspiracy. . . . I heard Murphy say, some time before the fort burnt, when the negroes were talking at Hughson's about the conspiracy, 'Damn me if I don't lend a hand to the fire as soon as anybody,'" Kane reported.

Mary vouched to Murphy's face that she also had seen him often at Hughson's and recalled his promising to give "Hughson and [the] negroes all the assistance in his power."

After his session with Horsmanden, Kane reported to the chief justice and fingered a white hatter arrested that morning. "I've often seen David Johnson at Hughson's when there were several negroes present, particularly since last Christmas. [Once] he was called from the company that came with him, into a room by Hughson and Ury the priest, and stayed in the room a considerable time. And Jerry Corker told me the day the town was to be fired, that Johnson said, 'Damn me if I'll not be as ready as any to do my part.' Corker told me that he told Johnson that the fire was to be on St. Patrick's night, if they could get their hands together," Kane said. Then he went to the grand jury where he focused on the man he now called "the priest" and elaborated on the religious ceremony he reported attending.

"At the christening were the priest, a countryman, Coffin, another man, three women, and Corker. The priest sprinkled the child and had salt on a plate and rubbed the child's mouth with it. Ury, Coffin, and the other man acted as priests," Kane said. Then he recalled a conversation between himself and the peddler Coffin on the docks only five days earlier, before either man's arrest.

"Shouldn't you go on board the privateer? All will come out," Coffin warned Kane.

"Not me. No one'll tell, unless some blabbing rascal might," the soldier scoffed, attempting to reassure the peddler that there was no need to set sail.

The irony of his own blabbing now apparently escaped Kane, but he certainly knew he had captured the officials' attention with his story implicating himself and other Irishmen from the Fort George garrison and the city in the talk at Hughson's and in Catholic ceremonies presided over by a priest.

The date was July 9.

# 14

## "Having Once Confessed Their Guilt"

JOHN URY'S ARREST as a suspected Catholic priest and the arrests of Irish soldiers such as William Kane and other whites, coming as they did on the heels of the rush to confession and round up of blacks, focused fresh attention on the conspiracy proceedings. Both townsfolk and others following news of the affair wondered where the king's men were headed now.[1]

Aroused as they were by the burning of Fort George and the fires that followed, most citizens had fixed their suspicions on slaves and eagerly accepted the officials' initial offering of what Attorney General Bradley called "Hughson's black guard." Popular outrage grew with the continuing revelations about Hughson's being a fence for goods blacks stole and his tavern's being a meeting place where slaves talked in undisguised tones against their holders and whites at large.

The similarities in the blacks' confessions convinced the people about the plot, and Mary Burton won both official and popular gratitude by providing the leads into Hughson's. At every turn since April the sixteen-year-old servant girl's reports had been corroborated, and she had served the prosecution as a continual star witness. Her motives for talking were clear enough in the officials' and citizens' minds: She wanted the reward, which meant both freedom and money for a fresh start to her young life. Further, people thought she simply was doing what was right by testifying against an evil design. The fact that virtually nothing was known about her until she entered Hughson's household as a servant during the summer of 1740 was accepted as commonplace, considering her youth and her status as a servant.

The growing talk that whites other than the Hughsons and Peggy were in the plot, however, raised questions about Mary. Horsmanden and his fellow officials were particularly vexed that for nearly three months the girl withheld mention of John Ury and other white men at Hughson's. Pressed on the reason for her reticence, Mary gave the grand jury virtually the same answer she had in April, when she had hesitated to talk about anything except the Hogg burglary: She said she was scared. "When Hogg's goods were found, John Earl said to me he'd rather have given twenty pounds than it was known and threatened to kill me if I discovered about the fire," Mary confided.

The pattern of her talking supported the idea that she was afraid, for the girl had tended to talk about both blacks and whites only after they were implicated by someone else or already in jail. Only after Ury's arrest did Mary identify him. She did the same with Kane, and it was only after the soldier implicated his garrison mates and other whites that Mary talked about them. She had, in fact, volunteered little and initiated almost nothing after declaring that Hughson hosted meetings of blacks who talked of burning the city and murdering whites.

Playing safe, Mary had opened herself to the charge of lying only in initially telling the officials she saw no whites other than the Hughsons and Peggy talking with the blacks about fires. But she seemed caught in a lie on July 9, when she told the grand jury that "of the white people who used to frequent Hughson's were Holt, the dancing master, a little man. I believe I've seen him in court on the trial of the negroes." That provoked fresh questions about her credibility because the grand jury and the judges knew Holt had skipped to the West Indies before the first trial.

⛓⛓⛓⛓⛓

Questions also lingered about the blacks' confessions, and a particularly strong current of doubt surfaced when Constable John Schultz approached Chief Justice DeLancey with reports that some slaves were recanting. Christopher Codwise's Cambridge, for example, declared that "what he had said . . . was a lie, that he didn't know in what part of the town Hughson lived, nor did he remember having heard of the man until it was a common talk over the town and country that Hughson was concerned in a plot with the negroes." Cambridge claimed he "had heard some negroes talking together in the jail [and saying] that if they didn't confess, they'd be hanged. That was the reason of his making that false confession," the constable told the chief justice.

Horsmanden rejected such notes out of hand earlier, and he raged now against the chief justice or anyone else who entertained the recanting. "A criminal confesses himself guilty at his own peril. It may be the only chance he has for saving his life. If he denies all and the crime is proved upon him, his case becomes desperate; but when once he confesses his guilt, it will be standing evidence against him. The remark upon negro recantations, once for all, is that one can scarce be thoroughly satisfied when it is that they do speak truth, unless what they say be confirmed by concurring circumstances. . . . Their having once confessed their guilt, a recantation and denial of it afterwards will scarce be thought an argument of sufficient force to prove their innocence," Horsmanden declared.[2]

Swelling with apparent frustration, the judge showed no desire to worry now if he and the king's other men had truly penetrated what he liked to call "the dark secret," especially not when he felt the climax close. He spilled himself in anger as he tried to dismiss the cries about recanting.

All Horsmanden's work since April rested largely on confessions, and he feared if they were retracted, the entire basis of the proceedings would crumble. Such a result threatened his reputation by showing his own judgments to have been deadly wrong; it threatened also to pervert what he saw as the basic lesson to be learned from the plot: Keeping slaves endangered society.

The judge contended that questioning the confessions' credibility was a ruse designed by slaveholders to reverse their mounting losses. And with nearly two hundred slaves implicated and in jail, many slaveholders in the city had grown anxious, indeed, about their own property being condemned and lost. Now that the danger of the plot seemed past, the toll of arrests and executions was turning holders against continuing the proceedings because the outcome no longer promised to remove a few troublesome slaves, but to rid the city of a third of its slave men.

Recalling the handling of the Antigua conspiracy, the judge noted that holders there were excluded from their slaves' trials. Indeed, the proceedings were closed to the public after spectators interrupted by shouting their own questions, answers, and accusations; and among the most obstreperous were the slaves' holders. "We soon discovered . . . how much masters were prone to countenance and excuse their slaves, and that slaves were emboldened by their masters' presence and witnesses intimidated," the West Indian island officials reported in 1736. Horsmanden quoted them as he expanded on his views of masters and slaves coupling insidiously in the face of justice.[3]

"In our own case, masters and owners of slaves were admitted as witnesses, which, all things considered, perhaps was too great an indulgence, for it is a known rule of law in civil cases that a party interested in the event of a suit cannot be a witness. And by parity of reason, it may be concluded that masters of slaves in criminal cases should not be witnesses, especially in matters of so much consequence to the public. And if any such like case should hereafter happen—which God forbid—upon the reason of that rule and the inconveniences which have happened from this indulgence, it may be necessary to vary from the practice," Horsmanden declared. He was convinced that property interests, particularly where trained and skilled male slaves were concerned, were inclining slaveholders to thwart continuing justice.

The judge's outburst flew in the face of Assembly Speaker Adolph Philipse, Chief Justice DeLancey's brother Peter, and other powerful men who testified in their slaves' behalf. The chief justice himself had to feel the sting of his colleague's words in the case of his personal manservant, the slave Othello; and in a clear attempt to show no favoritism on his part, DeLancey had already acquiesced in the court's sentencing the slave to burn at the stake, for Othello was one of three slaves who on the morning of July 10 pleaded guilty to conspiracy in hope of obtaining mercy.

☙☙☙☙☙

Young Sarah Hughson also found herself seeking mercy on Friday, July 10, for her time ran out in what Horsmanden called "the last experiment to bring her to . . . unfold this infernal secret." Sentenced to die on the morrow, Sarah reversed herself on saying she had never seen John Ury at Hughson's until mid-April.

"I've seen John Ury the priest often there when the negroes were there. He spoke to them, told them to keep secrecy and to be true and not tell on one another, [even] if they were to die for it, and that they should burn the town down and, in the night, cut their masters and mistresses' throats with knives. He told me not to discover what he siad. If I did, he said it'd be the death of me. He christened Vaarck's Caesar and others. I was sworn by him when Kane was, on a Sunday night. Things were generally done on Sunday nights," Sarah explained.

"Ury told us all that he could forgive sins if we did any misdemeanor, and said if I'd confess to him, he'd forgive me all my sins which was done and he could forgive all of them what they were to do in the business of the plot. I think he made my father and mother papists. He used to christen negroes at several times. Negroes said they went to him, and said he prayed for them. . . . Peggy was sworn and was a Roman [Catholic]. . . . He said if we discovered all our sins to him he could forgive them. I said, 'None but God could, if we prayed to Him.' He said, 'A priest can as well as God,'" the girl claimed.

Sarah sounded ready to save herself by sacrificing Ury to the judge's religious image, yet she refused to offer anyone else. She named only dead blacks, except for Walter's Quaco, who had joined Othello in pleading guilty that morning and received the same sentence—burning at the stake. The soldier Kane was the only white Sarah fully implicated besides Ury. Indeed, she spared one soldier and the white hatter by saying, "I don't know that Andrew Ryan was concerned, or David Johnson." She spoke less liberally on Private Edward Murphy but still refrained from directly connecting him to the plot; she said only, "I've seen Murphy often at the house since Christmas when Vaarck's Caesar asked him to drink a dram." And although she previously claimed to have heard Coffin's name and described him as "a fresh colored, long-haired man," when shown the peddler in a line-up, Sarah said, "I've not seen him before."

Sarah impressed Horsmanden by confessing to being sworn on the same Sunday in January 1741 as Kane and by reporting the blacks "standing around a circle made with chalk and saying, 'The devil fetch him and burn him that discovers'," much as

Kane also had confessed. Having two white witnesses reporting from inside the plot and agreeing on details meant a great deal to the judge.

Sensitive by now on the issue of prisoners' fabricating stories among themselves, Horsmanden tried to remove any question of taint from Sarah's words by noting that "she could scarce know that [Kane] had given such information, for . . . his examination was not out of the judges or grand jury's hands; [and] Kane and Sarah were confined in cells separate and distant from each other. . . . Such circumstances concurring with other evidence . . . puts the truth of the matter beyond doubt and, thereby, adds credit to the rest of her confession," the judge asserted.

Thus, on Saturday, July 11, when she was scheduled for the gallows, Sarah appeared before Justices DeLancey and Philipse and attorney John Chambers, who read her amended confession aloud and asked her if it were the truth. She hemmed and hawed, but perhaps hearing the hangman's footsteps drawing closer, she swore that all she said the previous day was true. Her reward was another stay of execution.

⛓⛓⛓⛓⛓

Hoping for at least a reprieve if not the full mercy he pleaded for, Othello also confessed. Many whites were anxious to hear what he had to say, because his position as the favored slave of the rich and powerful chief justice brought him notoriety. DeLancey was certainly interested, but trying to keep a proper distance, he absented himself from the session that Horsmanden recorded after church on Sunday, July 12.[4]

Othello said the butcher Carpenter's Albany introduced him to the plot at the beginning of the summer of 1740 by inviting him for a drink at Hughson's, after delivering meat to DeLancey's. Othello stayed in the yard when they reached the tavern, and Albany went in and brought back a two-penny shot of whiskey and a message that Hughson wanted Othello to wait and talk with him. "I said I couldn't stay then, but that I'd come there in the evening," Othello explained to the judge. "I went again about dusk. Albany wasn't there, [but] Hughson and I began to talk of the plot."

"Another time will do as well," Othello demurred, as the taverner pressed him to take the plotter's oath.

"If you'll swear, you'd never want for liquor. It'll not cost you anything. Bring your acquaintance with you, and I'll make them welcome," the taverner offered.

"Thanks," the slave said and left after about an hour. A few days later he returned to the tavern with Albany, following an early evening swim in the Hudson. Hughson again pressed him to swear, but Othello refused.

"If you won't [swear], you mustn't tell anybody what I've been talking about," Hughson insisted. Othello agreed to say nothing and continued to visit. "I've seen many soldiers at Hughson's, at different times, very great with Hughson, but I can't tell whether they knew or were concerned in the plot. But I know that Kane was one of them and believe he can name the rest. Hughson promised to find me a gun and cutlass and told me if I did any damage, I'd commit no sin thereby, [and] it wouldn't hinder me from going to heaven. Vaarck's Caesar told me that Rutgers's Quash was to find arms," Othello explained to Horsmanden. Also, he recalled once asking Philipse's Cuff, "You sworn?"

"Yes, aren't you?" replied Cuff.

"No, I've only promised to keep the secret," Othello said he answered. He insisted that since then he had spoken to nobody about the plot until being jailed on June 27. "Adam told me that he was to have killed his master and mistress, sure enough, and advised me to confess that I was to have killed my master and mistress, that that'd be a means of getting me off," Othello added.

Horsmanden was disappointed by the slave's story, and so were people who, following the common practice of transfering to a slave the like status of his holder, projected Othello as naturally important among blacks and thus a headman in the plot. According to the slave, he was hardly in the plot; at worst, he did no more than associate with the wrong crowd.[5]

If what Othello said were true, why had he pleaded guilty to conspiracy? That question bothered the judge, no doubt, because it created a predicament for him: If Othello had done only what he claimed, he seemed indeed to qualify for mercy like many of the other slaves recommended for pardon on condition of transportation; yet to let Othello live smacked of favoritism. The treatment of several other politicians' slaves had already produced mutterings about the justice being biased. Horsmanden's predicament in no way, of course, neared Othello's: The judge had only his and the court's reputation at stake; the slave stood to burn at the stake.[6]

Former assemblyman John Walter's Quaco stood in the same position as Othello but offered a somewhat different story to the judge that Sunday. His introduction to the plot came in May 1740 when Caesar, Cuff, and Prince invited him for a drink at Hughson's. "We got pretty merry with drinking," Quaco recalled.

"I want you for something, but you must swear not to tell it," Caesar said.

"I'll be cursed if I tell," Quaco responded.

"We don't care to trust Frank or John, nor many others who're apt to talk," Caesar continued, referring to Justice Philipse's Frank and former acting governor Rip Van Dam's John, then also at Hughson's. "If you'll agree to our proposal, it'll be better for you. When you come here, you'll never want for liquor."

Quaco accepted the offer and joined the plot. "Caesar, Cuffee and Prince swore at the same time to encourage me to swear. We all kissed a book. Then they told me of the plot," he told the judge and recalled more of the talk.

"Your master have any guns?" Hughson inquired.

"Two which I can get," Quaco answered.

"I've powder and shot enough, and I've bought some guns and have money to buy more. There are people up the river and on the other side of the water that are to come and help," the taverner boasted.

"Blacks or whites?" Quaco asked.

"I know who they are, and that's sufficient," Hughson huffed. Then in calmer tones he added, "If you bring any company here with you, I'll make them welcome."

"I understood . . . they were whites," Quaco explained about the people to whom Hughson referred. Further the slave said, "I remember seeing a gun hanging up at Hughson's [and] likewise a bag of large shot." Hughson and the others were certainly serious about their plans and recruited blacks and whites in and out of town and cached money to fund the deeds, Quaco said. He heard all that from Caesar when they were cellmates in April. One new white name the slave gave the judge from this hearsay was Robert Saunders, a tavern keeper along the docks.

Horsmanden's long craving for Quaco's hide apparently led him to pay as little attention to the slave's words as he had to his pleading guilty in hopes of obtaining mercy. The judge felt sure the slave was trying to get off cheaply by reporting hearsay and sounding as if he had done little more than once have a drink too many. Burning at the stake was what the slave deserved, the judge insisted, and that was his sentence. Only the date of execution remained unset.

✶✶✶✶✶

All the king's men began the week of July 13 intent on settling accounts with blacks and getting on against implicated whites. Horsmanden himself seemed as tired of the proceedings as his cohort; but determined to see no slave slip through the dragnet undeservedly, he called for new testimony against LeRoux's Quash, one of the two slaves released the previous week by the grand jury for lack of credible evidence. The judge quickly got enough to re-arrest the slave.

The continued digging turned embarrassing for Sheriff William Jamison, because his slave Cuffee was implicated and skipped town before anybody laid a hand on him. Also, a free black named Frans walked off from his job as a butcher before the constables arrived to arrest him. The judge further discovered to all the officials' chagrin that the long talked about firkins of butter, reportedly stolen by Caesar and taken in by John Romme, were unloaded through sale to New York's government as supplies for the troops in the Cuba expedition that had sailed in the autumn.[7]

Horsmanden produced more talk about "a Roman priest [who] swore the negroes to the plot and said he could forgive them all the sins that they did." He got Mary Burton to implicate several more whites, too. The girl identified one suspect simply as "an old man, a very old man, in old clothes, sometimes a red jacket. I believe he's not a soldier," she added, against speculation that the jacket was part of the regular British army uniform.

Another suspect was, the girl said, "a soldier [who] lives at the house behind the English churchyard." She had no name for him either. "Soldiers used to come to his house, and Hughson used to go up there and fetch them down" to the tavern, she said. Also, she drew in "a man by the Mayor's market. He lived at the shop where I used to fetch rum from." He looked and dressed like

185

Kane "but on Sunday used to have better clothes. I don't know his name. He lived in a sort of a cellar opposite the market. . . . I've seen another dancing master along with Holt and Kane at Hughson's talking about the plot," Mary offered. This was the dancing master she saw at the trials, not Holt, and she stammered at a surname with the initial letter "C." Not wanting to appear to be putting words in Mary's mouth, Horsmanden let her stumble along until she indicated where the man lived on Wall Street.

"Is his name Corry?" the judge asked.

"That's his name. I'd know him again if I saw him," the girl answered. The judge dismissed her and called in Kane.

"You know of any other dancing master besides Holt, that was among you at Hughson's when you were talking of the plot?"

"There's Pier's son-in-law who lives in that street," Kane answered instantly and pointed to Wall Street. Within minutes the constables had John Corry in custody.[8]

"I never spoke a word to Holt in my life, and never was in his company . . . [and was] never at Hughson's nor any other place on the North River within this city," Corry swore.

"Though as the proverb is 'Two of a trade can seldom agree,' it is much, very much, that these two dancing masters living in the same town for four or five years together should not have had one wrangle or exchanged one word neither in anger or civility in all that time. Surely he endeavors to prove too much, for they might possibly have talked together very innocently," Horsmanden noted, unconvinced by Corry's protest of not knowing Holt.

Mary returned to the hearing room, took a look at Corry, and nodded that he was the man she meant.

"I've never seen her before," Corry declared, denying all the girl said. She laughed at him and left. Then Kane entered and also identified the man, "but Corry knew him not," the judge noted.

The dancing master was ushered to jail despite his protests. With the thickening crowd of whites and throng of blacks, hardly any place then remained unoccupied. The efforts to relieve conditions in the cells had failed so far to do much because, although Governor Clarke cooperated fully with the judges' recommendations to pardon a growing list of blacks, none were to be released until their transportation from the colony was fully arranged. Only the executioner was thinning the prison population for the moment, as the prospect of more black deaths loomed on Wednesday, July 15, when eight including "Doctor" Harry, went on trial.

❦❦❦❦❦

Chief Justice DeLancey presided at the trial of the eight. It was his first jury case in the conspiracy proceedings and, also, the first full trial in almost three weeks. Joseph Murray, William Smith, and John Chambers prosecuted. Mary Burton and William Kane testified, and six blacks, including Murray's Adam, turned king's evidence. Combining pieces from the two whites and six blacks, the prosecutors placed all eight defendants at Hughson's during talk of the plot. Two witnesses appeared for the defense—Hermanus Wendover for his slave Toby and Jacob Walton for his slave Fortune. Walton protested that Burton failed to identify Fortune in a line-up and quoted the girl's saying earlier, "I've never seen him at Hughson's." It was to no avail.

The charge and evidence were basically the same as in the previous trials, and the expected outcome could only be the same unless the jury were willing to challenge the continuing popular belief in a massive plot. The verdicts in all the previous trials had to weigh on the jurors, for to acquit any of the eight defendants would certainly seem to suggest that earlier jurors had been wrong. Seven of the twelve men themselves had served on previous juries; they would be calling their own judgments into question. The verdict, then, was the same for one and all: Guilty.

"Doctor" Harry was ordered burned at the stake and the other slaves to hang—all on the day after their sentencing, the Saturday when Othello and Quaco were also scheduled to die. But, for the first time in the proceedings, muttering about political influence erupted in full voice as former assemblyman Walter pressed on his slave Quaco's behalf. Horsmanden fumed about "great solicitations made to his honor [Governor Clarke], for saving Quaco's life or, at least, if that could not be done, that his sentence might be changed from burning to hanging."

Clarke asked both Horsmanden and Philipse for a formal opinion on commuting the sentence, excluding DeLancey as Othello's holder. The focus fell only on the two slaves, because of the positions their holders occupied, but other elements intruded.[9]

Quaco had no claim to pardon or mercy, Horsmanden argued, but Philipse showed more compassion, perhaps because his own slave Frank also awaited fate's disposition. Both judges had to recognize the politics of the case and the chief justice's interest, although DeLancey sat close-mouthed and did not interfere on his slave's behalf. They had also to recognize the possibility of public outcry against blatant favoritism. At least one excuse for leniency existed however: Because Quaco and Othello pleaded guilty, there was no jury or public prosecution to overrule; the judges stood liable only for reversing their own instant decision to grant no mercy and burn the blacks.

Horsmanden stood steadfast in his belief that both slaves deserved exemplary punishment and, apparently feeling compelled to explain his view, wrote in review of the case histories that "The characters of these two miserable wretches were well known. They had more sense than the common rank of negroes. They had both kind and indulgent masters. They were two of the head negroes in town, both fellows of high spirits, and had both general acquaintance and great influence among the inferior sort of negroes. Their confessions were neither voluntary or free, but came from them very unwillingly and after much persuasion. Nor could the judges look upon them to be full. So . . . these criminals were deficient in all the particulars required by the proclamation as essential in a recommendation to mercy."

The judge was especially cutting on Quaco and scoffed at Walter and the slave by declaring, "It was well known how much idle time Quaco had, almost at his own disposal, as if he were his own master. And now, [when] at length the proofs that he was one of the conspirators came out to be strong against him and he had been impeached for a long while before indicted, what he pretended to call confessions were of little avail. . . . Quaco's insolence and ingratitude towards his master were very remarkable. . . . What virtues he might have had, if he had any, are best known to the family he belonged to, but it seemed agreed on all hand that Quaco was always much better fed than taught."

Taming his sarcasm, Horsmanden commented almost kindly on Othello. "This negro behaved upon this occasion with a great deal of composure and decency, [and] with an air of sincerity which very much affected [me], for from the intimacy I had the honor of with his master, I had frequent opportunities of seeing this negro at his house. Othello's case could not but move some compassion. But all things considered, when calmly reflected upon, one could not yield," the judge explained.

His kind note aside, Horsmanden declared that "the aptness and alacrity of these two criminals for mischief was monstrously remarkable. . . . Certainly it was not fit that two such cannibals, who could coolly engage to embrue their hands in the blood of innocent persons by wholesale—[persons] who could never have offended them—should be suffered any longer to breathe when the justice of the law had overtaken them. . . . The judges could by no means think them proper objects of mercy, and had they recommended them to the governor as such and his honor had pardoned them, such lenity towards them might have been deemed cruelty to the people," the judge concluded.

Philipse yielded to Horsmanden's position, and the two slaves would have burned at the stake if Governor Clarke had not weighed the issues and struck a compromise of sorts. He allowed the executions to proceed but changed the manner from burning to hanging.[10]

John Walter remained unplaced, to say nothing of Othello and Quaco's feelings. Walter and others questioned the decision in light of the pardons received by Alderman Pintard's Caesar, prominent merchant Peter Jay's Brash, and prosecutor Murray's Adam and Jack, among others.

The protests forced Horsmanden further to explain his judgments. "The other negroes concerned in this horrible undertaking were likewise of the head or chief slaves in town and principal agents, no doubt, among the conspirators of their own color. Some perhaps may object, why were not all, or at least Mr. Murray's own negroes, made examples of, as well as these two criminals [Othello and Quaco], for they may say they equally deserved it," the judge acknowledged. He argued, however, that several slaves "made large confessions and considerable discoveries, more especially [Pintard's] Caesar, [Jay's] Brash, [Murray's] Adam and Jack, insomuch that it was judged necessary to make use of them as witnesses; for which reason, considerably the pledge of the public faith, and as they made those large confessions and discoveries, conformable to and relying upon the proclamation for their indemnity with regard to their lives, their escape [from death] could not be avoided, though their crimes merited a more severe fate."

Taunting those who protested, Horsmanden revealed more of his personal feelings by declaring that "It is very true they all deserved exemplary punishment. But if all the conspirators in town had been executed, perhaps this would have been carrying the argument further than the objectors would have chosen it should, especially if any of their own slaves had been detected. Though indeed it were much to be wished that every negro in town concerned were transported or the place rid of them almost at any rate; and if so, it is probable there would be very few to trouble us,'' the judge wrote.

The protests were not without effect, aside from Othello and Quaco's changed sentences. Of the eight convicted on Wednesday and set for execution that Saturday, three were reprieved. The frenzy against blacks had peaked, but even in waning it remained deadly, for at noon that Saturday four from Wednesday's eight stood at the gallows with Othello and Quaco.

One of the blacks to be executed was Jacob Walton's Fortune, and he tried to cheat the hangman by jumping off the platform ''several times with the halter about his neck, as if sporting with death,'' Horsmanden reported. Both Othello and Quaco talked a bit more before being delivered to the crowd, but asked if he had any last words to add, Othello answered, ''I've nothing more to say than what I this morning declared to one of the judges.''

All six blacks then died together in sight of the rotting remains of John Hughson, Vaarck's Caesar, and Marschalk's York, still hanging in the Common. York's corpse was the freshest of the three, being on display only fifteen days. Caesar's was nearing eleven weeks and Hughson's five. The summer heat and sun turned the cadavers even more grisly than anyone imagined possible at the original hangings, and not knowing what to expect from corpses exposed that long led townspeople to speculate on the changes.

''The town was amused with a rumor that Hughson was turned negro and Vaarck's Caesar white,'' Horsmanden reported, noting that when York's corpse was hung in chains ''so much of Hughson as was visible—viz., face, hands, neck, and feet—were of a deep shining black, rather blacker than the negro placed by him, who was one of the darkest hue of his kind. The hair of Hughson's beard and neck—his head could not be seen for he had a cap on—was curling like the wool of a negro's beard and head. And the features of his face were of the symmetry of a negro beauty: the nose broad and flat, the nostrils open and extended, the mouth wide, lips full and thick. His body (which when living was tall, by the view upwards of six feet, but very meager) swelled to a gigantic size. An as to Caesar (who . . . was also of the darkest complexion) his face was at the same time somewhat bleached or turned whitish, insomuch that it occasioned a remark that Hughson and he had changed colors."

Spectators filed by daily to gawk. "Hughson's body dripped and distilled very much, as it needs must from the great fermentation and abundance of matter within him, as could not but be supposed at the time from the extraordinary bulk of his body. Though considering the force of the sun and the natural meagerness of his corpse, one would have been apt to imagine that long ere this it would have been disencumbered of all its juices," Horsmanden commented.

Shortly before the executions that Saturday, Hughson's corpse burst, spilling his putrid insides by the pailfuls. "The stench of it was very offensive," the judge noted, and in a last dig at the dead, he commented that "Hughson, [who] it seems let the worst happen to him in all events, declared as he was going to mount the cart which was to carry him to execution that he did not doubt but some remarkable sign would happen to show his innocence. And if his corpse becoming monstrous in size and his complexion (for once to use a vulgar similitude) as black as the devil can be deemed remarkable signs or token of his innocence, then some may imagine it was happened according to his expectation."

What was left of Hughson, Caesar, and York continued to hang as Othello and his mates' corpses were cut down and the crowd turned to await "Doctor" Harry's burning. "Several endeavored to persuade him to make a confession, but Harry's heart was hardened. He would discover nothing, as he had no hopes of benefiting himself by it in this world," Horsmanden sneered. Indeed, unlike others earlier who wagged as the flames neared, Harry held his tongue until the end when he screamed, "I know nothing of the plot of my own knowledge. If I did, I'd discover to save my soul. . . . It signifies nothing to confess."

The date was July 18.

# 15

## "An Ecclesiastical Person"

As THE LAST FULL WEEK of July began, the king's men had dealt with virtually every black implicated by name in the plotting. Those singled out as leaders had been executed, and all who remained were awaiting the officials' disposition. Several, such as the five convicted Spanish blacks, still sat under the death sentence. The task for Horsmanden and his colleagues then was simply to sort out whom to put on the lengthening list of pardons on condition of transportation and whom to simply release or execute.[1]

With his continuing desire to rid the city of slaves, Horsmanden resisted the growing pressure from holders to reclaim their slaves from jail. He rejected the argument that the execution of twenty-nine blacks had already removed the worst of the slaves and given sufficient warning to the rest. The judge stood adamant against releasing any of the implicated blacks.

Other officials, some with their own slaves at stake, were more yielding than the judge, and the grand jury continued the trickle released from jail on grounds of insufficient evidence. Among those dismissed were Justice Philipse's Frank, former acting governor Rip Van Dam's John, and Alderman John Moore's Caesar—his second slave to go unharmed.

Horsmanden complained as if the jurors and his fellow officials were growing soft-hearted and self-indulgent. He worried that even after three months of examples townspeople still failed to see that all slaves were dangerous. He wanted at least to banish all the jailed blacks, and he contended that there was "clear and positive evidence" that several of the slaves released by the grand jury had taken part in the plot.

Even for the judge, however, the immediate issue was no longer the black role in the plot, but the white role. Indeed, with the arrest of John Ury and the Irishmen who followed him to jail, the people at large had grown increasingly anxious to hear the king's case against the implicated whites.

The grand jury fed rumors of a round up of all whites who trafficked with slaves, by indicting ten taverners for "keeping a disorderly house [and] entertaining negroes." Judge Philipse marked such persons as virtual drug dealers when he charged the jury in April, before the terrifying reports of intemperance at Hughson's. At the time, his instructions sounded like only a note of personal pique, but now, with the townsfolk wide-eyed at the horrors alleged at Hughson's, those accused of feeding blacks' illicit habits stood liable for more than the usual warning of a wink and slap on the wrist.[2]

All ten taverners pleaded guilty in a bargain for mercy. No evidence put any of them in Hughson's league, but the court made examples by levying fines against each to match the proof of illicit liquor sales. Judged the worst offender, William Whitefield was fined £8—a year's wage for many. Not having the sum, he was jailed until he raised it. Michael Breton and John Christian each paid a £5 fine and were released from custody. Stephen Burdett and Nicholas Burger each paid £2. Israel Shadwick and three women innkeepers all paid ten shillings—half a pound. Robert Saunders paid half a shilling, which Horsmanden later lamented in noting that "This [was] supposed to be the man that Walter's Quaco understood, from what Vaarck's Caesar said to him, to be concerned in the plot. . . . But this was not thought of at that time."[3]

The quick punishment of the taverners served as a warning that the officials intended to crack down on all illicit relations between blacks and whites, but it distracted nobody from the pressing questions of the moment: Who were the whites at Hughson's, and what role had they played in the plotting?

Horsmanden and his colleagues pressed the questions with William Kane and Mary Burton. The soldier seemed ready to talk for all he was worth and on Tuesday, July 21, implicated James O'Brien and Thomas Evans, two more of his garrison mates. Also, Kane quoted Edward Murphy, another jailed soldier, as saying, "Damn me if I won't lend a hand to the fire as soon as anybody." Kane recalled the hatter David Johnson's telling him, "Damn you. Don't be downhearted. Never fear, for we'll have money enough by-and-by. . . . I'll help to burn the town and kill as many white people as I can." Clearly, the term *white people* meant *wealthy*.

Horsmanden dutifully recorded the evidence against the new suspects, but his focus fell on John Ury, who now sat indicted for conspiracy and also for "being an ecclesiastical person, made by authority pretended from the See of Rome, and coming into and abiding in this province." A New York law of 1700, entitled "An Act against Jesuits and Popish Priests" (11 William III), made such a person's presence illegal and punishable by "perpetual imprisonment . . . [or the] pains of death." The hatred of Catholics which had prompted the law originally had faded none over the years; and the charge of being a Catholic—especially of being a Catholic priest—remained a deadly affair.[4]

Ury pleaded not guilty to both counts and further declared, "I deny being anywise concerned in the conspiracy for burning the town and killing the inhabitants. I never was anywise acquainted with John Hughson or his wife or Margaret Kerry [Peggy]. Nor did I ever see them in my life, to my knowledge." But Mary, Kane, and Sarah Hughson swore the man had frequented Hughson's, and the authorities' discovered a diary of Ury's that darkened the suspicions about his background and religion.

Written like many diaries in a cryptic, personal shorthand, Ury's journal chronicled his arrival in Philadelphia on Saturday, February 17, 1739. Nothing was mentioned about where he came from, but he certainly followed an itinerant's path by circling the City of Brotherly Love and its suburbs before starting a stint of teaching during March in the town of London, Pennsylvania, just north of Maryland—then a haven for Catholics. In June 1739 he moved to Burlington, New Jersey, for the first of two stints; he did the second in January 1740. Then he stayed for awhile in a Pennsylvania place he called Penefuck. From July to October 1740 he taught in Dublin, Pennsylvania. He arrived in New York City on

Sunday, November 2, 1740, and boarded at John Croker's inn, The Fighting Cocks.[5]

Horsmanden and the grand jury focused particularly on several of Ury's entries. One read *"Naturo Johannis Pool*, 26th December, 1740.'' The judge speculated that the note indicated a birth where Ury performed some sort of rite. His suspicion was sharpened by another entry that read, ''Baptized Timothy Ryan, born 18th April 1740, son of John Ryan and Mary Ryan, 18th May 1741.''

The judge rushed to connect the entry to the Ryans who had lived at Hughson's, but he encountered a problem: Their names were Andrew and Eleanor, and they had no year-old son. Eleanor had testified in the Hughsons and Peggy's defense at their conspiracy trial. Andrew was in jail as one of the implicated soldiers from the Fort George garrison. So, although the names did not match, the couple remained under suspicion as plotters.

In casting about to match the entry with a couple other than Andrew and Eleanor, Horsmanden seemed to eye every Irishman as a Catholic. ''There was another Ryan, a married man . . . [and] a professed papist, who has it seems since withdrawn himself, but neither his nor his wife's name answers Ury's minute. But whosoever the infant belonged to, its being kept so long from baptism, in a place where there are so many protestant clergy of many denominations ready at hand, gives umbrage to the conjecture that this office was reserved for popish priest,'' the judge noted.

The final entry the king's men puzzled over was in Latin, *"Pater confessor Butler 2 Anni. non sacramentum non confessio."* Who Father confessor Butler was or what Ury meant by two years without sacrament or confession was a mystery to Horsmanden and his men, but they felt sure it meant Ury was a priest.

Still lingering in the shadow of death, Sarah Hughson stepped forward on July 22 and cast Ury firmly as a priest. ''I've seen Ury the priest at my father's house. He used to come there in the evening and at nights. I've seen him in company with the negroes and talking with them about the plot of burning the town and destroying the white people. I've seen him several times make a round ring with chalk on the floor and make all the negroes then

195

present stand around it. And he used to stand in the middle of the ring, with a cross in his hand, and there swore all the negroes to be concerned in the plot and that they shouldn't discover him nor anything else of the plot though they should die for it," the girl declared under oath to Chief Justice DeLancey.

"William Kane used often to come there with the negroes, and once, as I remember, he came there with Ury the priest who swore him into the plot and several negroes, in particular Vaarck's Caesar, Comfort's Jack, Auboyneau's Prince, Walter's Quaco, Philipse's Cuffee, [and] Peggy and me myself, and my father and mother. All this was done the last winter. Before Christmas, I think. . . . I saw Ury baptize the negroes . . . [I] named, or some of them, and tell them he made them Christians and forgave them all their sins and all the sins they'd commit about the plot, and [he] preached to the negroes. Kane was there also. I've heard Vaarck's Caesar, Philipse's Cuffee, and other negroes say that they used to go to Ury's lodging where they used to pray in private after the popish fashion and that he used to forgive them their sins for burning the town and destroying and cutting the people's throats," Sarah said. Then she recalled a conversation between her and the man.

"You must confess to me what sins you've been guilty of, and I'll forgive you them," Ury instructed.

"I've been guilty of no other sins but cursing and swearing in a passion," Sarah replied.

"As you've taken the oath to be concerned in the plot, I pardon you your sins."

"I don't believe anybody can forgive my sins but God."

"Oh, yes, I and all priests can if people but do as the priests bid them and follow all our directions," Ury said, according to the girl. She added that "Peggy used to confess in private to Ury, and I heard him tell her, if she'd confess all the wickedness she'd done in the world, he'd forgive her. . . . Peggy often told me she was a strong papist."

Horsmanden offered no complaint about Sarah's again naming only dead blacks and no whites other than Ury and Kane. Nor did he object to her saying, "Several of the soldiers used often to come to our house and call for liquor, but I don't know whether they knew of or were concerned in the plot or not." He also left unchallenged the discrepancies between her story and Kane's.

The judge seemed satisfied with Sarah's talk of Ury's baptizing slaves—a center of a generation-old controversy in New York over the christening of blacks being a sacrilege. At least some slaveholders continued to worry about slaves coming, perhaps too truly, to believe in Christian brotherhood. Protestants like Horsmanden had no questions at all on the issue of anybody but God forgiving sins: Any other idea in their mind was heresy. And he delighted also in the girl's talking, as Kane had, of a chalk circle and oath swearing.[6]

A confectioner named Elias DeBrosse added to the talk against Ury by reporting what he thought was a curious visit paid to his shop in May by the man and a carpenter named Joseph Webb.

"Do you have any sugar bits or wafers to sell?"

"I've no bits or wafers," the sweetsmaker recalled answering Ury and showing him other items made in animal shapes, thinking the man wanted treats for children.

"The Lutheran minister hasn't his wafers from you? Isn't the paste you showed me made of the same ingredients as the Lutheran minister's?" Ury pressed.

"If you've a congregation and want any such things, you might get any joiner for that purpose," DeBrosse advised, imagining Ury then as a new minister looking for communion bits and suggesting he needed no professional but simply a member of his church to make what he wanted. "Where's your congregation?" DeBrosse asked. Ury never answered.

Horsmanden considered the report clear evidence of Ury's seeking to minister secret communion, and the constables delivered Joseph Webb for questioning. The carpenter immediately confirmed DeBrosse's report, almost word for word, but his own story about Ury provided much more detail and revealed a knowledge of the man that nobody else in town admitted having.

Webb recalled first seeing Ury while doing carpentry for John Croker at The Fighting Cocks in early November 1740 and said that when he discovered the new man was a schoolteacher, he arranged for his son to join Croker's children in Ury's private classes. The tutoring fees were slight and the teacher's poverty rather easy to see, the carpenter suggested. Croker paid Ury with free room and breakfast, and Webb offered lunch and dinner at his own house. Ury accepted, and his almost daily presence at the carpenter's table from late November to early May created the basis of an apparent friendship.

Ury was indeed an ecclesiastical person and admitted being called to the cloth and pastoring a parish, Webb reported from their conversations. Yet the man was hardly the priest Horsmanden and others suspected him of being, the carpenter explained. Ury was a minister born, raised, and educated in England and ordained by an English bishop. He was a nonjuror, not a Catholic, the carpenter claimed. Confirmation offered hope of saving Ury's life even if it were likely to make him still unwelcome to High-Churchmen such as Horsmanden.[7]

Nonjurors stood as splinters from the Church of England and received their label from following those who refused in 1689 to take the oath of allegiance to William and Mary, the monarchs installed by Parliament after the overthrow of King James II in the Glorious Revolution of 1688–89. The issue with them was more political loyalty than religious fidelity, although the union of church and crown often allowed no distinction.[8]

Ury's present trouble with the law was in fact not his first on account of religion. The man had been arrested in London when the king's censors charged him with treason for a book he wrote. Stripped of his church position, cut off from a £50 annual income, and cast into prison, Ury was alive only because powerful friends of his family interceded to secure his release and his sailing for America, Webb reported.

Ury's table talk and other conversation frequently treated religious topics. "He'd give hints I could neither make head nor tail of," the carpenter conceded, but touching slaves and religion, he recalled enough to comment on Ury's ideas about preaching Christian salvation to blacks.

"They've souls to be saved or lost as well as other people," Webb reported himself once telling Ury during a discussion of blacks.

"They're not proper objects of salvation," Ury objected.

"What would you do with them then? What, would you damn them all?"

"No, leave them to that Great Being that made them. He knows best what to do with them. They're of a slavish nature. It's the nature of them to be slaves. Give them learning, do all the good you can, and put them above the condition of slaves, and in return, they'll cut your throats," Ury replied, not sounding at all like a man engaging in baptizing blacks and promising them freedom, riches, and salvation.

Webb's recollection cast Ury in a light that clearly clashed with the view presented by young Sarah Hughson. The king's men had to decide which view to accept, although Horsmanden claimed he saw no contradiction in using both. In the judge's eyes, Sarah showed the man as a priest and Webb showed that "Ury seemed to be well acquainted with the disposition of negroes." Believing deeply in the notion of black inferiority and ingratitude himself, Horsmanden took as truth the sentiments the carpenter attributed to the schoolteacher and construed them for his own purpose. All the evidence fitted together in the judge's perspective.

Ury had demonstrated his beliefs and interest in religion while in New York City and, indeed, had held services at Hughson's—but not in the manner previously reported to the authorities, Webb explained. The man performed ceremonies at the house in early May after young Sarah Hughson, her sisters, and Peggy's baby were evicted and John Campbell had become the tenant with Ury moving in as a boarder.

"I went there three times and heard him read prayers in the manner of the Church of England, but in the prayers for the king he only mentioned 'our sovereign lord the king' and not King George," the carpenter said, confirming his report of Ury's ministry and adherence to nonjuring principles.

Ury not only prayed but also preached at Hughson's former home. "The drift of his first sermon was against drunkenness and debauchery of life and against deists. The first part of his second sermon was much to the same purpose with the former, and the latter part was an admonition to every one to keep to their own minister: They that were of the Church of England, to the English minister; those that were of the Lutheran persuasion to keep to that, and those of the Presbyterian to keep to their ministers and not to have itching ears to run after every new minister. He didn't propose to set up a society for preaching. . . . 'I'm only giving a word of admonition at the request of the family [here] where I am,'" Webb reported Ury's saying.[9]

"At his third sermon, Mr. [Joseph] Hildreth [a schoolteacher] was present," the carpenter continued. "Ury therein took notice of two ministers that had lately preached in this city, whose doctrine he condemned. The particulars that I remember he took notice of were their preaching up that faith without works were sufficient for salvation. He said that this destroyed two grand attributes of God Almighty, His justice and mercy. He insisted that there must be good works. This was the Sunday before the king's proclamation day, and at the close, he warned the persons present that on the king's proclamation day [Wednesday, May 13], at five o'clock in the evening, he intended to preach upon the following words, among others: 'Upon this rock I will build my church and the gates of hell shall not prevail against it,' concerning St. Peter; and these other words, 'Whosoever sins ye remit, they are remitted, and whosoever sins ye retain, they are retained.' That's to the best of my remembrance, but I haven't heard that he preached according to that warning. I've heard Ury say that such and such a time was his sacrament day and that he must receive the sacrament. I think I've heard him say that he must administer the sacrament, but I cannot be positive.'' Webb concluded.

The carpenter left no doubt that Ury was a cleric, and his reports of the man's preaching disturbed many townsfolk, particularly the established ministers already irked by the intrusion of itinerant preachers and the frenzy of revivalism, which under the label the Great Awakening was maddening congregations throughout English America. Ury's comment on the old dispute over the doctrine of faith and good works threw him into the theological thicket and was sure to make him enemies.[10]

Yet the crucial question remained open: What was the man's faith? The texts (Matthew 16:18–19) projected for the proclamation day service fueled controversy. The first quotation irked many Protestants because the popes used the line to support the foundation of the Church of Rome and the idea of papal authority coming directly from Jesus Christ through St. Peter. The second quotation raised even more eyebrows because it was used as the basis for what Catholics called the Sacrament of Penance, which Protestants pilloried as an evil delusion.[11]

Webb's claim that he did not know if Ury actually preached on the texts stirred queries about what Ury might have said if he had preached the sermon. There also were questions about what Ury was referring to in speaking of a sacrament and sacrament days, as Webb reported. And why had Ury not mentioned King George by name; did he have some other king? Horsmanden was eager for answers.

The judge held steadfast in his belief that Ury was a Catholic, and the prosecutors worked on developing their case based on that belief. They intended to tie the man to Hughson's and the plot and to saddle him as a priest and, therefore, certainly a Spanish sympathizer and probably a spy. Their design suggested that the city's fires of March and April were simply part of a conspiracy that connected the current war between the English and Spanish and the centuries-old conflict between Protestants and Catholics. Horsmanden and his cohort looked to portray Ury as the insidious outsider who incited acts and ideas of insurrection among the domestic negroes, with Hughson and the condemned Spanish blacks helping.

⛓⛓⛓⛓⛓

The grand conspiracy theory of the king's men drew heavily on English history. Since King Henry VIII's break with the Church of Rome in 1534 and the creation of the Church of England, the Catholic-Protestant bitterness brewed in the Reformation stirred by German theologian and former priest Martin Luther had boiled over on English soil. The dregs spoiled Anglo-Spanish relations, too. Indeed, the soured grounds dripped from Henry's desire to divorce the first of his six wives, Katharine of Aragon—the aunt of Spain's King Charles I.[12]

England's shift from Catholicism to Anglicanism left a long legacy of religious bloodletting at home and abroad. The leeching grew almost as soon as Henry VIII died in 1547 and left his sole male heir, his child by third wife Jane Seymour, to become Edward VI—crowned king at age nine but dead at age fifteen. Mary I, Henry's only surviving child by his first wife Katharine, became queen in 1553. Her continuing Catholicism and marriage to the prince who became King Phillip II of Spain and pressed his claim to be crowned also a king of England, marked her as "Bloody Mary."

The religious contention and the Spanish claim to the English throne heightened when Mary I died in 1558 and Henry's daughter by his second wife, Anne Boleyn, became England's Queen Elizabeth I. Plots to kill Elizabeth and elevate Catholic Mary, Queen of Scots, to the English throne and continued pressure from Phillip II to become England's king led to increased bloodshed. Hostilities and suspicions ran particularly high when, in 1587, Elizabeth ordered Mary, Queen of Scots, beheaded after nineteen years of imprisonment and in 1588, when Phillip launched the ill-fated Spanish Armada against England.

The legacy perpetuated cries of conspiracy personified by Guy Fawkes, an English soldier executed for what became known as the Gunpowder Plot. Others, including the head of the Jesuit Order in England, also suffered death for that plot. The reported plan was to blow up King James I and Parliament at its opening ceremonies on November 5, 1605, and hopefully touch off an uprising by English Catholics seething at their persecution. Fawkes himself was caught in the Parliament's cellar with explosives and a fuse on the appointed day. Protestant Englishmen made the date an annual, popular holiday from then on, and their suspicions and torments of Catholics worsened.

Mayhem quickened with the English Civil War that started in 1642 and culminated in 1649 when King Charles I was dethroned and beheaded, partly for his Catholic sympathies and marriage to French Catholic Princess Henrietta Marie. The kingdom without a king became a republic known as the Commonwealth. For five years Oliver Cromwell ruled as Lord Protector, and the nation experienced Puritan reform which exacerbated the Catholic-Protestant tension.

When the crown was restored in 1660, Charles I's eldest son became England's King Charles II and his skills lessened tensions, although anti-Catholic hostilities flared in the so-called Popish Plot in 1678, which involved Titus Oates, an Anglican priest and one-time convert to Catholicism who falsely claimed Jesuits had hatched a plan to assassinate the king. The aborted Rye House Plot to kill the king and his brother in 1683 led—on what many considered flimsy grounds of guilt by association—to the execution of Algernon Sidney and Lord William Russell, leading Whig politicians noted for their opposition to the king.

Charles II's death in 1685 elevated his Catholic, younger brother to the throne as King James II, and a rash of troubles erupted when the new king filled offices with Catholics and suspended laws against them and dissenters. The contention cost James II his throne as Parliament revolted, deposed him, and imported Protestants William and Mary as monarchs in 1689.

English colonists transported the hostilities to America. The Puritan dissenters in Massachusetts Bay, for example, sought freedom of religion for themselves but tolerated others poorly. Catholics were unwelcomed in all the colonies except Maryland, specifically founded as a haven for them in 1634. New York—named in honor of James II when he was Duke of York—offered more than a common measure of toleration; most Protestants and Jews were allowed to worship in peace, but not Catholics.[13]

The imperial rivalry between Great Britain and Catholic France and Spain continually fed the religious hatred and insecurities among the English colonies, particularly in places like Georgia, which sat on a disputed border with Spanish Florida, and New York with its border on French Canada. The perceived threats on the frontier bred fearful intolerance, as politics and religion remained wedded in a mean union. And because of the Netherlands' long struggle to win independence from Spain—a goal achieved in the Thirty Years War (1618–1648)—the Dutch heritage aggravated the heavy anti-Catholic and anti-Spanish strains in New York.[14]

John Ury faced the offspring of old hatreds. His reported troubles with the censors in London had taken him to the Tower and although he escaped death then, he now faced it again as Horsmanden and the king's men in New York held him to account for his beliefs. The specter of treason lurked even if he proved himself a nonjuror, because refusal to profess allegiance to the king opened questions of his advocating revolt against George II in favor of James II's son, James Edward—born in 1688 and scorned with the title "Old Pretender" by those who worried that, like his father, the son was a Catholic and interested in pressing a claim to England's throne. Thus, the city's outlook clearly framed Ury's chances of living.[15]

As an outsider and apparent nonconformist, Ury needed the benefit of more tolerance than that displayed since early April. The chance of a break in the popular, hard-line perspective did emerge on the last Tuesday in July when a new grand jury replaced the old one that had helped Horsmanden and the prosecution almost eagerly since April. More than a third of the new grand jurors had personal experience with the proceedings: John Auboyneau's slave Prince had hanged; John Roosevelt's Quack had burned; and Hermanus Rutgers's Quash had burned and his Galloway had hanged. In all, eight of the twenty new jurors had suffered the arrest of their property, and six of their slaves were dead on account of the proceedings. Auboyneau and Roosevelt had appeared in court to defend their slaves, and so had Charles LeRoux who had succeeded in getting his slave Quash released from custody, after pledging to ship him from the province. Unlike their predecessors, the new jurymen were wary of the prosecution and in no rush to judgment. That boded well in calming the atmosphere for future indictments, but it promised no present help in Ury's case.[16]

The man's main hope lay in the hands of the twelve "good men" who would serve as the trial jury on his day in court. The king's men intended for the jurors to behold Ury as a man worse than the monster John Hughson was portrayed as. They aimed to have Ury replace the taverner as ringleader of the plot in the popular mind, and where Hughson's motives were attributed to ignorant greed, the prosecutors sought to impute Ury's to the cunning evil of deluded religion and treason.

Ury needed to disassociate himself completely from any hint of Catholicism. If he owned any notion of a sacrament of absolution or forgiving sins, or a communion of transubstantiation that changed bread and wine into what the Church of Rome called "the body and blood of Christ," or anything close to what the popes preached, he was likely to fall into the hands of the hangman.

Ury had to dispel from the minds of his trial jurors all suspicions about his being engaged in espionage and insurrection as the proffered "ecclesiastical person."

The date was July 28.

# 16

# "Hear Your Evidence"

*THE KING AGAINST JOHN URY* packed city hall on Wednesday, July 29. Observing every formality, the king's men anticipated an unimpeachable trial. To insure they had everything letter-perfect, they reindicted and rearraigned Ury because of a misprint in one of the original charges. They wanted everything to appear correct and nothing left open to question. No other trial received the attention of this one, for Horsmanden and his colleagues intended to explain finally the full extent and nature of the conspiracy.[1]

Chief Justice DeLancey presided with Philipse and Horsmanden. Attorney General Bradley led the prosecution, assisted by four of the most seasoned and successful lawyers in the city—James Alexander, John Chambers, Joseph Murray, and William Smith. John Ury stood alone to defend himself.

The proceedings opened with the court clerk's hushing the audience and the cryer's intoning the ritual to invoke the king's authority and summon prospective jurors. After having Ury hold up his hand to identify himself as the prisoner on trial, the clerk declared: ''These good men that are now called and here appear are those which are to pass between you and our sovereign lord the king, upon your life or death; if you challenge any of them, you must speak as they come to the book to be sworn, and before they are sworn.''

Chief Justice DeLancey advised Ury of his rights of peremptory challenge and challenge for cause, but the man exercised no objection to the first twelve men called, and they became his jury.

"You, gentlemen of the jury, that are now sworn, look upon the prisoner and hearken to his charge," the clerk instructed. Then he unveiled the first of the prosecution's surprises: The king's men offered only one count in this trial, and it was neither for conspiracy nor for being an ecclesiastical person. Holding those charges in reserve for subsequent trials, if necessary, they submitted only that Ury with "malice aforethought, wickedly, maliciously, voluntarily, wilfully, and feloniously, did counsel, abet, procure and encourage the aforesaid negro man slave called [Roosevelt's] Quack . . . [to] set on fire and burn and wholly consume and destroy, against the peace of our said sovereign lord the king, his crown and dignity, . . . a certain dwelling house of our said lord the king, which then was standing and being at the fort in the said City of New York. . . . Upon this indictment he has been arraigned and hath pleaded thereunto *not guilty*, and for his trial hath put himself upon God and his country, which country you are. Your charge is to inquire whether he is guilty of the felony whereof he stands indicted or not guilty."

With the preliminaries finished, Attorney General Bradley opened the prosecution's argument and made it clear that although the king's men were using only the indictment of Ury as an accessory to arson, they intended to present a case against him as a conspirator and as an alien churchman.

"We shall produce to you the following evidence, to wit: That the prisoner was actually concerned in the plot to burn the king's house and this city and murder the inhabitants. That he has frequently been at Hughson's house, in company with Hughson, his wife and daughter, and Margaret Kerry, and with divers negroes, talking with them about the plot and counselling and encouraging them to burn the king's house and the town, and to kill and destroy the inhabitants. That the negro Quack, who burnt the king's house, was present at one or more of those times when the prisoner counselled and encouraged the negroes as aforesaid. That he advised them what would be the fittest time to set the English church on fire; and that the prisoner, as a popish priest, baptized Hughson, his wife and daughter, and Kerry, and also divers negroes, and told them then, and at several other times, that he could forgive sins, and that he forgave them their sins relating to the plot,'' Bradley told the jurors.

To fathom Ury's part and the plot itself, one needed only to see Ury clearly as an agent of Catholicism—''that murderous religion''—the attorney general said. ''The popish religion is such that they hold it not only lawful but meritorious to kill and destroy all that differ in opinion from them, if it may anyways serve the interest of their detestable religion. . . . The Church of Rome has artfully devised to get an absolute dominion over the consciences, that they may the more easily pick the pockets of credulous people. Witness the pretended pardons and indulgences of that crafty and deceitful church and their masses to pray souls out of purgatory, which they quote, or rather wrest, scripture for, when no such thing is to be found there. It is but a mere invention and cheat of their own to gull the laity of their money. Then they have their doctrine of transubstantiation, which is so big with absurdities that it is shocking to the common sense and reason of mankind. For were that doctrine true, their priests by a few words of their mouths, can make a God as often as they please. But then they eat him too, and this they have the impudence to call honoring and adoring him. Blasphemous wretches! For hereby they endeavor to exalt themselves above God himself, inasmuch as the creator must necessarily be greater than his creature. These and many other juggling tricks they have in their hocus-pocus, bloody religion,'' Bradley declared.[2]

He was putting Ury on trial along with disputed tenets of theology, and he was confident of the outcome. ''I make no doubt but you will, for your oaths sake and for your own country's peace and future safety, find him *guilty*,'' the attorney general emphasized his concluding word.

George Joseph Moore, the court clerk, was the first witness for the king's case. As he had done previously, he attested to Quack's confessing at the stake to setting fire to Fort George. Like the Hughsons and Peggy before him, Ury failed to object to the slave's words being entered against him in court. No doubt an objection was likely to be overruled, yet the point seemed worth making: Under the law, a slave's word was inadmissible in court against a white person. The fact of Moore's reporting the slave's words only thinly disguised the violation.[3]

Mary Burton was next on the stand. Questioned by Prosecutor Chambers, she repeated her stories of seeing Ury with the Hughsons, Peggy, and blacks. "They talked of the plot, burning the fort first, then the Fly, and then the dock. Upon some of the negroes saying they were afraid of being damned for being concerned in the plot, I heard Ury tell them they needn't fear doing it, for he could forgive them their sins as well as God Almighty," she recalled.

"You say you have seen me several times at Hughson's. What clothes did I usually wear?" Ury cross-examined.

"I cannot tell what clothes you wore particularly."

"That's very strange, and know me so well."

"I've seen you in several clothes, but you chiefly wore a riding coat and often a brown coat trimmed with black," Mary rejoined, not to be outdone.

"I never wore any such coat," Ury countered. "What time of the day did I use to come to Hughson's?"

"You use chiefly to come in the nighttime, and when I've been going to bed I've seen you undressing in Peggy's room, as if you were to lie there. But I cannot say that you did, for you were always gone before I was up in the morning."

"What answer did the negroes make when I offered to forgive them their sins, as you said?"

"I don't remember," the girl sulked. Ury appeared satisfied and let her step down. His tactic of pressing for specifics was clear; it was also dangerous, for aiming simply to make logical points on gaps in the testimony ignored two essential facts: First, emotion rather than reason dominated the real charge against Ury, and second, disproving the testimony of the king's witnesses was not the same as proving his innocence.

The soldier William Kane replaced Mary on the stand and told the court, "I know the prisoner very well. I've seen him at Croker's, at Coffin's, and Hughson's, and particularly with Daniel Fagan, Jerry Corker, and Plummer [Thomas Plumstead], and several negroes at Hughson's. . . . Ury and Corker endeavored to persuade me to be a Roman Catholic. Ury said it was best to be a Roman, they could forgive sins for anything ever so bad. . . . Ury wanted to christen me, but I wouldn't. He wouldn't speak to me nor before me for a long time, for he couldn't abide me because I refused to become Roman, till after he knew that I was concerned in the plot, and even then, he didn't much care for me."

Testifying further that Ury baptized a baby at the peddler John Coffin's house and that he talked about burning Trinity

Church, the soldier pictured the man completely as a Catholic priest and then sketched him in the plot at Hughson. "Ury was present at Hughson's when John Hughson swore me and his father and brothers into the plot. Quack was there and forty or fifty negroes [were] there at the same time. We were to burn the town and destroy the people. . . . Ury was near me when I was sworn, and the Hughsons and I took him to be one of the head[men]. . . . Ury was by when Hughson swore eight negroes into the plot, in a ring, and it was then talked among them of burning the fort. Quack, who was present, was at that time pitched upon to do it," Kane concluded.

Ury cross-examined, using virtually the same questions he had asked of Mary—when and where he was at Hughson's, what he wore, and what he said. He in no way suggested he had not been at Coffin's or Hughson's.

Kane's quick tongue was ready with answers that made Ury's questions sound as if they called for confirmation of indisputable facts. Indeed, when Ury asked, "What did I offer in order to induce you to become a Roman Catholic?" the soldier replied with a touch of mockery, "Forgiveness of all my sins past and what I'd do in this case. And I said to you, 'What a fine thing it is to be of such a religion, when a priest can forgive sins and send one to Heaven.'"

The prosecution then called Sarah Hughson.

"I except against her being sworn, for she has been convicted and received sentence of death for being concerned in this conspiracy and, therefore, cannot be a witness," Ury objected, knowing the law prohibited felons from testifying.[4]

"But, Mr. Ury, she has received his majesty's most gracious pardon, which she has pleaded in court this morning, and it has been allowed of and, therefore, the law says she is good evidence," Attorney General Bradley countered, citing an appropriate text to bolster this surprise planned by the king's men.

"Her pardon has been pleaded and allowed, and by law she may be admitted," Chief Justice DeLancey overruled Ury's objection.

"Sarah, give the court and the jury an account of what you know of Ury's being concerned in this conspiracy," Prosecutor Chambers directed.

"I know him and have often seen him at my father's, late in last fall chiefly. I've seen him there at nights in company with negroes, when they've been talking of burning the town and killing the white people. I've seen him make a ring with chalk on the floor, which he made the negroes stand round and put their left foot in. He swore them with a cross in his hand, to burn and destroy the town and to cut their masters and mistresses' throats. . . . He asked me to swear to the plot, and said I'd have all my sins forgiven if I kept all secret. He swore me on an English book. My parents and Peggy were by, and he swore Peggy too. I heard him tell her that all the sins which she'd committed should be forgiven her; and he told her that priests could forgive sins as well as God, if they'd follow their directions. He used to christen negroes there. He christened Caesar, Quack, and other negroes, crossed them on the face, had water and other things, and he told them he'd absolve them from all their sins.''

Judge Horsmanden applauded Sarah's testimony. ''The behavior of this miserable wretch was, upon this occasion, beyond expectation. She was composed and decent and seemed to be touched with remorse and compunction. What came from her was delivered with all the visible marks and semblance of sincerity and truth, insomuch that the court, jury, and many of the audience looked upon her at this instant to be under real conviction of mind for her past offences—which was somewhat surprising to those who were witnesses to the rest of her conduct since her condemnation and several reprieves,'' he later commented.

The judge failed to note any inconsistencies in the testimony— where Sarah either contradicted previous witnesses or her own earlier statements. For example, Sarah claimed Ury drew the reported chalk circle, but Kane suggested the girl's father had done it. Also, the girl previously claimed Ury swore her and the soldier at the same time, but Kane testified that Hughson swore him to the plot. Further, Sarah testified to details she never mentioned before.

Horsmanden insisted that Sarah simply remembered the facts. He denied that ''there could have been any confabulation'' between Sarah and the soldier, because ''Sarah was underground before and all the time Kane had been committed . . . nor could Mary Burton have intercourse with either.'' To the judge's mind, the servant girl, the soldier, and Sarah's testimony confirmed each others' word because they simply spoke the truth, proving the king's case. He dismissed all contrary evidence.

Ury picked at none of the inconsistencies and cross-examined Sarah in the same fashion he used with Mary and Kane, starting by asking, "How did I swear you?"

"On a book. I believe it was an English book."

"Who was present when I swore you?"

"My parents, Peggy, Kane, and others."

"You say I baptized several people. Pray, what ceremony did I use at baptizing?"

"When you baptized the negroes, you made a cross upon their faces and sprinkled water, and you used something else, but I cannot tell what, and you talked in a language which I didn't understand."

"Whom did I baptize?"

"Caesar, Prince, Bastian, Quack, Cuffee, and several other negroes," Sarah answered, and Ury let her go. He appeared to be simply eliciting information. He challenged nothing, denied nothing. He let the answers stand as facts.

Prosecutor Joseph Murray then rose and offered another surprise from the king's men, introducing as an exhibit a letter from General James Oglethorpe, governor of Georgia. "I only offer this by way of inducement and illustration of what is strictly evidence, and what I think by law I may. It is to show in general that there was a plot," Murray explained and cited precedent.

"Mr. Murray, you must prove that signing to be General Oglethorpe's hand," Chief Justice DeLancey noted, and the prosecutor presented the proof of signature. The court accepted the letter and had it read.

*Frederica, in Georgia, May 16, 1741*

To the honorable George Clarke, Esq.

Lieutenant Governor of New York

Sir—A party of our Indians returned the eighth instant from war against the Spaniards. They had an engagement with a party of Spanish horse, just by [St.] Augustine [on the Atlantic coast, about seventy miles below the St. Mary's River which served as a disputed border between Spanish Florida and English Georgia]. And [they] brought one [Spaniard] prisoner to me. He gives me an account of three Spanish sloops and a snow—privateers who are sailed from Augustine to the northward, for the provision vessels bound from the northward to the West Indies, hoping thereby to supply themselves with flour, of which they are in want. Besides this account which he gave to me, he mentioned many particulars in his examination before the magistrates.

Some intelligence I had of a villainous design of a very extraordinary nature and, if true, very important, viz. that the Spaniards had employed emissaries to burn all the magazines and considerable towns in the English North America, thereby to prevent the subsisting of the great expedition and fleet in the West Indies. And for this purpose, many priests were employed who pretended to be physicians, dancing masters, and other such kinds of occupations, and under that pretence to get admittance and confidence in families. As I could not give credit to these advices, since the thing was too horrid for any prince to order, I asked [the prisoner] concerning them, but he would not own he knew anything about them.

> I am, sir,
> your very humble servant,
> James Oglethorpe

The prosecution argued that the letter indicated a grand Spanish design to burn places such as Fort George, using priests in disguise for the mission—the basic notion of the king's case against Ury.[5]

"Mr. Murray, have you any more witnesses?" the chief justice asked, after the letter was duly entered into the court record without objection from Ury.

"We shall rest here at present," the prosecutor informed the court.

⛓⛓⛓⛓⛓

Ury started his defense with a prepared statement, evidently thinking he had the same opportunity as the prosecution to offer an opening argument. But he was cut short.

"If you have any witnesses to examine, it is more proper you should do that now and make your defense afterwards," Chief Justice DeLancey advised.

Ury yielded to the rebuke without protesting and called to the stand John Croker, owner of The Fighting Cocks coffeehouse and inn.[6]

"As I have lodged at your house for some time, you can best give an account of my manner of life and conversation. And, pray, first inform the king's judges and the jury if you ever saw any negroes come after me?''

''I never saw any negroes come after you,'' Croker answered and proceeded to report that Ury had first come to his inn in the summer of 1739 and stayed for a week before returning to teach in Burlington, New Jersey. Ury visited Croker's again in November 1740 and talked of moving on shortly, but Croker said he persuaded Ury to stay as a tutor for his son, paying him with room and board. Ury picked up Colonel Henry Beekman's daughter and Richard Norwood's children as students also; his classes in reading, writing, and Latin grew enough for schoolmaster John Campbell to take him in as a partner in April 1741.[7]

Croker testified that Ury had kept decent hours and spent most evenings alone in his room; the only nights he spent out were during a spring visit to New Jersey: That contradicted Mary Burton's saying Ury was often at Hughson's late at night. He noted that Ury was hired to preach in Staten Island once and sometimes shut himself in his room with a lighted candle in the daytime—which he thought was odd. But as for the man's being a priest, Croker said he had seen or heard no evidence of Catholicism or secret ceremonies. And as for reports of Ury's offering to save blacks from their sins, Croker said it sounded unlikely because Ury insisted blacks were not what he called ''proper objects of salvation.''

The attorney general pressed Croker under cross-examination but succeeded in squeezing out only an admission that Ury came home a few times around midnight and that the innkeeper was away from home for a day or two and, thus, could not say where Ury spent those nights. Bradley pushed also about Ury's reported preaching, and Croker recalled hearing Ury once. But what he reported made the king's men frown, for he said, ''In his prayer before sermon, he prayed for His Majesty King George [II] and all the royal family.'' The mention of Ury's praying for the sovereign by name was, Horsmanden noted, ''beyond what any other witness says, and contrary to Ury's own pretended principles as a nonjuror.'' Croker was dismissed.

The carpenter Joseph Webb took the witness stand and recounted his hiring Ury to tutor his son and his inviting Ury for meals and conversation at his home. He cast Ury as a serious, religious man, but certainly not a Catholic nor a person who trafficked with blacks.

Bradley challenged Webb's testimony, particularly on Ury's religion. The carpenter confirmed that he accompanied Ury to a confectioner's to buy wafers and that he had heard Ury talk about sacraments. He also admitted to building Ury a stand the king's men were calling an altar, but he cast it as a simple table or desk. "It was two pieces of boards which formed a triangle and was raised against the wall, at the bottom of which was a shelf. On each side there was a place to hold a candle," Webb said.

"Do you think if a man wanted a shelf or other place to lay a book on to read or set a bottle or glass on, he would make it in that form?" Bradley taunted.

"I can't say. People may have odd humors," Webb retorted.

The attorney general continued, pressing for a crack in the image Webb built for the defense, but the carpenter held steady on a final probe about blacks and responded, as he had before, by quoting Ury as saying, "Negroes are of a slavish nature. It is the nature of them to be slaves. Give them learning, do them all the good you can and put them beyond the condition of slaves and, in return, they will cut your throats." The prosecution had no further use for the carpenter.

John Campbell and his wife, Alice, then testified in turns. Campbell said he never knew Ury to have visited Hughson's. "I never saw him there till I went to take possession of the house at May Day last. And, then, as we were going there together, he said he didn't know the way thither. When we came down, he took Gerardus Comfort's house for it. As for anything else, I know nothing more of him, for I took him for a grave, sober, honest man."

"Sarah Hughson swore and curse at me," Mrs. Campbell said, recalling the scene when she, her husband, and Ury went to move in and found Hughson's daughters still occupying the house although they had lost their lease.

"How dare you talk so impertinently and saucily to an old woman, you impudent hussy! Go out of the house or I'll turn you out," Ury told the girl.

"You've a house now, but shan't have one long," she retorted.

"Sarah then swore miserably," Mrs. Campbell recalled. Clearly thankful for Ury's intervention, she ended her testimony with a few kind notes by saying, "I've often heard him pray and sing psalms, and he prayed by a sick woman. I never saw any harm by him. My husband and he were to keep school together.''

The prosecution did not bother cross-examining the Campbells. Instead, Attorney General Bradley called for rebuttal witnesses on the issue of Ury's religion.

Schoolteacher Joseph Hildreth came forward. ''What I have to say, sir, I have committed to writing,'' he told Bradley, showing himself clearly prepared for the questions.

''You must not read the paper, but you may look into it to refresh your memory,'' Chief Justice DeLancey cautioned.

Stealing glances at his notes then, Hildreth recited lengthy detail about his acquaintance with Ury since first hearing of him in February 1741, when Joseph Webb asked if he were interested in ''a good sober sort'' for a partner to teach English, Greek and Latin. He did not know who Webb was referring to then, but he rejected the idea. ''I'm inclined to be master of my own school alone, though it's not so large as if I had a partner,'' Hildreth explained. He met Ury about eight weeks after Webb's approach. They had coffee together and discussed their classes, teaching methods, and readings.

Hildreth described Ury as secretive and unconventional in his thinking. He recalled Ury's having a book on the 117th psalm at their first meeting but not letting him examine even its title page to see who wrote it or where and when it was published. He thought that odd and said his suspicions about Ury grew during their later conversations about religion.

Once the two men privately debated an exchange between two prominent English evangelists, the Reverends George Whitefield and John Wesley, on the source of the grace mankind required for salvation. Wesley, a founder of Methodism, pushed the idea of free grace, and Whitefield, who preached heavily in America during the colonies' Great Awakening, held to the idea of predestination and, also, favored treating blacks as objects of salvation.

''Ury believed it was through the great encouragement the negroes had received from Mr. Whitefield we had all the disturbance and that he believed Mr. Whitefield was more of a Roman [Catholic] than anything else; and he believed he came abroad with no good design,'' Hildreth claimed. The king's men thought it significant that Ury's reported comment attributed not only a religious element, but a Catholic connection, to the plot. They ignored Ury's sounding critical of the connection.[8]

Hildreth reported, as Webb had, that Ury professed himself a nonjuror. "I asked him what was the signification of a nonjuror, as I understood he pretended to be, and he answered that they would not take the oath of allegiance, as he did not. I asked him why? He says, 'Can you swear one to be a bastard? No, no more can they say King James was one. The difference between we nonjurors and others is this: We, in the prayers for the king and royal family, mention no names, as they do.' I asked him if they prayed for the pretender? He said, 'For him, let him be who he will, that was the king.' He mentioned no names," Hildreth said.

The king's men picked a hint of treason out of Ury's reported refusal to take the oath of allegiance, and they welcomed Hildreth's testifying that Ury said, "You talk so much against popery. I believe though you speak so much against it, you will find you have, or I think you will have, a pope in your belly. The absolution of the Church of Rome is not half so bad as that of the Church of England at the visitation of the sick." Horsmanden construed the comment as Ury's approving of the Catholics' practice of confession.

Hildreth stressed the idea of Ury's having a Catholic connection. "I observed several times he said, 'we priests,'" he told the court and added that Ury admitted to baptizing a child in the city. He reported also that Ury kept wafers in a locked box in his room. He had seen them himself, eaten one, and heard Ury talk of transubstantiation, the Catholic belief in wafer and wine being turned into the body and blood of Christ during the Mass—one of the beliefs Attorney General Bradley had ridiculed as absurd. Hildreth recalled Ury's saying that "the wafer is more pure and no bread [is] pure enough to represent the body of our Lord" and admitting that the stand in his room was an altar.

Ury held private services at Hughson's—after the Campbells took the house, Hildreth said. He reported attending one service where Ury preached about false prophets and heresies, taking his text from St. Peter's Second Epistle, verses 1–3. He implied that Ury's message followed the line of there being only one true church—an essential, Catholic idea. He noted also that Ury argued against predestination and salvation by faith, beliefs held by many Protestants but rejected by Catholics.[9]

Hildreth finished his testimony with a further insinuation of Ury's having a Catholic connection. Corroborating Webb's recollections, he said Ury announced as the text for his next sermon

Matthew 16:18–19 and John 20:23. Hildreth had not heard that sermon, but his recalling the texts was enough for the king's men as both sets of verses were well connected to Catholic beliefs. The first contained the line, "thou art Peter, and upon this rock I will build my church," on which the popes based their authority and the belief in there being one, true church. The second was the line, "Whose soever sins ye remit, they are remitted unto them, and whose soever sins ye retain, they are retained," on which Catholic based their sacrament of penance—the forgiving of sins that Ury was accused of preaching.

Attorney General Bradley was clearly delighted by Hildreth's testimony, for in his mind it cast ample and sinister light on Ury, and he was almost taunting when he turned the witness over for cross-examination.

Ury ignored the baiting and let his rival schoolteacher leave the stand without a single question.

The prosecution called Richard Norwood who had hired Ury in December 1740 to teach his children to read and write but had not been pleased with Ury's services. "In conversation with him, he talked in such a manner that I suspected him to be a popish priest. He used very often to miss coming to teach my children at the school time, and made frivolous excuses. At last, I was very angry with him and discharged him," Norwood explained.

Ury's missing classes had irked Norwood to the point of thinking about checking on his whereabouts. Norwood said he was particularly suspicious of Ury's excusing himself in the evenings to visit a sick person who lived near Trinity Church. "I had often a mind to have dogged him, to have seen where he went. I don't know how it happened, but I never did," Norwood told the court. Considering the current charges, he sounded apologetic for not checking if Ury really had visited the sick or Hughson's, which was off Broadway, near the church.

Norwood said he had not been alone in suspecting Ury's behavior. "One day I met Campbell the schoolmaster in the street. He said to me, 'What do you think? Webb has taken away his son from me and has put him in a schoolmaster that lodges at Croker's.' Campbell said, 'Damn him, he's a popish priest.' At last, having a bad opinion of him, I discharged him—lest he should inveigle my children. I told him I'd have nothing more to say to him."

Ury let Norwood go, like Hildreth, without cross-examination. He made no objection to the picture of professional delinquency or to the jealous sounding words reported from Campbell before the two became partners.

That concluded the testimony.

❊❊❊❊❊

Prosecutors Joseph Murray and William Smith asked and received the court's permission to enter a few remarks before summation, in effect preempting Ury's turn to make his defense summation immediately after the rebuttal witnesses and, also, giving the prosecution a double chance at summation.

"That the prisoner is a Romish emissary sent according to the intimation in General Oglethorpe's letter, I think must be concluded from what has been given in evidence," Murray asserted. Smith repeated the assertion and emphasized particular points of Catholic belief and the ceremonies of baptism and absolution, which he said the king's witnesses had related to Ury. "This is all that we shall mention at present, that if the prisoner pleases, he may take notice of them in his defense and show, if he can, that he had another warrant than the Church of Rome for the like practices proved by the witnesses," Smith finished.

Ury had his chance now to make his defense. Reading a statement he wrote before the trial, he told the court that "It is very incongruous to reason, to think, that I can have any hand or be anyway concerned in this plot, if these things be duly weighed."

As if lecturing a class in elementary logic, Ury began with a series of rhetorical propositions. If he were guilty as charged, would he have remained in town and advertised his presence by calling for students after the plot seemed crushed by the mass arrest of blacks and John Hughson's conviction? His friend Webb and attorney Chambers had warned him in June, before his arrest, that he was suspected of being a priest and connected with the plot, he said. "I answered my innocency would protect me and I valued not what the world said."

If he had encouraged Roosevelt's Quack to burn the fort, why had Quack not named him in his confession, as he had named Hughson and others? If he were a priest and chief conspirator as alleged, would not Hughson, his wife, Peggy, or any of the executed blacks have named him to save themselves? "Doubtless, they would have been eager to have betrayed me when the scheme was discovered. . . . If I had been engaged, they would have soon informed, thinking to have saved their own lives, knowing how this government stands [towards priests]. . . . All that have been put to death did not once name me," Ury noted. Then he declared, "I never knew or saw Hughson, his wife, or the creature [Peggy] that was hanged with them to my knowledge—living, dying, or dead—or the negro that is said to have fired the fort, excepting in his last moments."

If he had frequented Hughson's as alleged, would he have argued with Sarah Hughson as he did when he went with the Campbells to move into the house? And even if he had frequented Hughson's, would his mere presence there mean he was in the conspiracy? "Is it reasonable to think that all or any man being seen at Hughson's must make him or them culpable or chargeable with his villainy?" Ury queried, hitting at the idea of guilt by association and noting that Hughson's was a place open to the public.

"All this trouble of mine springs from and is grounded upon the apprehensions of my being a Roman priest and, therefore, must be a plotter—some believing there can be no mischief in a country but a priest, if there, must be in it," Ury noted. But thinking him a priest was absurd, particularly on the face of the evidence against him, he suggested.

"I stand charged with being an ecclesiastic person made by authority from the See of Rome, that I have celebrated masses, given absolutions, and that I have acknowledged myself to be a priest of the Church of Rome: All of that cannot be and is not proved. As to my professing myself to be an ecclesiastic of the Church of Rome, it is very improbable, if it be considered that no gentlemen who is a priest would be so childish as to tell any person out of communion that he is a priest," Ury said.

Showing he knew something of Catholic practice, Ury then described the rites he was accused of performing and indicated that the witnesses against him had not known what they were talking about. "Now, how come these persons to know so much, to be acquainted with priests and their secrets, who know not what mass is nor what the difference of a vesper from a compline or a compline from a nocturn, nor the hours of mass?" he asked in a dig at the witnesses.[10]

"As to my books and writings, I cannot be deemed a Roman Catholic, either a spiritual person or laic. I believe it cannot with reason be concluded that a person having a mass book in possession must, therefore, be a papist. If so, a man having the Alcoran must be a Mahometan and a Presbyterian with a Book of Common Prayer must, from thence, be a [Anglican] churchman. But I believe that will not be allowed by any," Ury contended, referring to parts of his diary and notes uncovered by the king's men. Besides, he said, Parliament had declared in the case of Algernon Sidney that a person's private papers were unreasonable proofs in the case of conspiracy.

"Gentlemen, the mistake the major part of the world lies under is their apprehending that a nonjuring priest must be a popish priest, whereas there is no truer Protestants: For they are far from having any regard to a pretender or for setting on the throne a popish prince to be head of a Protestant church. The doctrines they assert and stand by is nonresistance and passive obedience, which is now as vigorously maintained as ever it was in any reign. I believe that there is no nonjuror, either clergy or laity, but would show themselves such true subjects to the present King George as to take the oaths of allegiance and supremacy," Ury declared in defense of his own religious beliefs.

"I have now no more to say, but hope and pray that what has been offered will be considered with minds unprejudiced, minds prepossessed with no opinions, with minds in a diligent search after truth. You [are] gentlemen, I hope, [who believe in] fearing God, reverencing conscience, hating partiality, lov[ing] truth and innocency, and having a tender regard to life," Ury closed, his eyes and hopes resting on the jury.

William Smith then delivered the prosecution's summation and assured the jury that the conspiracy was finally and fully fathomed. "The secret springs of this mischief lay long concealed . . . [and] opened by slow degrees. But now, gentlemen, we have at length great reason to conclude that it took its rise from a foreign influence and that it originally depended upon causes that we ourselves little thought of," he said.

"The monstrous wickedness of this plot would probably among strangers impeach its credit; but if it be considered as the contrivance of the public enemy and the inhuman dictate of a bloody religion, the wonders cease," Smith declared. Launching a history lecture on the bloodshed in the Protestant Reformation and in England's religious fratricide, he called the Catholic church "the scarlet whore" and revived the images of Guy Fawkes, the Glorious Revolution in England, and New York City's calamities of March and April.[11]

"Gentlemen, if the evidence you have heard is sufficient to produce a general conviction that the late fires in this city and the murderous design against its inhabitants are the effects of a Spanish and popist plot, then the mystery of this iniquity—which has so long puzzled us—is unveiled and our admiration ceases. All the mischiefs we have suffered or been threatened with are but a sprout from that evil root, a small stream from that overflowing fountain of destruction that has often deluged the earth with slaughter and blood and spread ruin and desolation far and wide," the prosecutor told the jury.

"The principle point in this trial is to prove the prisoner was an accessory to the burning of the king's house in the fort," Smith said, finally mentioning the specific indictment. But he did not pause on the evidence. Continuing his anti-Catholic play against Ury, he concluded simply: "If you find also that he is a Roman priest, . . . of that corrupt and apostate church whereof he is a member, all that the witnesses have declared against him is the more easy to be believed. Gentlemen, I shall add no more but leave you to the direction of the court and your own consciences."

Chief Justice DeLancey charged the jury, and the twelve men retired to reach the verdict.

❦❦❦❦❦

Ury had asked for the jurors to weigh the case against him without bias. Repeatedly using the word *if*, he had asked for the men to follow his logic. He had offered few facts, except in displaying his detailed knowledge of Catholic ceremonies, and there he was, perphaps, too wise for his own good. He had swallowed the prosecution's line with its religious baiting and not snapped at the fact that the trial was—as Prosecutor Smith's summation conceded in a single, brief sentence—on the charge of accessory to arson. Ury saw he was doomed unless he shook the hook of popery. Yet he left the jurors to their own wits in sorting out issues that easily demanded a jury of theologians.

Ury proved no match for the king's men in courtroom skills although he was clearly the most educated and articulate of all those tried in the proceedings and had shown a sense of the fine points of argument. The question was had he had been too fine? Had he pressed hard enough on the burden of proving himself innocent? He had been weak in examining witnesses. Certainly his attempts to trip up Kane, Mary Burton, and Sarah Hughson were feeble, and he had not confronted Hildreth or Norwood at all. Ury had laid his defense on simple reason, but the prosecutors had played on strong emotion, arguing *ad hominem* and asking *if* questions where the jurors were likely to suppose only what they already believed.

Ury seemed truly to believe that, as he said, "innocency would protect me." And perhaps he intended to show his good faith by not challenging prospective jurors, but his accepting the first twelve to sit loomed as blind faith. Only one of the men had shown any previous sign of opposition to the proceedings: That man was Gerardus Beekman who had testified in Quack's behalf during the first conspiracy trial, back on May 29. He was a brother of Colonel Beekman, whose daughter Ury had tutored, and this was his first as a trial juror during the conspiracy prosecution. It was also the first for three others on the jury. But the remaining eight jurors had served in earlier trials—all more than once and one man five times. Certainly Ury had cause to challenge those men: In every case they had returned guilty verdicts.[12]

As if to confirm a fundamental error in Ury's judgment, his jury deliberated about fifteen minutes and returned its verdict: Guilty.

The date was July 29.

# 17

## "Called Up to Judgment"

HORSMANDEN AND HIS COLLEAGUES of the bench and bar accepted the guilty verdict against Ury as the ultimate justification of their proceedings against the reported conspiracy. Indeed, the king's men viewed their case against the man as the final answer to questions nagging New York City since Fort George's burning on March 18. By and large, the townsfolk also accepted the verdict and the officials' view of it. Thus, Ury's fate seemed sealed even before his sentencing by Chief Justice DeLancey on Tuesday, August 4.[1]

Death was the punishment prescribed by law for conviction as an accessory to arson, and that was the sentence requested by the prosecution. Resigned to his end, Ury offered no objection to Attorney General Bradley's motion for death and requested only that the court allow him time to settle his affairs.

The chief justice rendered the final judgment. Summarizing the case made by the king's men, he left no doubt about his own view of Ury as a priest engaged in what he called, ''the dangerous and pernicious tendency of the doctrines of the Church of Rome which embolden her disciples to embark in the most hazardous, wicked, and inhumane enterprises.'' He exhorted Ury to confess publicly and gave him eleven days to live, scheduling him to hang on Saturday, August 15.

With Ury convicted and condemned as the chief conspirator and a final solution to the puzzle of the March and April fires and the reports of seditious talk at Hughson's in hand, the king's men turned to close their proceedings after nearly four months. Looking now to clear away the remaining pieces, the officials made their first order of business disposing of the jailed blacks, and they began by indicting and arraigning Murray's Adam, Carpenter's Tickle, Livingston's Tom, and Niblet's Sandy for conspiracy.

The four pleaded guilty and put themselves at the mercy of the court. They sat then in the position of many before them—fellow slaves whom they helped convict and send to the gallows or the stake, by turning king's evidence. They had talked in hope of saving themselves, and now their time of truth had come.

Sandy's first words to the grand jury suggested his fear that even if he talked and served the whites' purposes, they would kill him as they had killed other blacks who confessed in the past. The boy could only wait and see if the king's men honored their promise to pardon him. In the meantime, he had to wonder why they made him plead if they intended to keep their word to him and those like him.

Horsmanden and his colleagues were not completely agreed on how to handle the blacks, but they were agreed on having the legal record clear about who had been implicated and how. So they issued fresh arrest warrants to bring in blacks who had been named during the proceedings but not yet jailed. The city's constables went as far as Brooklyn to search for four black men, three of whom they captured and delivered to city hall. But the officials showed no intention of prosecuting more blacks; they acted as if they wanted simply to record the arrests, to show that no suspect at hand had escaped them. If fact, that was part of the reason Sandy and his three fellows were made to plead; the larger reason was to establish their crime and guilt, for only then were they eligible for pardon. And the king's men did agree that pardons were to be the order of the day for most of the blacks.

Governor Clarke issued the writs. The conditions were that, in Horsmanden's legal terms, "The persons pardoned should be transported to the dominion of some foreign prince or state, or the island of Newfoundland. And if any of the negroes or slaves should at any time after be found in any of his majesty's dominions, except Newfoundland, the letters patent as to all and every person and persons so found will be null, void, and of no force or effect." In simple language, the pardoned blacks were to be shipped off and stand liable to execution if ever found on English soil again. Thus, an exodus started.[2]

Seventy-two slaves received pardon. Twenty-seven of them were banished to Madeira, the largest in the group of five Portuguese islands off the coast of Morocco. Twenty-six went to Hispaniola, the large Caribbean island between Cuba and Puerto Rico: Seventeen of these, including Niblet's Sandy, were placed on the eastern side of the island, in what became the Dominican Republic; nine went to Cape François on the western side that became Haiti. Five went to Curaçoa, the largest island of the Netherland Antilles in the West Indies. Three were sent north to Newfoundland. Four of the five condemned Spanish blacks were spared execution: Three were sent to the Spanish West Indies and the fourth to the Dutch island of Statia in the Caribbean. One slave was shipped to Portugal. The remaining six embarked without a recorded destination.[3]

Thirty-three jailed blacks were simply released to their owners, to slave as before. Most of these blacks had never been indicted, but a few like Hermanus Wendover's Toby had been convicted and condemned to death. They escaped execution because of their owner's influence, bonds to assure their future good behavior, and the new grand jury's decision that the evidence against them was weak. Horsmanden scowled and warned that these slaves "were enemies of their own household."

The judge received perhaps a bit of satisfaction in settling the score against one condemned black, for the court ordered the execution of Juan de la Sylva, who alone remained of the five convicted Spanish blacks. All four of his mates—like Antonio de la Cruz, whom Chief Justice DeLancey's brother Peter held as a slave—were among those banished. None of them had faced the same animosity as Juan, because he stood condemned for lighting fires at the Fly Market and at Ben Thomas's and Agnes Hilton's homes, which flanked his holder Jacob Sarly's house. The neighbors had seized Juan in April for the obvious acts of arson. The judges decided the evidence against him was too strong to ignore.[4]

Juan went to his death on Saturday, August 15. Ury also was scheduled to die that same morning, but Governor Clarke accepted the man's petition for a stay. Thus, Juan alone visited the gallows, and Horsmanden reported with apparent approval that "He was neatly dressed in a white shirt, jacket, drawers [i.e. long, tight pants], and stockings. He behaved decently, prayed in Spanish, kissed a crucifix and insisted on his innocence to the last.''

⛓⛓⛓⛓⛓

Ury's lingering presence enlivened questions about his character and the character of the grand conspiracy portrayed by the prosecution; and as skeptics increased their muttering against the proceedings, Horsmanden and his colleagues labored to reassure everyone that justice had been done, not only in Ury's case but in all the trials.[5]

The majority of the city folk backed the pronouncements of the king's men, for labelling Ury a Catholic priest and sticking him at the center of the talk of burning and looting and killing satisfied the popular desire to replace fears of the unknown with an explanation that fit the image of the world as most New Yorkers and their neighbors believed it to be. All the proceedings, in fact, reflected the prevailing psychology that assigned an evil cause to all misfortune.[6]

For the like-minded citizenry, the evidence of the reported plot's reality had fallen into place, piece by piece, from the first bits offered by Mary Burton to the full testimony at Ury's trial. The flames of late winter and early spring were beyond doubt. Everyone in town saw the rash of blazes—ten of which occurred within five days. The remnants of Fort George and other gutted structures still lay as visible reminders that the fires were facts.

The signs of arson were clear in several places: the two straw beds heaped in Thomas's loft; the tow wedged into Hilton's wall; the hay piled to the roof at Quick and Vergereau's stable in the Fly; and the coals in Murray's haystack, with a trace of embers outside.

The slaves' confessions clinched the case of arson for the people. Roosevelt's Quack admitted to setting the fort on fire. Philipse's Cuff owned the blaze at the Philipse storehouse. Sleydall's Jack confessed to putting the coals at Murray's. Peck's Caesar acknowledged that he and Gomez's Cuffee torched Van Zant's warehouse.

Griffith Evans's charred corpse was also a fact that people remembered as they thought back on the fires, particularly the holocaust at the fort which claimed the soldier's life and threatened the whole town. The thefts accompanying the blazes were real, and

226

there was no question that Vaarck's Caesar and Auboyneau's Prince burglarized Hogg's or that John Hughson and his wife and Peggy handled the loot. Massive gatherings of blacks at Hughson's were not in doubt either, because the constables had broken up such groups at the tavern.

The mutinous talk attributed to Irish soldiers at Hughson's surprised few citizens. Continual troubles with the constables, townspeople, and the troopers' desertion rate cast them as naturals for the roles in which the prosecutors put them. And the talk reported from black mouths—talk of wanting to be free and of revenging themselves on holders—fit the popular fears about slaves. The accusations of arson and theft also fit the profile of blacks in the city's records which showed such crimes to be among those most frequently committed by slaves. The fact of the slave uprising in 1712, which left nearly two dozen white men killed or maimed, reinforced the popular belief in a conspiracy to do the same in 1741.[7]

The people who looked at the general pattern without closely examining the particular threads readily accepted the prosecution's design. Even the few who had doubts did not challenge the authenticity of motives. They accepted the angry talk by slaves and soldiers and the eagerness of fortuneless whites, such as Hughson, to grab more for themselves.

The doubtful worried that Horsmanden and his fellows had woven whole cloth from genuine pieces. Suspecting the prosecution of having stretched at almost every point to create a design of total death and destruction by blacks and their white accomplices, the doubters questioned if a grand conspiracy ever existed. What split the fabric, in the their view, was the king's men casting John Ury as the spying chief priest of a Spanish-Catholic conspiracy.

The doubts and questions enraged Horsmanden. Lambasting the skeptics and the few who dared openly to criticize the prosecution, he called them "wanton, wrongheaded persons . . . who took the liberty to arraign the justice of the proceedings and set up their private opinions in superiority to the court and grand jury, though God knows—and all men of sense know—they could not be judges of such matters. But, nevertheless, they declared with no small assurance—not withstanding what we *saw* with our eyes and *heard* with our ears, and everyone might have judged with his intellects, that had any—*that there was no plot at all*!" the judge emphasized derisively.[8]

Horsmanden hoped to settle the issue with facts he gathered from inquiries sent out when Ury was arrested, for the outlines of a test were developing from a single question: Who was John Ury? The overdrawn lines shaped the consequence of the answer simply: If Ury was a priest, then the conspiracy theory of the king's men was correct; and if he was no priest, the entire prosecution was wrong.

⛓⛓⛓⛓⛓

At Ury's arrest in June almost nobody in the city seemed to know him, but as controversy about him developed, people appeared suddenly to recall experiences with him. His manner was mimicked and his sermons were quoted. He became a shadowy folk figure. Children began to play games that mocked him in the caricature presented by their elders. A few persons with the influence to gain access visited the man in jail, to see him up close and personal, perhaps to have their own questions about him answered directly.

Ury allowed interviewers glimpses to broaden the popular view of his life, telling how he came from a once-comfortable English family that fell on hard times when his father died in the ruin resulting from the so-called South Sea Bubble. He said his father was a secretary in the South Sea Company founded in 1711 with a monopoly on trade with the South Seas and South America. The venture was a public stock corporation, and as its prospects for huge profits peaked in 1720, a surge of speculation sent the price of a share soaring from £128 to £1000. But the huge run up proved a fraud, and when that was discovered, the price plummeted and ruined many.[9]

The financial collapse virtually killed his father and left his family destitute, Ury said. A gentleman friend of the family took him in for rearing, and it was from this benefactor that he was exposed to the nonjurors. Ury confessed that later in life he suspected the gentleman of actually being a Jesuit—reputed by Protestants to be the most fanatic of Catholics—rather than a true nonjuror. But Ury insisted that his own faith was never corrupted and that after being educated at two universities, which he never named, he became a nonjuring clergyman associated with the prominent English nonconformist divine Samuel Clarke.[10]

Ury said he won a lucrative position as a rector, receiving £50 a year, and anticipated brightening his prospects by writing a book on church history and theology, but his writing proved his undoing. Like Sir Thomas More, the famed Catholic and Lord Chancellor of England sent to death by Henry VIII in 1535, Ury said he found himself in the Tower of London on account of King George II's censors construing his book as treasonous. Only the character and interest of his friends allowed him to escape death and flee to America.

Ury reported landing at Philadelphia, as his diary indicated, and said he had sought to make a living by putting his classical education to work. Emphasizing that he was no Catholic, he suggested that the misunderstanding of his religious views followed him to New York.

Horsmanden scoffed at Ury's account, which was clearly vague in places. While confirming that Ury's father was a secretary in the South Sea Company, the judge noted that his own inquiries contradicted much of Ury's story. He reported, for example, that the senior Ury was dismissed long before the bubble of 1720 and had neither profited from the boom nor been ruined in the collapse. The family never had much money and on the father's death was put in dire straits, indeed.

Ury was not taken in and educated by a gentleman; he worked as a messenger, never attended any university, and his ambition as a boy was to be a valet in service to some prominent person, Horsmanden reported from his unnamed sources. He quoted one—"a gentleman of distinguished worth and character in London"—as saying that he "never heard nothing of [Ury's] writing against the government, nor believed him capable of it, being without education."

The judge himself demeaned Ury's education by carping about the lack of grammar in the scribbled defense statement Ury had read in court. Pointing to misspellings and lack of punctuation, he cackled that "it may be remarked that those who were somewhat acquainted with the man were of the opinion he was not very capable." But Horsmanden's own writing was itself no model of clarity, and if grammar alone marked the educated, more than Ury were liable to be expelled from the class.

Neither Horsmanden nor his informants accounted for Ury's abilities in Greek and Latin. The man's performance in court, his conversations with Hildreth, and the sermons reported by Webb showed a degree of learning. Indeed, had Ury not demonstrated uncommon education, he might never have sat condemned as a priest versed in Catholic lore. The judge ignored that. He also ignored the fact that one of Ury's misspellings was Hewson for Hughson—which might have suggested that Ury really had not known the taverner. The judge further ignored the fact that the same source which he used to contradict Ury's autobiographical sketch noted that Ury "professed great religion, went often to worship with the dissenters, but always communicated with the Church of England."

People from Philadelphia who knew Ury, belatedly attested to his character and education, but none of the protests about the man's not being a Catholic moved Horsmanden. He seemed simply to emphasize what he wanted from the answers to his inquiries and to ignore the implications of what failed to fit with his own ideas—even though, to his credit, he dutifully noted the information that contradicted his own view. None of the searching exchange altered Ury's fate beyond the extension of his life for a few days.

⛓⛓⛓⛓⛓

John Ury mounted the gallows amid a throng of onlookers on the final weekend of August 1741, exactly one month after his trial. He stood meekly, unlike the haggling Hughson or the haughty Caesar. The carpenter Joseph Webb stood by him to the end, ready to preserve his last words, and Ury had more than a few, for he had prepared a final speech addressed to "Fellow Christians."

"In the presence of this God, the possessor of heaven and earth, I lift up my hands and solemnly protest I am innocent of what is laid to my charge. . . . I protest that the witnesses are perjured. I never knew the perjured witnesses but at my trial," Ury declared after invoking the image of Christ's execution and the chief priests and Pharisees' false witnesses.

"I have no more to say by way of clearing my innocence, knowing that to a true Christian of unprejudiced mind I must appear guiltless. . . . Indeed, it may be shocking to some serious Christians that the holy God should suffer innocence to be slain by the hands of cruel and bloody persons—I mean the witnesses who swore against me at my trial. Indeed, there may be reasons assigned for it, but as they may be liable to objections, I decline them and shall only say that this is one of the dark providences of the great God in His wise, just and good government of this lower earth.

"In fine, I depart this waste, this howling wilderness, with a mind serene, free from all malice, with a forgiving spirit—so far as the gospel of my dear and only redeemer obliges and enjoins me to—hoping and praying that Jesus, who alone is the giver of repentance, will convince, conquer and enlighten my murderers' souls that they may publicly confess their horrid wickedness before God and the world, so that their souls may be saved in the day of the Lord Jesus," Ury said. Concluding in the style of a revival minister, he added a final admonition.

"Oh, sinners, trifle no longer! Consider life hangs on a thread, here today and gone tomorrow. Forsake your sins ere ye be forsaken forever. Hearken, now is God awfully calling you to repent, warning you by me, his minister and prisoner, to embrace Jesus, to take, to lay hold on him for your alone savior in order to escape the wrath to come. No longer delay, seeing the summons may come before you are aware and you, standing before the bar of a God who is consuming fire out of the Lord Jesus Christ, should be hurled [and] be doomed to that place where their worm dies not and their fire is never quenched."

The swarming spectators hardly halted their buzzing during the speech. They had come to see Ury die, not to listen to him preach. Yet his martyr's look and his echo of St. Luke's gospel (23:34)—"Father, forgive them; for they know not what they do"—drew some to take in what he said and ponder a belated question: What truly had this man done?

The date was August 29.

# 18

## "Not Yet Out of Danger"

URY WAS SLATED to be the last to die, for none of the remaining prisoners sat under the death sentence. The grand jury had handed up no fresh indictments, and the prosecutors had not pushed for any more trials after his conviction. So as his corpse was cut down and carried away for burial, the parade to the gallows seemed at an end.[1]

Four whites and seventeen blacks had now been hanged, and thirteen blacks had been burned at the stake in connection with the plot. But Justice Horsmanden was not yet satisfied that he and his fellow officials had done enough. Stopping short of eradicating every hint of conspiracy seemed a retreat in the judge's view, and he was ready neither to stop or retreat; he wanted to finish what he had started to rid New York of all its troublesome blacks, their whites consorts, and others whom he considered "strangers and suspicious persons."[2]

Neither Chief Justice DeLancey nor Justice Philipse shared Horsmanden's desire. They were inclined—like the prosecutors, the grand jury, and the people at large—to do little more than quietly clear away the residue and wash their hands of the proceedings now that the full, official explanation of the plot had been validated by the verdict condemning Ury and sending him to his death.

When the Supreme Court convened on Monday, August 31, to dispose of the remaining prisoners, Horsmanden was left with little more to do than grumble. The task at hand promised only a few minutes' work, since the bulk of jailed blacks were already marked for banishment. There were simply a handful of whites remaining.[3]

John Corry was the first prisoner called for review. Jailed since July 13, when Mary Burton and William Kane fingered him as someone who frequented Hughson's and joined in talk of the plot, the young dancing master never wobbled in denying he visited the tavern or associated with those who had. The prosecutors produced no evidence of missteps; indeed, nobody other than Burton and Kane ever claimed Corry so much as teetered in the wrong direction. But gossip followed his arrest, and with Horsmanden's promise to glare at his every step, Corry was left in an awkward position although the judges discharged him. Harnessed with a lingering hint of suspicion, the dancing master faced exclusion from the social circles on which his livelihood depended. Only the roads leading out of the city looked inviting for him.

David Johnson was next in court. Jailed on the same day as Corry, the hatter sat accused of saying, "Damn me, but we'll burn the Dutch and get their money." That report came from Kane. Nobody else ever implicated Johnson in plotting at Hughson's, although tongues did wag about his scheming as a ladies' man and drinking heavily. Sobered, no doubt, by his seven weeks in a cell, Johnson was discharged to hang his hats elsewhere, according to Judge Horsmanden's suggestion.

John Coffin followed. Arrested on July 6, after Kane's account of Ury's baptizing a year-old child in Catholic fashion at Coffin's home and Coffin's visiting Hughson's, the peddler suffered from the cloud of suspected conspiracy and Romanism. Young Sarah Hughson claimed she heard the man named among her father's visitors as an accomplice in the plot, but she failed to recognize him in a line up, and when he was pointed out to her, she declared that she had never seen him at Hughson's. Thus, Kane's word stood alone against Coffin and he departed court. His eight week ordeal convinced him to peddle his wares away from the city.

Peter Connolly came next. Arrested on June 23, he was the first of the Irish soldiers seized as suspected Catholics and conspirators. Nobody linked him directly to the plot until Kane came to jail on July 4 and turned king's evidence, and still having only

Kane's word, the court dismissed Connolly on the assurance that military transfer would rid the province of him.

Edward Kelly, another of the soldiers, followed Connolly. Arrested on June 25, he sat in dire straits after Ward's Will implicated him while confessing at the stake; and when Kane decided to talk to save himself, Kelly seemed sunk. Will's execution left only Kane's word weighing against the soldier however, and the court discharged him to join the transfer list.

Private Edward Murphy joined the parade. Implicated by Kane for saying, "Damn me, if I won't lend a hand to the fires as soon as anybody," Murphy was jailed on July 8. Mary Burton quoted his saying much the same thing and accused him of trafficking in stolen rings and jewelry with the Hughsons. Young Sarah confirmed that he was one who frequented Hughson's. Having the word of three witnesses, Horsmanden was anxious to try Murphy, but the judge was isolated in this desire. The court released this soldier, too, for service elsewhere.

Andrew Ryan was the last of the jailed Irish soldiers in court. He was the target of suspicions because he lodged at Hughson's during part of the winter of 1740–1741. His wife Eleanor's testimony for the defense in the conspiracy trial of the Hughsons and Peggy helped none, and when the king's men discovered Ury's diary entry on the baptism of a baby surnamed Ryan, Horsmanden tried to close the web of conspiracy on the soldier and his wife. Mrs. Ryan was never jailed, but her husband was on July 9. Mary Burton then put the finger on the private, but nothing firm emerged, and the court sent Ryan packing with his wife and fellow troopers.

Much to Horsmanden's dismay, three implicated Irish soldiers disappeared shortly after the fire at the fort and, thus, escaped the sniping that caught the garrison regulars. Chief among them was Jerry Corker, whom Kane quoted as saying, "By God, I've a mind to burn the fort." Corker assisted the plumber at welding the gutter on Governor Clarke's roof the day it caught fire, and he was one of the men who reportedly talked of burning Trinity Church. Daniel Fagan, the second absent soldier, was implicated for being in the discussions of the blazes, but not even Kane recalled anything Fagan said before slipping away quietly. The third missing soldier was Thomas Plumstead: Judy Pelham implicated him for saying, shortly before the fort burned, "There'll be bloody times in York before harvest, and I must be in the middle of it." Kane also referred to the man during Ury's trial, calling him Plummer and saying he was one of the group of regulars at Hughson's. Horsmanden craved to question all three of these soldiers, sure that they were Catholics and subversives, as he suspected other Irishmen of being; but none of the king's other men showed much desire to pursue them further.

Only the lone Irish soldier, William Kane, had wagged his tongue for the prosecutors, and they used him gladly to fetch suspects. Turning king's evidence assured Kane's release after he testified against Ury, but it brought him no thanks. Kane failed to convince Horsmanden that he told the whole truth and nothing but the truth about his role in the plot. The judge wanted the soldier gone from the city, not just his cell. Kane found no welcome in the garrison either, for turning on comrades to save himself violated the brotherhood of arms. With no promise of forgetting or forgiving, Kane faced limited options: He was willing enough to quit the garrison and the city, but at age forty, either he had soldiered too long to try another trade or he simply liked the king's army. He sought his peace, paradoxically, by volunteering for duty on the West Indies' battle front.

Like Kane, Sarah Hughson also talked for the prosecution; but unlike the soldier, the girl held her tongue against almost everybody except the dead. Ury alone seemed her target, and testifying against him seemed her last chance to escape hanging by grabbing a pardon. True to the words she uttered when arrested in May—that if ever released she hoped never to set foot again in the city, Sarah gathered her orphaned three sisters and Peggy's now ten-month-old baby and headed northward. Her grandmother Elizabeth Luckstead lived in Yonkers, as did the women and children of the Hughson clan headed by Sarah's grandfather Thomas Hughson. But he and her uncles Richard, Nathaniel, Walter, and William still sat in Westchester County's jail on conspiracy charges.

On Thursday, September 24—which Governor Clarke proclaimed as "a day of public and general thanksgiving to Almighty God for his late mercies vouchsafed unto us in delivering his majesty's subjects of this province from the destruction with which they were so generally threatened by this horrible and execrable conspiracy"—the five Hughson men petitioned the Supreme Court in writing:[4]

May it please your honors,
Our being so long confined in prison, and at this season of the

year, has almost reduced our families to become a public charge, and we are likely to perish should we be continued here the approaching winter.

We are innocent of the crime laid to our charge and hope it would appear, were we to be tried. We humbly pray that, if the law will admit of it, we may be delivered on bail, which we can procure, until you shall think proper to try us. But if the law will not admit us to be bailed, rather than to suffer here and our wives and children should perish at home or be burdensome to their neighbors, we are willing to accept of a pardon to prevent our being further molested on account of the indictment found against us and to depart this province and never to make any settlement any more therein. We humbly pray your honors to procure the same for us and in such manner that we may be released as soon as possible.

We remain your most obedient, though distressed, humble servants.

Horsmanden and his colleagues took their time in responding to the plea, and the Hughson men continued to languish until allowed to make bail in mid-October, when the judges recommended pardoning them "upon condition of their leaving the province."

Governor Clarke consented to pardoning the men, and on October 21 the released Hughsons packed up for parts unknown. The reported sins of a single son had thus visited the entire clan, preventing father and brothers from reaping what they had sown and pushing them from their lands and their livelihoods.

One family remained to account for—the Rommes. Implicated as a fence by Caesar's holder John Vaarck, Mary Burton, and Peggy, John Romme had absconded in March, during the initial investigation of the burglary at Hogg's. For weeks Peggy insisted Romme was a chief in the plot, but the gentleman's status or his kinship with Alderman William Romme made Horsmanden and others loath to believe the charge. A letter written to John by his wife Elezabet fueled the suspicions, however, and landed her in jail in May, after the authorities intercepted the message. John shortly followed his wife to jail after being captured in New Jersey. "The devil couldn't hurt me, for I've a great many friends in town, and the best in the place'll stand by me," Romme reportedly boasted once. In the end, his bragging appeared based on fact, for both he and his wife were released without indictment. They simply posted bond and slipped from the province.

Of the whites tied to Hughson's only one lingered in New York: Mary Burton. The sixteen-year-old indentured servant's initially reluctant testimony to the grand jury in April turned a routine burglary investigation into a broad conspiracy inquiry. She kept pace with the prosecutors at every turn during the proceedings, providing new twists and corroborating leads along the way to make her evidence as crucial in August as it was in April.

The king's men hovered about her during the investigations and trials and dangled the £100 reward from the city council; but as the proceedings closed, the officials left the girl in the cold and abandoned the promise of freedom. She remained a servant, her indenture seized as part of John Hughson's forfeited property. Clinging to her hopes, Burton fastened on the king's men to get her reward, but her scratching produced nothing in 1741.[5]

❦❦❦❦❦

Mary was not alone in complaining. Testy about their losses, holders whose slaves were executed or banished as a result of the conspiracy proceedings griped about the prosecution's methods and scope. Publication of Ury's last words as a broadside in New York and Philadelphia provoked further muttering that he had not received a fair trial.[6]

Horsmanden was particularly sensitive to the growing criticism about the handling of the conspiracy, but he never wavered in arguing that he and his cohort acted in a manner that was beyond reproach. The only failing he saw was that the deadly dosages he prescribed were cut short. Indeed, in January 1742 Horsmanden began to reissue his call for harsh remedies while moaning "that this city and people were not yet out of danger from this hellish confederacy."

Certain that the halt in sweeping the city clean as he wanted had left contagious black elements, Horsmanden envisioned an imminent outbreak of fresh plotting. He warned his colleagues and citizens at large that "It seemed probable that the like attempts would be renewed, notwithstanding the many examples that had been made by executions and the number of slaves sent out of the province."

The judge pointed to the "many cabals of negroes . . . discovered in diverse parts of the country" and, particularly, to what he called the "daring piece of insolence" of several dozen blacks in

Queens who armed themselves and formed a troop during Christmastime 1741. Caught during their gathering near Nassau, Long Island, the blacks said they were simply playing, but Horsmanden saw nothing entertaining in the scene nor did the local magistrates who had the blacks whipped.

Governor Clarke and Attorney General Bradley joined the judge in worrying aloud about the dangers from blacks and called for a renewed crackdown on slaves. Clarke issued a circular letter to the magistrates of "every city, borough and county within this government" urging them "to put the people upon their guard." In the message dated January 20, 1742, he warned that "there are too many yet remaining among us who were of the late conspiracy. Though we have felled the tree, I fear it is not entirely rooted up." The governor "strictly charged and required [the magistrates] to see the laws against negroes duly and punctually executed, suffering no meetings of them within your city and county and several districts."

Noting what he, Horsmanden, and Bradley saw as insolent and dangerous behavior by blacks, Clarke called for the constables throughout New York to search out offending slaves and "all persons as shall be found to harbor negroes, confederate or consort with them." And he directed that his letter "be read from time to time at your general quarter sessions and that you give it in charge to the grand juries, that they make inquiries concerning the offenders."

Clarke not only exhibited continuing fears, his words enlarged the 1741 plot beyond the prosecutions' reports of blacks having planned to destroy New York City. He envisioned all of New York threatened now, and he virtually pleaded for citizens to accept the view of blacks as perennially dangerous and needing the strictest controls.

"After the providential discovery of the late most execrable conspiracy and the hellish and barbarous designs of a perverse and blood-thirsty people for the ruin and destruction of the whole province and the inhabitants thereof and that even at a time when all things were ripe for execution and the intended desolation was so nigh at hand, one would think our signal preservation could never be forgot and that no one could be so blind to himself and regardless of his future safety as to suffer the negroes to have private or public meetings and caballings together, thereby giving them any opportunity of forming new designs or another conspiracy, knowing them to be a people whom no example can reclaim, no punishment deter or lenitives appease," the governor declared.[7]

Clarke's circular further stirred rumors already circulating about slaves in South Carolina plotting to set Charleston afire on the coming March 25—almost the anniversary of the Fort George blaze. Remembering Georgia Governor Oglethorpe's writing about the Spanish instigating plots to burn the principal cities of the English colonies, many of New York's citizens began again to worry of their being threatened.[8]

⛓⛓⛓⛓⛓

Amid the fresh worries, the Court of General Quarter Sessions of the Peace for the City and County of New York opened on February 2, for its first term of 1742. Horsmanden appeared in court that day to read Clarke's letter and to add his own injunctions in his capacity as the city's recorder. He urged the opening of a 1741-style investigation, and trying to draw the pattern from the previous year to the present, he focused on a single suspect then awaiting arraignment. The man Horsmanden used was William Whitefield, the taverner who received the heaviest fine among the ten indicted in July 1741 for trafficking with blacks and who now stood before grand jury on a similar charge.

Horsmanden portrayed Whitefield as a Hughson-like character, but to the judge's chagrin, the grand jurors rejected his appeal for an indictment and investigation. Deciding that they "could get no sufficient information . . . whereon to found an accusation," the jurors released the man. They were not ready to rush to judgment as the first grand jurors had in 1741.

Within two weeks of Whitefield's release, neither the juror; nor citizens at large who had shied away from repeating the pre vious year's prosecutions were so sure the judge was wrong abou the city's not yet being out of danger, for at about six o'clock o the morning of Monday, February 15, 1742, flickers of fire lappe at Walter Hyer's house, next to the Dutch churchyard in the Dock Ward.

The flames made little headway because a carpenter named Cornelius Hendricks spotted the smoke while beginning his work at a new house on Hyer's street. Hendricks roused Hyer from bed, and together they smothered the sparks.

Arson was clear. There were "live coals in the gutter next to the shed, towards the churchyard and likewise a brand's end or the bark of a brand's end on the other side of the house next [to] Ratsey's," Hendricks and Hyer reported.

Mayor John Cruger convened the city council at ten o'clock "to consult what steps to take in order to discover the incendiaries," the recorder noted. The entire council went to investigate and questioned Hyer's neighbors, who cooperated fully knowing that any flames endangered all their townhouses.

The common suspicion immediately fixed on Tom, a slave held by the widow Divertie Bradt whose yard ran along the rear of Hyer's and Ratsey's. Nicknamed "Monkey" by neighborhood blacks, Tom was described as "a simple, half-witted boy," and constables fetched him from work at Bradt's bakery.

Tom turned out to be no boy. He was twenty-two years old and "a lusty, well-set fellow, of a man's growth, . . . [whose] natural countenance was none of the pleasantest, but his appearance on this occasion betokened symptoms of guilt. It was thought that baker's servants, from the nature of their business must be up early and have always a command of fire, which administered some color of suspicion, which the looks of the fellow very much heightened, and therefore he was without ceremony committed" to jail, Horsmanden reported.

At three o'clock the city council reconvened in city hall and without preliminaries asked Tom, "How come you put fire to Hyer's house? Who advised and assisted you in it?"

The slave responded by confessing on the spot and giving the officials the names of four other slaves. Captain Jasper Farmar's Jack was chief on the list, for Tom said that while he was pitching pennies with Jack and three other blacks in Farmar's yard on Sunday, February 7, Jack approached him.

"Your mistress's cross with you," Jack said. "You should take fire and throw it upon the offdackye [New York Dutch for shed] and set them on fire. If you don't do it, I'll poison you. . . . If you fire the shed, that'll fire the house of Captain Ratsey and your mistress's house, too, and her in it. . . . In firing the shed, that'll fire the whole town, and then the negroes in town, with the negroes that'll come from Long Island, will murder the white people."

"When the negroes come from Long Island, they could do it all at once [and] murder the white people. And we'll . . . help in murdering the whites, and then we'll be rich like the Backarara," chorused John Tudor's Peter, Samuel Dunscomb's Michael, and Charles Crooke's Rob, using slave slang in referring to their holders.

"Throw fire upon the offdackye early on Monday morning come [a] week," Jack directed.

Tom said he simply did as told. "I rose early, about five o'clock, lit a candle, made a fire in the bakehouse, heated water to melt the sugar and, then, took a lighted coal of fire and threw it upon the roof of the shed. . . . The coal, in falling, broke into several smaller coals [and] the wind blew the sparks into the little street. Soon after, I heard knocking at Walter Hyer's door. I was then still in my mistress's yard, and hearing the knocking, I was afraid to be discovered and run into my mistress's bakehouse and sat myself down at the fireside. Being afraid I be followed, I bolted the side door which leads into the yard."

The slave's story enlivened the echoes of 1741 for Horsmanden, who resumed his old patterns by starting further interrogation on Tuesday, February 16. He got Tom to say that the day before the fire Jack told him, "You shouldn't forget tomorrow morning. The wind blows hard now, and if it does so tomorrow morning, then you must fire the shed. But if the wind doesn't blow hard, then you shouldn't do it."

The morning wind was right, Tom said. Expanding his confession, he claimed Jack sent him word to be sure that he knew it was right. "I heard a knocking at my mistress's gate, went and opened it, and found a negro man there whose name I don't well know, unless it be Jack, who told me that Farmar's Jack had sent him to tell me to fire the offdackye immediately. This negro brought with him a piece of walnut wood bark which was on fire at one end and not on the other. This negro put that fire between the house of Captain Ratsey and Walter Hyer's house and ran away when the knocking was at Hyer's house, [going] over the churchyard fence."

Trying to billow the fire for his own use, Horsmanden brought Tom and Farmar's Jack together. The confrontation generated two flashes. One illuminated Dunscomb's Michael, who, according to Tom, chided Jack about the arson scheme by saying, "Oh, hey, why do you put such a little boy upon putting fire?" Jack reportedly retorted, "He's big enough." The other flash revealed a lie about a black coming to Bradt's and helping with the fire at Hyer's, for Tom switched from his earlier story and said, "I put this fire all alone, and nobody was with me or helped me. There was a negro [who] came for fire that morning and took it, having knocked at the gate for that purpose, and then went out at the gate again. . . . [I] don't know who he was."

The fresh twists sparked controversy, particularly after checking proved Dunscomb's Michael was nine miles out of town on the day when, according to Tom, he was trading words with Jack. Horsmanden dismissed the discrepancy by remarking, "So Tom was at least mistaken as to the Sunday, which is no uncommon thing for negroes to mistake in point of time." The holders of the slaves named by Tom took a different view, and so did many other slaveholders who feared another wave of property losses like those they had suffered in 1741: They demanded full verification of everything Tom said, before the authorities acted against any other slaves.[9]

Horsmanden's attempts to enlarge the fire into a plot were doused on February 25, when Tom declared all his earlier talk about other slaves to be a lie and accepted full blame for the arson. All four blacks he named denied knowing anything about the fire, although they admitted playing pennies at Farmer's, as Tom said in his first confession.

"This fellow having thus prevaricated, no use could be proposed to be made of him as an evidence to convict others," Horsmanden conceded, but he refused to believe the slaves had not plotted. "It can scarce be imagined that Tom—who was really no fool nor any of the wisest—had framed this scheme and made this attempt merely on his own bottom, which should so correspond with the villainous confederacy of the last year," the judge complained. Hoping still to uncover a dark designed, he proposed to bring Tom to trial.

⛓⛓⛓⛓⛓

The Supreme Court was out of session until April, and nobody proposed to wait that long to proceed. So, as provided in New York's slave code, Tom went before a court where five freeholders sat in judgment with at least one justice of the peace, but he got more than the minimum.

When the trial convened on March 2, Judge Horsmanden sat with Mayor Cruger and six of the city's seven aldermen, all acting as justices of the peace. The selected freeholders included distinguished citizens: James Alexander, a member of the prosecution in 1741; Assemblyman David Clarkson; Robert Livingston, Sr., of the powerful landed and merchant clan; and soon-to-be assemblyman Paul Richards. Peter Van Burgh Livingston, Robert's thirty-one-year old nephew, was called to be the final member of the panel, but having not yet come into his full inheritance, he lacked legal title to a freehold and was excused. The merchant James Searle replaced him.[10]

Four counts faced Tom. The first alleged conspiracy with Farmar's Jack, Dunscomb's Michael, Tudor's Peter, and Crooke's Rob. The second was for arson. The third was for attempted murder, because the house he was charged with setting fire to was occupied. The fourth was for attempted arson against the entire city.

Tom pleaded not guilty to all but the second count. No real need for a trial existed after his pleading guilty to arson, but the panel proceeded anyway.

William Smith prosecuted the case, calling Hendricks and Hyer as witnesses to the actual and potential damage of the fire on February 15. Introducing Tom's confessions, Smith joined Horsmanden in trying to enlarge the issue from a single fire to a conspiracy to burn the city.

Tom had no counsel and offered no defense.

After the public show of evidence, the packed court was cleared for the panel to deliberate. The issue was not Tom's guilt, but its implications and his punishment. Horsmanden wanted a verdict linking Tom to the four blacks named in the conspiracy count and leading to a 1741-style investigation. The majority of the panel shunned his idea and confined themselves to the one count of arson. Horsmanden was allowed only to pronounce judgment, and he used the opportunity to display his continuing concerns about slave conspiracy and his discontent with the prevailing view of the evidence in Tom's trial.

Tying all four counts together as proven facts, Horsmanden lashed out against slaves in general and turned Tom's sentencing into a sermon replete with 1741 images and phrases. "You negroes are treated here with great humanity and with tenderness.

You have no hard taskmasters. You are not laden with too heavy burdens, but your work is moderate and easy. . . . Such worthless, detestable wretches are many, it may be said most, of your complexion that no kindnesses can oblige you. There is such an untowardness, as it should seem, in the very nature and temper of you, that you grow cruel by too much indulgence," Horsmanden asserted.

The judge's loathing of blacks was as clear as his sense that they ought to have been grateful to be enslaved. "So much are you degenerated and debased below the dignity of human species that even the brute animals may upbraid you, for the ox knoweth his owner and the ass his master's crib. Even the very dogs also will, by their actions, express their gratitude to the hand that feeds them, their thankfulness for kindnesses. They will fawn and fondle upon their masters. Nay, if anyone should attempt to assault them, they will defend them from injury, to the utmost of their power. Such is the fidelity of these dumb beasts. But you, the beasts of the people, though you are clothed and fed and provided with all the necessaries of life, without care, in requital of your benefactors, in return for blessings, you give curses and would scatter firebrands, death and destruction around them, destroy their estates and butcher their persons. Thus monstrous is your ingratitude," he declared.

Horsmanden wanted to burn Tom at the stake but reluctantly settled for hanging, in the face of the panel's opposition to harsher punishment. He scoffed that blacks were "so hardened and stupefied . . . in villainy that no examples, though ever so severe, no terrors of punishment, can affright you. You will even defy the gallows and commit your bodies to flames rather than not risk the chance of gratifying your savage cruel and insatiable thirst for blood."

The panel set Tom's execution for Friday, March 5, but Governor Clarke issued a stay to allow Horsmanden more time to pump the slave for leads to accomplices. During the following week the judge dredged up several names, among them James De-Brosse's Primus, who had confessed and been spared during 1741, and a white indentured servant named Abraham, who was with the blacks at Farmar's when they pitched pennies. Horsmanden's real find was Marston's Orinoko who confessed that Farmar's Jack had indeed put Tom up to the fire. The judge confronted Tom with Orinoko, but the condemned man refused to reverse himself then by repeating his original story.

Tom went to the gallows on Saturday, March 13, and his last words were, "Now that I'm sure I must die, I'll tell the truth: Farmar's Jack, [Gerardus] Duychinck's Philip, William Gilbert's Cuffee, and David Van Horne's Corah were the persons who put me upon setting the fire."

Immediately after the execution, Corah, Cuffee, and Philip were jailed for questioning, "but nothing could be got out of them," Horsmanden lamented.

⛓⛓⛓⛓⛓

Two days after Tom's hanging, fire visited the city's northeast end section called Beekman's swamp. The alarm sounded shortly after noon, calling people from unfinished lunches, and none too soon, because the fire seemed to roar from its start. Rumbling with the loud breath of a hard-blowing northwest wind, the blaze burst through John Stevens's tannery and swallowed its immediate surroundings. Ripe for a hungry fire, the area was packed with oak skins peeled from barks heaped for crushing to make tannin, the yellowish acid used to turn hides into leather. Flammables lay everywhere. The lone element lacking for endless burning was heartwood. Only isolation kept the blaze from immediately threatening homes and lives.

The fire fighters hustled to save the section, and for the most part, they succeeded although Stevens lost everything. His new barkhouse building, his adjoining stable, his millhouse, and his workhouse all burned. He and his fellow operators muttered a single question: Was the blaze an accident or arson?

Fire was an ever-present tool in tanning, and although workers in the pits learned quickly to use the element with care, mishap had to be considered as a cause of that Monday's conflagration. Investigators found, in fact, that three of Stevens's men built a fire in the yard outside the workhouse, to ward off the chills of the March morning.

Stevens's slave Sam, the foreman of the three man crew, insisted that the heating flames were well enclosed, guarded against the wind, and carefully watched for safety's sake. He noted that the workhouse sat between the buildings where the blaze centered and the yard where the men had warmed themselves. Further, he pointed out that the wind blew away from the buildings and, thus, could not have carried any coals or sparks from the heater onto the buildings. Besides, he said, the flames which consumed the pit started after the men's fire was doused for their lunch break, during which they went home. He firmly ruled out the workers' fire as a cause of the blaze.

Stevens's slave Tom and an indentured servant named John Bass, the other two crew workers, confirmed the precautions, but their story failed to corroborate Sam's completely. Both admitted, during questioning by Horsmanden and others, that they had not actually seen Sam put out the heating fire. Tom noted that Sam sent him to fetch tea water for their meal. After hesitating, perhaps because he was sensitive about taking orders from a slave, Bass declared that Sam had sent him to help Tom fill the jug: That contradicted Sam's claiming that the white boy had helped him close things down for lunch. Bass declared further that "When me and Tom did return with the water, we didn't find Sam near the place where the [heating] fire had been. Nor did we stand there with him. I didn't see Sam till I passed the workhouse, and then Sam stood within five yards of Mr. [Daniel] Bonnett's lime house." Tom corroborated Bass's version.

The investigation intensified in the days that followed. Several of the fire fighters agreed with Sam's contention that the heating fire was not a possible cause of the blaze. Their opinion was that the fire was arson. One man said, "I don't believe that the fire, which broke out on the roof [of the barkhouse], did proceed from the fire that was made in the yard at the side of the workhouse. I believe it was set on fire on purpose." Echoing the same sentiment another said, "This fire couldn't, I believe, proceed from the fire that was in the yard at the side of the workhouse, but I believe it was set on fire by hand."

Accident was thus ruled out, and the question became, who set the fire?

William Rogers, one of Bonnett's workers, helped concentrate suspicions on Sam by reporting recent trouble with the slave. Ten days before the blaze, Sam had asked Rogers to change a gold, double doubloon. The blackened condition of the Spanish coin and its value—probably more than a quarter of Rogers's annual wages—led the white man to suspect that something was wrong with the slave's having the coin.[11]

Instead of changing the money as Sam asked, Rogers delivered it to Stevens who immediately whipped the slave for having the money and not telling him. The day after the coin deal, Sam and Rogers had another exchange.

"Well, William, you've occasioned my master's whipping of me. He said he'd whip me again. But I'll be even with you for it," Sam warned.

Not liking the sound of the black's words, the white man again reported him to Stevens.

"Don't fear him. He'll not hurt you. He's a harmless fellow," the holder told Rogers.

Horsmanden hardly thought Sam harmless, however, and harboring his own suspicions, he launched an investigation. "There seemed too much reason to apprehend [that] there were yet remaining among us many of the associates in that execrable confederacy, who might yet be hardy enough to persist in the same wicked purposes and make new attempts," the judge commented, using Sam as an example and tying in two fresh alarms on March 17,1742. "Had but the last taken effect when a strong wind favored the design, perhaps St. Patrick's Day might have been an anniversary in our calendar, to have been commemorated by the colony with fasting, weeping and mourning," Horsmanden noted.

A new scare added to the judge's worries on March 23, when Robert Benson's east-end brewhouse caught fire. Investigation revealed arson: The flames started from lighted coals placed on the roof. Horsmanden and the magistrates tried to uncover the culprit, "but no particular person being suspected of the fact, nothing could be made of it," the judge lamented.

⛓⛓⛓⛓⛓

When the Supreme Court opened its spring 1742 term on April 20, the judge sat determined to seize the recent fires as the starting point for a grand jury probe in the manner of 1741. But rejecting Horsmanden's direction, the jurors reported no evidence to pursue in the Benson fire, and although they indicted Sam, the charge was not arson but theft connected with the Spanish coin. The slave had room to rejoice, for he faced a whipping instead of death. The judge was disappointed.

Nursing his anger for months, Horsmanden appeared at the General Quarter Sessions of the Peace when it opened the third of its yearly four sittings. Vehement as ever, the judge continued in his antislave crusade to stir the city's people, in his words, "from a supine security and put them upon their guard against these latent enemies.''

Horsmanden repeated Governor Clarke's January circular and told the new grand jury that ''In order for you to pursue the good intention of his honor's letter, it is necessary that you make diligent inquiry into the economy and behavior of all the mean alehouses and tippling houses within this city and to make out all such, to this court, who make it a practice—and a most wicked and pernicious one it is—of entertaining negroes and the scum and dregs of white people in conjunction, who to support such expense are tempted and abetted to pilfer and steal that they may debauch each other upon the plunder and spoils of their masters and neighbors.'' He wanted to start again where he had in 1741.

Conjuring up images of Hughson's, Horsmanden argued that such places gave ''opportunities for the most loose, debased and abandoned wretches amongst us to cabal and confederate together and ripen themselves in these schools of mischief, for the execution of the most daring and detestable enterprizes. I fear there are yet many of these houses amongst us, and they are the bane and pest of the city. It was such that gave the opportunity of breeding this most horrid and execrable conspiracy.''

The judge asked the jurors ''to inquire concerning all lodgers that are strangers within this city [and] obscure people that have no visible way of subsistence; for that the popish emissaries have been despatched from abroad to steal in among us under several disguises such as dancing masters, schoolmasters, physicians, and such like, whereby, as it is calculated, they may easily gain admittance into families, work underground like a mole in the dark, and accomplish the works of the devil and other of our declared enemies.''

Horsmanden knew his view had lost popular appeal, but he persisted. ''Notwithstanding the great pains and industry, as it should seem, [that] has been taken to bring the notion of a plot into contempt and ridicule by some people among us of phlegmatic tempers, who have endeavored to make light of it, dozed themselves into a lethargic security and have set at naught the evidence of their own senses—for they have seen and heard and, methinks, they might have felt, too, nevertheless, I shall not forbear expressing my fears and apprehensions also that the enemy is still at work within our bowels,'' he declared. ''Let us therefore, gentlemen, think seriously and take better heed to these things . . .

and make proper use of the warning that has been given us, by providing for our own safety and security,'' the diatribe continued.

When the grand jurors' turn came to respond, they indicted nine tavern owners for trafficking with blacks but ignored the judge's appeal to repeat the proceedings of 1741. One murderous purge of slaves, strangers, and suspicious persons was evidently quite enough for the men. They scorned Horsmanden's appeal. The popular inclinations to jump at rumors of revolt had reached the end.

The date was August 3, 1742.

# AFTERWARD

# "The Actual Existence of a Plot"

Horsmanden doted on the events of 1741. As if obsessed by a matter of conscience and honor and, also, motivated by a stipend from the city council, he collected records of the proceedings—transcripts of the trials and interrogations, notes of the prosecutors and judges, including his own jottings, minutes of the magistrates, depositions, and confessions. He envisioned shaping the materials into "a standing memorial of so unprecedented a scheme of villainy."[1]

Intending his work to display the reality of the conspiracy and the justness of the proceedings, the judge expected to refute critics and silence skeptics for all time. The prejudice of his own self-righteousness, which convinced him that right-minded readers would see the facts as he saw them, and the presence of opponents sure to quibble at any false hint kept him honest in his accounting.

To offer the utmost assurance that he had not tampered with the evidence and to underscore his own insistence that the evidence spoke virtually for itself, Horsmanden presented his product not as his personal narrative but as a day-by-day record that ran from the Hogg burglary on February 28, 1741, until September 2, 1742, when Mary Burton finally received her reward—£81 in cash and £19 to pay off the remainder of her indenture, which finally made her free.[2]

In explaining his choice of form, the judge wrote: "A *journal* would give more satisfaction inasmuch as in such a kind of process the depositions and examinations themselves, which were the groundwork of the proceedings, would appear at large—which most probably would afford conviction to such as have a disposition to be convinced and have *in reality* doubted whether any particular convicted had justice done them or not—notwithstanding they had the opportunity of *seeing* and *hearing* a great deal concerning them. And others who had no such opportunities, who were prejudiced at a distance in their disfavor by frivolous reports, might the readier be undeceived. For as the proceedings are set forth in the order of time they were produced, the reader will thereby be furnished with the most natural view of the whole and be better enabled to conceive the design and dangerous depth of this *hellish* project, as well as the justice of the several prosecutions."[3]

Horsmanden hoped that "the people in general might be persuaded of the necessity there is for everyone that has negroes to keep a very watchful eye over them and not indulge them with too great liberties which we find they make use of to the worst purposes, caballing and confederating together in mischief in great numbers when they may. . . . The principal inducement, therefore, to this undertaking was *the public benefit*: that those who have property in slaves might have a lasting memento concerning the nature of them; that they may be thence warned to keep a constant guard over them; since what they have done, they may one time or other act over again, especially if there should in future times appear *such monsters in nature*, as the *Hughsons, Ury the priest, and such like* who dare be so wicked as to attempt the seducing [of] them to such execrable purposes. And if any should think it not worth their while to learn from the ensuing sheets what by others perhaps may be esteemed *a useful lesson*, the fault will be their own."

Even those who disagreed with Horsmanden's conclusions seemed to agree that he correctly rendered the facts, such as they were, and his journal raised no cavils from contemporaries when it appeared in 1744. The only complaint was the judge's own that "the thing dies away and is almost forgotten," less than three years after the twenty-one hangings and thirteen burnings at the stake.

251

Few besides Horsmanden appeared interested in extending the public memory. The prominent New York politician and writer Cadwallader Colden preserved an anonymous letter he received from Massachusetts in the summer of 1741, criticizing the trials as a "Bloody Tragedy" akin to the notorious Salem witchcraft trials of 1692; but Colden cast suspicion on the letter's sentiments and elaborated no view of his own in any of his writings. Even William Smith, the zealous prosecutor, avoided any significant reference to the conspiracy in his writings. His son, William Smith, Jr., gave the events of 1741 two harsh pages in his classic *History of the Late Province of New York, from its Discovery to 1762*, mentioning his father once but in no way suggesting his prominence in the proceedings. The public silence suggested that the episode became an embarrassment to the city and its citizens who thought the less said the better.[4]

The apparent desire of Horsmanden's contemporaries to remain tight-lipped about the proceedings failed to keep the episode from having a noticeable effect in at least two areas. First, the mass banishment of black men and the suspicions raised about them at the height of prosecution—when nearly half the city's male slaves sixteen years or older were jailed—helped to change the character of the slave population and the predominant role of slavery in the city.

The New York census of 1746, the first after the conspiracy, showed men at 46.6 percent of the black population. In the previous census taken in 1737, they accounted for 52.5 percent of blacks. The declining percentage of black men hinted at a shift to a more domestic role for slaves, one emphasizing household and personal service with preference for females over males, who were perennially noted as difficult to control and as troublesome competition for white craftsmen and laborers. New York was far from abandoning slavery, however: The 1746 census indicated that the slave population had grown to an all-time high of 20.9 percent of the city's total population.[5]

In the conspiracy's aftermath, there was also a change in New York's political leadership. Admiral George Clinton arrived as governor in 1743, displacing George Clarke from his role as acting governor, and Daniel Horsmanden, Esq., was removed from New York's city council and the bench of the Supreme Court in 1744. Horsmanden proved himself a survivor however, and when he died in 1778, three months past his eighty-fourth birthday, he was New York's chief justice—the last of the colonial era. He remained a king's man to the end.[6]

⛓⛓⛓⛓⛓

Horsmanden never escaped a cloud about his behavior during 1741, and both his reputation and the conspiracy he so faithfully reported languished in historical oblivion. The episode was resuscitated briefly in 1810 when the Manhattan publishing house of Southwick & Pelsue reprinted the *Journal*. The anonymous editor of that second edition remarked that "The History of the Great Negro Plot of 1741 has always been a subject of curiosity. . . . After a lapse of nearly three-quarters of a century, we look back with astonishment on the panic occasioned by the negro plot and the rancorous hatred that prevailed against the Roman Catholics. To judge from tradition and [Horsmanden's] 'Journal of the Proceedings against the Conspirators,' no doubt can be had of the actual existence of a plot, but its extent could never have been so great as the terror of those times depicted."[7]

Referring to the episode as a "singular event in our colonial history," the 1810 editor noted that "the very mode adopted to discover abettors by mutual criminations and confessions tended, in the progress of the trials, to inculpate every negro slave in the city." To explain the historical context, he wrote further that "Insurrections and conspiracies were, at this juncture, frequent in the West India islands, and great apprehensions were entertained of an invasion by the French and Spanish. These circumstances aggravated the horrors of a domestic plot to such a degree that the white inhabitants, regarding every negro slave as an incendiary and an assassin, carried their apprehensions and resentments beyond all bounds."

In the editor's view, the indisputable truth that New Yorkers plunged off the deep end with the prosecutors' grand conspiracy theory increased the inherent interest of the episode. But scholars of the event have seldom shared the editor's view. Instead, they focused largely on the overdrawn lines of the king's men and, finding them faulty, denied there was anything to the conspiracy story. Particularly as Horsmanden's compilation of documents became the most complete primary source of information on the proceedings, many researchers dismissed the evidence out of a presumption that the journal was as hopelessly biased as the judge. They refused to concede, as the 1810 editor did, that "no doubt can be had of the actual existence of a plot."[8]

By virtual consensus, historians have usually passed lightly over the events of 1741 or mentioned the proceedings only to write them off as a popular delusion. The eminent American historian Charles A. Beard called the plot "imaginary," and a "massacre" that exemplified "plagues of popular frenzy." Ulrich B. Phillips, in his monumental and controversial volume *American Negro Slavery*, gave the episode a single sentence and said it was simply "a panic among the white people." Herbert Aptheker's classic work *American Negro Slave Revolts*—which labored to challenge "American historians [who] have generally tended to minimize or deny the discontent among the Negroes slaves in the United States"—denied the plot was "a complete hoax or an unaccountable mob delusion," yet labelled it "the hysteria of 1741."[9]

Simple notes of the official grand plot theory became the common legacy of the New York Conspiracy. Even as an example of colonial justice gone wrong or as a dark illustration of what historian Richard Hofstadter called "the paranoid style in American politics," the events of 1741 received little attention, in contrast to similar episodes. The Salem witchcraft trials of 1692, for example, have been an often-told and long-studied tale. Perhaps a fascination with witches or with the nineteen whites who hanged and the one pressed to death in the Massachusetts town has accounted for that episode's continuing celebrity in contrast to the rare references to rebellious blacks and the twenty-one who hanged and thirteen who burned at the stake in 1741.

The absence of whites killed directly by black hands, as in Nat Turner's famous rebellion in Virginia during 1831, the Stono Rebellion in South Carolina in 1739 or in the New York uprising of 1712, certainly diminished the recognition of slave unrest in the events of 1741. Also, the fact that the episode occurred in a northern city during the colonial era lent the events little of the character that a growing national concern about slavery in the South bestowed on the plotting and conspiracy charged against Gabriel Prosser and other blacks in Henrico County, Virginia, in 1800 or against Denmark Vesey in Charleston, South Carolina, in 1822.[10]

Historical opinion has tended to sketch the conspiracy episode only along the lines of the hollow case constructed by Horsmanden and the prosecution. The substance of the events of 1741 languished then. Not only what actually happened but what lay beneath the events fell into a sinkhole of oblivion. The character of the entire episode thus became a victim of the prosecution's infamy.

⛓⛓⛓⛓⛓

No doubt can exist that the king's men were wrong in 1741. For example, their attempt to float John Ury as a Catholic priest, a Spanish spy, and the chief plotter failed on the face of the evidence. Nothing presented in court proved Ury was a Catholic, although he certainly harbored dissident religious views. And if he was a minister, there was no sign that he was a priest. His penniless circumstances hardly sustained an argument that he was employed as a spy or anything other than as a teacher who earned meager lodging and meals. Nor was there any proof that Ury was dispatched by Spain.

The case against Ury was clearly fabricated. Star witness Mary Burton swore to little more than seeing Ury at Hughson's. The soldier William Kane and Young Sarah Hughson never agreed on their sightings, although they testified about the same scenes. Sarah's reported run in with Ury when the Campbells came to dispossess her and her sisters supplied the grounds for a grudge sufficient to taint what she said. Her receiving a pardon in exchange for testimony against Ury added to reasonable suspicions that she lied to serve herself. Burton and Kane's testimony against Ury suffered also from the taint of self-interest: The servant girl saw her reward, with its promise of freedom, hanging on the trial's outcome; the soldier saw the matter as life or death.

None of the other conspiracy trials had such obvious flaws as Ury's, and none were as crucial to the contemporary and historical image of the events of 1741. In other trials the prosecution had at least circumstantial evidence, corroborated testimony, or subsequent confessions. They had the facts of arson, and theft, and illicit meetings. Against Ury, however, the king's men had only their own and the public's dreadful conception of the events of 1741.

The king's men cast Ury as a Catholic outsider in order to satisfy their own prejudices and to explain the reported plot's timing and character. They believed that only the presence of an outside influence could account for the open rebellion they saw among the city's slaves for the first time in a generation. Also, the public belief that blacks were incapable of serious thinking and planning created the expectation that there was a white leader. Hughson qualified, of course, but schoolteacher Ury was clearly more plausible as the brains of the extensive conspiracy that the prosecution described. Further, the consensus held that not even those whom Horsmanden called "the scum and dregs" of the city's whites would on their own stoop so low as to reject the society's basic values by making common cause with blacks. In the official and public view, only an outsider or someone bewitched or thoroughly corrupted by foreign ideas—like Catholicism—could conceive a black-white coalition.

The war with Spain promoted the idea of infiltration and allowed the king's men to play on the hateful image of an outsider armed with subversive ideas lurking in the city. Thus did prosecutor William Smith proclaim to the jury in Ury's trial that "if the evidence you have heard is sufficient to produce a general conviction that the late fires in this city and the murderous design against its inhabitants are the effects of a Spanish and popish plot, then the mystery of this iniquity, which has so much puzzled us, is unveiled."[11]

Ury's case served then as a capstone. It was fashioned to cover the grand design Horsmanden and his cohort created during their months of building on the foundation discovered at Hughson's. The illicit structure formed by the likes of Caesar and the taverner was not enough for the officials' purposes. Having pictured all the city ablaze and citizens burning to death—as Griffith Evans had in the fire at Fort George, the king's men saw the presentation of an overarching scheme as the only suitable point for concluding their work. But they so overburdened the evidence that the entire proceedings collapsed.

⛓⛓⛓⛓⛓

The law of conspiracy lent itself to the prosecutors' designs and led them into a thicket of issues that have grown increasingly controversial since 1741. The legal theories underlying the general charge were only in nascent stages in 1741, but the character of the crime was the same then as now: an agreement or intention between at least two persons to act illegally or in secret.[12]

Simply announcing an intention or agreement to commit a crime is technically conspiracy, whether or not the act agreed to or intended is ever attempted. Also, agreeing to act in secret may constitute conspiracy even if the intended act is not itself a crime. For example, if two persons secretly agreed to talk against someone, intending thereby to destroy the person's reputation, that agreement could constitute conspiracy although what the two actually said was no crime. In short, if either an act or the means to commit an act are illegal and two or more persons agree to the act or means, they stand liable for conspiracy. Agreeing is the crime, and no proof of any other overt act is needed.

What one conspirator says about the common design is chargeable against all connected in the agreement. Thus, a path running close to guilt by association may open in the web of conspiracy. A person's mere presence in a place where loose talk roams freely may be seen as a sign of agreement in some evil design, and silence may be deemed consent. Also, what one alleged conspirator intends may not be the same as another, but they may all stand equally to blame for what anyone of them announces as an intention.

By definition, evidence of conspiracy resides almost completely outside public view. Indeed, a glimpse may provide the only basis available to judge if the crime exists in any case. Recognizing that secrets and personal intentions make tricky targets to capture and display in court, the law permits prosecutors broad range. Opponents have lambasted the conspiracy charge as a blunderbuss because prosecutors can use it for random action that can scatter abuse against suspects and standard legal procedures. What, in other circumstances, might seem a weak catch may suffice for indictments and convictions for conspiracy.[13]

Fallout from the explosive legal theory of conspiracy combined with exposure of the grand conspiracy theory to contaminate the events of 1741 in the eyes of many past researchers and largely accounted for their slighting the episode. Focusing simply on the fearful fantasy created by Horsmanden and his cohort chronically distracted attention by confusing the priority of questions: It mistakenly elevated the phantom existence of the prosecutors' conspiracy, instead of the underlying realities of how the episode occurred.

While the scenario was not as fantastic as the prosecutors portrayed it, slaves and whites at Hughson's were guilty of plotting and committing crimes. Beyond any reasonable doubt, Vaarck's Caesar and Auboyneau's Prince planned the burglary at Hogg's and carried off the crime with John Hughson, his wife, and Peggy as accomplices. They had the loot in hand to prove the crime. There was no need to argue about agreement or intent. The same was true about the large meetings of blacks at Hughson's. The slaves' gathering in numbers greater than three was a crime, and the Hughson's entertaining them and providing liquor were also crimes—agreed to, intended, and committed.

The illegal behavior by blacks and the whites catering to them were fundamental elements of the New York Conspiracy. Intending at least to shake off their shackles for a few hours or an evening, slaves clearly reached out for more than the law allowed them, and whites like Hughson agreed to aid them. That was a fact exhibited in the city's life almost daily. It was the persistence of slave crime that maddened Horsmanden and his fellow citizens.[14]

The slaves' wrath was all too clear. Instead of being gratefully obedient as slaveholders hoped, blacks seethed with resentment. Roosevelt's Quack resented Governor Clarke's prohibiting him from visiting his wife, the governor's cook. Ward's Will likewise resented Abraham Van Horne's interference when Will wanted to be with his wife, one of Van Horne's house slaves. The patterns of slaveholding and housing in the city multiplied the examples of Quack and Will because slave couples were often forced to live apart and spend time together usually only once a week, on Sundays. Like other black men, Will sought ways to defeat such regulation. Quack's fights with the sentry at the fort, during repeated attempts to get to his wife, showed the slave's determination not to let the governor or anybody else thwart his desire.

Black resentment ranged widely and surfaced in piques against particular sore spots and slavery in general. Mrs. Carpenter's Tickle complained about being treated meanly and not having decent clothes. Several slaves complained about being worked hard and seldom getting any leisure. Todd's Dundee muttered about his mistress's nagging and about Mr. Todd's dogging him on errands. Niblet's Sandy echoed the sounds of a pervasive black sentiment in saying, "God damn all the white people, if I had it in my power, I'd burn them all."

Angry talk no doubt flowed as liberally as the liquor among blacks at Hughson's and at the party Comfort's Jack hosted while his holder was away from home. Too many slaves corroborated the general fretting to doubt it. There was no doubt that slaves vented steam against their individual holders and the society or that they announced desires to reverse the roles on whites who enslaved them.

"A great many people have too much and others too little," Philipse's Cuff once complained, capturing an underlying black tone. He hankered to share his holder's wealth. "In a short time, I'll have more and my old master less," the slave announced. Marshall's Ben saw enough of his holder's good life to want it for himself. Other slaves said the same.

Some slaves did seem resigned to their station and content with how their holders treated them. DeBrosse's Primus contended that his master and mistress were kind to him, and he wished them no harm. Alderman Pintard's Caesar claimed he lived well enough. But Ben and Rutgers's Quash captured the prevailing sentiment among most slaves, declaring that "it's a hard case upon the poor negroes . . . [who] couldn't so much as take a walk after church-out, but the constables took them up." Ben insisted that blacks had to strike a blow "in order to be free."

The surfeit of discontent was not confined to blacks. Whites struggling like the Hughsons or outcasts like the sailors and soldiers, particularly the Irish among them, had grievances aplenty which accounted for someone like Private Edward Murphy reportedly saying, "Damn me if I won't lend a hand to the fires as soon as anybody." That whites in the city's underclass shared grievances with blacks and talked of taking revenge was indisputable.[15]

The broadcast of discontent carried enough rebellious seeds for conspiracy to grow in the hothouse climate and liquor at Hughson's, but ripening revolution was a bogus crop. Horsmanden and his cohort falsely advertised a wholesale harvest of a scorched city with slaughtered white men and ravished white women. The actual forecast at Hughson's called for nothing so improbable.

Talk at the tavern took occasional flights of fancy about capturing the city, but the sober reality centered on much more limited goals and on specific targets. Strategic points such as Fort George and the Fly Market, warehouses like Philipse's and Van Zant's, and residences like Thomas's and Hilton's were the places fixed for burning—not the whole city. Particular whites were marked for murder, not the whole population. And the issue was not so much blacks against whites, as haves against havenots—a fact made plain by whites at Hughson's joining in with blacks. The talkers' common motivation seemed simply a desire to kick back at the society's oppression and to get something more than they had for themselves. Settling some personal scores, stealing, and escaping were the aims.

The scenarios used to project the talk were not as farfetched as the prosecutors' case made them appear. For example, a French and Spanish invasion of the city was talked of at Hughson's as a contingency, not an impending fact. As Vaarck's Bastian explained, "we were to stay till the Spaniards and French came, about a month and a half, and if they didn't come in that time, we were to begin ourselves."

A clear gap yawned between the talk and the action. The slaves who whet their knives with Comfort's Jack were ready enough to join in his boasting of having a blade "so sharp that if it came across a white man's head, it'd cut it off." But when it came to the test most shrank like Todd's Dundee who confessed, "I was to fire my master's house the same evening after the fort was burned, but was afraid lest I'd be catched and hanged."

The talk sounded less than serious at times, as when slaves spoke of starting fires one weekend, working during the week, and finishing their illicit acts on the following weekend. At least part of the reason for the gap issued from the reported methods of recruiting slaves: Threatening to cut someone's throat or shoot him, plying him with drinks, or asking him to swear to do something before telling him the proposition were hardly ways to build a reliable cadre.

Some slaves acted out part of their talk. Roosevelt's Quack confessed to lighting fire to the governor's house at Fort George—that was his revenge for Clarke's denying him conjugal visits. Five separate reports confirmed Quack's arson. Cuff likewise confessed to setting fire at the Philipse storehouse. Peck's Caesar confessed to his and Gomez's Cuffee's committing arson at Van Zant's warehouse. Sleydall's Jack confessed to setting the coals in Murray's haystack. Sarly's Juan never confessed, but the evidence confirmed his setting fire to the houses on both sides of Sarly's. What the slaves intended was never fully demonstrated, and any orchestration they planned was never performed. There were only the few solo acts.

White New Yorkers like Horsmanden worried about what blacks might have done, as well as about what they had actually done. The conspiracy proceedings were, after all, not the product of simple retaliation or retribution; they were designed as "a terror for the evildoer," to use Justice Philipse's words, for New York existed on a basis of terror—like all slave societies. The flood of executions flowed from the wellsprings of insecurity about the prevailing terror being supplanted or reversed enough to let citizens taste violence as victims.

Horsmanden and his cohort simply wrapped New York's recent events with the perennial insecurities and produced a ready-made package that most citizens accepted without question because they had samples to validate the official bill of goods. They had the troubling facts of persistent black crime, and the facts from the Hogg burglary showed townspeople beyond doubt that whites like Hughson had combined in crime with blacks like Caesar. The fact of the ten tippling houses whose owners were indicted and fined suggested widespread black carousing with whites beyond the gatherings at Hughson's. Also, townsfolk had the fact of Luke Barrington, an Irish schoolteacher in New York's Ulster County, who in March 1741 publicly drank a toast to Spain's King Philip V and declared that "King Philip's my king, and if he'd come over with his army, I'd take up arms for him and knock the English on the head."[16]

The war news bolstered the common beliefs the prosecutors presented in court. New Yorkers continually read reports like one in December 1740 about enemies plotting "to turn the tables upon the English in America by exciting revolts and disturbances in their possessions and by doing everything in [their] power to traverse the designs and even to distress the English." The townspeople also knew the history of the burning and killing by blacks during the uprising of 1712.[17]

The belief that black men planned to seize white women sprang also from established facts. Affairs between white women like Peggy and black men like Caesar were facts, and the sharp imbalance that had developed in the city's sex ratio during the lean economic years of the 1730s was also a worrisome fact for many New Yorkers. In 1731 there had been 117 white men for every 100 white women in the city; by 1737, however, there were only 91 white men per 100 white women, and the number was still falling. It was around 89 in 1741 and fell later in the 1740s to 77.5 white men per 100 white women. At the same time, the ratio between black men and women ran contrary to the ratio among whites, for the number of black men increased significantly. In 1731 there were 99 black men for every 100 black women. By 1737 there were 111 black men per 100 black women, and the ratio was still rising. It was around 119 in 1741 and reached 127 black men per 100 black women later in the 1740s. The increasing number of black men and white women left without matches among their own color, along with the examples of black men taking up with white women, held frightening implications for those who hoped, in Governor Clarke's words, to see New York "replenished with white people."[18]

❈❈❈❈❈

The conspiracy proceedings preyed on facts. Economic depression, aggravated by war and a wretched winter, deepened popular anger against familiar targets—blacks, Catholics, and strangers. To be sure, a paranoid style emerged. Hysteria certainly prevailed in the shouts of "the negroes are rising" and the mobbing of blacks on the Monday of the many fires. But frenzy did not sustain the tiring interrogations and trials from April thru August. The prosecutors and public simply followed the dictates of their political culture.[19]

The world, as Judge Horsmanden and his cohort believed it to be, was a place where deception and disorder constantly threatened their very survival. They felt their enemies and evil always at hand, plotting their destruction. And they were not alone, for the feeling was not limited to New York in 1741. As historian Gordon S. Wood has noted in a study of conspiracy and the paranoid style in the eighteenth century, "The conspiratorial interpretations of the age were a generalized application to the world of politics of the pervasive duplicity assumed to exist in all human affairs."[20]

New York's officials indulged themselves and the public in acting out their fears. But they played no hoax. They set out to deceive no one. They simply deceived themselves by systematizing real disorders into a single scheme where all the enemies of the English world suddenly surfaced—from the forces of evil, personified by Hughson whom prosecutors called the devil's agent, to England's arch rival Spain, to strangers such as Ury, and to truly troublesome blacks like Caesar.

The prosecution's misguided rhetoric caused many people to blanch after the proceedings because the officials' case could hardly withstand scrutiny. But exposing their errors without recognizing the real discontent and daily struggle by slaves and others to seize liberty and a living for themselves has previously shrouded the enduring value of the conspiracy episode as an exhibition of a seldom-seen, dark side of life in colonial America.

The burning of thirteen black men and the hanging of seventeen more, along with two white men and two white women, in an attempt to restore a sense of stability in the city through a public catharsis has forever marked the New York Conspiracy's tragic reality. The murderous events sprang from authentic causes—not simply spurious charges. The undercurrent of practical and symbolic issues such as defeating the Spanish, policing slaves, recovering from economic depression, and insuring a "white man's country" played their parts. The source of the tragedy lay in the tangled undergrowth of the society's self-conception where people were directed to see others not as themselves but as greater or lesser, good or evil, depending on their class, color, origin, or religion. A world of prejudice and injustice ensnared the New Yorkers of 1741, and not them alone, in rumors of revolt.

# Sources and Notes

THE PRINCIPAL PRIMARY SOURCE on the conspiracy episode is Daniel Horsmanden's *Journal of the Proceedings in the Detection of the Conspiracy formed by Some White People in Conjunction with Negro and Other Slaves for Burning the City of New-York in America and Murdering the Inhabitants* (New York: James Parker, 1744). In 1747 it was reprinted in London by John Clarke. A second edition was published in New York during 1810 by Southwick & Pelsue, with the title *The New-York Conspiracy or a History of the Negro Plot with the Journal of the Proceedings against the Conspirators at New-York in the Years 1741–2.* An abridged version of the text appeared in four parts, edited by William B. Wedgwood, under the title *The New York Conspiracy in the City of New York in 1741* (New York: G. W. Schoot, 1851). Also, a fifty-eight-page partial edition was published under the title *The Trial of John Ury* (Philadelphia: M. I. J. Griffin, 1899). In 1971 two complete editions appeared: a photocopy reprint of the 1810 edition, done by Negro Universities Press with the same title as the 1810 edition, although the heading on the book's spine mistakenly read "History of the Negro Plot 1711–2," and an entirely reset reprint entitled *The New York Conspiracy*, edited with an introduction by Thomas J. Davis and published by Beacon Press.

A source bearing Judge Horsmanden's mark naturally attracts serious questions about its validity and reliability, but the questions are no different from those that historians necessarily ask when dealing with any source, and the criteria used in evaluating the *Journal* are the traditional ones of objectivity, opportunity, and transmission.

No question exists about Horsmanden's opportunity to observe the events he recorded. As trial judge, city recorder (thus, a member of the city council), and member of the governor's council, he was an insider to the official activity. Indeed, directing much of the action as he did, Horsmanden was privy to the aims and objects of the proceedings in public and private. He was both an eyewitness and a participant, and as a source on his thinking and the official action, the *Journal* is unimpeachable.

Horsmanden's admissions run so much against his self-interest as an impartial judge that they stand as convincing evidence of the facts of his belief. Yet the prejudice he demonstrated during the proceedings and his reputation as a career partisan in New York politics leave no question about his objectivity. On that basis alone many scholars have immediately dismissed the *Journal*. Conceding his bias, however, answers neither the question about the judge's accuracy as a recorder nor about the *Journal*'s value as a source. Horsmanden's opinion and the facts in the *Journal* are not the same.

The structure of the *Journal* sustains its reliability as a source on the proceedings, for it is a documentary compilation commissioned by the New York City council as an official report on the affair. The original does not bear Horsmanden's name on the title page but simply indicates that the compilation was done "by the Recorder of the City of New-York." The actual court proceedings—in the form of abstracts and transcripts—comprise about sixty-five percent of the text. Confessions, depositions, and interrogations account for twenty percent. Less than fifteen percent represents direct commentary from Horsmanden, and it appears in the form of a preface, which in the 1971 Beacon Press edition runs eight pages, an introduction running twenty-three pages, a twenty-seven page conclusion, and scattered footnotes.

An admittedly singular perspective predominates in the *Journal*. The proffered outlook is that of Horsmanden and his fellows, but the benefits of that view provide rare insights to the officials' actions and thoughts, while not impairing the details of the fires, robberies, trials, and executions nor the picture of interactions among the officials, between them and the accused, or between blacks and whites at large in the city. The examinations, sworn statements, and trial testimony draw upon a variety of individual points of view that provide proportion to the official outline.

The problem of perspective arises most acutely in considering the contents of the confessions and examinations of the accused, particularly the slaves, for they were taken largely in private, and for the most part, only evidence from the *Journal* itself exists as a check on them. That eliminates the test of contemporary scrutiny which stands for the court proceedings conducted in full public view, where outside of wholesale collusion neither Horsmanden nor any other official had any chance to alter the substance.

The issue with the slave confessions and examinations is more one of transmission and meaning, rather than one of intentional tampering. The mass of confessions taken between June 20 and July 3 clearly outdistanced the recorders' abilities to keep pace, as the officials themselves admitted. As an expedient, the transcribers took down what they considered to be the gist of what the slaves said. Also, the circumstances of their origins raise questions about the confessions and examinations.

The fact that whites transcribed what slaves said in 1741 and put the words into standard English also raises significant but hardly new questions. Controversy about such problems in transmission has long raged, and the pros and cons of accepting the products as sound have been argued rather fully in treatments of the Denmark Vesey case and the case of Nat Turner's revolt. For example, see John W. Lofton, *Insurrection in South Carolina: The Turbulent World of Denmark Vesey* (Yellow Springs, Ohio, 1964); Richard C. Wade, "The Vesey Plot: A Reconsideration," *Journal of Southern History* 30 (May 1964): 143–161; Sterling Stuckey, "Remembering Denmark Vesey," *Negro Digest* 15 (February 1966): 28–41; and Robert S. Starobin, ed., *Denmark Vesey: The Slave Conspiracy of 1822* (Englewood Cliffs, N. J., 1970). Also, see Herbert Aptheker, *Nat Turner's Slave Rebellion: Including the Full Text of the So-Called "Confessions" of Nat Turner Made in Prison in 1831* (New York, 1966) and the significant stir created in this area by William Styron, *The Confessions of Nat Turner: A Novel* (New York, 1967), and the reaction in John Henrik Clarke, ed., *William Styron's Nat Turner: Ten Black Writers Respond* (Boston, 1968), and John B. Duff and Peter M. Mitchel, eds., *The Nat Turner Rebellion: The Historical Event and the Modern Controversy* (New York, 1971).

The full meaning and range of black thinking is forever moot in the case of 1741. In fact, completely independent black testimony from colonial America is all too rare. The prime value of the confessions and examinations in 1741 lies in the patterns they reveal about the detail of slave life and social relations, more than in the exact expressions contained in the reports. The words may not have been completely the slaves', but the evidence of their experience stands free from the style and limitations of the recorded language. For example, although the filtering by white hands no doubt missed nuances of black thought, the recurrent resentment of slaves and their interaction with one another and with whites constantly surface.

In the rush to avoid judgment, many of the slaves seemed hardly to be confessing "freely and fully," but trying "to come off as cheaply as they could," to use Horsmanden's words. No doubt, they slanted their stories to tell what they thought the officials wanted to hear. Some admitted discussing what they should say to escape execution. They tried not to create whole cloth, but to hide patches, and their efforts did not alter the substance of their lives and relationships.

The circumstances were not the same for all the confessions. Cuff and Quack's statements, for example, were virtual dying declarations. Their admissions of guilt promised nothing by themselves. They needed to give the authorities verifiable facts. So did the other slaves who might have sought to lie in part to save themselves. The confessions can be checked for validity by comparing them with one another in the context of other facts and the continuity of references. What they failed to tell is not recoverable, but most of their content is verifiable against contradiction.

No definitive resolution seems likely to arise about the slaves' intentions. But the historical events are clearer and stand not on the *Journal* alone, for other primary sources confirm the detail. For example, although apparently ignored before now in connection with the conspiracy episode, the *Calendar of Historical Manuscripts in the Office of the Secretary of State, Albany, N.Y.*, Part II, edited by Edmund B. O'Callaghan (Albany: Weed, Parsons and Company, 1866), contains 182 entries on the proceedings, running from March 4, 1741, to March 16, 1743. These documents comprise the first 148 pages in volume 74 of the "English Manuscripts in the Historical Manuscripts of the [New York] Secretary of State," available at the New York State Library, Manuscripts and Special Collections Division, Albany, New York.

Also available are council and court records for the city and county of New York: See *Minutes of the Common Council of the City of New York, 1675–1776*, 8 vols. (New York, 1905); "Minutes of the Circuit Court of Oyer and Terminer and Gaol Delivery" (1721–1749)—two bound folio volumes copied from the original manuscript—Library of the Association of the Bar of the City of New York; "Minutes of the Mayor, Deputy Mayor and Alderman of New York City" (1733–1742), microfilm copy in Queens College Historical Documents Collection, Roll MC 27; "Minutes of the Court of General Quarter Sessions of the Peace" (1691–1776), microfilm copy in Queens College Historical Documents Collection, Rolls CMS1–CMS2. The minutes of the Supreme Court have not survived for 1741: See "Minute Books of the Supreme Court of Judicature" (1704–1740; 1750–1781), microfilm copy in Queens College Historical Documents Collection, Rolls SC1–SC8. These court records furnish a context for the 1741 proceedings.

Among other official documents and records useful here are: "Calendar of Council Minutes, 1668–1783," New York State Library, *Bulletin* 58 (March 1902), edited by Berthold Fernow; *Journal of the Votes and Proceedings of the General Assembly of the Colony of New York, 1691–1765*, 2 vols. (New York: Hugh Gaine, printer, 1764–1766); *The Colo-*

*nial Laws of New York from the Year 1664 to the Revolution*, 5 vols. (Albany: James B. Lyon, 1894); and Charles Z. Lincoln, ed., *Messages from the Governors, Comprising Executive Communications to the Legislature and Other papers Relating to Legislation from the Organization of the First Colonial Assembly in 1683 to and Including the Year 1906*, 11 vols. (Albany: J. B. Lyon, 1909).

A variety of avenues exists for research on the events of 1741 within the context of historical and theoretical models of racial violence and community development in New York and, more broadly, in eighteenth-century America. This work is informed by such works as Paul Boyer and Stephen Nissenbaum's *Salem Possessed: The Social Origins of Witchcraft* (Cambridge, Mass., Harvard University Press, 1974); Peter H. Wood's instructive treatment of the Stono Rebellion of 1739 in *Black Majority: Negroes in South Carolina from 1670 through the Stono Rebellion* (New York, Alfred A. Knopf, 1974); Douglas Greenberg's *Crime and Law Enforcement in the Colony of New York 1691–1776* (Ithaca, N.Y. Cornell University Press, 1976); Richard Maxwell Brown's "Living Together Violently: Black and Whites in America From the Colonial Period to 1970," in *Strains of Violence: Historical Studies of American Violence and Vigilantism* (New York, 1975), 185–235; Darrett B. Rutman's "The Social Web: A Prospectus for the Study of Early American Community," in William L. O'Neill, ed., *Insights and Parallels* (New York, 1973); and Thomas Bender's *Community and Social Change in America* (New Brunswick, N.J., 1978).

By reconstructing the events of 1741 in a narrative that seeks as faithfully as possible to depict what happened as it happened, *A Rumor of Revolt* aims to broaden understanding of the conspiracy episode. It lays no claim to providing wholly new evidence. Rather, it seeks a new perspective that explains how the cry of conspiracy started, what sustained it, and how the thirty-four victims came to be accused and executed.

The bulk of the quotations used in this book comes directly from the *Journal*. Punctuation and spelling have been modernized and the words put in direct address for dialogue, but otherwise there is no alteration in the quotations. The chronological structure of the text allows for reference to any edition of the *Journal* in checking quotations. The Beacon Press reprint of 1971, which contains an index, is the edition used here, and the opening note for each chapter indicates the pages from which *Journal* quotations come. Quotations from sources other than the *Journal* are individually noted.

### Abbreviations Used in Notes

CHM          *Calendar of Historical Manuscripts in the Office of the Secretary of State, Albany, N.Y.*, 2 vols. (Albany, 1866)

DHNY          *Documentary History of New York*, 4 vols. (Albany, 1849–1851)

DRCHNY        *Documents Relative to the Colonial History of New York*, 15 vols. (Albany, 1856–1887)

Eng. Mss.      *"English Manuscripts in the Historical Manuscripts of the [New York] Secretary of State,"* in the New York State Library, Manuscripts and Special Collections Division, Albany, N.Y.

MCC           *Minutes of the Common Council of the City of New York, 1675–1776*, 8 vols. (New York, 1905)

NY Col. Laws    *Colonial Laws of New York from the Year 1664 to the Revolution*, 5 vols. (Albany, 1894)

## Chapter 1

1. For quotations and description of Caesar's life and death, see Daniel Horsmanden, *The New York Conspiracy*, edited with an introduction by Thomas J. Davis (Boston, 1971), especially 13–22, 41–48, 188–191, 446–452.
2. On size and composition of New York's population, see Thomas J. Davis, "Population and Slavery in Eighteenth Century New York" (M.A. thesis, Columbia University, 1968); and Thomas J. Davis, "New York's Long Black Line: A Note on the Growing Slave Population, 1626–1970," *Afro-Americans in New York Life and History* 2 (1978): 41–59.
3. On the law of slavery in New York, see *NY Col. Laws*, 1:679–688, giving summary act passed 29 October 1730, entitled "An Act for the more Effectual Preventing and Punishing the Conspiracy and Insurrection of Negro and other Slaves; for the better regulating them and for repealing the Acts herein Mentioned Relating thereto." Also, see Edgar J. McManus, *A History of Negro Slavery in New York* (Syracuse, 1966); Oscar R. Williams, "The Regimentation of Blacks on the Urban Frontier in Colonial Albany, New York City and Philadelphia," *Journal of Negro History* 63 (1978): 329–338; Oscar R. Williams, "Blacks and Colonial Legislation in the Middle Colonies" (Ph.D. dissertation, The Ohio State University, 1969); A. Leon Higginbotham Jr., *In the Matter of Color: Race and the American Legal Process: The Colonial Period* (New York, 1978); Thomas J. Davis, "Slavery in Colonial New York City" (Ph.D. dissertation, Columbia University, 1974); Edwin Olson, "The Slave Code in Colonial New York," *Journal of Negro History* 29 (1944): 147–165; and Carl Nordstrom, "The New York Slave Code," *Afro-Americans in New York Life and History*, 4 (1980): 7–26.

4. On general law enforcement, see Julius Goebel, Jr., and T. Raymond Naughton, *Law Enforcement in Colonial New York: A Study in Criminal Procedure, 1664–1776* (New York, 1944); Douglas S. Greenberg, " 'Persons of Evil Name and Fame': Crime in the Colony of New York, 1691–1776" (Ph.D. dissertation, Cornell University, 1974)—particularly on methodological problems posed in researching in the records of the criminal courts in New York—see 52–57 and 190–193; also, see Greenberg, *Crime and Law Enforcement in the Colony of New York, 1691–1776* (Ithaca, N.Y., 1976), an excellent book derived from his dissertation. Focusing on defendants in colonial New York's criminal courts, Greenberg says that "slave crime was more frequent in the city. In New York, slaves accounted for a larger proportion (10.7%) of prosecutions than they did in the colony as a whole, but this was still smaller than their relative position in the population. These figures can, of course, be interpreted in several ways" (ibid., 44). Greenberg and I differ in interpreting the relative troublesomeness of slave crime in the city, largely because he deals with cases that went to the regular criminal courts, although he acknowledges the existence of a significant volume of slave crime that, in his words, "would never be reported to the courts" (ibid.).

Also, see Greenberg's chap. 2, "The Demography of Crime: The Accused," especially 43–46, and his chaps. 6–8 on the effectiveness of law enforcement. For a general description of the "Watch" or early police forces in New York City, see Arthur E. Peterson and George William Edwards, *New York as an Eighteenth Century Municipality*, 2 vols. (New York, 1917; reprinted 1967 as two volumes in one), 1:151–168; 2:109–127. Note that there were a variety of watches—the constables watch, the citizens watch, and the military watch. For regulations, see *MCC* 1:64, 71–72, 90–94, 134–135, 147, 153–154, 205–209; and 5:77, for troubles around 1741. Also, see Augustine E. Costello, *Our Police Protectors: A History of the New York Police from the Earliest Period to the Present Time* (New York, 1885); and James F. Richardson, *The New York Police: Colonial Times to 1901* (New York, 1970).

On problems with theft in New York City, see Peterson and Edwards, *New York*, 2:116–118; Goebel and Naughton, *Law Enforcement*, 216–220; and Greenberg, *Crime and Law Enforcement*, especially 69, where he writes, "The court records confirmed a variety of notions about crime and the people of New York: blacks were thieves; the Dutch were tendentious and antipathetic to authority, but highly individualistic and economically secure; many English residents of New York, men and women alike, were transported felons who continued their thieving ways on the shores of the New World; women who ran taverns were usually prostitutes, and their activities could be clearly associated with theft; invariably, cities bred disorderly houses and disorderly houses bred crime; and finally, New York society was unstable and subject to a variety of difficult social problems directly attributable to the composition of the population.''

5. On ideas of law enforcement and theory of punishment, see Goebel and Naughton, *Law Enforcement in Colonial New York*, 13–15, 701–710; Olson, ''The Slave Code in Colonial New York,'' 147–165; Greenberg, *Crime and Law Enforcement*, 138–153; James Heath, ed., *Eighteenth Century Penal Theory* (Glasgow, 1963); Christopher Hibbert, *The Roots of Evil: A Social History of Crime and Punishment* (Boston, 1963); Leon Radzinowicz, *A History of English Criminal Law and Its Administration from 1750*, 2 vols. (New York, 1948–1957); M. J. Heale, ''Humanitarianism in the Early Republic: The Moral Reformers of New York, 1776–1825,'' *Journal of American Studies* 2 (1968):161–163.

6. On Romme family connection, see Howard S. F. Randolph, ''The Rommen-Romme-Van Langstraat Family and the Romme Family: Showing Connections between These Two families and the Elsworth Family of New York City,'' *New York Genealogical and Biographical Record*, 44 (1933): 330–341; and ''The Elsworth Family of New York, with the Related Families of Rommen-Romme-Van Langstraat and Roome,'' ibid., 154–166, 255–267; and Peter Roome Warner, *Descendants of Peter Willemse Roome* (New York, 1883). Note variation in spelling of Romme/Roome. Horsmanden used the Romme spelling in his *Journal*, and that is the spelling used here throughout the text, although other sources use the Roome spelling.

7. For details of the Hogg robbery and investigation, see Horsmanden, *The New York Conspiracy*, 13–22. Also, see deposition of Rebecca Hogg, dated 14 April 1742, ibid., 445–449. The Hoggs' shop was at the corner of Broad and South William Streets, according to Martha J. Lamb, *History of the City of New York*, 3 vols. (New York, 1877–1896), 1:581.

8. On crimes of theft, see Greenberg, *Crime and Law Enforcement in Colony of New York*, especially 52–58, 61–64, 92, 115–117.

9. See warrant for commitment of Caesar and recognizance for the appearance of Prince, *CHM*,2:552; *Eng. Mss.*, 74:1–2.

10. See deposition of Anne Kannady, dated 13 April 1742, Horsmanden, *The New York Conspiracy*, 443–445. On presence of indentured servants in New York, see William Stuart, ''White Servitude in New York and New Jersey,'' *Americana* 15 (1921): 19–37; Charles M. Haar, ''White Indentured Servants in Colonial New York,''

*Americana* 34 (1940): 370–392; Samuel D. McKee, Jr., *Labor in Colonial New York, 1664–1776* (New York, 1935), chap. 3. Also, see Abbot Emerson Smith, *Colonists in Bondage: White Servitude and Convict Labor in America, 1607–1776* (Chapel Hill, 1947); and on origins and characteristics of indentures, see David Galenson, *White Servitude in Colonial America* (New York, 1982).

11. New York City's council at the time was officially called the Common Council. Presided over by the mayor, who after 1731 was elected instead of appointed annually by the governor, the council contained an alderman and an assistant elected annually from each of the city's wards. The aldermen were empowered as magistrates to administer and enforce the law and to act as justices of the peace. Also, there was a recorder, essentially the corporation counsel, and a clerk—sometimes called the town clerk or common clerk—who minuted council meetings, acted as court stenographer and keeper of the city court records, filed tax collections, and was the official city petitioner to the provincial government: Both the recorder and the clerk were appointed by the governor.

For the structure and organization of the city government, see *NY Col. Laws*, 2:575–639; *MCC*, 4:38–41; 5:190–195, 340. For comments and explanations, see Chancellor James Kent, *The Charter of the City of New York with Notes* (New York, 1851); David Thompson Valentine, *Manual of the Corporation of the City of New York*, 25 vols. (New York, 1834–1867)—a sort of yearbook hereafter referred to by the year for which published; Valentine, *Manual of New York for 1860*, 167–173; Peterson and Edwards, *New York*, especially 2:1–41; John Franklin Jameson, "The Origin and Development of Municipal Government in New York City" (Ph.D. dissertation, Johns Hopkins University, 1882); Bayrd Still, "New York's Mayoralty," *New-York Historical Quarterly* 47 (1963): 239–243; and Bruce Wilkenfeld, "The New York City Common Council, 1698–1800," *New York History* 52 (1971): especially 252–255.

In 1741 the city had seven wards: the Dock Ward, the East Ward, the Montgomerie Ward (named in honor of Governor John Montgomerie, who died in office on 1 July 1731, after a brief but well-received tenure that began with his appointment on 15 April 1728), the North Ward, the Out Ward, the South Ward, and the West Ward.

The aldermen were Christopher Bancker, Simon Johnson, John Marshall, John Moore, John Pintard, William Romme, and Gerardus Stuyvesant. The assistants were Robert Benson, Henry Bogert, George Brinkerhoff, Samuel Lawrence, Philip Minthorne, and Isaac Stoutenburgh. The mayor was John Cruger, Sr.

The recorder was Daniel Horsmanden, and the clerk was John Chambers.

City Hall was located at the intersection of Broad and Wall Streets: See, Lamb, *History of the City of New York*, 1:505.

12. The undersheriff served as prison keeper, and the basement of city hall, completed in 1700, contained the only prison in the New York City until 1759 when the "new gaol" was built in what was called the "Fields," at the northeast corner of present City Hall Park. The undersheriff received rooms, with a place for his family, and a stipend per prisoner. See *NY Col. Laws*, 4:355-357; *MCC*, 4:422; Peterson and Edwards, *New York*, 1:192; 2:102-104.

13. See deposition of Mary Burton, 4 March 1741, *CHM*, 2:552; *Eng. Mss.*, 74:5.

14. See deposition of John Hughson, 4 March 1741, *CHM*, 2:552; *Eng. Mss.*, 74:6.

15. See recognizance for appearance of Prince, warrant for Peggy, recognizance for appearance of John Hughson, and recognizance for appearance of Sarah Hughson, all dated 4 March 1741, *CHM*, 2:552; *Eng. Mss.*, 74:1-6.

16. See deposition of "John Varrick" (Vaarck), dated 4 March 1741, *CHM*, 2:552; *Eng. Mss.*, 74:7.

## Chapter 2

1. See Horsmanden, *Journal*, 22-31. On celebration of St. Patrick's Day, see Maymie R. Krythe, *All about American Holidays* (New York, 1962), 58-64; Marguerite Ickis, *The Book of Festival Holidays* (New York, 1964), 44-47. As a popular but unofficial holiday, St. Patrick's was only a few years old in New York City, where the idea of celebrating in public fashion had spread from Boston's Irish, starting in 1737. Also, note comments in Horsmanden, *Journal*, 409-410, 415: Taking note of activities in 1742 and suggesting a contrast to the festivities of the day, Horsmanden wrote "perhaps St. Patrick's day might have been an anniversary in our calendar, to have been commemorated by the colony with fasting, weeping and mourning" (ibid., 409-410).

2. For a description of Fort George and its prominence, see Isaac Newton Phelps Stokes, *The Iconography of Manhattan Island, 1498 to 1909*, 6 vols. (New York, 1915-1928), 5:562. Also, see Jerry E. Patterson, *The City of New York: A History Illustrated from the Collections of the Museum of the City of New-York* (New York, 1978); Lamb, *History of the City of New York*, 1:579.

3. For a description of the fire at the fort, see New York *Weekly Journal*, 23 March 1741. On the city's provisions for fighting flames,

see *MCC*, 4:56, 82–83; 5:22. For story of early fire fighting, see George W. Sheldon, *The Story of the Volunteer Fire Department of the City of New York* (New York, 1882), especially chap. 1; Augustine E. Costello, *Our Firemen: A History of the New York Fire Departments, Volunteer and Paid* (New York, 1888), especially 23–37. For problems and regulations, see Peterson and Edwards, *New York*, 1:169–181, 2:128–141.

4. On Cornelius Van Horne, note his political activity and being selected as mayor-designate in 1736 by Rip Van Dam, during the dispute when Gov. William Cosby died. See Lamb, *History of New York*, 1:564n.

5. On damage done, see New York *Weekly Journal*, 23 March, and 8 June 1741, which discuss repairs to fort after the fire, noting that the Assembly "Resolved, That 260£ be allowed for building a New Secretary's Office within *Fort George*, 42 foot long, 20 foot wide[,] of one story 10 foot high. [And] that there be allowed and paid 900£ for building New Barracks for the soldiers in *Fort George*." Expenditures were also voted for batteries and armaments. Also, see *DRCHNY*, 6:215. On poor condition of fort and requests for money to make repairs prior to fire, see *Journal of the Legislative Council of the Colony of New York*, 2 vols. (Albany, 1861), 1:726; and *Journal of the Votes and Proceedings of the General Assembly of the Colony of New York, 1691–1775*, 2 vols. (New York, 1764–1766), 1:750. Following the fires, the city ordered a new fire engine in June 1741; see *MCC*, 5:22. By 1750 the city possesses six fire engines: See the New York *Weekly Post-Boy*, February 12, 1750.

6. On the change in calendar, note that the Gregorian calendar presently in use was not accepted officially in England and its American colonies until 1752. For the period before its adoption, the Gregorian style is referred to as New Style (N.S.) and the Julian as the Old Style (O.S.). Because New Style years began January 1 and Old Style usually on March 25, both styles are sometimes given for dates between January and April, and rendered as 1741/2 or 1741/42. See Harold Watkins, *Time Counts: The Story of the Calendar* (New York, 1954), and Frank Freidel, ed., *Harvard Guide to American History*, 2 vols., rev. ed. (Cambridge, 1974), 1:23–25. The dates in the text are rendered in New Style; in the notes, the 1741/42 convention is used in referring to materials where confusion might otherwise arise.

7. On regulations requiring men to report to fires, see *MCC*, 4:436–438, 5:43; and NY Col. Laws, 2:1064–1067. Starting in 1737, the city appointed firemen and organized them on the basis of the ward in which they resided. The men were unpaid. See Peterson and Edwards, *New York*, 2:135–136.

8. On the continuing fire hazards from chimneys and the city's regulations concerning them, see *MCC*, 4:82; 7:330–331, 409. Also, note the hazard of wooden structures was so great by 1761 that the New York Assembly, which convened in the city as capital of the province, ordered all new buildings south of the Fresh Water Pond to be of brick and stone and roofed with slate or tile. This law passed in 1761 took effect on January 1, 1766: See *NY Col. Laws*, 4:571–573. Also, see *Manual of New York for 1850*, 427–428. For examples of prosecutions arising from dirty chimneys, see Minutes of the Court of General Sessions of the Peace, [1691–1776]," microfilm roll CMS1–CMS2, Historical Documents Collection, Queens College of the City University of New York, CMS2: 9 February 1744, and 3 February 1748. For a contemporary comment on the fire situation, see Peter Kalm, *Travels in North America*, 2 vols. (London, 1770; reprint, New York, 1966), 1:249.

9. On Abigail Earle and Lydia George, see their depositions dated 9 May 1741: *CHM*, 2:556; English Mss. N.Y., 74:38.

10. For mention of losses at the fort and private reward offered, see New York *Weekly Journal*, 13–27 April 1741.

11. On the Spanish Negroes' being captured and condemned, see Charles M. Hough, ed., *Reports of Cases in the Vice Admiralty Court of the Province of New York and in the Court of Admiralty of the State of New York, 1715–1788* (New Haven, 1925), 17: See the case of "Capt[.] John Lush Ag't Sloop La Solidad." Also, see indictment of Antonio *et al.* in *CHM*, 2:555; *Eng. Mss.*, 74:27.

12. On Vernon (1684–1757) and the course of fighting in the West Indies, which was part of the War of Jenkins' Ear (1739–1741) and became part of the War of the Austrian Session (1740–1748) and King George's War (1741–1748) in the colonies, see Cyril H. Hartmann, *The Angry Admiral: The Later Career of Edward Vernon* (London, 1953); Russell W. Ramsey, "The Defeat of Admiral Vernon at Cartagena in 1741," *Southern Quarterly* 1 (1963): 332–355; John T. Lanning, "The American Colonies in the Preliminaries of the War of Jenkins' Ear," *Georgia Historical Quarterly* 11 (1927): 129–155; Albert Harkness, Jr., "Americanism and Jenkins' Ear," *Mississippi Valley Historical Review* 37 (1950): 61–90; David Syrett, "American Provincials and the Havana Campaign," *New York History* 49 (1968): 375–390; Joseph A. Devine, Jr., "The War of Jenkins' Ear: The Political, Economic and Social Impact on theBritish North American Colonies" (Ph.D. dissertation, University of Virginia, 1964); Howard J. Peckham, *The Colonial Wars, 1689–1762* (Chicago, 1964); Robert Leckie, *The Wars of America*, 2 vols. (New York, 1968), 1:28–30.

For news and reaction to war in New York City, see New York

*Weekly Journal* from March 1740 onward, but especially the issues 2, 16, 23 February, 2, 23 March, and 6 April 1741.

13. On drumming up patriotism, see ditty on war (ibid., 2 February 1741):

> Let's revenge the wrongs of Britain,
> And support our injur'd Trade;
> The True Spirit of the Nation
> In our honest Hearts we bring,
> True tho' in an humble Station
> To our Country and our King.
>
> Spain no longer shall assume Boys
> The true Ocean as their own,
> For the Time at last is come Boys,
> We'll her Topsails lower down,
> Tho' in politicks contesting
> Round to Round they veer about
> All their shifts and manifesting,
> We will with our Broad Sides rout.
>
> Hark the British Canon thunders,
> See my Heart's six ship appear,
> Britain acting wonders,
> Fills the southern world with fears,
> Porto Bello sam'd the story,
> Now at length submits to fate,
> VERNON'S courage gains us glory
> His March proves us great.
>
> May all English hearts like you Boys,
> Prove on shore true hearts of Gold
> To their King and Country true Boys,
> And be neither bought or sold;
> Let the Land Men without party
> Act like brethern of the blood,
> To one cause alone be hearty,
> And be that for England's Good.
>
> Yet thro' all the mighty Ocean,
> The English Cross shall honor find,
> Far as Wave can feel a Motion,
> Far as Flag can move with Wind;
> The insulting Monarch showing
> More regard shall humble be,
> The Sole Truth of Britain knowing,
> As their brave they will be free.

*Chapter 3*

1. On reaction to fires, see New York *Weekly Journal*, 13–27 April 1741; *Journal of the Legislative Council of the Colony of New York*, 2 vols. (Albany, 1861), 1:298–302. On New Yorkers' character and animosities, see Patricia U. Bonomi, *A Factious People: Politics and Society in Colonial New York* (New York, 1971), especially "Political Factionalism: A 'divided' and 'contentious' People," 10–16, and chap. 3, "Economic Interests and Political Contentions," 56–102; Greenberg, *Crime and Law Enforcement in the Colony of New York*, 37–69; Thomas J. Archdeacon, *New York City, 1664–1710: Conquest and Change* (Ithaca, 1976), chap. 2, "The People of New York City," 32–57.

2. Ibid.; Bonomi, *A Factious People*, "A mixture of Nations," 18–28.

3. Archdeacon, *New York City, 1664–1710*, chap. 3, "The Merchants," 58–77, and chap. 6, "Ethnic Politics," 123–146; Bonomi, *A Factious People*, especially 60–69, 97–102.

4. Ibid., 18–28; Archdeacon, *New York City, 1664–1710*, 32–57.

5. Ibid., especially 44–52.

6. Ibid.

7. See Joyce D. Goodfriend, "Burghers and Blacks: The Evolution of a Slave Society at New Amsterdam," *New York History*, 59 (1978): 115–131; Rhoda Golden Freeman, "The Free Negro in New York City in the Era before the Civil War" (Ph.D. dissertation, Columbia University, 1966), 9–16; Harry Yoshpe, "Record of Slave Manumissions in New York during the Colonial and Early National Periods," *Journal of Negro History*, 26 (1941): 78–107; E. V. Morgan, "Slavery in New York: The Status of the Slave under the English Colonial Government," *Papers of the American Historical Association*, 5 (1891): 335–350; William R. Riddell, "The Slave in Early New York," *Journal of Negro History*, 13 (1928): 53–86; Samuel D. McKee Jr., *Labor in Colonial New York, 1664–1776* (New York, 1935), 140; Olson, "The Slave Code in Colonial New York," 147; James G. Lydon, "New York and the Slave Trade, 1700–1774," *William and Mary Quarterly*, 35 (1978): 375–394.

8. On fears of revolt and crimes, see McManus, *Slavery in New York*, especially, 85, 121–126; Herbert Aptheker, *American Negro Slave Revolts* (New York, 1943), chap. 2, "Fear of Rebellion," 18–52; Greenberg, *Crime and Law Enforcement in the Colony of New York*, 37–69. The discussion of the Stono uprising and events in South Carolina is drawn from Peter H. Wood's outstanding work, *Black Majority: Negroes in South Carolina from 1670 through the Stono Rebellion* (New York, 1974), especially 285–326.

9. Ibid., 312; W. Noel Sainsbury, comp., Records in the British Public Record Office Relating to South Carolina, 1663–1782, 36. vols., South Carolina Department of Archives and History, Columbia, S.C., 20:40–41. Also, see J. H. Easterby and Ruth S. Green, eds., *The Journal of the Commons House of Assembly, 1736–1750,* 9 vols. (Columbia, 1951–1962), 19 January 1739, 590–596.

10. Wood, *Black Majority,* 314–317; "A Ranger's Report of Travels with General Oglethorpe, 1739–1742," in Newton D. Mereness, ed., *Travels in the American Colonies* (New York, 1916), 223.

11. Wood, *Black Majority,* 315.

12. Ibid., 319–323; Robert Pringle to Capt. Andre Pringle, 27 December 1739, in Walter B. Edgar, ed., *The Letter Book of Robert Pringle, 1737–45,* 2 vols. (Columbia, 1972).

13. Wood, *Black Majority,* 321–323. On New Yorkers, see *New-York Weekly Journal,* 20, 27 April 1741; Horsmanden, *The New York Conspiracy,* 351–353n, 418–420.

14. On order for a military watch, see *Journal of the Legislative Council of the Colony of New York,* 2 vols. (Albany, 1861), 1:298–302.

15. On New York City charter of 1731, sometimes called the Montgomerie Charter, see *NY Col. Laws,* 2:575–639; *MCC,* 4:38–41; 5:190–195, 340.

16. On Anne Hyde Clarke, see Lamb, *History of the City of New York,* 1:580; and see obituaries in the New York *Gazette,* 26 May 1740, and New York *Weekly Journal,* 26 May 1740.

17. For biographical detail on George Clarke (1676–1760), see Charles W. Spencer's entry on him in Allen Johnson and Dumas Malone, eds., *Dictionary of American Biography,* 10 vols. (1928–1937), 2:151–152; E. B. O'Callaghan, ed., *Voyage of Geo. Clarke, Esq. to America* (Albany, 1867); E. B. O'Callaghan, ed., *Letters of Isaac Bobin, Esq., Private Secretary to Hon. Geo. Clarke* (Albany, 1872); Morgan Dix, *History of the Parish of Trinity Church in the City of New York,* 4 vols. (New York, 1898–1906), 1:209–232; Lamb, *History of the City of New York,* 1:579; Stokes, *Iconography,* 5:557.

18. On Clarke's appointment as lieutenant governor and controversy surrounding it, see Lamb, *History of the City of New York,* 1:563–565; Beverly McAnear, "Politics in Provincial New York, 1689–1761" (Ph.D. dissertation, Stanford University, 1935); Nicholas Varga, "New York Government and Politics during the Mid-Eighteenth Century" (Ph.D. dissertation, Fordham University, 1960); and Bonomi, *A Factious People,* 130–134. Also, see Cadwallader Colden, "History of Gov. William Cosby's Administration and of Lt. Gov. George Clarke's Administration through 1737," New-York Historical Society, *Collections* 68 (1935): 283–355; especially note Colden's closing remarks: "Mr. Clarke's party who

were before so exceedingly popular[,] now [that] they were thought to join with the Governor lost every day ground with the People & divided among themselves[.] Some were so fond of the offices in the Governor[']s power that for the sake of them they risked their popularity[.] Others blamed them & would only stand upon that foundation on which their strength lay[,] but all were so much affray'd of loosing their popularity that none of them would be seen to converse with the Governor. Such was his case[,] his Ennemies were equally strong with his friends[,] if they may be so call'd[,] who were in perpetual distrust of him & would not converse with him[.] He found it then necessary after continueing near a year in this State to indeavour to Change hands" (Ibid., 355).

On Zenger's trial, see James Alexander, *A Brief Narrative of the Case and Trial of John Peter Zenger, Printer of the New York "Weekly Journal,"* ed. Stanley N. Katz (Cambridge, 1963). Alexander's is a contemporary account, originally printed in 1736; and Alexander is the same lawyer associated with the prosecution in 1741. William Smith also assisted in defending Zenger: See Lamb, *History of New York City*, 1:550–557. Several other sources also contain the Zenger trial text and accounts: See Frank L. Mott, ed., *The Case and Tryal of John Peter Zenger* (Columbia, Mo., 1954), which reprints the pamphlet Zenger himself printed about his trial; Livingston Rutherford, *John Peter Zenger* (New York, 1904), provides trial text plus a biography of Zenger; Vincent Buranelli, ed., *The Trial of Peter Zenger* (New York, 1957), offers the trial text and sketches of the participants, including Attorney General Bradley.

On impact of Zenger case, see Leonard W. Levy, ed., *Freedom of the Press from Zenger to Hamilton* (Indianapolis, 1966); Sidney Kobre, "The Revolutionary Colonial Press—A Social Interpretation," *Journalism Quarterly* 20 (1943): 193–212; Warren C. Price, "Reflections on the Trial of John Peter Zenger," ibid. 32 (1955): 161–175; Harold L. Nelson, "Seditious Libel in Colonial America," *American Journal of Legal History* 2 (1959): 160–172.

Also see "Freedom of the Press vindicated," *Harper's New Monthly Magazine* 57 (July 1878): 296–305, which provides a lively description of the Zenger trial and its setting; and Bernard C. Steiner, "Andrew Hamilton and John Peter Zenger," *Pennsylvania Magazine*, 20 (Summer 1896): 405–421, which emphasizes Hamilton's role as Zenger's defense lawyer.

19. Clarke's commission as lieutenant governor was dated 30 July 1736, Edmund B. O'Callaghan, ed., *Calendar of New York Colonial Commissions, 1680–1770* (New York, 1929), 33; Philip Livingston to James Alexander, 14 August 1736, Rutherford Collection,

New-York Historical Society, New York City, 2: 185; Bonomi, *A Factious People*, 130–132.

20. For comments on the weather, see Horsmanden, *The New York Conspiracy*, 69, 72–74; William Smith, *The History of the Late Province of New York, from the Discovery, to the Appointment of Governor Colden in 1762*, 2 vols. (New York, 1829–1830), 2:69. Also, note John Peter Zenger's comments: "Our streets are filled with confused heaps of snow, so that the lovers of sled-riding can scarcely use them without danger. The whole mass fell in one night's time, and now the cold is so excessive that while I am writing in a warm room, by a good fire, the ink freezes in the pen," New York *Weekly Journal*, 29 December 1740. "We have now here a second Winter more severe than it was some weeks past, and the navigation of our river is again stopp'd by the ice, and the poor [are] in great want," New York *Weekly Journal*, 2 February 1740/41. "By our accounts from the Country, the people here are in so great want of Fodder for their Cattle, in several places four cows were given to have one delivered in May, and that the Cold had been so severe that even Deer, Squirrells and Birds have been froze to Death and great quantities of Sheep have perished. And this day Wood has been sold for forty Shillings per Cord," New York *Weekly Journal*, 23 February 1740/41. On patterns of weather, see David Ludlum, *Early American Winters, 1604–1820* (Boston, 1966).

21. On location and specialization of city markets, see Peterson and Edwards, *New York*, 2:71–72.

22. On prices, see New York *Gazette* and New York *Weekly Journal*, from October 1740 through May 1741. Especially note bakers' demands and price list for bread in New York *Weekly Journal*, 18 May 1741. The city regulated the price of bread at the time and pegged it to the price of wheat. The cost of a loaf was one penny, but the weight of the loaf varied. For continuing problems, see *NY Col. Laws*, 4:1096–1098.

23. On poorhouse, see *NY Col. Laws*, 2:617; MCC, 4:240–241, 250–251, 307, 459; and Lamb, *History of New York*, 1:559–560. On treatment of poor, see Peterson and Edwards, *New York*, 2:96–108; David M. Schneider, *The History of Public Welfare in New York State, 1609–1866* (Chicago, 1938); Raymond A. Mohl, "Poverty in Early America, a Reappraisal: The Case of Eighteenth Century New York," *New York History* 50 (1969): 5–28.

24. On wheat, depression, and agricultural base, see Ulysses P. Hendrick, *A History of Agriculture in the State of New York* (Cooperstown, 1933), especially 331–332; George E. Mingay, "The Agricultural Depression, 1730–1750," *Economic History Review* 8 (1956): 323–338; William S. Sachs, "Agricultural Conditions in the Northern

Colonies Before the Revolution," *Journal of Economic History* 13 (1953): 274–290; C. R. Ball, "History of Wheat Improvement," *Agriculture History* 4 (1930): especially 48; Percy W. Bidwell and John I. Falconer, *History of Agriculture in the Northern United States, 1620–1860* (Washington, D.C., 1925), chap. 3: Virginia D. Harrington, "The Place of the Merchant in New York Colonial Life," *New York History* 13 (1932): 366–380. On lingering social conflict, see Irving Mark, *Agrarian Conflicts in Colonial New York, 1711–1775* (New York, 1940), especially chap. 3; and Bruce Wilkenfeld, "The Social and Economic Structure of the City of New York, 1695–1796" (Ph.D. dissertation, Columbia University, 1973). Also, see Richard A. Lester, "Currency Issues to Overcome Depression in Delaware, New Jersey, New York, and Maryland, 1715–1737," *Journal of Political Economy* 47 (1939): 182–217.

25. Ibid. On rise of neighboring colonies and trade patterns, see Carl R. Woodward, *The Development of Agriculture in New Jersey, 1640–1880* (New Brunswick, 1927), especially chaps. 3–5; Duane Ball and Gary M. Walton, "Agricultural Productivity Change in Eighteenth Century Pennsylvania," *Journal of Economic History*, 26 (1976): 102–117; James T. Lemon, *Best Poor Man's Country: A Geographical Study of Early Southeastern Pennsylvania* (Baltimore, 1972), especially 149–152; Herbert C. Bell, "The West India Trade before the American Revolution," *American Historical Review*, 22 (1917): 274–285; Richard Pares, *War and Trade in the West Indies, 1739–1763* (Oxford, 1936); Curtis Nettels, "The Economic Relations of Boston, Philadelphia, and New York, 1680–1715," *Journal of Economic and Business History* 3 (1931): 185–215; Gary B. Nash, "Maryland's Economic War with Pennsylvania," *Maryland Historical Magazine*, 60 (1965): 231ff.

26. For George Clarke's comments, see Charles Z. Lincoln, ed. *Messages from the Governor, Comprising Executive Communications to the Legislature and Other Papers . . . 1683–1906*, 11 vols. (Albany, 1909), 1:256–261.

27. On prices, see Herman M. Stoker, "Wholesale Prices at New York City, 1720–1800," *Cornell University Agricultural Experiment Station Memoir*, 142 (November 1932), Part 2; Arthur H. Cole, *Wholesale Commodity Prices in the United States, 1700–1861* (Cambridge, Mass., 1938); and U.S. Department of Commerce, Bureau of the Census, *Historical Statistics of the United States: Colonial Times to 1970*, 2 vols. (Washington, D.C., 1975), 2:1197, "Average Annual Wholesale Prices of Selected Commodities in Philadelphia: 1720 to 1775."

28. On labor situation, see McKee, *Labor in Colonial New York, 1664–1776*; Arnett G. Lindsay, "The Economic Condition of the Negro

in New York prior to 1861," *Journal of Negro History* 6 (1921): 190–200.

29. For Clarke's comments, see Lincoln, *Messages from the Governor*, 1:260. On population, see Davis, "New York's Long Black Line: A Note on the Growing Slave Population, 1626–1790," 41–59; DHNY, 1:694–695; and Evarts B. Greene and Virginia D. Harrington, *American Population before the Federal Census of 1790* (New York, 1932), 98–99. On importations, see DRCHNY, 5:814; Elizabeth Donnan, ed., *Documents Illustrative of the History of the Slave Trade to America* (Washington, D.C., 1935), 3:462–509; Lydon, "New York and the Slave Trade, 1700–1774," 375–394; and *Historical Statistics of the United States*, 2:1173, "Slave Trade in New York: 1701–1764."

30. On fear of slaves, see Edwin V. Morgan, "Slavery in New York, with Special Reference to New York City," in Maul Wilder Goodwin *et al.*, *Half-Moon Series: Papers on Historic New York*, 2 vols. (New York, 1899), 1:12; Aptheker, *American Negro Slave Revolts*, chap. 2; McKee, *Labor in Colonial New York*, chap. 4.

31. Lincoln, *Messages from the Governor*, 1:260.

32. On general background of war, see Harkness, "Americanism and Jenkins' Ear," 61–90.

33. On New York's reaction, see New York *Weekly Journal*, 2, 23 March, 6 April 1741. On shipping problems, see embargo announced in New York *Weekly Journal*, 2 March 1740/41; Clarke's instructions from London, dated 16 August 1739, to commission privateers: DRCHNY, 6:147; and E. B. O'Callaghan, comp., *Calendar of New York Colonial Commissions* (New York, 1929), 334. Also, see Pares, *War and Trade*, chaps. 1–3; Bell, "The West India Trade before the American Revolution," 284ff.; Violet Barbour, "Privateers and Pirates in the West Indies," *American Historical Review*, 16 (1911): 529ff. Also, see retort to those concerned about injury to personal interests, in New York *Weekly Journal*, 13 April 1741: "If all the King's Subjects in *America* could suffer themselves to be strictly honest, and just to the Interest of the Nation but for a very few Months, we should have but little Occasion for Guns, or Swords in the West Indies. But Oh thou Gain!"

34. On Clarke and the assembly, see Lincoln, *Messages from the Governors*, 1:288–289, 290–292; *Journal of the Votes and Proceedings of the General Assembly of the Colony of New York, 1691–1775*, 2 vols. (New York, 1764–1766), 1:778–808; *Journal of the Legislative Council*, 1:755ff.

35. Note Clarke's complaining of the assembly showing signs of a "Thirst for Power, that no Consideration how equitable, prudential or beneficial so ever must stand in its way. . . . They in effect

subverted the Constitution, assuming to themselves an undoubted and essential Branch of his Majesty's Royal Prerogative." Clarke also noted that "A Jealousy . . . for some years has obtained in England that the Plantations are not without Thoughts of throwing off their dependence on the Crown of England." Lincoln, *Messages of the Governors*, 1:293. Also, see New York *Weekly Journal*, 27 April 1741. The difficulty over revenue was tied to the assembly's struggle for power that began before the war. In reply to Clarke's contentions about rebellious inclinations, the assembly replied that "Not one single person in the colony has any such thought or desire, for under what government can we be better protected, or our liberties and properties so well secured?" See Lincoln, *Messages of the Governors*, 1:293n.

36. On New York troops, see *Journal of the Assembly of New York*, 1:778–808; DRCHNY, 6:185; Syrett, "American Provincials and the Havana Campaign," 375–390. Note that on July 1, 1740, Clarke transmitted to the assembly a copy of his "eighth instruction" sent from London. It said, "We trust and expect that our Assembly of New York will provide victuals, transports, and all other necessaries for the troops to be raised in our Province, except their clothes, tents, arms, ammunition, and pay, until their arrival at the General Rendezvous in the West Indies." The assembly acted promptly and on July 12, 1740, appropriated monies. See Lincoln, *Messages from the Governors*, 1:288; and *NY Col. Laws*, 1740, chap. 603. On September 9, 1740, Clarke told the assembly that "At your last sitting you gave a sum of money for transporting and victualling five hundrd men to be employed in the expedition against the Spaniards, that being the number you then thought would be raised in this Province for that service, but there being now another company of one hundred men raising and almost complete, I recommend it to you in his Majesty's name to give a further sum." The assembly declined any further payment. See Lincoln, *Messages from the Governors*, 1:289–290.

37. On New York's invasion fears, see Lois Mulkearn, "The English Eye the French in North America," *Pennsylvania History* 21 (1954): 316–337; Douglas Edward Leach, *The Northern Colonial Frontier, 1607–1763* (New York, 1966); Lawrence Henry Gipson, *The Coming of the Revolution, 1763–1775* (New York, 1954), chap. 2; Devine, "The War of Jenkins' Ear: The Political, Economic and Social Impact on the British North American Colonies." Note comment in New York *Weekly Journal*, 16 February 1740/41: "We are told that the *French* Privateers are very brisk in the West Indies, and it may not be long before we may expect them on this Coast."

Also, see protective measures ordered, *Journal of Assembly*, 1:758–769; *DRCHNY*, 6:147.

38. On proclamation, see New York *Weekly Journal*, 20 April 1741.

## Chapter 4

1. Horsmanden, *The New York Conspiracy*, 31–35. On council action, see *MCC*, 5: 14–19, 21; *CHM*, 2:553; *Eng. Mss.* 74:8
2. For membership of city council, see chap. 1, n11; *MCC*, 5:14–19.
3. On ward boundaries, see *MCC*, 4:39–41; *NY Col. Laws*, 2:599–602; Peterson and Edwards, *New York*, 143–144. On distribution of slaves, see Thomas J. Davis, "'These Enemies of their Own Household'," *Journal of the Afro-American Genealogical Society* 6 (1985): 33–51, especially table 4; and, Archedeacon, *New York City, 1664–1712*, 89–90.
4. On prevalent suspicions about the fires and robberies, see the New York *Weekly Journal*, 23 March 1740/41; and comments in the Boston *Weekly News-Letter*, 7–14 May 1741. On liabilities, see Olson, "The Slave Code in Colonial New York," 147ff.; Nordstrom, "The New York Slave Code," 7–26.
5. On use of slaves, see McKee, *Labor in Colonial New York*, 114–169; McManus, *Negro Slavery in New York*, 41–58. On identification of slaveholders, see "A List of Negroes Committed on Account of Conspiracy," Horsmanden, *The New York Conspiracy*, appendix.
6. Cf. chap. 1, n11. For a sidelight on John Chambers, see Edmund B. O'Callaghan, "John Chambers: One of the Justices of the Supreme Court of the Province of New York," *New York Genealogical and Biographical Record* 3 (April 1872): 57–62.
7. For warrants of commitments, see *CHM*, 2:553; *Eng. Mss.*, 74:8.
8. Horsmanden, *The New York Conspiracy*, 31.
9. For details of Horsmanden's life, see Charles W. Spencer's entry on him in *Dictionary of American Biography*, 9:236–237; David McAdam, *et al.*, eds., *History of the Bench and Bar of New York*, 2 vols. (New York, 1897), 1:361–362; E. A. Jones, *American members of the Inns of Court* (New York, 1924); and Mary P. McManus, "Daniel Horsmanden, Eighteenth Century New Yorker" (Ph.D. dissertation, Fordham University, 1960); Lamb, *History of New York*, 1:576.
10. On city-colony relations, see Peterson and Edwards, *New York*, 2:13–41, 190–205; Edward Durand, *Finances of New York City* (New York, 1898), chap. 1; Bayrd Still, "The Personality of New York City," *New York Folklore Quarterly* 14 (1958): 83–92; Michael Kam-

men, *Colonial New York: A History* (New York, 1975), especially chaps. 3–5; Bonomi, *A Factious People*, 25–26, 32–37, especially 80–81; Charles W. Spencer, "Sectional Aspects of New York Provincial Politics," *Political Science Quarterly*, 30 (1915): 397–424. For examples of politics, see *Journal of the Legislative Council*, 2:95–99, 101, 109–110, 916–917. For extension of theme, see David M. Ellis, " 'Upstate Hicks' versus 'City Slickers'," *New-York Historical Society Quarterly* 43 (1959): 202–220.

11. For official note of rewards, see *MCC*, 5:16–18; New York *Weekly Journal*, 20 April 1741; and "Proclamation offering a reward of one hundred pounds to any white person who shall discover the person or persons who set fire to the several houses and other buildings in the city of New York," dated 17 April 1741, in *CHM*, 2:553; *Eng. Mss.*, 74:10.

12. For rewards stipulations, see preceding note and *MCC*, 5:16–18. Also, note ibid., 4:483, which states city revenue for 1739 at £301. On city revenues, see "Municipal Revenue from Franchises and Properties in Pounds, over Five-Year Periods," in Peterson and Edwards, *New York*, 2:197; and Durand, *Finances of New York City*, 19. On wage scales, see McKee, *Labor in Colonial New York*, especially 54–61, 126–130.

13. For comments on search, see New York *Weekly Journal*, 20 April 1741. On the number of houses in the city, see "A plan of the city and environs along with principle land marks, drawn from memory in 1813 by David Grim then 76," in *Manual of New York for 1855*, 584–586. Grim's plan shows 1141 houses: 129 on the west side of Broadway to the Hudson; 232 on the east side of Broadway to the west of Broad Street; 324 on the east side of Broad Street to the west side of Williams Street; 242 on the east side of Williams Street to the west side of Pearl Street; and 214 on the east side of Pearl Street to the East River.

On time calculation, allow 13 hours (780 minutes) from dawn to dusk and 14 men (7 aldermen plus 7 assistants) searching separately: That yields a total searching time of 10,920 minutes; dividing by the number of houses produces 9.6 minutes per house.

14. On Philipse, see Bonomi, *A Factious People*, 67–68, 93–99, 130, 133; he was the speaker in the twenty-second assembly, 1739–1743; Lamb, *History of New York City*, 1:602, 692; 2:514, 541, 575.

15. On law of conspiracy, see James W. Bryan, *The Development of the English Law of Conspiracy* (Baltimore, 1909); Peter W. Winfield, *The History of Conspiracy and Abuse of Legal Procedure* (New York, 1921); and Robert Hazell, *Conspiracy and Civil Liberties* (London, 1974).

## Chapter 5

1. See Horsmanden, *The New York Conspiracy*, 37–47. On official positions, see Edgar A. Werner, *Civil List and Constitutional History of the Colony and States of New York* (Albany, 1888), 561. Also, see McAdam, *History of the Bench and Bar of New York*, which contains background and biographical sketches. For operation and position of the bench, see volume one of Paul Hamlin and Charles E. Baker, eds., *Supreme Court of Judicature in New York, 1691–1704*, 3 vols. (New York, 1959), which provides an introduction to the court, especially 1:149–158, on judges' charge to grand jury, and 1:149–158, on operation of grand jury; and Goebel and Naughton, *Law Enforcement in Colonial New York*, 80–90; Carter R. Pitman, "Judicial Supremacy in America: Its Colonial and Constitutional History," *Georgia Bar Journal* 16 (1953): 148–165.

2. On DeLancey's being in Rhode Island, note his being a member of the commission "determining the bounds of Narragansetts bay, and the eastern boundary of Rhode Island": See *CHM*, 2:552; *Eng. Mss.*, 73:144–146.

3. On Frederick Philipse II (1698–1751), see Bonomi, *Factious People*, 95, 110, 114; and Lamb, *History of New York City*, 1:602, 692.

4. The full roster of grand jurors included Henry Beekman, Jr., John Cruger, Jr., Isaac DePeyster, Thomas Duncan, Rene Hett, Abraham Keletass, Jeremiah Latouche, John McEvers, John Merritt, David Provoost, Joseph Reed, Anthony Rutgers, Adoniah Schuyler, George Spencer, David Van Horne, Winant Van Zant, Robert Watts, foreman. Van Zant, aside from having his warehouse burned in 1741, suffered earlier trouble with slaves in 1735, when a coroner's jury acquitted him for "accidentally" whipping to death a slave of his arrested by the night watch for being on the street without a pass after dark. The jury ruled that "the Correction given by the Master was not the Cause of [the slave's] death, but that it was by the visitation of God." See New York *Weekly Journal*, 5 January 1735/36.

5. The "gentlemen of the bar" who appeared were James Alexander (1691–1756), John Chambers, William Jamison, Abraham Lodge, Joseph Murray (c1694–1757), Richard Nicolls, and William Smith (1697–1759). For some biographical notes on individuals, see *Dictionary of American Biography*, 1:167–168, on Alexander; 7:363–364 on Murray; 9:352–353 on Smith. Also see, Lamb, *History of New York City*, 1:503–504, 557–573, and obituary in New York *Gazette or Weekly Post Boy*, 5 April 1756 on Alexander; Lamb, 1:552–554, 638–647, and O'Callaghan, "John Chambers: One of

the Justices of the Supreme Court of the Province of New York,''
57–62, on Chambers; Lamb, 1:507n, 678, on Nicolls. On other
service of men to colony, see McAdam, *History of the Bench and Bar
of New York*; and Werner, *Civil List*; and Goebel and Naughton,
*Law Enforcement in Colonial New York*.

6. For review of the action in 1712, see Kenneth Scott, ''The Slave
Insurrection in New York in 1712,'' *New-York Historical Society
Quarterly* 45 (1961): 43–74. Also, see Joshua Coffin, *An Account of
Some of the Principal Slave Insurrections* (New York, 1860), 10–11;
William R. Riddell, ''The Slave in Early New York,'' *Journal of
Negro History*, 13 (1928): especially 70–74; Harvey Wish, ''Ameri-
can Slave Insurrections before 1861,'' ibid., 22 (1937): 308ff.;
Goebel and Naughton, *Law Enforcement in Colonial New York*, 118–
119; Aptheker, *American Negro Slave Revolts*, 172–173.

  The term Cormantine also appears elsewhere as ''Coroman-
tee'' or ''Coromantyn'' and was used in the English colonies as a
common appelation for slaves from Africa's Gold Coast region.
The term particularly denoted Africans of Akan origin. Also, note
that the name Cuffee derives from the Akan language name Cofi.
See Orlando Patterson, ''Slavery and Slave Revolts: A Sociohistorical Analysis of the First Maroon War, 1665–1740,'' *Social
and Economic Studies* 19 (1970): 289–325; and W. W. Claridge, *A
History of the Gold Coast and Ashanti* (London, 1964).

  The term Pawpaws referred to blacks from the area of Petit
Popo and Grand Popo in the Bight of Benin area of Africa. See Patrick Manning, ''The Slave Trade in the Bight of Benin, 1640–
1890,'' in Henry A. Gemery and Jan S. Hogendorn, eds., *The Uncommon Market: Essays in the Economic History of the Atlantic Slave Trade*
(New York, 1979): 107–141, especially 115.

  Also on Cormantines and Pawpaws, see Donnan, *Documents Illustrative of the History of the Slave Trade to America*, 1:392n, 398.

  For contemporary report on action, see Governor Robert
Hunter's comments, Hunter to Lords of Trade, 23 June 1712, in
*DRCHNY*, 5:341–342; and Hunter to Lords of Trade, 14 March
1713, ibid., 5:356–357. Note that the action occurred after mid-
night, and thus, on the morning of 7 April 1712. In his letter of 23
June, Hunter misdated the events as occurring on April 6. Both
*Minutes of the General Sessions of the Peace*, 2:229–230; and Horsman-
den, *The New York Conspiracy*, 59n, give April 7.

7. On deaths and contemporary description, see Coroner's Inquisi-
tion, 9 April 1712, in New-York Historical Society, Miscellaneous
Manuscripts, New York City, box 4; *Minutes of the General Sessions
of the Peace*, 2:229–230; and Boston *Weekly News-Letter*, 7–14, 14–21
April 1712.

8. For quotations, see [Rev.] John Sharpe to Secretary [of Society for the Propagation of the Gospel in Foreign Parts], 23 June 1712, in Roswell R. Hoes, "The Negro Plot of 1712," *New York Genealogical and Biographical Record* 21 (1890): 162–163; and Boston *Weekly News-Letter*, 7–14, April 1712. Also, see Aptheker, *American Negro Slave Revolts*, 172.

9. For summary of punishments and comments, see Sharpe to Secretary, 23 June 1712, in Hoes, "The Negro Plot of 1712," 162–163. Also, see McKee, *Labor in Colonial New York*, 151–152.

10. For Governor Robert Hunter's comments, see Hunter to Lords of Trade, 23 June 1712, in *DRCHNY*, 5:341–342; and Hunter to Lords of Trade, 14 March 1713, ibid., 5:356–357. On Hunter himself, see the excellent biography, *Robert Hunter, 1666–1734: New York's Augustan Statesman* (Syracuse, 1983), by Mary L. Lustig.

   In reaction to the uprising, the slave code was tightened by the colonial assembly on 10 December 1712, and further by the city council on 3 March 1713: See, *NY Col. Laws*, 1:762–767; and *MCC*, 3:30–31. Also, see added restrictions by council, ibid., 3:277–278, 296; 4:86–90.

   On Leisler's sentencing and punishment, see Lawrence H. Leder, ed., "Records of the Trials of Jacob Leisler and His Associates," *New-York Historical Society Quarterly*, 26 (1952): 440–452; Sloughter to Sec'y Blathwayt, July 1691, *DRCHNY*, 3:789. For good brief discussion, see Archdeacon, *New York City, 1664–1712*, chap. 5, "Leisler's Rebellion," 97–122.

11. On regulations for summary justice and trials for slaves, see Olson, "The Slave Code in Colonial New York," 147–165; Nordstrom, "New York Slave Code," 7–26; and *NY Col. Laws*, 1:762–767. Also, note debate on extent to which summary proceedings were used against slaves in colonial New York: See Goebel and Naughton, *Law Enforcement in Colonial New York*, 418, which states that while slaves "sometimes [were] accorded the usual indictment process and trial available to freemen . . . the usual practice was to try them summarily." That view is contested by Leo Hershkowitz, "Tom's Case: An Incident, 1741," *New York History* 52 (1971): 63–71, which states that "a study of the cases in New York City, however, reveals that the indictment process was used more often than not." Ibid., 64–65n. Note that Hershkowitz's article presents the transcript of the legal proceedings and execution of a slave in Kingston, New York, and is not connected to the New York Conspiracy. The indictment process was used throughout the proceedings in 1741, as indicated by the warrants and indictments issued during the proceedings: See *CHM*, e.g. 2:8–18. No notice of these warrants and indictments appears in Horsmanden,

*The New York Conspiracy*, and the existence of these manuscript documents bearing on the proceedings has largely been overlooked, as noted above in my remarks on sources.

12. On court terms and cancellation of circuit courts because of extension of the supreme court's term, see *Calendar of Council Minutes*, 338. Also, see Hamlin and Baker, *Supreme Court of Judicature in New York, 1691–1704*, 1:278–279, 291.

13. On background of problems of Dutch being suspected and having difficulty with English, see Greenberg, *Crime and Law Enforcement in Colony of New York*, 64–65, 141; Langdon G. Wright, "Local Government in Colonial New York, 1640–1710" (Ph.D. dissertation, Cornell University, 1974); Archdeacon, *New York City, 1664–1710*, chap. 6, "Ethnic Politics, " 123–146.

## Chapter 6

1. See Horsmanden, *The New York Conspiracy*, 47–66. On indictments, see *CHM*, 2:554; *Eng. Mss.*, 74:20–22. On coverage in colonial press, see Boston *Weekly News-Letter*, 7–14 May 1741. Reporting on the events appears in Boston *Weekly News-Letter*, 9 April, 25 June, 16, 23 July, 27 August, 8 October 1741; and in the New York *Weekly Journal*, 23, 30 March, 9, 20, 27 April, 18, 25 May, 8, 15, 22, 29 June, 6, 13, 20, 27 July, 10, 31 August, 14 September, 14 October 1741. Also, see *South Carolina Gazette*, 9 April, 23, 30 July 1741.

2. On fires and execution of slaves in Hackensack, see New York *Weekly Journal*, 4 May 1741; Boston *Weekly News-Letter*, 14 May 1741; William Nelson, ed., *Archives of the State of New Jersey*, 1st series, 13 vols. (Trenton, 1901–1917), 12:88–99; *Proceedings of the New Jersey Historical Society for 1874* (Trenton, 1876), 179; Henry S. Cooley, *A Study of Slavery in New Jersey* (Baltimore, 1896), 40–43; Aptheker, *American Negro Slave Revolts*, 194. Also, on arson and other threats by slaves in New Jersey, see Harry B. Weiss and Grace M. Weiss, *Crime and Punishment in Colonial New Jersey* (Trenton, 1960), 45–55. Also, see belated report in the *South Carolina Gazette*, 30 July 1741.

3. On segregation of prisoners, note that the authorities placed the blacks in the regular prison cells in city hall's basement and placed the whites on the upper floors. That accounts for Peggy's referring to "the two poor fellows below." On use of basement, see Peterson and Edwards, *New York*, 2:102–103.

4. On Mrs. Romme's arrest, see "warrant for commitment of Elizabeth, wife of John Romme," dated 8 May 1741; *CHM*, 2:556; *Eng. Mss.*, 74:36.

## Chapter 7

1. See Horsmanden, *The New York Conspiracy*, 66–88.

2. On usual racial segregation in jail, see note 3, chapter 6; and for further elaboration on conditions, see Greenberg, *Crime and Law Enforcement*, 125–127. Jail conditions were apparently rotten; indeed, city hall itself was declared rotten in 1738: See, *MCC*, 4:443.

3. On Horsmanden's connection with Trinity Church, see McManus, "Daniel Horsmanden," 172; and Lamb, *History of the City of New York*, 1:577–578. On general observance of proclamation day, see New York *Weekly Journal*, 18 May 1741. On Burton's deposition, see *CHM*, 2:556; *Eng. Mss.*, 74:40.

4. Various forms of currency were used in colonial New York. The official monetary unit was the English pound sterling, symbolized £; one £ equals twenty shillings or two hundred and forty pence. A shortage of currency induced colonists to use more than the English units, and particularly, Spanish coins were circulated. The American dollar owes its origin, in part, to the Spanish coin called the *dollar*, which was also referred to as a piece of eight. The American phrase two bits reflects the Spanish connection, for two bits of a piece of eight equals a quarter.

    On colonial monetary units, see Simon L. Adler, "Money and Money Units in the American Colonies," *Rochester Historical Society*, Public Fund Series, 8 (1929): 143–173; Henry Chapman, "The Colonial Coins of America Prior to the Declaration of Independence," *Numismatist* 61 (1948): 75–87. Also, see Leslie V. Brock, *The Currency of the American Colonies, 1700–1764* (New York, 1975); E. James Ferguson, "Currency Finance: An Interpretation of Colonial Monetary Practices," *William and Mary Quarterly* 10 (1953): 153–180; M. L. Burstein, "Colonial Currency and Contemporary Monetary Theory: A Review Article," *Explorations in Entrepreneurial History*, 2nd series, 3 (1966): 220–223; Charles J. Bullock, *Essays on the Monetary History of the United States* (New York, 1900); Curtis P. Nettels, *The Money Supply of the American Colonies before 1720* (Madison, 1934); and Joseph A. Ernst, *Money and Politics in America, 1755–1775* (Chapel Hill, 1973). Series Z599–610, "Paper Money Outstanding in American Colonies: 1705–1775," in *Historical Statistics of the United States*," 2:1200, may be of interest. Also, see Lester, "Currency Issues to Overcome Depression," 182–217; and James H. Hickcox, *A History of Bills of Credit or Paper Money Issues by New York from 1709 to 1789* (Albany, 1866).

    On Peggy's deposition, see *CHM*, 2:556; *Eng. Mss.*, 74:42.

## Chapter 8

1. See Horsmanden, *The New York Conspiracy*, 89–117.
2. Stoutenburgh later (1761) became keeper of the city's fire engines; *MCC*, 6:255.
3. On slave's position in court and giving "negro evidence," see Olson, "The Slave Code in Colonial New York," 147–165; Wilbert E. Moore, "Slave Law and the Social Structure," *Journal of Negro History* 26 (1941): 171–202; and *Colonial Laws of New York*, 1:761–767, 2:679–688; and Hamlin and Baker, *Supreme Court of Judicature in New York, 1691–1704*, 1:160–162.
4. On operation of legal theory, see Hamlin and Baker, *Supreme Court of Judicature in New York*, 1:141–245; Goebel and Naughton, *Law Enforcement in Colonial New York*, 573–576, 629, and chap. 7; Richard B. Morris, "The Sources of Early American Law: The Colonial Period," *West Virginia Law Review* 40 (1934): 212–234; George A. Billias, ed., *Law and Authority in Colonial America: Selected Essays* (Barre, Mass., 1965); Zechariah Chafee, Jr., "Colonial Courts and the Common Law," *Proceedings of the Massachusetts Historical Society* 68 (1952): 132–159; Carter R. Pittman, "The Colonial and Constitutional History of the Privilege against Self-Incrimination in America," *Virginia Law Review* 21 (1935): 763–789; Leonard W. Levy and Lawrence H. Leder, " 'Exotic Fruit': The Right against Compulsory Self-Incrimination in Colonial New York," *William and Mary Quarterly* 20 (1963): 3–32; Arthur P. Scott, *Criminal Law in Colonial Virginia* (Chicago, 1930); Greenberg, *Crime and Law Enforcement in the Colony of New York*, chap. 8; and Henry W. Scott, *The Courts of the State of New York* (New York, 1909).
5. On position of justices, see "Prestige of the Court" in Hamlin and Baker, *Supreme Court of Judicature in New York*, 1:412–422; Goebel and Naughton, *Law Enforcement in Colonial New York*, 73–79; Pittman, "Judicial Supremacy," 148–165; William R. Riddell, "Notes on the Pre-Revolutionary Judiciary in English Colonies," *Canadian Bar Association Review*, 11 (1933): 317–324, 376–384. Also, see Felix Rackow, "The Right to Counsel: English and American Precedents," *William and Mary Quarterly* 11 (1954): 3–27.
6. On prevailing white attitudes toward blacks, see Winthrop D. Jordan, *White Over Black: American Attitudes toward the Negro, 1550–1812* (Chapel Hill, 1968), especially chap. 3. Also, note similarities in Smith's argument with antebellum defense of slavery: See, Eric L. McKitrick, ed., *Slavery Defended: The Views of the Old South* (Englewood Cliffs, N.J., 1963), especially 34–69.
7. On plight of free blacks in New York, see Freeman, "The Free Negro in New York City," especially 10–17.

8. On slave rebelliousness and white fears, see Aptheker, *American Negro Slave Revolts.*, especially chap. 2; Aptheker, "Slave Resistance in the United States," in Nathan I. Huggins *et al.*, eds., *Key Issues in the Afro-American Experience*, 2 vols. (New York, 1971), 1:161–173; Aptheker, "Maroons within the Present Limits of the United States," *Journal of Negro History*, 24 (1939): 167–84; and Aptheker, *To Be Free: Studies in American Negro History* (New York, 1948), especially 11–30, "Slave Guerrilla Warfare"; Jordan, *White Over Black*, especially 122–135; Eugene D. Genovese, *From Rebellion to Revolution: Afro-American Slave Revolts in the Making of the Modern World* (Baton Rouge, 1979), especially chap. 1; and Marion D. deB. Kilson, "Towards Freedom: An Analysis of Slave Revolts in the United States," *Phylon* 25 (1964): 175–187.
9. On punishment, see William R. Riddell, "Judicial Execution by Burning at the Stake in New York," *American Bar Association Journal*, 15 (1929): 373–376; Greenberg, *Crime and Law Enforcement in the Colony of New York*, 39, 223; and Goebel and Naughton, *Law Enforcement in Colonial New York*, 701–710. Also, note that Governor Clarke sent a transcript of Quack and Cuff's trial to London, with a cover letter commenting on his view of the plot, its origins and consequences: See Clarke to Lords of Trade, 20 June 1741, in *DRCHNY*, 6:198.

## Chapter 9

1. See Horsmanden, *The New York Conspiracy*, 117–138.
2. On New York's handling of problems with disorderly houses and their proprietors, see Greenberg, *Crime and Law Enforcement in the Colony of New York*, especially 67–68, 91–98.
3. On colonial officials' aversion to ordering prison sentences, see ibid., 125; and Goebel and Naughton, *Law Enforcement in Colonial New York*, 701–710. For further development, see Leon Radzinowicz, *A History of English Criminal Law and its Administration from 1750*, 2 vols. (New York, 1948–1957).
4. On rights of accused, see Goebel and Naughton, *Law Enforcement in Colonial New York*, 411–442, 513–514, 574–477; Rackow, "The Right to Counsel," 3–27; Milton M. Klein, "Prelude to Revolution in New York: Jury Trials and Judicial Tenure," *William and Mary Quarterly* 17 (1960): 439–462.
5. On position of women, see Carl Holliday, *Woman's Life in Colonial Days* (Boston, 1922); and Mary S. Benson, *Women in Eighteenth Century America: A Study of Opinion and Social Usage* (New York, 1935). For pattern of treatment of female defendants in New York courts, see Greenberg, *Crime and Law Enforcement in the Colony of*

*New York*, especially 42, 51–53, 76–83. Also, see comment on "Women Attorneys" in Hamlin and Baker, *Supreme Court*, 1:108, which notes that "in New York women . . . appeared in court to plead either for themselves or for others . . . but in every case that has been found, their appearances were for the purposes of representing themselves as unmarried women, or to defend their husbands' interests."

## Chapter 10

1. See Horsmanden, *The New York Conspiracy*, 138–167.
2. On requests and handing of pardons for capital crimes, see Greenberg, *Crime and Law Enforcement in the Colony of New York*, 127–132; Goebel and Naughton, *Law Enforcement in Colonial New York*, 748–761. On appeals, see ibid., chap. 4. The governor and council heard appeals on writs of error in cases of judgment by the supreme court; and the king and council represented ultimate appeal: See ibid., 237. Also, see Richard B. Morris, "Judicial Supremacy and the Inferior Courts in the American Colonies," *Political Science Quarterly*, 55 (1940): 429–434.

## Chapter 11

1. See Horsmanden, *The New York Conspiracy*, 168–196.
2. On capture of Spanish blacks, see Hough, *Reports of Cases in the Vice Admiralty Court*, 17; and on presumption of color, see Carl N. Degler, "Slavery and the Genesis of American Race Prejudice," *Comparative Studies in History and Society*, 2 (1959): 49–66; Winthrop D. Jordan, "Modern Tensions and the Origins of American Slavery," *Journal of Southern Slavery*, 27 (1962): 18–33; and Richard B. Morris, "The Measure of Bondage in the Slave States," *Mississippi Valley Historical Review*, 41 (1954): 219–240. On other problems with military prisoners, see Smith, *Colonists in Bondage*, 198–203.
3. On rules of evidence, see Goebel and Naughton, *Law Enforcement in Colonial New York*, especially 629; Olson, "The Slave Code in Colonial New York," 147–165; and *Colonial Laws of New York*, 1:761–767, and 2:679–688. On war worries, see Devine, "The War of Jenkins' Ear," especially chap. 3.
4. On "Mr. Ogilvie," note his being a missionary to Mohawks and later pastor of Trinity Church. See Lamb, *History of New York*, 1:585.

5. For background on Indian slavery, see Almon W. Lauber, *Indian Slavery in Colonial Times within the Present Limits of the United States* (New York, 1913): and Allen W. Trelease, *Indian Affairs in Colonial New York: Seventeenth Century* (New York, 1960). Also, see Alden T. Vaughan's instructive discussion of early American attitudes toward Indians, "From White Man to Redskin: Changing Anglo-American Perceptions of the American Indian," *American Historical Review*, 87 (1982): 917–953. For illustration of relations between blacks and Indians, see James H. Johnston, "Documentary Evidence of Relations of Negroes and Indians," *Journal of Negro History* 14 (1929): 21–43; and Kenneth W. Porter, "Relations between Negroes and Indians within the Present Limits of the United States," *Journal of Negro History* 17 (1932): 282–321.
6. On proclamation of June 19, see *CHM*, 2:559; *Eng. Mss.*, 74:68; and New York *Weekly Journal* 29 June 1741. Also, see Clarke to the Lords of Trade, 20 June 1741, *DRCHNY*, 6:198–199; and his references to the plot in his opening address to Assembly, 14 April 1741: Lincoln, *Messages of the Governors*, 1:297–298; and note Assembly's fortifications act and act for providing military watches, in *NY Col. Laws*, chaps. 707 and 708, both passed June 13, 1741.

## Chapter 12

1. See Horsmanden, *The New York Conspiracy*, 196–278. Also, see "Names of negroes examined; places were examined; names of the negroes accused by them, and circumstances elicited by their testimony" and "List of negroes whose confessions were taken, with remarks": *CHM*, 2:562–563; *Eng. Mss.*, 74:88, 99, 100, 105.
2. On Van Cortlandt family, see L. E. DeForest, *The Van Cortlandt Family* (New York, 1930); Sung Bok Kim, "The Manor of Cortlandt and Its Tenants, 1697–1783" (Ph.D. dissertation, Michigan State University, 1966); Lamb, *History of New York City*, 1:600; and on Frederick Van Cortlandt, see Hamlin and Baker, *Supreme Court of Judicature in New York*, 3:192–195.
3. On education of blacks in colonial New York, see Carleton Mabee, *Black Education in New York State from Colonial to Modern Times* (Syracuse, 1979), especially chaps. 1–2; Carter G. Woodson, *The Education of the Negro Prior to 1861: A History of the Education of the Colored People of the United States from the Beginning of Slavery to the Civil War* (New York, 1915), especially chaps. 1–3; Enid V. Barnett, "Educational Activities by and in Behalf of Negroes in New York, 1800–1830," *Negro History Bulletin* 14 (1951): 99.
4. On doubloons' usage and value, see Adler, "Money and Money

Units in the American Colonies," 143–173; Chapman, "The Colonial Coins of America," 75–87. Also, see Burton Hobson and Robert Obojski, *Illustrated Encyclopedia of World Coins* (New York, 1970), s.v. "Doubloon"; and Robert Friedberg, *Gold Coins of the World Complete from 600 A.D. to 1958: An Illustrated Standard Catalogue with Valuations* (Chicago, 1958), 289–292.

5. On dancing master Holt, see his advertisement in New York *Gazette*, 13 February 1739, for a performances of "The Adventure of Harlequinne and Scaracouch, or the Spaniard Tricked."

6. On colonial fears of epidemic, see John Duffy, *Epidemics in Colonial America* (Baton Rouge, 1953); and John B. Blake, "Diseases and Medical Practice in Colonial America," *International Record of Medicine* 171 (1958): 350–363. On New York particularly, see Claude E. Heathon, "Medicine in New York during the English Colonial Period, 1664–1775," *Bulletin of the History of Medicine* 29 (1955): 99–115; Carl Bridenbaugh, *Cities in the Wilderness* (New York, 1938), 239–241, 399–401; and especially Cadwallader Colden, "Observations on the Fever that Prevailed in the City of New York in 1741 and 2," *American Medical and Philosophical Register* 1 (1811): 310–330; and Dix, *History of Trinity Church*, 1:224, which notes that yellow fever or something closely akin actually broke out in the late summer of 1741 and claimed 217 lives. For example of New York City's precautions, see *MCC*, 4:429.

7. On debt imprisonment, see Goebel and Naughton, *Law Enforcement in Colonial New York*, 537–540; and Edwin T. Randall, "Imprisonment for Debt in America: Fact and Fiction," *Mississippi Valley Historical Review*, 39 (1952): 89–102; Edward Ryan, "Imprisonment for Debt—Its Origin and Repeal," *Virginia Magazine of History and Biography* 42 (1934): 53–58. Also, see Robert A. Feer, "Imprisonment for Debt in Massachusetts before 1800," *Mississippi Valley Historical Review*, 48 (1961): 252–269.

8. On use of pardons on condition of transportation, see Goebel and Naughton, *Law Enforcement in Colonial New York*, 754–759. On exchange of pardon for confession, see ibid., 592. Also, see Greenberg, *Crime and Law Enforcement in the County of New York*, 127–131.

9. On Will, see "Information of John Williams of New York; lived next door to Mr. Ward, the clockmaker" and "Evidence of John Williams, as to confession of Ward's Will"; *CHM*, 2:564; *Eng. Mss.*, 74:111–112. On slave rebelliousness in Antigua, see comments in *South-Carolina Gazette*, 23 April and 30 July 1737; also, see references to West Indies in Jordan, *White over Black*, 151–180; and comparison and general discussion, mentioning Antigua and St. John, in Gabriel Debien, "Le marronage aux Antilles Françaises aux XVIIe siécle," *Caribbean Studies* 6 (No. 3, 1966): 3–44, and es-

pecially 6–7. Also, instructive are Patterson, "Slavery and Slave Revolts: A Sociohistorical Analysis of the First Maroon War, 1665–1740," 289–325; Elsa V. Goveia, *Slave Society in the British Leeward Islands at the End of the Eighteenth Century* (New Haven, 1965); and Michael Craton, *Testing the Chains: Resistance to Slavery in the British West Indies* (Ithaca, 1982).

## Chapter 13

1. See Horsmanden, *The New York Conspiracy*, 211–293.
2. On background of anti-Catholicism, see Colman J. Barry, "Some Roots of American Nativism," *Catholic Historical Review* 44 (1958): 137–163; Mary A. Ray, *American Opinion of Roman Catholicism in the Eighteenth Century* (New York, 1936); John D. G. Shea, *A History of the Catholic Church Within the Limits of the United States, from the First Attempted Colonization to the Present Time*, 4 vols. (New York, 1886–1892); and Joseph M. Ives, "The Catholic Contribution to Religious Liberty in Colonial America," *Catholic Historical Review* 21 (1935): 283–298.
3. On xenophobia, see Gustavus Myers, *A History of Bigotry in the United States* (New York, 1943); on schoolteacher Elias Neau and 1712 uprising, see [Rev.] John Sharpe to Secretary of Society for the Propagation of the Gospel in Foreign Parts, 23 June 1712, in Roswell R. Hoes, "The Negro Plot of 1712," *New York Genealogical and Biographical Record* 21 (1890): 162–163; Scott, "The Slave Insurrection in New York in 1712," 67–69.
4. On image of Pope, see Ray, *American Opinion of Roman Catholicism in the Eighteenth Century*, especially chap. 1; also on religious aspect, see Trevor R. Reese, "Religious Factors in the Settlement of a Colony: Georgia in the Eighteenth Century," *Journal of Religious History*, 1 (1961): 205–216. On sorties, see Herbert W. Richmond, *The Navy in the War of 1739–48*, 4 vols. (Cambridge, Eng., 1920), 3:268–278. On imperial rivalries and impact on colonial borders, see James G. Johnson, "The Colonial Southeast, 1732–1763: An International Contest for Territorial and Economic Control," *University of Colorado Studies* 19 (1932): 163–226; Norman W. Caldwell, "The Southern Frontier during King George's War," *Journal of Southern History* 7 (1941): 37–54; Leach, *Northern Colonial Frontier*, especially chap. 4; and Max Savelle, *The Origins of American Diplomacy: The International History of Anglo-America, 1492–1763* (New York, 1967); and Felix Gilbert, "The English Background of American Isolationism in the Eighteenth Century," *William and Mary Quarterly* 1 (1944): 138–160.

Also, note Governor Clarke's comments in reports to London saying that he saw "the hand of popery in this hellish conspiracy" and that "the hand of Popery is in it": Clarke to Lords of Trade, 20 June 1741, and 24 August 1741, *DRCHNY*, 6:198, 201.

5. On New York's problems with and treatment of women connected with disorderly houses, see Greenberg, *Crime and Law Enforcement in the Colony of New York*, especially 51–53, 67–68, 76–83, 91–98. Also see Goebel and Naughton, *Law Enforcement in Colonial New York*, 100–101.

6. On Trinity Church's place in the city community, see Dix, *History of the Parish of Trinity Church of the City of New York*, especially 1:14–60; and William Berrian, *An Historical Sketch of Trinity Church, New York* (New York, 1847).

7. On imprisonment for debt, see Goebel and Naughton, *Law Enforcement in Colonial New York*, 245, 534–540. Also, note John Campbell's offering bond for Hughson and his wife at their arrest on March 4; see "Recognizance. John Hushson . . ." [sic], 4 March 1741, *CHM*, 2, 551; *Eng. Mss.*, 74: 3.

8. On malpractice issue, see "Declaration of negro doctor Harry," *CHM*, 2:556; *Eng. Mss.*, 74:129. On context of 'Doctor' Harry's practice, see Oliver S. Heaton, "Three Hundred Years of Medicine in New York City," *Bulletin of the History of Medicine*, 32 (1958): 517–530; Ezell D. Stiles, "Regulation and Licensing of Physicians in New York," *New York Journal of Medicine* 57 (1957): 543–554; Byron Stookey, *A History of Colonial Medical Education in the Province of New York* (Springfield, Ill., 1962). Also, see M. O. Bousfield, "An Account of Physicians of Color in the United States," *Bulletin of the History of Medicine*, 17 (1945): 61–84.


## Chapter 14

1. See Horsmanden, *The New York Conspiracy*, 294–326. Also, note the *South Carolina Gazette* of 30 July 1741 reported the plot as one "calculated not only to ruin and destroy [New York] City, but the whole Province, and it appears that to effect this their Design was first to burn the Fort, and if Opportunity favoured[,] to seize and carry away the Arms in store there, then to burn the whole Town, and kill and murder all the Male Inhabitants thereof (the Females they intended to reserve for their own Use) and this to be effected by seizing their Master's Arms and a general Rising, it appears also we are informed, that these Designs were not only carried on in this City, but had also spread into the country. . . . And so far had they gone that the particular Places to be burnt were laid out,

their Captains and Officers appointed, and their places of general Rendezvous fixed, and the Number of Negroes concern'd is almost incredible, and their barbarous Designs still more so.''

2. On law regarding confessions, see Goebel and Naughton, *Law Enforcement in Colonial New York*, 591–594. Also, see Levy and Leder, "The Right against Compulsory Self-Incrimination in Colonial New York," 3–32; Pittman, "The Colonial and Constitutional History of the Privilege against Self-Incrimination," 763–789.

3. On Antigua, see comments in *South-Carolina Gazette*, 23 April and 30 July 1737; and chap. 12, n9.

4. On practice of confession in connection with plea for mercy, see Goebel and Naughton, *Law Enforcement in Colonial New York*, 593, 597–598.

5. On expectations about Othello's confession, see John Shultz to Judges Philipse and Horsmanden, 17 July 1741, *CHM*, 2:566; *Eng. Mss.*, 74:127.

6. On question of partisanship in proceedings, see comments in Horsmanden, *The New York Conspiracy*, 324n, 440–442; Colden to Clarke, (no day) August 1741, *Letters and Papers of Cadwallader Colden*, 8:272–273.

7. On Havana campaign, see "Syrett, "American Provincials and the Havana Campaign," 375–390.

8. On Corry's arrest, see "Warrant for the arrest of _____ Curry," *CHM*, 2:564; *Eng. Mss.*, 74:121.

9. On political lines drawn among some of participants, see Klein, "Politics and Personalities in Colonial New York," 2–15; Stanley N. Katz, *Newcastle's New York: Anglo-American Politics, 1732–1753* (Cambridge, Mass., 1968), especially chaps. 7–8; and Bonomi, *A Factious People*, especially chaps. 4–5. Also, see comments on personalities in Colden, "History of William Cosby's Administration as Governor of Province of New York, and of Lieutenant Governor George Clarke's Administration through 1737," especially 351–355.

10. See Philipse and Horsmanden to Clarke, 17 July 1741; *CHM*, 2:566; *Eng. Mss.*, 74:128.


## Chapter 15

1. See Horsmanden, *The New York Conspiracy*, 326–337.

2. On disorderly houses see Greenberg, *Crime and Law Enforcement in the Colony of New York*, especially 51–53, 67–68, 76–83, 91–98. Also, note citizens' concerns expressed in a petition to the Assembly regarding more effective laws for preventing blacks from at-

tending "Public Houses" and plotting: New York *Weekly Journal,* 29 June 1741.

3. On monetary units, note one £ equals twenty shillings or two hundred and forty pence. Cf. chap. 7, n4. Also, see Goebel and Naughton, *Law Enforcement in Colonial New York,* 96, on value of coin.

4. On 1700 act, see *NY Col. Laws,* 1:302. Also, see warrant to commit John Ury, dated 24 June 1741, *CHM,* 2:560; *Eng. Mss.,* 74:80; Valentine, *Manual of New York for 1870,* 769–770; Joseph C. Carroll, *Slave Insurrections in the United States, 1800–1865* (Boston, 1938), 26–31; Lamb, *History of New York City,* 1:444; Clarke to Lords of Trade, 20 June and 24 August 1741, *DRCHNY,* 6:198–202. Cf. chap. 13, n1, esp. Ray, *American Opinion of Roman Catholicism,* chap. 1.

5. For diary extracts, see Horsmanden, *The New York Conspiracy,* 315–316; and *CHM,* 2:566; *Eng. Mss.,* 74:135.

6. On controversy over baptizing slaves and their Christianity, see (New York Governor Richard Coote,) Earl of Bellomont to the Lords of Trade, 27 April 1699, *DRCHNY,* 5:510–511; *NY Col. Laws,* 1:597–598, 631; Sharpe to Secretary, in Hoes, "The Negro Plot of 17!2," 162–163; Scott, "The Slave Insurrection in New York in 1712," 67–69; McManus, *Slavery in New York,* 70–75; Frank J. Klingberg, "The S.P.G. Program for Negroes in Colonial New York," *Historical Magazine of the Protestant Episcopal Church* 8 (1939):306–371; Edwin T. Corwin, ed., *Ecclesiastical Records of the State of New York,* 7 vols. (Albany, 1901–1916), 1:508, 548. Also, see Marcus W. Jernegan, "Slavery and Conversion in American Colonies," *American Historical Review* 21 (1916):504–529; Jordan, *White over Black,* 180–193. On larger issue of slavery and religion, see David B. Davis, *The Problem of Slavery in Western Culture* (Ithaca, N.Y., 1964).

7. On long-standing contention over nonjurors in New York, see Dix, *A History of the Parish of Trinity Church,* 1:215ff. Also, note antagonism toward nonjurors shown by George Clarke in 1715, when he attacked minister William Vesey for alleged nonjurist tendencies. Vesey was rector of Trinity Church in 1741, and his widow later became Daniel Horsmanden's first wife. See, *DRCHNY,* 5:564; and Lamb, *History of New York City,* 1:504–505, for Clarke attack. On Horsmanden's connection to Trinity and Mrs. Vesey, see Dix, 224, and Lamb, 1:557–78. For a sketch of Rev. Vesey, see Lamb, 1:436.

8. On principles and history of nonjurors, see J. H. Overton, *Law, Nonjuror and Mystic* (London, 1881), and *The Nonjurors: Their Lives, Principles and Writings* (London, 1902); S. L. Ollard, *et al.,* eds., *A*

*Dictionary of English Church History*, 9th ed. (London, 1970), s.v., "Nonjuror"; and William H. Harris and Judith S. Levey, eds., *The New Columbia Encyclopedia* (New York, 1975), s.v. "Nonjuror." Also, see Norman Sykes, *Church and State in England in the Eighteenth Century* (London, 1934); and D. B. Horn and Mary Ransome, eds., *English Historical Documents, 1714–1783* (New York, 1957), 341–409.

9. On deist controversy, see Herbert M. Morais, *Deism in Eighteenth Century America* (New York, 1934).

10. On background of controversy over faith versus good works, see Dewey D. Wallace, Jr., *Puritans and Predestination: Grace in Protestant Theology, 1525–1695* (Chapel Hill, 1982). On the impact of the Great Awakening, see Charles Maxson, *The Great Awakening in the Middle Colonies* (New York, 1920); Alan Heimert, *Religion and the American Mind from the Great Awakening to the Revolution* (Cambridge, 1966); Alan Heimert and Perry Miller, eds., *The Great Awakening: Documents Illustrating the Crisis and its Consequences* (New York, 1967); Frederick L. Weis, "The Colonial Clergy of New York, New Jersey, and Pennsylvania 1628–1776," *Proceedings of the American Antiquarian Society* 66 (1956):167–351. Also, see account of Rev. George Whitefield's arrival and reception in New York City in November 1739, when William Vesey, pastor of Trinity Church, denied Whitefield permission to preach in the church. Whitefield was denied use of the New Dutch Church also. See [Boston] *New England Journal*, 4 December 1739.

11. On controversy over papal authority and penance in this context, see E. I. Watkins, *Roman Catholicism in England from the Reformation to 1950* (London, 1957), especially chaps. 1–3; Howard R. Marraro, "Rome and the Catholic Church in Eighteenth Century Magazines," *Catholic Historical Review* 32 (1946):157–189; Ray, *American Opinion of Roman Catholicism in the Eighteenth Century*; Paolo Brezzi, *The Papacy: Its Origins and Historical Evolution* (New York, 1958). Roman Catholic doctrine does not contend that priests forgive sins but act only as agents of God, who alone can forgive sins. On Roman Catholic sacrament of penance, see Franz J. Heggen, *Confession and the Sacrament of Penance*, trans. Peter Tomlinson (Notre Dame, Ind., 1968).

12. For the background of English political and religious troubles, see: Alfred F. Pollard, *Political History of England, 1547–1603* (London, 1910); H. M. Smith, *Henry VIII and the Reformation* (London, 1948); G. R. Elton, *England Under the Tudors* (London, 1953); Neville Williams, *The Life and Times of Elizabeth I* (London, 1972) and his *All the Queen's Men* (London, 1972); Alison Plowden, *The Catholics under Elizabeth I* (London, 1973); John Langdon-Davies,

ed., *The Gunpowder Plot* (London, 1964); John Gerard, *What Was the Gunpowderr Plot?* (2nd ed., London, 1897); S. R. Gardiner, *What the Gunpowder Plot Was* (London, 1897; reprint ed., London, 1971); H. Ross Williamson, *Charles and Cromwell* (London, 1946); Christopher Hill, *The Century of Revolution, 1603–1714* (London, 1961); C. V. Wedgewood, *A Coffin for King Charles* (London, 1964); William Ogg, *England in the Reigns of James II and William III* (London, 1955; reprint ed., London, 1969); John Kenyon, *The Popish Plot* (London, 1972); A. C. Ewald, *Algernon Sidney*, 2 vols. (London, 1873); George M. Trevelyan, *The English Revolution, 1688–1689* (London, 1938); Lucile Pinkham, *William III and the Respectable Revolution* (London, 1938).

13. On anti-Catholicism, see chap. 13, n2. On religious toleration in general, see Ray A. Billington, *The Protestant Crusade, 1800–1860: A Study of the Origins of American Nativism* (New York, 1938), especially chap. 1; Sidney E. Mead, "From Coercion to Persuasion: Another Look at the Rise of Religious Liberty and the Emergence of Denominationalism," *Church History* 25 (1956): 317–337; Philip Sandler, "Earliest Jewish Settlers in New York," *New York History* 36 (1955): 39–50; Matthew P. Andrews, "Separation of Church and State in Maryland," *Catholic Historical Review*, 21 (1935): 164–176; Nelson P. Mead, "Growth of Religious Liberty in New York City," *Proceedings of the New York Historical Association*, 17 (1919): 141–153; Max Savelle, *Seeds of Liberty: The Genesis of the American Mind* (New York, 1948), 568–573; Also, note John Higham, *Strangers in the Land: Patterns of American Nativism 1860–1925* (New York, 1965), 4–5, which states: "By far the oldest and—in early America—the most powerful of the anti-foreign traditions came out of the shock of the Reformation. Protestant hatred of Rome played so large a part in pre-Civil War nativist thinking that historians have sometimes regarded nativism and anti-Catholicism as more or less synonymous."

14. On rivalries, see chap. 13, n4. Also, see Peter Geyl, *Revolt of the Netherlands*, 2nd ed. (New York, 1958); and George L. Smith, *Religion and Trade in New Netherland: Dutch Origins and American Development* (Ithaca, N.Y., 1973).

15. On worries about the "Pretender," James Edward, see Lamb, *History of New York City*, 1:590–591.

16. The new grand jurors were John Auboyneau, Abraham Boelen, Henry Cuyler, Abraham DePeyster, Gerardus Duychinck, Edward Hicks, Peter Jay, Henry Lane, Jr., Charles LeRoux, James Livingston, Abraham Lynsen, John Provoost, Joseph Robinson (foreman), Jacobus Roosevelt, John Roosevelt, Hermanus Rutgers, Jr., Peter Rutgers, Joseph Ryall, Peter Schuyler, and Stephen Van Cortlandt, Jr.

## Chapter 16

1. See Horsmanden, *The New York Conspiracy*, 338–355. The trial transcript appears in ibid., 338–375.

2. Bradley referred for authority on his characterization of Catholicism to Archbishop John Tillotson (1630–1694), see Leslie Stephen and Sidney Lee, eds., *Dictionary of National Biography*, 22 vols. (London, 1885–1890; reprint 1921–1922), 19:872–878; and Thomas Birch, ed., *The Life and Collected Works of John Tillotson*, 3 vols. (London, 1752).

3. On rules of evidence, see *NY Col. Laws*, 1:597–598. Also, for comments and notes on legal points in the trials, see Goebel and Naughton, *Law Enforcement in Colonial New York*, 624, 627, 640, 645, 651–653, 660, 662; and Alden Chester, *The Legal and Judicial History of New York*, 3 vols. (New York, 1911), 1:257.

4. On rule of evidence from felons, see Goebel and Naughton, *Law Enforcement in Colonial New York*, 645, which discussed precedents for Sarah's being allowed to testify. Also, see McManus, *Slavery in New York*, 130.

5. On introduction of Oglethorpe's letter, see discussion of issue and legal precedents in Goebel and Naughton, *Law Enforcement in Colonial New York*, 651–652. On Oglethorpe and Florida-Georgia connection, see Allen D. Chandler, comp., *Colonial Records of the State of Georgia*, 24 vols. (Atlanta, 1904–1915), 4:275–284; Clarke to Lords of Trade, 24 August 1741, *DRCHNY*, 6:202. Also, corresponding with Oglethorpe's comments about the Spanish fleet and provisions, note worries about Spanish successes in southern war theater and their pressure on Charleston, S.C. The New York *Weekly Journal*, 8 June 1741, reported a "rumor that the Spanish had taken Havanna. The Truth thereof was much doubted, but it now gains Credit every Hour. All sorts of Provisions are extremely dear here, flour is from 7 to 8£ Currency per hundred, and Corn from 22s 6d to 27s 6d per Bushel." Oglethorpe exhibited continual worries about the Spanish being connected to slave rebellions, for examples, see Alexander Hewat, *An Historical Account of the Rise and Progress of the Colonies of South Carolina and Georgia*, 2 vols. (London, 1779), 2:72–74; "A Ranger's Report of Travels with General Oglethorpe, 1739–1742," in Mereness, ed., *Travels in the American Colonies*, 222–223; Jordan, *White Over Black*, 120; McManus, *Slavery in New York*, 132–133. For other reports of Spanish conspiracy connection, see Boston *Gazette*, 1 December 1740; *South-Carolina Gazette*, 25 December 1740; [Philadelphia] *Pennsylvania Gazette*, 1 January 1741.

6. See part of Ury's speech delivered before interruption, Horsmanden, *The New York Conspiracy*, 352–355; for full speech, also, see

"Address. John Ury to the jury on his trial," *CHM*, 2:566; *Eng. Mss.*, 74:134.

7. See New York *Weekly Journal*, 30 March, 6–27 April 1741, which carry ads by John Campbell, schoolmaster, for classes at Bridge Street. Ury's name does not appear in the ads.

8. On controversy stirred by Reverend George Whitefield's preaching about blacks, see New York *Weekly Journal*, 2 March 1741, which noted Whitefield's arrest in Charleston, S.C., on January 15. Also, see *The Querist: The Rev. Mr. Whitefield, the Rev. Mr. Barden's Letter and the Causits* (New York, 1741), a pamphlet printed and sold by John Peter Zenger; *Three Letters from the Reverend Mr. G. Whitefield . . . Letter III. To the Inhabitants of Maryland, Virginia, North and South-Carolina, Concerning Their Negroes* (Philadelphia, 1740); [Boston] *New England Weekly Journal*, 29 April 1740. Among other things, Whitefield said, "Blacks are just as much, and no more, conceived and born in Sin, as White Men are. Both, if born and bred up here, I am persuaded, are naturally capable of the same improvement." Ibid.

Richard Charlton, a missionary of the Society for the Propagation of the Gospel in Foreign Parts (S.P.G.), said Whitefield's "imprudence and indiscretion" on the subject of slaves gave "great countenance" to the unrest in New York—the point Hildreth reported Ury making. See Charlton to [S.P.G.] Secretary, 30 October 1741, S.P.G. Manuscripts, B9, no. 62, Library of Congress, Washington, D.C. Also, see Jordan, *White over Black*, 180–181, 214–215.

On life of Whitefield, see A. A. Dallimore, *The Reverend George Whitefield* (London, 1970). On Wesley, see L. Tyerman, *The Life and Times of the Rev. John Wesley, M.A., Founder of the Methodists*, 3 vols. (London, 1870–1871). See Whitefield to Wesley, 22 March 1751, ibid., 2:132, for an exchange between them on the subject of slavery.

Also, cf. chap. 15, n10, on Whitefield's troubles in New York in 1739; and see section on Whitefield in Richard L. Bushman, ed., *The Great Awakening: Documents on the Revival of Religion, 1740–1745* (New York, 1969), 19–38.

9. Hildreth introduced controversy over the Nicene creed (from the Latin *credo*, "I believe"), see Paul T. Fuhrmann, *Introduction to the Great Creeds of the Church* (Philadelphia, 1960); and J. H. Leith, *Creeds of the Churches* (New York, 1963). The Nicene Creed refers to the creed adopted by the Council of Nicaea in 325, as revised by the First Council of Constantinople in 381, which added the *Filioque* clause—*qui ex Patre Filioque procedit*, "who proceeds from the Father and the Son"—in referring to the Holy Spirit as an equal element in the divine Trinity. Roman Catholics, some Protes-

tants, and members of the Eastern Orthodox Church use forms of the Nicene Creed as their official creed.

The phrase Hildreth reported in his testimony about Ury suggests a reference to the opening lines of the creed, but differs from the Catholic version which reads, "I believe in one God, the Father Almighty, Maker of heaven and earth, and of all things visible and invisible. And in one Lord Jesus Christ, the only begotten Son of God, born of the Father before all ages." See, Rev. Raymond A. Tartre, *et al.*, eds., *The Blessed Sacrament Missal* (New York, 1958), 21. The Catholic version used since Vatican II differs. Also, on Hildreth's testimony, see John G. Shea, "The Negro Plot," in *Manual of New York for 1870*, 760–771; and "Relation by Joseph Hildreth, of New York, schoolmaster, concerning John Ury," in *CHM*, 2:566; *Eng. Mss.*, 74:134.

10. In the Roman Catholic Church, vespers is the sixth of the seven canonical hours or parts of the day set aside for prayers and refers also to the prayers for that time. Compline is the seventh hour or last prayer in the sequence. Nocturn is the early morning set of prayers. See *The New Catholic Encyclopedia*, 15 vols. (New York, 1967), s.v. "Vespers."

11. See chap. 15, n12, for background to historical references used by Smith in his summation. Especially see, Horn and Ransome, *English Historical Documents, 1714–1783*, 341–409.

12. The jurors were Gerardus Beekman, Thomas Bohenna, John Breese, Sidney Breese, Peter Fresneau, William Hamersley (foreman), John Hastier, Brandt Schuyler, Daniel Shatford, John Shurmur, James Tucker, Thomas Willet.

On Beekman family, see Philip L. White, *The Beekmans of New York in Politics and Commerce, 1647–1877* (New York, 1956).


## Chapter 17

1. See Horsmanden, *The New York Conspiracy*, 375–383.

2. On pardon procedure, see and Goebel and Naughton, *Law Enforcement in Colonial New York*, 748–761.

3. For numbers and destinations of those pardon, computations made from "A List of Negroes Committed on Account of the Conspiracy," in Horsmanden, *The New York Conspiracy*, appendix. Also, see lists in *CHM*, 2:562, 566; *Eng. Mss.*, 74:132.

4. On final determination on Juan and four other Spanish blacks, see order by governor and his council, *Calendar of Council Minutes*, 338.

5. On questioning of proceedings, see undated anonymous letter to Cadwallader Colden in *The Letters and Papers of Cadwallader Colden*, 8.270–272; Colden commented that it was "a letter which I re-

ceiv'd the 8th of July," but the editor of Colden's papers appended "*Sic* for August 8, 1741." Colden noted further that the letter was "inclosed in one from my Daughter DeLancey & which she says came by the Post. It was under a cover directed To the Honourable Cadwallader Colden Esq at New York. The direction and the letter appear to be wrote in a feign'd hand." See Colden to George Clarke, [8?] August 1741, which Colden sent with a copy of the anonymous letter and comments, "On Saturday last Sr I received the inclosed letter under cover from my Daughter. All she says of it is [']I inclose a letter which I receiv'd by the Boston Post[']. I can make no conjecture about it otherwise than any person may who reads it. Whether the writer sincerely discloses his own Sentiments or designs only to impose such a belief upon others I am of Opinion it may be Proper to publish the Priests Tryal & the other Material Evidences of the Plot to prevent such an Opinion. Mr Nicolls upon viewing the Cover may perhaps recollect whether such a letter really came by the Post or whether it came in the Boston bag or only by the Post man for it may have been sent to my Daughter as from the Post house tho' otherwise. Another reason of my sending the Letter to you & the Cover as I receiv'd it is because sometimes Discoveries are made by unexpected things as by something of the hand writing (tho this be certainly a feign'd hand) by the Seal or the paper or the manner of its being sent & by comparing them with other writings which perhaps may be propagated or things which may be found at the same time." Ibid.; also, see Clarke's reply to Colden, 18 August 1741, ibid., 273–274, indicating Clarke showed the anonymous letter to Chief Justice DeLancey and lamented that "I fear it will be difficult to discover the author." Also, see Daniel Horsmanden to Cadwallader Colden, 7 August 1741, ibid., 2:224–227; Clarke to Lords of Trade, 24 August 1741, *DRCHNY*, 6:202.

6. On idea of evil causes, see Gordon S. Wood, "Conspiracy and the Paranoid Style: Causality and Deceit in the Eighteenth Century," *William and Mary Quarterly* 39 (1982): 401–441.

7. On New York's perennial trouble with troopers, see Peterson and Edwards, *New York*, 2:109–113; Greenberg, *Crime and Law Enforcement in the Colony of New York*, 121–124. Also, note Governor Clarke's complaining to the Assembly in September 1740 that "Desertions from his Majesty's ships of war and land forces in the Province have of late been so frequent that unless some good law be passed to prevent the like for the future, they may be unable to protect either your trade or country. By passing such a law you will show your zeal for his Majesty's service and the welfare of your country." See Lincoln, *Messages from the Governors*, 1:290. The

Assembly declined to act on desertions, and on September 26, 1740, reported its opinion that Parliament's acts relating to desertions were sufficient. See ibid., n3.

8. See Horsmanden, *The New York Conspiracy*, 10–11.
9. On the South Sea Company and its "bubble," see Lewis S. Benjamin *South Sea Bubble* (New York, 1967; reprint of 1921 ed.).
10. On Jesuits, see Christopher Hollis, *The Jesuits: A History* (New York, 1968), especially 106–117. On Samuel Clarke (1684–1750), see *Dictionary of National Biography*, 4:446–447. Clarke authored *The Saints' Inheritance; being a Collection of the Promises of Scripture*, a popular and oft-reprinted religious volume of the period, and he pastored a nonconformist congregation at St. Albans in Hertfordshire, southeastern England.

## Chapter 18

1. See Horsmanden, *The New York Conspiracy*, 381–413.
2. For the judge's continuing concerns, see Horsmanden to Colden, 7 August 1741, *The Letters and Papers of Cadwallader Colden*, 2:224–227. In dating this letter, Horsmanden notes his being "on Board Admiral Winne near the Mouth of the Highlands," having taken a brief cruise to recuperate from the trials. He wrote, "Ever since the fire at the Fort w[hi]ch was on the 18th March I've been engag'd in perpetual hurry, insomuch that I've been forced to dedicate part of my resting time to the publick Service in presenting an Enquiry into ye rise & occasion of Our Late Disorders in the City of New York, but I think the Labour bestowed has not been in Vain; for tho' the Mystery of Iniquity has been unfolding by v[e]ry Smal[l] & Slow Degrees, it has at length been discovered. . . ."
3. On remaining prisoners, see "Petition of Andrew Ryan *et al.*," dated 31 August 1741, *CHM*, 2:567; *Eng. Mss.*, 74:136.
4. See Hughson's petition from Westchester jail, 24 September 1741; *CHM*, 2:567; *Eng. Mss.*, 74:137. On proclamation day, see New York *Weekly Journal*, 29 September 1741.
5. On Burton's troubles, see Horsmanden, *The New York Conspiracy*, 434–442. The judge noted Burton's complaining "that she had been ill used; that her life had been threatened by conspirators of both complexion, and frequently insulted by people of the town for bringing their negroes in question, and that people did not believe what she said, so what signified speaking?" Burton also suggested that "there were some people *in ruffles* that were concerned" in the plot. Horsmanden underscored the phrase and noted its meaning,

"persons of better fashion than ordinary." Indeed, when pressed to speak up further, Burton "named several persons which she said she had seen at Hughson's among the conspirators, talking of the conspiracy, who were engaged in it; among whom she mentioned several of known credit, fortunes and reputations, and of religious principles superior to a suspicion of being concerned in such detestable practices; at which the judges were very much astonished . . . ; but it came out at last, that one of them was a doctor (a professed papist, as common fame had it), whom she had seen several times afterwards in the streets, and who upon sight of her, always turned another way to avoid meeting her. However it was, this person had the discretion to remove himself out of this province soon after. . . . But upon the whole, there was reason to conclude that this girl had at length been tampered with," Horsmanden concluded. See ibid., 440–441. Also, see Horsmanden comments in Horsmanden to Colden, 7 August 1741, *Letters and Papers of Cadwallader Colden*, 2:224–225; and comments on Burton in Lamb, *History of New York City*, 1:581–585; "Petition of Mary Burton, spinster, for the reward," dated 9 April 1742, *CHM*, 2:567; *Eng. Mss.*, 74:142; and "Order referring to the justices of the Supreme Court, the petition of Mary Burton," dated 9 April 1742, *CHM*, 2:567; *Eng. Mss.*, 74:143.

6. See Horsmanden, *The New York Conspiracy*, 381, 429–430, where the judge noted that the transcript of Ury's speech "differs from that supposed to have been printed at Philadelphia soon after Ury's execution, which perhaps might have been altered and corrected by some of his associates." The judge further suggested that Ury copied his own speech from "Langhern's dying speech, State Trials, 2d volume." The "Langhern" Horsmanden referred to was Richard Langhorne, executed in 1679 as a victim in the Titus Oakes Affair. Langhorne was a lawyer, admitted a member of the Inner Temple (which Horsmanden himself later attended) in 1646 and to the bar in 1654. See *Dictionary of National Biography* 11:543–544. Horsmanden's reference to "State Trials" indicates the repeatedly updated English compilation. Langhorne's trial may be found in Thomas Bayly Howell and Thomas Jones Howell, eds., *State Trials*, 33 vols. (London, 1809–1826), 7:417. For note of publication history of the State Trials, see *Dictionary of National Biography* 10:117, in discussion of Thomas B. Howell's editing, which was continued by his son, Thomas J. Howell.

On slaveholders' resistance, note city petition to assembly for restitution of losses connected with execution of slaves: See *Journal of the Assembly*, 1:835, 22 October 1742.

7. On Clarke's basic concerns about unrest among slaves and their

being incited, see Clarke to Lords of Trade, 20 June and 24 August 1741, *DRCHNY*, 6:198–202.

8. On slave unrest in South Carolina and other colonies, see Aptheker, *American Negro Slave Revolts*, 191–192, 195–196; Jordan, *White over Black*, 120–122; Wood, *Black Majority*, 324–326; *South-Carolina Gazette*, 15 Aug. 1741; *New-York Weekly Journal*, 14 September, 18 October 1741.

9. Note city petition to assembly for restitution of losses connected with execution of slaves: See *Journal of the Assembly*, 1:835, 22 October 1742.

10. On freeholders' court for slaves, see *NY Col. Laws*, 1:761–767; 2:679–688; *DHNY*, 1:471–472, 4:120. Also, see Hamlin and Baker, *Supreme Court of New York*, 1:182–183, 183n, on qualification of freeholders, which was a personal estate of £50. Smith, *History of Late Province*, 2:26, says that in 1735 New York county contained "less than a thousand freeholders qualified as jurors."

11. On value of doubloon, see Hobson and Obojski, *Illustrated Encyclopedia of World Coins*, s.v. "Doubloon"; Friedberg, *Gold Coins of the World Complete from 600 A.D. to 1958: An Illustrated Standard Catalogue with Valuations*, 289–292. Also, see Adler, "Money and Money Units in the American Colonies," 143–173; Chapman, "The Colonial Coins of America," 75–87.

## Afterward

1. See Horsmanden, *The New York Conspiracy*, 5–12.

2. On Burton's receiving her reward, see ibid., 413–414. Also, see *Calendar of Council Minutes*, 341. As Burton was legally a minor, George Joseph Moore, the court clerk and deputy provincial secretary, was appointed her guardian to handle the money as trustee for Burton. Also, see Burton's petition, 9 April 1742, *CHM*, 2:567; *Eng. Mss.*, 74:142; and "Order referring to the justices of the Supreme Court, the petition of Mary Burton, for reward . . ."; *CHM*, 2:567; *Eng. Mss.*, 74:143.

3. The original, full title of Horsmanden's book was *A Journal of the Proceedings in the Detection of the Conspiracy formed by Some White People in Conjuction with Negro and Other Slaves for Burning the City of New-York in America, and Murdering the Inhabitants* (New York: James Parker, 1744). The New York Public Library, Rare Book Room, owns a copy of the first edition, as does the New-York Historical Society.

4. See anonymous letter to Cadwallader Colden, undated, 67:270–272; Colden to George Clarke, August 1741, ibid., 272–273. See

Clarke's reply to Colden, 18 August 1741, ibid., 273–274. Cf. note 4, chap. 18. Also, note Colden's comment on fresh fears of a plot in 1747, Colden to his wife, 18 April 1747, ibid., 345. On Colden himself, see Alice M. Keys, *Cadwallader Colden: A Representative Eighteenth Century Official* (New York, 1906); Siegfried B. Roland, "Cadwallader Colden: Colonial Politician and Imperial Statesman, 1718–1760" (Ph.D. dissertation, University of Wisconsin, 1952); Miriam E. Murphy, "Cadwallader Colden, President of the Council, Lieutenant Governor of New York, 1760–1775" (Ph.D. dissertation, Fordham University, 1957); and Allan R. Raymond, "The Political Career of Cadwallader Colden" (Ph.D. dissertation, The Ohio State University, 1971).

On Smith, note his giving two pages to the events and another page to general commentary against slavery; his tone is harsh, but he mentions his father—referred to as "Mr. Smith"—only once, in passing, and in no way suggests the prominent role played by the senior William Smith. See Smith, *The History of the Late Province of New-York*, 2:74–75.

5. On population, see Davis, "New York's Long Black Line," especially 46–47, and cf. note 17, below. On slavery's eventual ending in New York, see McManus, *Slavery in New York*, 161–179; Arthur Zilversmit, *The First Emancipation: The Abolition of Slavery in the North* (Chicago, 1967), especially 87–92. On shift, see Davis, "Slavery in Colonial New York City," chap. 6; and McKee, *Labor in Colonial New York*, 123–131, 168–169.

6. On Clinton's coming to New York and subsequent political manuvering, see New York *Weekly Journal*, 26 September 1743; *Calendar of Council Minutes*, 343; *Journal of Assembly*, 1:839; Bonomi, *A Factious People*, 149–166. On Horsmanden, see McManus, "Daniel Horsmanden," 164–178; and *Dictionary of American Biography*, 9:236–237.

7. For quotations from 1810 edition, see Horsmanden, *The New York Conspiracy*, 1–3.

8. On historiography of 1741, see Ferenc M. Szasz, "The New York Slave Revolt of 1741: A Re-Evaluation," *New York History* 48 (1967): 215–230; Jordan, *White over Black*, 115–120; McManus, *Slavery in New York*, 126–139; Annette K. Dorf, "The Slave Conspiracy of 1741" (M.A. thesis, Columbia University, 1958); T. Wood Clarke, "The Negro Plot of 1741," ibid., 25 (1944): 167–181; Joseph C. Carroll, *Slave Insurrections in the United States, 1800–1860* (Boston, 1939), 26–31; Henry H. Ingersoll, "The New York Plot of 1741," *The Green Bag* 20 (1908): 135–153; Walter F. Prince, "New York 'Negro Plot' of 1741," [New Haven] *Saturday Chronicle*, 28 June and 23 August 1902, typescript, The New York Public

Library; unsigned, "Negro Plot in New York," *The National Magazine: A Monthly Magazine of American History* 18 (1893): 128–131.

9. On classic interpretations, see Charles A. and Mary P. Beard, *The Rise of American Civilization*, 2 vols. (New York, 1927), 1:81; Ulrich B. Phillips, *American Negro Slavery* (New York, 1918), 470–471; Aptheker, *American Negro Slave Revolts*, 192–195.

10. On paranoid style idea, see Richard Hofstadter, *The Paranoid Style in American Politics and Other Essays* (New York, 1964); also, see Wood, "Conspiracy and the Paranoid Style: Causality and Deceit in the Eighteenth Century," 401–441. On Salem, see Paul Boyer and Stephen Nissenbaum, *Salem Possessed: The Social Origins of Witchcraft* (Cambridge, 1974). On Stono, see Peter H. Wood, *Black Majority: Negroes in South Carolina from 1670 through the Stono Rebellion* (New York, 1974), especially 285–326. On Turner, see John B. Duff and Peter M. Mitchell, eds., *The Nat Turner Rebellion: The Historical Event and the Modern Controversy* (New York, 1971). On Prosser, see Gerald W. Mullin, "Gabriel's Insurrection," in Peter I. Wood, ed., *Americans from Africa*, 2 vols. (New York, 1970), 2:53–73. On Vesey, see Robert S. Starobin, ed., *Denmark Vesey: The Slave Conspiracy of 1822* (Englewood Cliffs, N.J., 1970).

11. For Smith's words, see Horsmanden, *The New York Conspiracy*, 370.

12. On history of conspiracy law, see James W. Bryan, *The Development of the English Law of Conspiracy* (Baltimore, 1909); Peter W. Winfield, *The History of Conspiracy and Abuse of Legal Procedure* (New York, 1921); and Robert Hazell, *Conspiracy and Civil Liberties* (London, 1974).

13. On criticism of conspiracy law, see sources cited in previous note. Also, see Paul Marcus, *Prosecution and Defense of Criminal Conspiracy Cases* (New York, 1978); and Herbert L. Packer, "The Conspiracy Weapon," *New York Review of Books* 13 (6 November 1969): 24–30. Note that in the late 1960s and early 1970s, the law of conspiracy became the center of controversy due to several widely publicized trials such as the Chicago 8 case and the Panther 21 case in New York: See, Judy Clavir and John Spitzer, eds., *The Conspiracy Trial* (Indianapolis, 1970), and Peter L. Zimroth, *Perversion of Justice: The Prosecution and Acquittal of the Panther 21* (New York, 1974).

14. On unsettling connections of slave crime, see Thomas J. Davis, "The New York Slave Conspiracy of 1741 as Black Protest," *Journal of Negro History* 56 (1971): 17–30.

15. For example of the extension of discontent from the underside of white society, see Jesse L. Lemisch, "The American Revolution Seen from the Bottom Up," in Barton J. Bernstein, ed., *Towards a*

*New Past* (New York, 1968), 3–45; and Lemisch, "Jack Tar in the Streets: Merchant Seamen in the Politics of Revolutionary America," *William and Mary Quarterly*, 25 (1968): 371–407.

16. On Barrington episode in Ulster County, see *The Letters and Papers of Cadwallader Colden, 1711–1767*, 8:228–229; and Horsmanden, *The New York Conspiracy*, 352n.

17. On war news, see Boston *Gazette*, 1 December 1740; [Charleston] *South Carolina Gazette*, 25 December 1740; [Philadelphia] *Pennsylvania Gazette*, 1 January 1741. Also, see Clarke to Lords of Trade, 20 June and 24 August 1741, *DRCHNY*, 6:198–202.

18. On sex ratio, see Davis, "New York's Long Black Line," especially 47. Note that the sex ratios reported here are for population not counted as children: In the 1731 and 1737 censuses, the cut off age used was ten years; in 1746 it was sixteen years; this accounts for what may seem a discrepancy in reporting that the percentage of males in the black population fell from 52.5 in 1737 to 46.6 in 1746. In actual number, in 1731 there were 599 black males over ten, 607 black females over ten, 186 black males under ten, and 185 black females under ten; in 1737 there were 674 black males over ten, 609 black females over ten, 229 black males under ten, and 207 black females under ten; in 1746 there were 671 black males over sixteen, 569 black females over sixteen, 419 black males under sixteen, and 735 black females under sixteen. Thus, in 1746 the sex ratio between black men and black women, that is those over sixteen years of age, was 126.7; for blacks under sixteen the sex ratio was 57.0; and for all blacks it was 87.4: The comparable ratios among whites was 77.5, 105.2, and 88.9. The key to the shifting within the black population was in the under-sixteen age group where females increased and males decreased in relative number. See ibid.; Davis, "Population and Slavery in Eighteenth Century New York," especially 35–36, 65–66; and Greene and Harrington, *American Population*, 97–99.

   For quotation from Clarke, see Lincoln, *Messages from the Governors*, 1:260.

19. On blacks, Catholics, and strangers as scapegoats, see Barry, "Some Roots of American Nativism," 137–146; Higham, *Strangers in the Land*, 5–6. On social psychology of confluence of hatreds, see Gordon Allport, *The Nature of Prejudice* (New Haven, 1954). On connection to paranoid style, see Hofstadter, *The Paranoid Style*, 3–40, especially 19–23.

20. Wood, "Conspiracy and the Paranoid Style: Causality and Deceit in the Eighteenth Century," 427.

# Index

*Note:* Slaves are listed in the index by their given name followed by the possessive of their holders' surname in parentheses; where several holders shared a surname, the initial of the holders' first name also appears in the parentheses.

Index